America in an anti-American demonstration.

The Kitchen Clash with Khrushchev: A spontaneous and dramatic confrontation, in a Moscow kitchen, of democracy versus Communism, which put to the test every ounce of Mr. Nixon's calm, wit, and resourcefulness—and an account of the hitherto unreported private meeting in K's *dacha*, which revealed the Premier to the author as "Communist man at his most dangerous best."

The Campaign of 1960: The self-imposed inner struggle in deciding the best way to serve the people if elected President; the tedious and all-consuming campaign; the emergence of a stronger man in the face of defeat.

SIX CRISES is an original, exciting, captivating book by a man who has been in public service for many years. It is a close-up of a dynamic man, revealing the demands placed upon him, the thinking behind his decisions, and the pressures of political life.

Mr. Nixon's story is one of challenge, not only to himself but also to the nation. His is the story of six great events in the history of the United States—six turning points, six decisions, SIX CRISES.

SIX CRISES

RICHARD M. NIXON

SIX CRISES

1962

DOUBLEDAY & COMPANY, INC., GARDEN CITY, NEW YORK

Library of Congress Catalog Card Number 62–8074
Copyright © 1962 by Richard M. Nixon
All Rights Reserved
Printed in the United States of America
First Edition

To PAT
she also ran

NOTE OF ACKNOWLEDGMENT

Among the many who so generously gave me the benefit of their advice and assistance in preparing this book, I would particularly like to thank Bill Henry, Earl Mazo, Charles McWhorter, Raymond Moley and Kyle Palmer.

And to Alvin Moscow, for his skilled professional services in directing research and organizing material, my special appreciation.

—R. N.

Introduction

THE last thing I ever intended or expected to do after the 1960 election was to write a book. I had received the usual offers for publication of my memoirs which are tendered to political leaders who have retired—voluntarily or involuntarily. But although anyone who goes through a presidential campaign feels immediately afterward that he has lived enough for a lifetime, I still did not believe I had reached the point in life for memoir-writing. Since I had never kept a diary, I was not in a position even to write a detailed account of my eight years as Vice President. Three people exerted particular influence in changing my mind.

Shortly after the election, I had the honor of sitting by Mrs. Eisenhower at a White House dinner. I told her that one of the reasons I had decided against writing a book was my belief that only the President could write the story of his Administration and that, by comparison, any other account would be incomplete and uninteresting. She answered, "But there are exciting events like your trips to South America and to Russia which only you can tell, and I think people would be interested in reading your account of what really happened."

In April, I visited President Kennedy for the first time since he had taken office. When I told him I was considering the possibility of joining the "literary" ranks, of which he himself is so distinguished a member, he expressed the thought that every public man should write a book at some time in his life, both for the mental discipline and because it tends to elevate him in popular esteem to the respected status of an "intellectual."

The one who had the greatest influence on my decision was Adela Rogers St. Johns. From the time I entered public life, as a Congressman in 1947, she has been a close friend and adviser. Through the years she has insisted that I should take time off to write a book. Until January 20, 1961, I could always plead that I was too busy. When I left Washington and returned to California, she took matters into her own hands. I received a phone call from her in April informing me that Ken McCormick of Doubleday and Company was flying to California to see me the next day. I protested, as I had many times before, that I did not have a subject which seemed to me worth writing about. "You let Ken decide that," was her reply.

The night before McCormick arrived, I tried to jot down some ideas which might form a basis for discussion. I decided that what particularly distinguished my career from that of other public figures was that I had had the good (or bad) fortune to be the central figure in several crisis situations with dimensions far beyond personal consideration. I made notes covering a dozen such situations and then selected six of them—the chapter headings of this book—for presentation to McCormick. He approved the concept, told me how easy and enjoyable I would find writing a book to be, and finally convinced me that I should undertake the venture.

It turned out to be the seventh major crisis of my life, and by far the most difficult from the standpoint of the mental discipline involved. My respect for those who write books, already high, has gone up a hundredfold. But my personal attitude toward undertaking any more such assignments in the future can probably best be described by one of my favorite Eisenhower anecdotes.

President Eisenhower gave up smoking in 1945. I asked him once whether he was ever tempted to resume the habit. "No," he said, and then added: "I can't say that I might not start again. But I can tell you one thing for sure: I'll never quit again!" My attitude toward writing a book runs along somewhat similar lines: I might start another one, but I am sure I will never finish it!

I would like to add a word as to what this book is—or tries to be—and what it is not.

I have not attempted to set forth a complete and detailed account of all the events surrounding each crisis situation. What I have tried to do is describe my personal reactions to each one and then to distill out of my experience a few general principles on the "crisis syndrome."

On the other hand, I do not presume to suggest that this is a scholarly treatise on conduct in crisis. The experts will have to judge what contribution my observations may make to a better understanding of that intriguing and vitally important subject.

My own limitations in this respect were brought home to me in a letter I received from James A. Robinson and Thomas W. Milburn of Northwestern University, two political scientists now engaged in a study of crisis behavior. Among the questions they suggested I try to answer were these:

Is it possible to be rational at all in crisis situations? Can you separate what were really factual and empirical matters as opposed to emotional reactions?

Do crises seem to have many elements in common?

Does the participant seem to learn from one crisis to another?

Did you feel a sense of exhilaration or enjoyment of any, or all, of the six crises about which you are writing?

Do you feel you have learned anything new about basic strengths in your personality, or did you discover any personal weaknesses about which you were previously unaware?

Have you found that you had extra strength which you had not anticipated when you were confronted by a crisis?

Could you recall your feelings after the crisis had passed? Was there any sense of relief from tension or anxiety?

As a result of these several crises have you formulated any "rules of thumb" to guide your behavior in subsequent crisis situations?

Several of these questions I will try to answer—but, let me emphasize, from a personal rather than a general viewpoint. Because there is one lesson, from my own experience, that seems especially clear: reaction and response to crisis is uniquely personal in the sense that it depends on what the individual brings to bear on the situation—his own traits of personality and character, his training, his moral and religious background, his strengths and weaknesses.

Among my personal conclusions, which will be spelled out in greater detail in the following pages, are these:

One factor common to all six of these crises is that while each was an acute personal problem, each also involved far broader consequences which completely overshadowed my personal fortunes. In one way, the fact that so much more rides on a crisis than personal considerations makes it more difficult to bear. But in another, this very factor may prove to be an asset. We often hear it said that truly "big" men are at their best in handling big affairs, and that they falter and fail when confronted with petty irritations—with crises which are, in other words, essentially personal.

From my own experience, the bigger the problem, the broader its consequences, the less does an individual think of himself. He has to devote his entire concentration to the much larger problem which confronts him. "Selflessness" is the greatest asset an individual can have in a time of crisis. "Selfishness" (in its literal rather than its lay sense) is the greatest liability. The very fact that the crisis is bigger than the man himself takes his mind off his own problems. The natural symptoms of stress in a period of crisis do not become self-destructive as a result of his worrying about himself but, on the other hand, become positive forces for creative action.

A second general point can best be illustrated by an anecdote. Shortly after I returned from South America in 1958, I attended a Washington reception for Congressional Medal of Honor winners. One of the guests of honor came up to me and, pointing to his ribbon, said, "You should be wearing this, not I. I could never have done what you did in Caracas." I answered: "And I could never have done what you did during the Battle of the Bulge." Perhaps we were both wrong. No one really knows what he is capable of until he is tested to the full by events over which he may have no control. That is why this book is an account not of great men but rather of great events—and how one man responded to them.

I do not believe, for example, that some men are just "naturally" cool, courageous, and decisive in handling crisis situations, while others are not. "He doesn't have a nerve in his body" is a popular cliché. Of course some men may be stronger, less emotional, quicker, smarter, bolder than others. But I think these attributes are for the most part acquired and not inherited, and many times acquired suddenly under stress. The public likes to glamorize its leaders, and most leaders like to glamorize themselves. We tend to think of some men as "born leaders." But I have found that leaders are subject to all the human frailties: they lose their tempers, become depressed, experience the other symptoms of tension. Sometimes even strong men will cry.

I should like finally to list some of the lessons I have learned from the six crises described in this book. I offer them not as inflexible rules, but only as tentative guides.

Confidence in crisis depends in great part on adequacy of preparation—where preparation is possible.

Coolness—or perhaps the better word is "serenity"—in battle is a product of faith. And faith, apart from that which stems from religious heritage and moral training, comes to an individual after he has gone through a necessary period of indecision, of doubt and soul-searching, and resolves that his cause is right and determines that he must fight the battle to the finish.

Courage—or, putting it more accurately, lack of fear—is a result of discipline. Any man who claims never to have known fear is either lying or else he is stupid. But by an act of will, he refuses to think of the reasons for fear and so concentrates entirely on winning the battle.

Experience is a vitally important factor. When a man has been through even a minor crisis, he learns not to worry when his muscles tense up, his breathing comes faster, his nerves tingle, his stomach churns, his temper becomes short, his nights are sleepless. He recognizes such symptoms as the natural and healthy signs that his system is keyed up for battle. Far from worrying when this happens, he should worry when it does not. Because he knows from experience that once the battle is joined, all these symptoms will disappear—unless he insists on thinking primarily of himself rather than the problem he must confront.

A man will look forward to the end of the battle. He thinks, "Just as soon as this is over I'll feel great." But except for a brief period of exhilaration if the fight ended in victory, he will then begin to feel the full effects of what he has been through. He may even be physically sore and mentally depressed. What has happened, of course, is that he is just too spent emotionally, physically, and mentally to enjoy the fruits of victory he so eagerly anticipated.

The easiest period in a crisis situation is actually the battle itself. The most difficult is the period of indecision—whether to fight or run away. And the most dangerous period is the aftermath. It is then, with all his resources spent and his guard down, that an individual must watch out for dulled reactions and faulty judgment.

I find it especially difficult to answer the question, does a man "enjoy" crises? I certainly did not enjoy the ones described in this book in the sense that they were "fun." And yet, life is surely more than simply the search for enjoyment in the popular sense. We are all tempted to stay on the sidelines, to live like vegetables, to concentrate all our efforts on living at greater leisure, living longer, and leaving behind a bigger estate. But meeting crises involves creativity. It engages all a man's talents. When he looks back on life, he has to answer the question: did he live up to his capabilities as fully as he could? Or were only part of his abilities ever called into action?

One man may have opportunities that others do not. But what counts is whether the individual used what chances he had. Did he risk all when the stakes were such that he might win or lose all? Did he affirmatively seek the opportunities to use his talents to the utmost in causes that went beyond personal and family considerations?

A man who has never lost himself in a cause bigger than himself has missed one of life's mountaintop experiences. Only in losing himself does he find himself. Only then does he discover all the latent strengths he never knew he had and which otherwise would have remained dormant.

Crisis can indeed be agony. But it is the exquisite agony which a man might not want to experience again—yet would not for the world have missed.

And since we live in an age in which individual reaction to crisis may bear on the fate of mankind for centuries to come, we must spare no effort to learn all we can and thus sharpen our responses. If the record of one man's experience in meeting crises—including both his failures and his successes—can help in this respect, then this book may serve a useful purpose.

SIX CRISES

The Hiss Case

The ability to be cool, confident, and decisive in crisis is not an inherited characteristic but is the direct result of how well the individual has prepared himself for the battle.

"IF it hadn't been for the Hiss case, you would have been elected President of the United States." This was the conclusion of one of my best friends after the election of 1960.

But another good friend told me just as sincerely, "If it hadn't been for the Hiss case, you never would have been Vice President of the United States or candidate for President."

Ironically, both of my friends may have been right.

The Hiss case was the first major crisis of my political life. My name, my reputation, and my career were ever to be linked with the decisions I made and the actions I took in that case, as a thirty-five-year-old freshman Congressman in 1948. Yet, when I was telling my fifteen-year-old daughter, Tricia, one day about the subjects I was covering in this book, she interrupted me to ask, "What was the Hiss case?"

I realized for the first time that a whole new generation of Americans was growing up who had not even heard of the Hiss case. And now, in retrospect, I wonder how many of my own generation really knew the facts and implications of that emotional controversy that rocked the nation twelve years ago.

It is not my purpose here to relate the complete story. What I shall try to do in these pages is to tell it as I experienced it—not only as an acute personal crisis but as a vivid case study of the continuing crisis of our times, a crisis with which we shall be confronted as long as aggressive international Communism is on the loose in the world.

The Hiss case began for me personally on a hot, sultry Washington morning—Tuesday, August 3, 1948—in the Ways and Means Committee hearing room of the New House Office Building. David Whittaker Chambers appeared before the House Committee on Un-American Activities to testify on Communist infiltration into the federal government. Never in the stormy history of the Committee was a more sensational investigation started by a less impressive witness.

Chambers did not ask to come before the Committee so that he could single out and attack Alger Hiss, as much of the mythology which has since grown up around the case has implied. The Committee had subpoenaed him in its search for witnesses who might be able to corroborate the testimony of Elizabeth Bentley. Miss Bentley had caused a sensation three days earlier when she named thirty-two government officials who she said had supplied her with classified documents which she, as courier for a Soviet spy ring, had then put on microfilm and passed to Russian agents in New York for transmittal to Moscow. The individuals named by Miss Bentley had been called before the Committee. The majority of them refused to answer questions on the ground that the answers would tend to incriminate them. Others categorically denied having given assistance to any spy ring. The charges were significant and sensational—but unsubstantiated.

We then learned from other sources that Whittaker Chambers, a Senior Editor of *Time,* had been a Communist functionary in the 1930's, and we subpoenaed him to testify on August 3. I first saw Chambers in a brief executive session which was held in the Committee office prior to the public hearing. Both in appearance and in what he had to say, he made very little impression on me or the other Committee members. He was short and pudgy. His clothes were unpressed. His shirt collar was curled up over his jacket. He spoke in a rather bored monotone. At first, he seemed an indifferent if not a reluctant witness. But his answers to the few questions we asked him in executive session convinced us that he was no crackpot. And so we decided to save time by going at once into a public session. None of us thought his testimony was going to be especially important. I remember that I considered for a moment the possibility of skipping the public hearing altogether, so that I could return to my office and get out some mail.

There were relatively few in the hearing room when Chambers began his public testimony. The spectator section was less than one-third full and the only reporters present were those who covered the Committee as a regular beat. The public address system was out of order and Chambers constantly had to be reminded to keep his voice up so that the Committee members and the press could hear what he was saying. He identified himself and began reading a prepared statement in a rather detached way, as if he had an unpleasant chore to do which he wanted to get out of the way as quickly as possible. As he droned on, I found my thoughts wandering to other subjects. He was halfway through the statement before I realized that he had some extraordinary quality which raised him far above the run of witnesses who had appeared before our Committee. It was not how he spoke; it was, rather, the sheer, almost stark eloquence of phrases that needed no histrionic embellishment.

He explained that he had joined the Communist Party in 1924 because he had become convinced that Communism was the only sure way to progress, and that he had left the Party in 1937, at the risk of his life, when he became convinced that it was a form of totalitarianism which meant slavery to all mankind.[1] And then, speaking with what seemed to me almost a sense of sadness and resignation, he said: "Yet so strong is the hold which the insidious evil of Communism secures upon its disciples that I could still say to [my wife] at the time—'I know that I am leaving the winning side for the losing side but it is better to die on the losing side than to live under Communism.'" From that moment, I came more and more to realize that despite his unpretentious appearance, Chambers was a man of extraordinary intellectual gifts and one who had inner strength and depth. Here was no headline-seeker but rather a thoughtful, introspective man, careful with his words, speaking with what sounded like the ring of truth.

Chambers went on in his statement to name four members of his underground Communist group whose purpose, he said, was not espionage but rather "Communist infiltration of the American government." The four were: Nathan Witt, former Secretary of the National Labor Relations Board; John Abt, former Labor Department attorney; Lee Pressman, former Assistant General Counsel for the Agricultural Adjustment Administration, later Counsel for the Works Progress Administration, and later still, General Counsel for the CIO; and Alger Hiss who, as a State Department official, had had the responsibility for organizing the Dumbarton Oaks world monetary con-

[1] Actually, as Chambers later testified and as he recounts in his book, *Witness*, both these dates are wrong. He entered the Party in 1925 and left it in 1938. But in both cases, what was involved was a process rather than a single moment—a whole series of events and not one sharp entrance or break—which makes his lapse all the more understandable.

ferences, the U. S. side of the Yalta Conference, and the meeting at San Francisco where the UN Charter was written and adopted.

Under further questioning, Chambers also identified two more as Communists: Donald Hiss, Alger's brother, who had been in the Labor Department; and Henry Collins, who had also been in the Labor Department, and later served with the U. S. Occupation Forces in Germany. He named as a "fellow traveler" Harry Dexter White, who had reached the position of Assistant Secretary of the Treasury before leaving government service. Most of the questioning that day, in fact, pertained to White because Elizabeth Bentley had also named him and because he had held the highest government position of all those she had accused of espionage activity. Chambers said that Mrs. Alger Hiss, too, was a Communist, but just as categorically he stated that Mrs. Donald Hiss was not. This was not a man who was throwing his charges about loosely and recklessly. Still, because his accusations did not involve espionage, they made little impression on me or the other Committee members.

This was the first time I had ever heard of either Alger or Donald Hiss. My attention that morning centered on another phase of Chambers' testimony, and it was the only point on which I questioned him during the time he was on the stand. What disturbed me was that Chambers testified he had told his story to government officials nine years before—and nothing had happened. Not only that, but Chambers stated that on three other occasions since then he had repeated the story to representatives of the government—at their request—and still, so far as he knew, no action had been taken to investigate his charges.

Chambers testified that he left the Communist Party in 1937 but said nothing to government officials about his past affiliation for two years thereafter. But in 1939 the signing of the Hitler-Stalin pact was so frightening to him that he felt he could no longer keep silent. Even though he was risking his own reputation and safety, he went to Washington as a "simple act of war" and told his story to Adolf A. Berle, Jr., who was then Assistant Secretary of State for Intelligence. Berle, whom Chambers was careful to identify as an anti-Communist, became very distraught by what he heard and took extensive notes on the conversation. But Chambers' charges were so incredible and the temper in Washington at that time was such that when Berle reported the story to his superiors, he was told in so many words to "go jump in the lake." Years passed during which Chambers heard nothing whatever about what action, if any, had been taken with regard to his charges.

Then, in 1943, agents from the FBI visited him at his farm in Westminster, Maryland, and Chambers repeated his story in detail. Again, nothing happened. In 1945, and in 1947, he told the same story to FBI agents but, to his knowledge, no action was taken. It should be emphasized that during this period, J. Edgar Hoover, to his eternal credit, was conducting constant investigations of Communist infiltration in the United States generally and the government in particular, despite the fact that the official Administration policy was to "get along with Stalin." But Hoover had the power only to conduct investigations. He could not follow them up with prosecutions or other required action without the approval of his superiors in the Justice Department and in the White House.

As Chambers testified that morning in his low, rather monotonous voice, most of the Committee members and the reporters at the press table yawned, took sporadic notes, and waited for the "spy stories" which never came.

His testimony made headlines the next day, but they were not nearly as sensational as those Elizabeth Bentley had drawn. For my own part, I gave very little thought to Chambers or his testimony that evening or the following morning, until Robert Stripling, the Committee's chief investigator, phoned me to say that the Committee had received a telegram from Alger Hiss requesting an opportunity to appear in public session to deny under oath all the allegations made about him by Chambers. Hiss was the only one named by Chambers who volunteered in this way. His request was granted immediately, and his appearance was set for the next day, August 5.

Hiss's performance before the Committee was as brilliant as Chambers' had been lackluster. The hearing was held in the caucus room of the Old House Office Building, which was much larger than the room in which Chambers had testified. It was filled to capacity. The press section was crowded with newsmen, many of whom were acquainted with Hiss and had gained respect for the ability he had demonstrated as head of the Secretariat at the San Francisco Conference which set up the UN organization. In this position, one of his jobs had been to brief the press and, in the process, he had earned their respect for his intelligence and over-all competence.

When he appeared on the morning of the fifth, Hiss immediately went on the offensive.

He told the Committee in a clear, well-modulated voice: "I was born in Baltimore, Maryland, on November 11, 1904. I am here at my own request to deny unqualifiedly various statements about me which were made before this Committee by one Whittaker Chambers the day before yesterday.

"I am not and never have been a member of the Communist Party. I do not and never have adhered to the tenets of the Communist Party. I am not and never have been a member of any Communist front organization. I have never followed the Communist Party line directly or indirectly. To the best of my knowledge none of my friends is a Communist."

Hiss next reviewed his government career, and it was impressive to everyone in the room. After graduating from Johns Hopkins University and the Harvard Law School, he had served for a year as Clerk to Supreme Court Justice Oliver Wendell Holmes, a signal honor for any Harvard Law graduate, had practiced law for three years, and then had come to Washington—in 1933—and became Assistant General Counsel (along with Lee Pressman) to the Agricultural Adjustment Administration. In 1934, he became Counsel to the Senate Committee Investigating the Munitions Industry (the Nye Committee). From there, he went to the office of Solicitor General Stanley F. Reed, who was later to be appointed to the U. S. Supreme Court. In September 1936, at the request of Assistant Secretary Francis B. Sayre, he joined the State Department, where he remained until January 1947. He resigned from government to accept the presidency of the Carnegie Endowment, one of the most respected private organizations in the field of foreign affairs. Its Board Chairman was John Foster Dulles.

Dulles, at the time of this hearing, was the chief foreign policy adviser to the Republican nominee for President, Governor Thomas E. Dewey. Hiss told the Committee that it was Dulles who had asked him to take the job at the Carnegie Endowment.[2]

Hiss described his work in the State Department—including his preparing the draft of the U. S. position for the Yalta Conference and then accompanying former President Roosevelt to the conference. His manner was coldly courteous and, at times, almost condescending.

[2] Later I learned that Dulles had first offered this position to Adlai Stevenson and that Stevenson, in declining the offer, had, in a letter to Dulles, suggested three other names he might consider. One of the three was Alger Hiss. But Dulles and Stevenson were to end up on different sides when Hiss finally was tried for perjury. Stevenson gave a sworn deposition that Hiss's "reputation for veracity, for integrity, and for loyalty was good." Dulles testified against Hiss.

Had he concluded his testimony at this point—after denying any Communist affiliations or sympathy—he would have been home free. Hundreds of witnesses had denied such charges before the Committee in the past and nothing more had come of it because it was then simply their word against that of their accusers. In fact, this was one of the primary reasons the Committee itself was under such attack in the press at that time.

But here Hiss made his first and what proved to be his irreversible mistake. He was not satisfied with denying Chambers' charge that he had been a Communist. He went further. He denied ever having heard the name Whittaker Chambers. "The name means absolutely nothing to me," he said.

When Robert Stripling, the Committee's chief investigator, handed him a photograph of Chambers, he looked at it with an elaborate air of concentration and said, "If this is a picture of Mr. Chambers, he is not particularly unusual looking." He paused and then, looking up at Congressman Karl Mundt, the acting Chairman of the Committee, added: "He looks like a lot of people. I might even mistake him for the Chairman of this Committee."

Hiss's friends from the State Department, other government agencies, and the Washington social community sitting in the front rows of the spectator section broke into a titter of delighted laughter. Hiss acknowledged this reaction to his sally by turning his back on the Committee, tilting his head in a courtly bow, and smiling graciously at his supporters.

"I hope you are wrong in that," Mundt shot back quickly.

"I didn't mean to be facetious," Hiss replied, "but very seriously I would not want to take oath that I had never seen that man. I would like to see him and then I would be better able to tell whether I had ever seen him. Is he here today?"

He then looked from side to side, giving the impression that he did not have the slightest idea who this mysterious character might be and that he was anxious to see him in the flesh.

"Not to my knowledge," answered Mundt.

"I hoped he would be," said Hiss, with an air of apparent disappointment.

It was a virtuoso performance. Without actually saying it, he left the clear impression that he was the innocent victim of a terrible case of mistaken identity, or that a fantastic vendetta had been launched against him for some reason he could not fathom. But even at that time I was beginning to have some doubts. From considerable experience in observing witnesses on the stand, I had learned that those who are lying or trying to cover up something generally make a common mistake—they tend to overact, to overstate their case. When Hiss had gone through the elaborate show of meticulously examining the photograph of Chambers, and then innocently but also somewhat condescendingly saying that he might even mistake him for the Chairman, he had planted in my mind the first doubt about his credibility.

Karl Mundt, an experienced and skillful investigator, came back at Hiss strongly. He said, "You realize that this man whose picture you have just looked at, under sworn testimony before this Committee, where all the laws of perjury apply, testified that he called at your home, conferred at great length, saw your wife pick up the telephone and call somebody who he said must have been a Communist, pleaded with you to divert yourself from Communist activities, and that when he left you, you had tears in your eyes and said, 'I simply can't make the sacrifice.'"

"I do know that he said that," replied Hiss. "I also know that I am testifying under those same laws to the contrary."

And so it went through the balance of the hearing. He so dominated the proceedings that by the end of his testimony he had several members of the Committee trying to defend the right of a congressional committee to look into charges of Communism in government.

But looking over my notes on his testimony, I saw that he had never once said flatly, "I don't know Whittaker Chambers." He had always qualified it carefully to say, "I have never known a man by the name of Whittaker Chambers." Toward the end of his testimony, I called Ben Mandel, one of the members of our staff, to the rostrum and asked him to telephone Chambers in New York and find out if he might possibly have been known under another name during the period he was a Communist functionary. The answer came back too late. After the hearing was over, Chambers returned the call and said that his Party name was Carl and that Hiss and the other members of the Communist cell with which he had worked had known him by that name.

As the hearing drew to a close, Karl Mundt, speaking for the Committee, said, "The Chair wishes to express the appreciation of the Committee for your very co-operative attitude, for your forthright statements, and for the fact that you were first among those whose names were mentioned by various witnesses to communicate with us, asking for an opportunity to deny the charges."

John Rankin of Mississippi added, "I want to congratulate the witness that he didn't refuse to answer the questions on the ground that it might incriminate him. And he didn't bring a lawyer here to tell him what to say."

When the hearing adjourned Rankin left his seat to shake hands with Hiss. He had to fight his way through a crowd for, when the gavel came down, many of the spectators and some of the press swarmed around Hiss to congratulate him. He had won the day completely. It would not be an exaggeration to say that probably 90 per cent of the reporters at the press table and most of the Committee members were convinced that a terrible mistake had been made, a case of mistaken identity, and that the Committee owed an apology to Hiss for having allowed Chambers to testify without first checking into the possibility of such a mistake. Most of the news stories the next day and the editorials during the week were to express the same opinion—blasting the Committee for its careless procedures and, for the most part, completely overlooking the possibility that Chambers rather than Hiss might have been telling the truth.

One of the reporters who regularly covered the Committee came up to me afterwards and asked, "How is the Committee going to dig itself out of this hole?" Mary Spargo of the Washington *Post*, who had been covering the Committee for some time, told me bluntly, "This case is going to kill the Committee unless you can prove Chambers' story." I ran into another barrage of questions when I went to the House restaurant after the hearing for lunch. Ed Lahey of the Chicago *Daily News*, whom I respected as one of the most honest and objective reporters in Washington, walked up to me literally shaking with anger. His eyes blazed as he said, "The Committee on Un-American Activities stands convicted, guilty of calumny in putting Chambers on the stand without first checking the truth of his testimony."

As I was eating lunch I got the report of President Truman's opinion of the case. At his press conference he labeled the whole spy investigation a "red herring," cooked up by a Republican Congress to avoid taking action on price controls, inflation, and other legislation important to the welfare of the people. Later, a Presidential Order directed that no federal agency was to release information on government personnel to committees of Congress, thus blocking that avenue of investigation.

When the Committee reconvened in executive session later that afternoon, it was in a virtual state of shock. Several members berated the staff for not checking Chambers' veracity before putting him on the stand.

One Republican member lamented, "We've been had. We're ruined."

Ed Hébert, a Louisiana Democrat, suggested that the only way the Committee could get "off the hook" would be to turn the whole file over to the Department of Justice and hold no more hearings in the case. "Let's wash our hands of the whole mess," he said. That appeared to be the majority view, and if Hébert had put his suggestion in the form of a motion, it would have carried overwhelmingly. I was the only member of the Committee who expressed a contrary view, and Bob Stripling backed me up strongly and effectively.

I argued, first, that turning the case over to the Department of Justice, far from rescuing the Committee's reputation, would probably destroy it for good. It would be a public confession that we were incompetent and even reckless in our procedures. We would never be able to begin another investigation without having someone say, "Why do you amateurs insist on getting into these cases? Why don't you leave the job where it belongs—to the experts in the Department of Justice?" Beyond that, I insisted that we had a responsibility not to drop the case but rather, now that we had opened up the whole question, to see it through. I reminded the Committee members that Chambers had testified that on four different occasions he had told his story to representatives of government agencies and that no action had ever been taken to check the credibility of his charges. Judging from that record, we could only assume that if we turned the investigation over to the Department of Justice, the case would be dropped. And the truth would never be determined.

I pointed out my suspicions: that while Hiss had seemed to be a completely forthright and truthful witness, he had been careful never to state categorically that he did not know Whittaker Chambers. He had always qualified his answer by saying that he did not know a man "by the name of Whittaker Chambers." I argued that while it would be virtually impossible to prove that Hiss was or was not a Communist—for that would simply be his word against Chambers'—we should be able to establish by corroborative testimony whether or not the two men knew each other. If Hiss were lying about not knowing Chambers, then he might also be lying about whether or not he was a Communist. And if that were the case, the charges were so serious— in view of the vitally important and sensitive positions Hiss had held— that we had an obligation running to the very security of the nation to dig out the truth.

Bob Stripling, speaking from his years of experience as an investigator of Communist activities, made one very telling argument in support of my position. He reported that before and during the hearing, a calculated whispering campaign had been initiated against Chambers. The rumors were that he was an alcoholic, that he had been in a mental institution, that he was paranoiac. This, of course, did not establish that Chambers was telling the truth or that Hiss was a Communist. But, Stripling pointed out, this was a typical Communist tactic always employed to destroy any witness—and particularly any former Communist—who dared to testify against them.

Finally my arguments prevailed and Karl Mundt, as acting Chairman, appointed me to head a Sub-committee to question Chambers again—this time in executive session, with no spectators or press present. Stripling was directed to subpoena Chambers to a hearing in New York two days later, on August 7.

When I arrived back in my office that afternoon, I had a natural sense of achievement over my success in preventing the Committee from dropping the case prematurely. But as I thought of the problems ahead of me I realized for the first time that I was up against a crisis which transcended any I had been through before.

I had put myself, a freshman Congressman, in the position of defending the reputation of the Un-American Activities Committee. And in so doing, I was opposing the President of the United States and the majority of press corps opinion, which is so important to the career of anyone in elective office. Also, my stand, which was based on my own opinion and judgment, placed me more or less in the corner of a former Communist functionary and against one of the brightest, most respected young men following a public career. Yet I could not go against my own conscience and my conscience told me that, in this case, the rather unsavory-looking Chambers was telling the truth, and the honest-looking Hiss was lying.

Life for everyone is a series of crises. A doctor performing a critically difficult operation involving life and death, a lawyer trying an important case, an athlete playing in a championship contest, a salesman competing for a big order, a worker applying for a job or a promotion, an actor on the first night of a new play, an author writing a book—all these situations involve crises for the individuals concerned. Crisis, by its nature, is usually primarily personal. Whether an individual fails or succeeds in meeting and handling a crisis usually affects only his own future and possibly that of his family and his immediate circle of friends and associates.

Up to this time in my own life, I had been through various crises which had seemed critical at the time. In college, each examination was a minor crisis; I had to get high enough grades to qualify for a scholarship if I were to be able to go on to law school. Passing the California Bar Examinations in which for three days, seven hours a day, of written tests I was in effect putting on the line everything I had learned in four years of college and three years of law school—this had been the most difficult experience of my prepolitical career. My first day in court and my first jury trial seemed to me crucial experiences at the time. But these crises had been primarily personal as far as their outcome was concerned.

Only when I ran for Congress in 1946 did the meaning of crisis take on sharply expanded dimensions. The outcome of the election would naturally have a profound effect on me. If I failed, my family and close friends would share my disappointment. But, in addition, I realized in that campaign that I must not only do the best I could because of my personal stake in the outcome but also that I must call up an even greater effort to meet the responsibility of representing the institution which had nominated me for office, the Republican Party, as well as fulfilling the hopes of literally thousands of people I would never meet, Republicans and Democrats, who were working for my election and would vote for me.

But on that evening of August 5, as I reviewed Hiss's testimony, I realized that this case presented a crisis infinitely greater and more complex than anything I had faced running for Congress in 1946.

The most immediate consequence of whatever action I took would be its effect on the lives of two individuals, Hiss and Chambers. One of them was lying and therefore guilty of perjury. But on the other hand, one of them was an innocent man who would, in my opinion, never be proved innocent unless someone on the Committee diligently pursued the search for the truth.

Beyond the fate of these two individuals, I recognized that the future of the Committee on Un-American Activities was at stake. The Committee in 1948 was under constant and severe attack from many segments of both press and public. It had been widely condemned as a "Red-baiting" group, habitually unfair and irresponsible, whose investigations had failed to lead to a single conviction of anyone against whom charges had been made at its hearings. It was, the critics said, doing more of a disservice to the country because of its abridgment of civil liberties than any alleged services it might be rendering in uncovering Communist subversives.

The Committee had survived many past attacks for its failure to prove the charges of witnesses appearing before it. But I was convinced that a failure in this case would prove to be fatal. The President of the United States himself, the great majority of the press corps, and even some of the Committee's own members were mounting an all-out attack on its alleged "sloppy" procedures.

No one was more aware than I that the Committee's past record had been vulnerable to attack. This was due in part to how it had conducted its investigations, but possibly even more to what it was investigating. The extent to which congressional investigations are generally approved is largely determined by whose ox is gored. If it is a J. P. Morgan, a Jimmy Hoffa, or a Frank Costello being investigated, most of the press and the public couldn't seem to care less what procedures the Committee uses. But particularly in those years immediately after World War II, a congressional investigation of Communist activities was just like waving a red flag in the face of potential critics. This was not because the critics were pro-Communist—only a small minority could be accurately so designated. It was, rather, because such investigations seemed in that period to involve an attack on the free expression of ideas. The Communist Party, in most intellectual circles, was considered to be "just another political party" and Communism just "an abstract political idea"—a generally unpopular one to be sure, but one that any individual should have the right to express freely without running the risk of investigation or prosecution.

The Hiss case itself and other developments in the period between 1947 and 1951 were to effect a significant change in the national attitude on these issues. But I recognized on that August evening in 1948 that even though a committee investigating Communism followed impeccably correct procedures and proved to be right, it would receive very little credit. Where its procedures were loose and it proved to be wrong, it would be subjected to scathing and merciless attack—and along with it, all its members who participated in the investigation.

Despite its vulnerabilities, I strongly believed that the Committee served several necessary and vital purposes. Woodrow Wilson once said that congressional investigating committees have three legitimate functions: first, to investigate for the purpose of determining what laws should be enacted; second, to serve as a watchdog on the actions of the executive branch of the government, exposing inefficiency and corruption; third, and in Wilson's view probably most important, to inform the public on great national and international issues. I had served on the Committee long enough to realize that congressional investigations of Communist activities were essential to further all these purposes. I knew that if the Committee failed to follow through on the Hiss case, the effectiveness of all congressional investigations, and particularly those in the field of Communist activities, might be impaired for years.

But more important by far than the fate of the Committee, the national interest required that this investigation go forward. If Chambers were telling the truth, this meant that the Communists had been able to enlist the active support of men like Alger Hiss—in education, background, and intelligence, among the very best the nation could produce. If this were the case, then surely the country should be informed and Congress should determine what legislative action might be taken to deal with the problem.

When I listened to the radio later that evening and saw the next morning's newspapers, I had some second thoughts about the wisdom of my insisting on continuing the investigation. I knew there was a strong bias against the Committee among the press corps, and I had expected some critical comment. But I was not prepared for an assault on the Committee and its members which, in fury and vehemence, had never even been approached in the Committee's past history. The overwhelming majority of the reporters seemed to assume that Chambers was an out-and-out liar bent on destroying an innocent man. And almost every one of my Republican colleagues in the House who expressed an opinion the day after Hiss testified voiced doubts as to Chambers' credibility and as to the wisdom of continuing the investigation.

What particularly disturbed me was a conversation I had with Congressman Christian Herter of Massachusetts, for whom I had developed great respect and admiration. I had served as a member of a special Committee he had headed the year before to study United States foreign aid programs in Europe. Herter had always voted for the appropriations for the Committee on Un-American Activities and I knew he had some good contacts in the Department of State. When I asked him about the Hiss case, he told me that the consensus in the State Department and among people who knew Hiss was that he was not a Communist. "I don't want to prejudge the case," said Herter, "but I'm afraid the Committee has been taken in by Chambers."

I replied that it was too late to turn back now, that I myself honestly did not know which man was telling the truth, but that I thought the Committee had an obligation to see the case through: "If Chambers is lying, he should be exposed. If Hiss is lying, he should be exposed."

Herter said that he thoroughly approved of this course of action.

That night I read and reread the testimony of both men. I tried to disregard those sections which bore on Chambers' charge that Hiss had been a Communist. I concentrated my sole attention on one question—had Hiss known Chambers?—because it was obvious from reading Chambers' testimony that not only did he claim to know Hiss, but that he knew him very well.

What should one man know about another if he knew him as well as Chambers claimed to know Hiss? I worked into the small hours of the morning making notes of literally scores of questions that I might ask Chambers which would bear on this point.

After the experience of the last two days, I was determined never to go into another hearing of the Committee on Un-American Activities without being at least as well prepared as the witnesses themselves.

August 7 was a Saturday and the Committee met in a large empty wood-paneled courtroom on the first floor of the Federal Courthouse in New York's Foley Square. Chambers sat alone on one side of a long counsel table in the front of the courtroom, with the members of the Sub-committee—Congressmen Hébert, John R. McDowell, Pennsylvania Republican, and myself—across from him. Stripling sat with us and behind us were the Committee's three other investigators—Louis Russell, Donald Appell, and Charles McKillips—and Ben Mandel, our research director. The only other person present was the Committee's stenographer, who recorded the official transcript.

After Chambers had taken the oath as a witness, I began the questioning by going straight to the main issue: since he claimed to know Hiss and Hiss denied knowing him, I asked him to tell the Committee everything he knew about Hiss. Then, for almost three hours, I bombarded him with questions covering every fact I could think of which one man should know about another if they were friends. The answers came back one after another, unequivocally, and in the most minute detail.

He had first met Hiss in 1935 and had seen him on scores of occasions through 1937.

He had collected Communist Party dues from him.

He had stayed at the Hiss home on several occasions, once for a week.

Hiss and his wife had a cocker spaniel dog which they had boarded at a kennel on Wisconsin Avenue in Washington when they went on vacations to Maryland's eastern shore.

Hiss was called "Hilly" by his wife; he called her "Dilly"; friends commonly referred to them as "Hilly" and "Dilly," but not in their presence.

He described Mrs. Hiss as a short, highly nervous woman with a habit of blushing bright red when she was excited or angry. He told us Mrs. Hiss's maiden name, her birthplace, her background.

He described Hiss's stepson.

He told us of Hiss's boyhood hobby of fetching spring water from Druid Hill Park and selling it in Baltimore.

He described the interiors and exteriors of three different houses the Hisses lived in while he knew them.

All of this information, I realized, he might have obtained by studying Hiss's life without actually knowing him. But some of the answers had a personal ring of truth about them, beyond the bare facts themselves.[3]

[3] Chambers' memory of minute details was one of the very things, incidentally, that raised doubts in the minds of some Committee members as to his credibility. How could he possibly recall names, places, and events with which he had last been associated over ten years before? In retrospect, I believe that two factors contributed to his ability to do so. First, even his most bitter enemies had to agree that Chambers was a man of extraordinary intelligence. In addition, as a Communist underground agent, he had to train himself to carry vast quantities of information in his head so that he could reduce to the minimum the risk of ever being apprehended with documents on his person. As a result, his mind's retentive capacities were developed to an astonishing degree.

For instance, when I asked him how the Hiss family lived and about the kind of meals they served, he replied, "I think you get here into something else. Hiss is a man of great simplicity and a great gentleness and sweetness of character, and they lived with extreme simplicity. I had the impression that the furniture in that house [on Twenty-eighth Street in Washington] was kind of pulled together from here or there. Maybe they got it from their mother or something like that, nothing lavish about it whatsoever, quite simple. Their food was in the same pattern, and they cared nothing about food. It was not a primary interest in their lives."

I got a similar impression when I asked him, "Did he have any hobbies?"

"Yes, he did. They both had the same hobby—amateur ornithologists, bird observers. They used to get up early in the morning and go to Glen Echo out the canal, to observe birds. I recall once they saw, to their great excitement, a prothonotary warbler."

John McDowell, a bird fancier himself, interrupted to comment, "A very rare specimen." And Chambers said, "I never saw one. I am also fond of birds."

But while testimony like this was very convincing, some of the things Chambers told us that day were so close to unbelievable that they raised a doubt in our minds about all the rest.

For example, I asked him, "Did they have a car?"

"Yes, they did," Chambers replied. He described a 1929 Ford roadster, black and dilapidated, which had windshield wipers that had to be worked by hand. Then he told what seemed to be an unlikely story of how Alger Hiss bought another car in 1936 and wanted to give the old Ford to the Communist Party. "It was against all the rules of the underground organization—and I think this investigation has proved how right the Communists are in such matters. But Hiss insisted. Much against Peters' [J. Peters was at that time the head of the Communist underground in the United States] better judgment, he finally got us to permit him to do this thing," Chambers said.

Hiss turned the car over to a Communist in a Washington service station and it was later transferred to another Party member. "I should think the records of that transfer would be traceable," Chambers concluded.

As he came to the end of his testimony, I asked, "Would you be willing to submit to a lie detector on this testimony?"

"Yes, if necessary," he answered, without hesitation.

"You have that much confidence?"

"I am telling the truth," he said quietly.

While listening to Chambers testify that Saturday afternoon, I felt sure that he was telling the truth. But on the train ride back to Washington, some of my doubts began to return.

Could Chambers, by making a careful study of Hiss's life, have concocted the whole story for the purpose of destroying Hiss—for some motive we did not know?

It was difficult back in 1948, before the scope of the Communist underground movement had become generally known, to believe a man like Chambers over a man like Hiss. Consider Chambers' background. He had been a City Editor of the *Daily Worker*, written for the *New Masses*, and served as a paid functionary of the Communist Party underground, then had repudiated the Party, and for months had slept with a gun under his pillow for fear of assassination. Could such a man be believed? Wasn't it more plausible to conclude that he was bent on destroying an innocent man?

Hiss, on the other hand, had come from a fine family, had made an outstanding record at Johns Hopkins and Harvard Law, had been honored by being selected for the staff of a great justice of the Supreme Court, had served as Executive Secretary to the big international monetary conference at Dumbarton Oaks in 1944, had accompanied President Roosevelt to Yalta, and had held a key post at the conference establishing the United Nations at San Francisco. Was it possible that a man with this background could have been a Communist whose allegiance was to the Soviet Union, even during the period when the Communists and Nazis had been allies, in 1939–41?

The Committee could not go off half-cocked again, particularly with such great stakes involved. We had a grave responsibility to be sure of our facts before any more charges were aired in public.

In the next nine days, from August 8 to August 16, the Committee staff under Stripling's direction worked round the clock in a search for documentary or other proof, if it existed, of Chambers' story. They questioned real estate agents for leases pertaining to the three houses in which Chambers said Hiss lived from 1935 to 1937. They found the dog kennel in Georgetown where the Hisses had left their cocker spaniel when they went on vacation. They searched for anyone who might possibly have seen the two men together in the neighborhoods where

Hiss had lived. And in detail after detail, where the Chambers story could be checked with third parties, it proved to be true. But they were unsuccessful in their search for one vitally important piece of documentation: they could not find the Motor Vehicle records to substantiate Chambers' strange story about Hiss's giving his car to a Communist Party functionary.

In this same period, I tried to resolve some of my own doubts by reading and rereading Chambers' testimony and by seeking counsel from men of varying views whose opinions I respected. The question I asked over and over again was whether Chambers' testimony constituted a prima facie case against Hiss, justifying a further pursuit of the investigation. Or should I agree with the Committee's original inclination after hearing Hiss testify that we turn the case over to the Justice Department?

I was to learn during this period a lesson about the nature of crisis which would serve me for years to come.

Making the decision to meet a crisis is far more difficult than the test itself. One of the most trying experiences an individual can go through is the period of doubt, of soul-searching, to determine whether to fight the battle or to fly from it. It is in such a period that almost unbearable tensions build up, tensions that can be relieved only by taking action, one way or the other. And significantly, it is this period of crisis conduct that separates the leaders from the followers. A leader is one who has the emotional, mental, and physical strength to withstand the pressures and tensions created by necessary doubts and then, at the critical moment, to make a choice and to act decisively. The men who fail are those who are so overcome by doubts that they either crack under the strain or flee to avoid meeting the problem at all.

On the other hand, if one is to act and to lead responsibly he must necessarily go through this period of soul-searching and testing of alternate courses of action. Otherwise he shoots from the hip, misses the target, and loses the battle through sheer recklessness.

Even in a struggle as clear-cut as that between Communism and freedom, there are gray areas. But there are intrinsic principles which must be adhered to. Anyone who shirks this inner debate in waging this struggle acts irresponsibly. It is this soul-searching and testing which ultimately gives a man the confidence, calmness, and toughness with which to act decisively.

In the period between August 7 and August 16, when Hiss was to testify again, I not only insisted that the Committee staff, by the most intensive possible investigation, try to establish the truth or falsity of Chambers' testimony by corroborative evidence but, in addition, I tried to check the objectivity of my own judgment against the opinions of men whom I respected.

I asked Bert Andrews, chief Washington correspondent of the New York *Herald Tribune,* to come to my office. I felt he would be predisposed to believe Hiss rather than Chambers. He had recently won a Pulitzer Prize for a series of articles attacking the fairness of the State Department's loyalty program. Along with James Reston of the New York *Times,* he had recommended Hiss to Dulles for the Carnegie post. From my brief acquaintance with Andrews and from his reputation among his colleagues in the press corps, I was convinced he would be objective. He had the rare quality which distinguishes a great reporter from just a good one—he never allowed his prejudices or emotions to get in the way in his search for and reporting of the truth. He once told me, "An editor has the right to write from his heart. But a reporter must never allow his heart to override what his head tells him are the facts. The trouble with too many reporters who cover the State Department, for example, is that they forget that their job is to write *about* the Secretary of State and they proceed to write as if they *were* the Secretary of State."

I asked Andrews to read the testimony, with the understanding that he could write nothing about it until it was released for publication to all papers. When he finished his reading, he turned to me and said, "I wouldn't have believed it, after hearing Hiss the other day. But there's no doubt about it. Chambers knew Hiss."

The next day I asked William P. Rogers, who was then chief counsel for the Senate Internal Security Sub-committee investigating the Bentley charges, to read the testimony. Rogers, who was later to become Attorney General, had made a brilliant record as one of Tom Dewey's young prosecutors in New York, and I felt that he would be a good judge of Chambers' credibility. He reached the same conclusion as Andrews.

That night I had dinner with Congressman Charles J. Kersten, Republican of Wisconsin, with whom I served as a member of the Labor Committee and who was a keen analyst of Communist tactics and strategy. After Kersten read the testimony he made a suggestion which was not only to have a great bearing on my own conduct of this case but on the course of my career in the years ahead. He told me he had heard that Hiss was trying to get John Foster Dulles and other members of the Carnegie board to make statements in his behalf. He suggested that I should give Dulles the opportunity to read the testimony.

The following morning, August 11, I telephoned Dulles and he said he would be willing to see me that night at the Roosevelt Hotel in New York, where he was working on the Dewey presidential campaign. Kersten and I took the train to New York that afternoon and met Dulles in his hotel suite. His brother Allen, who later was to become head of the Central Intelligence Agency, was also there. Both men read the testimony. When they had finished, Foster Dulles paced the floor, his hands crossed behind him. It was a characteristic I was to see many times in the years ahead when we discussed important issues. He stopped finally and said, "There's no question about it. It's almost impossible to believe, but Chambers knows Hiss." Allen Dulles reached the same conclusion.

I asked Foster Dulles whether he thought I was justified in going ahead with the investigation. He replied without hesitation, "In view of the facts Chambers has testified to, you'd be derelict in your duty as a Congressman if you did not see the case through to a conclusion."

I was so wrapped up with the problems of making my own decision that I did not fully realize at the time the political courage and integrity Dulles demonstrated by this statement. He was Dewey's chief foreign policy adviser in the campaign. If and when Dewey was elected President, which most people thought was pretty certain at that time, it was generally assumed that Foster Dulles would be named Secretary of State. As Chairman of the Board of the Carnegie Endowment he had approved the appointment of Hiss to his present position. It would be acutely embarrassing to him if Hiss should be discredited —or worse, proved to be a Communist. He could have suggested that I delay the proceedings until after the election. But both Foster Dulles and his brother Allen, in this instance and in every case in which I was to work with either of them during my years as Vice President, put the cause of justice and the national interest above any personal or political considerations.

Still I was not satisfied. I decided to see Chambers again, this time alone and informally, not so much to get more information from him as to gain a more intimate impression of what kind of man he really was. I thought that if I could talk to him alone, I would be better able to sense whether or not he was telling the truth. To avoid any publicity, I made the two-hour trip from Washington to his farm by car. We sat on some dilapidated rocking chairs on his front porch overlooking the rolling Maryland countryside. It was the first of many long and rewarding conversations I was to have with him during the period of the Hiss case, and through the years until his death in 1961. Like most men of quality, he made a deeper impression personally than he did in public. Within minutes, the caricature drawn by the rumormongers of the drunkard, the unstable and unsavory character, faded away. Here was a man of extraordinary intelligence, speaking from great depth of understanding; a sensitive, shy man who had turned from complete dedication to Communism to a new religious faith and a kind of fatalism about the future. One thing that especially impressed me was his almost absolute passion for personal privacy. He seemed particularly to want to spare his children any embarrassment from what he had hoped was a closed chapter in his life. His wife, Esther, was exactly like him in this respect.

Why then was he willing to sacrifice this privacy and risk his own financial security by testifying against Hiss and by testifying as he had before our Committee? I told him bluntly that many of those who questioned his credibility believed he must have some personal motive for doing what he had to Hiss.

Chambers replied, "Certainly I wouldn't have a motive which would involve destroying my own career." He had come forward out of necessity, he said, as a kind of duty to warn his country of the scope, strength, and danger of the Communist conspiracy in the United States. It would be a great pity if the nation continued to look upon this case as simply a clash of personalities between Hiss and himself. Much more was at stake than what happened to either of them as individuals. Turning to me, he said with great feeling, "This is what you must get the country to realize."

The visit was not too productive in obtaining any additional information about his relationship with Hiss. But one incident occurred to confirm my conviction that when he spoke of Hiss, he was talking about someone he knew rather than someone whose life he had studied. I happened to mention the fact that I was a member of the Society of Friends. He said that he and his family attended the Friends' meeting in Westminster. He recalled that Mrs. Hiss, at the time he knew her, also had been a Friend.

Then his eyes lit up, he snapped his fingers, and he said, "That reminds me of something. Priscilla often used the plain speech in talking to Alger at home."

I knew from personal experience that my mother never used the plain speech in public but did use it in talking with her sisters and her mother in the privacy of our home. Again I recognized that someone else who knew Priscilla Hiss could have informed Chambers of this habit of hers. But the way he told me about it, rather than what he said, again gave me an intuitive feeling that he was speaking from first-hand rather than second-hand knowledge.

Two days later I asked Bert Andrews to drive with me to Chambers' farm so that I could get his impression as well. Andrews grilled him as only a Washington newspaperman can, and Chambers met the test to Andrews' complete satisfaction. On this visit another small but somewhat significant item came up which seemed to corroborate Chambers' story. I asked him if he had anything in the house which Hiss might have given him during the time that he knew him. Chambers brought out a volume of Audubon prints which he said Hiss had given him one Christmas. As we thumbed through it, he pointed to a drawing of a hooded warbler and said, "As I recall, the Hisses had this in the dining room of one of the houses they lived in."

As a final test, two days before Hiss was to appear on August 16, I asked Bob Stripling to drive to Westminster with me. Stripling had almost a sixth sense in being able to distinguish the professional "Red-baiters" from those who were honestly trying to help the Committee in its work of exposing the Communist conspiracy. He, too, had been convinced by this time that Chambers knew Hiss. But as we drove back to Washington, he made a most perceptive observation: "I don't think Chambers has yet told us the whole story. He is holding something back. He is trying to protect somebody."

When our Sub-committee met again in executive session in Washington on August 16, we found a very different Alger Hiss from the confident, poised witness who had appeared before us in public session just ten days before. Then he had succeeded in giving the impression of being completely honest and forthright—trying his best to enlighten some clumsy Congressmen who had either been taken in by a vicious maniac or who were fooled in a terrible case of mistaken identity.

Now he was twisting, turning, evading, and changing his story to fit the evidence he knew we had. Despite our efforts to keep Chambers' testimony of August 7 secret, Hiss had learned that Chambers had been able to give us intimate details of their association together.

After a few preliminary questions, I had the Committee clerk show Hiss two pictures of Chambers. Then I asked him: "After looking at those pictures, I ask you if you can remember that person, either as Whittaker Chambers or as Carl or as any other individual you have met."

Ten days before, he had given everyone at the public hearing the distinct impression that the face was completely unfamiliar to him. Now Hiss was to make the first of several subtle but significant changes in his story. He said: "In the public session when I was shown another photograph of Mr. Whittaker Chambers, I testified that I could not swear that I had never seen the man whose picture was shown me. Actually the face has a certain familiarity—I cannot recall any person with distinctness and definiteness whose picture this is, but it is not completely unfamiliar."

I continued to question him, trying to widen this first tiny crack in his claim that he did not know Chambers. He fought stubbornly and skillfully every inch of the way and his answers became increasingly lengthy and evasive.

He finally began to argue with the Committee. "I have been angered and hurt," he said to me, "by the attitude you have been taking today that you have a conflict of testimony between two witnesses—one of whom is a confessed former Communist and the other is me—and that you simply have two witnesses saying contradictory things as between whom you find it most difficult to decide on credibility. I do not wish to make it easier for anyone who, for whatever motive I cannot under-stand, is apparently endeavoring to destroy me. I should not be asked to give details which somehow he may hear and then may be able to use as if he knew them before."

I replied that the questions I had asked him and Chambers had regard to facts that "could be corroborated by third parties" and that under no circumstances would the Committee use his testimony so that Chambers would be able to "build a web" around him.

Then he attacked on another front. He said: "The issue is not whether this man knew me and I don't remember him. The issue is whether he had a particular conversation that he said he had with me, and which I have denied, and whether I am a member of the Communist Party or ever was, which he has said and which I have denied."

But it was Hiss himself who in the public session had deliberately raised the issue of whether Chambers knew him. He had taken a calculated risk in raising that issue, and now he had to pay the price for his bold gamble.

I pressed him on this critical point. "When Mr. Chambers appeared," I said, "he was instructed that every answer he gave to every question would be material and that answers to a material question would subject him to perjury. Membership in the Communist Party is one thing, because that is a matter which might be and probably would be concealed. But items concerning his alleged relationship with you can be confirmed by third parties, and that is the purpose of these questions."

Hiss obviously recognized that he had come to the end of the road of detours. "I have written a name on this pad in front of me of a person I knew in 1933 and 1934 who not only spent some time in my home but sublet my apartment," he said. "I do not recognize the photographs as possibly being this man. I have given the name to two friends of mine before I came to this hearing. I don't think in my present frame of mind that it is fair to my position that I be asked to put down here a record of personal facts about myself which, if they came to the ears of someone who had for no reason I can understand a desire to injure me, would assist him in that endeavor."

For fifteen minutes he sparred with me and with Stripling. He kept insisting that if he answered our questions—questions to which Chambers had already replied, on the record and under oath, in great detail—Chambers would somehow learn what his answers had been and use this information against him.

At this point, Ed Hébert burst out with what to Hiss must have felt like a blockbuster. Hébert, a Democrat from Louisiana, was respected by both Republicans and Democrats in the Congress because, while he always fought hard for his party's positions, he had made it known on several issues in the past that he was no rubber stamp for Democratic administrations. He had been a member of the Sub-committee which had questioned Chambers in New York on August 7. After that hearing, he had made it clear that he still had great doubts about Chambers' credibility.

But now he had had enough. He said: "Mr. Hiss, let me say this to you now—and this is removed from all technicalities, it's just a man-to-man impression of the whole situation. . . . I will tell you exactly what I told Mr. Chambers so that it will be a matter of record, too: either you or Mr. Chambers is lying . . . and whichever one of you is lying is the greatest actor that America has ever produced. Now, I have not come to the conclusion yet which one of you is lying and I am trying to find the facts. Up to a few moments ago you have been very open, very co-operative. Now, you have hedged.

"We met Mr. Chambers forty-eight hours after you testified in open session. Mr. Chambers did not know or have any indication as to the questions that we were going to ask him and we probed him for hours . . . and we literally ran out of questions. There wasn't a thing that came to our minds that we didn't ask him about, those little details to probe his own testimony or rather to test his own credibility.

"Now if we can get the help from you and, as I say, if I were in your position, I certainly would give all the help I could, because it is a most fantastic story. What motive would Chambers have? You say you are in a bad position, but don't you think that Chambers destroys himself if he is proven a liar? What motive would he have to pitch a $25,000 position as a respected Senior Editor of *Time* magazine out the window?"

Hiss was shaken to his toes by this blast. Up to this time he had, not without considerable support from the press and from President Truman himself, tried to imply that the entire hearing was a "Republican plot" to smear the New Deal. Now for the first time, a Democrat had begun to question his story. Hiss reacted by counterattacking Hébert as hard as he could.

"It is difficult for me to control myself," he exclaimed. "That you can sit there, Mr. Hébert, and say to me casually that you have heard that man and you have heard me and you just have no basis for judging which one is telling the truth. I don't think a judge determines the credibility of witnesses on that basis."

But Hébert, not to be cowed, fired back: "I absolutely have an open mind and am trying to give you as fair a hearing as I could possibly give Chambers or yourself. The fact that Mr. Chambers is a self-confessed traitor . . . and a self-confessed former member of the Communist Party—has no bearing at all on the alleged facts that he has told . . ."

"Has no bearing on his credibility?" interrupted Hiss.

"No, because, Mr. Hiss, I recognize the fact that maybe my background is a little different from yours," replied Hébert, who had been a New Orleans newspaper editor for many years. "But I do know police methods, and you show me a good police force and I will show you the stool pigeon who turned them in. We have to have people like Chambers to come in and tell us. I am not giving Mr. Chambers any great credit for his previous life. I am trying to find out if he is reformed. Some of the greatest saints in history were pretty bad before they were saints. Are you going to take away their sainthood because of their previous lives? Are you not going to believe them after they have reformed? I don't care who gives the facts to me, whether a confessed liar, thief, or murderer—if it is facts. That is all I'm interested in."

Hiss had a bear by the tail. He tried to change the subject. "I would like to raise a separate point," he said. The real issue, he again insisted, was not whether Chambers knew him or he knew Chambers; it was whether he and Chambers had had the one particular conversation to which Chambers had testified.

I answered by saying, "If Chambers' credibility on the question of whether he knew you or not is destroyed, obviously you can see that this statement that he had a conversation with you and that you were a member of the Communist Party, which was made on the basis of this knowledge, would also be destroyed. And that is exactly the basis upon which this questioning is being conducted. If we prove that he is a perjurer on the basis of his testimony now, the necessity of going into the rest of the matter will be obviated."

After a few more questions, I asked Chairman J. Parnell Thomas to declare a recess so that Hiss could phone his wife, Priscilla, and make arrangements for her to appear before the Committee.

Five minutes later, when Hiss returned to the Committee room, he was ready to talk. He said: "The name of the man I brought in—and he may have no relation to this whole nightmare—is a man named George Crosley. I met him when I was working for the Nye Committee. He was a writer. He hoped to sell articles to magazines about the munitions industry."

This man Crosley, he went on, had sublet his apartment on Twenty-eighth Street and had moved in with his wife and "one little baby." "My recollection is that he spent several nights in my house because his furniture van was delayed. The apartment wasn't very expensive and I think I let him have it at exact cost."

"His wife and he and little baby did spend several nights in the house with you?"

"This man Crosley, yes," Hiss replied.

"Can you describe his wife?" I asked.

"Yes, he answered. "She was a rather strikingly dark person. Very strikingly dark."

I was the only one in the room to whom that answer was significant. I had seen Esther Chambers and I knew that she was indeed strikingly dark.

Hiss insisted, however, that he could not say that Crosley and Chambers were one and the same person. He described Crosley as a "deadbeat" who stayed in the apartment during the summer months of 1935 and never paid any rent.

"What kind of automobile did that fellow have?" Stripling asked.

"No kind of automobile," Hiss replied. "I sold him an automobile. I had an old Ford that I threw in with the apartment, that I had been trying to trade in and get rid of. A slightly collegiate model. It wasn't very fancy, but it had a sassy little trunk on the back."

"You sold him that car?" I asked.

"I threw it in," Hiss replied. "He wanted a way to get around and I said, 'Fine. I want to get rid of it. I have another car. We kept it for sentimental reasons—not worth a damn.' I let him have it along with the rent."

"You gave this car to Crosley?" I asked.

"I threw it in along with the apartment—charged the rent and threw the car in at the same time," Hiss replied.

"In other words, added a little to the rent to cover the car?"

"No, I think I charged him exactly what I was paying for the rent and threw the car in in addition. I don't think I got any compensation."

From there I went on with the other questions which I had asked Chambers. In virtually every detail, Hiss's answers matched those of Chambers. He had a brown cocker spaniel which he boarded at a kennel near Rock Creek Park when he went on vacation to the eastern shore of Maryland. He used to fetch water from the Druid Hills spring as a boy of twelve to sell in Baltimore.

"What hobby, if any, do you have, Mr. Hiss?" I asked.

"Tennis and amateur ornithology," he replied.

"Did you ever see a prothonotary warbler?" McDowell asked.

"I have, right here on the Potomac. Do you know that place?" Hiss replied. ". . . They come back and nest in those swamps. Beautiful yellow head. A gorgeous bird."

The lease on the apartment expired in September 1935, Hiss said. "And I think I saw him several times after that. I think he told me he moved from here to Baltimore."

"Even though he didn't pay his rent, you saw him several times?" I asked.

"He was about to pay it and was going to sell his articles. He gave me a payment on it on account once. He brought a rug over which he said some wealthy patron gave him. I have still got the damned thing."

"Did you ever give him anything?" I asked.

"Never anything but a couple of loans. Never got paid back," Hiss replied.

"Have you ever heard of him since 1935?" I asked.

"No. Never thought of him again until this morning on the train," Hiss answered.

Hiss said that to his knowledge Crosley was not a member of the Communist Party and that they had never discussed Communism. Crosley claimed to have written for *American Magazine* and for *Cosmopolitan,* but Hiss said he had never seen Crosley's name on any articles and that he personally had never seen anything Crosley had written. Apart from the rug, he had paid only $15 or $20 on the rent —which would have been $225 for the three-month summer period.

I told Hiss that Chambers had indicated his willingness to take a lie detector test with regard to this testimony and asked him if he would also be willing to do so. Hiss said that he would like to have an opportunity for further consultation as to the accuracy of such tests before he gave his answer.

Just before the end of the session, the Committee voted to hold a public hearing on Wednesday, August 25, in the caucus room of the Old House Office Building—at which time Chambers and Hiss would have the opportunity to confront one another. Hiss agreed to be present.

That evening Stripling and I spent several hours in my office comparing notes on our reactions to Hiss's testimony. We were convinced that Crosley and Chambers were the same man. Chambers did know Hiss. But the key question remained: which man was telling the truth as to the character of that relationship?

Hiss's story was plausible. But could an argument over his failure to pay a $200 rent bill cause Chambers—thirteen years later—to risk his reputation, a $25,000-a-year job, and a prison term for perjury, in order to get revenge on Hiss? Where was the motivation?

And then there was the testimony about the car. Why would Hiss, who was not a wealthy man, give even an old car in those depression days to a "deadbeat" free-lance writer with whom he had only a casual acquaintance? I recalled, too, that Hiss had spoken with rather strange and uncharacteristic vehemence when we asked him about the car. "It wasn't worth a damn," he had said. And he seemed to have a similar reaction when we spoke of Chambers giving him the rug. "I still have the damn thing," he had exclaimed. Was there something about the car and the rug that especially worried him? Like Lady Macbeth, was he saying, in effect, "Out, damned spot!"[4]

But we had not been able to find the records on the car, and Chambers had not even mentioned the rug. Stripling and I decided that every available member of our small Committee staff should concentrate between now and August 25 in trying to find out what had happened to that "slightly collegiate model Ford with the sassy little trunk on the back."

Stripling left my office shortly before midnight, but I continued to appraise the testimony of both Hiss and Chambers. I knew that we had reached the critical breaking point in the case. Timing now became especially important.

If Hiss's story about Crosley were true, why had he not disclosed it to the Committee when he first appeared in public session? Why had he first tried so desperately to divert the Committee from questioning him on the facts Chambers had previously testified to? The longer I thought about the evidence, the more I became convinced that if Hiss had concocted the Crosley story, we would be playing into his hands by delaying the public confrontation until August 25, thus giving him nine more days to make his story fit the facts. With his great influence within the Administration and among some of his friends in the press, he might be able to develop an enormous weight of public opinion to back up his story and to obscure the true facts in the case. The more I thought about it, the more I became convinced that we should not delay the confrontation. Only the man who was not telling the truth would gain by having additional time to build up his case.

So, at two in the morning, I called Stripling on the phone. I told

---

[4] Tom Murphy, the government prosecutor in the perjury trials, was to prove that Hiss had good cause for worry on both counts. The car and the rug became incriminating pieces of evidence which Hiss could not explain away.

him to summon both Chambers and Hiss before the Sub-committee in New York City that same afternoon. Desiring as much privacy as possible, we decided to have the meeting in a suite in the Commodore Hotel.

That afternoon, riding on the train from Washington to New York, we read in the papers that Harry Dexter White, who had denied Chambers' and Elizabeth Bentley's testimony that he had participated in Communist activities, had died of a heart attack. The Committee was subsequently to be accused of arranging the Hiss-Chambers confrontation on August 17 in order to divert attention from White's death. All I can say is that this accusation—like so many others against the Committee—while plausible, is completely untrue. I myself had made the decision on the confrontation well before I learned of White's death.

At 5:35 P.M. on August 17, John McDowell opened the meeting of our Sub-committee by swearing in Alger Hiss as our first witness.

Room 1400 of the Commodore was an average-size hotel sitting room. Only one feature of it was in keeping with the high drama of the Hiss-Chambers case: the pictures on the wall were Audubon prints.

McDowell and I sat on separate chairs, our backs to the window, with a lamp table to serve as the presiding officer's rostrum. Parnell Thomas arrived later. We had Hiss sit in a chair about eight or ten feet from the table, facing us. We reserved a place for Chambers on the couch, which was against the wall directly on Hiss's right. The only others present were four members of the Committee staff and the official reporter recording the proceedings. Hiss entered the room accompanied by Charles Dollard of the Carnegie Corporation staff.

I opened the questioning by informing Hiss that, since he had raised the possibility of a third party who might be involved in the case—I was referring, of course, to "George Crosley"—the Committee had concluded that Hiss and Chambers should confront each other at the earliest possible time. I told him he would have the opportunity to see Chambers at this hearing.

From the beginning, Hiss dropped all previous pretensions of injured innocence. He was on the defensive—edgy, delaying, belligerent, fighting every inch of the way. When he found that the Committee hearing might take longer than fifteen minutes, he complained that he had a six o'clock appointment at the Harvard Club and asked that a call be made explaining his delay. Dollard offered to make the call for him so that we could proceed.

Then Hiss commented, "I would like the record to show that on my way downtown from my uptown office, I learned from the press of the death of Harry White, which came as a great shock to me, and I am not sure that I feel in the best possible mood for testimony. I do not for a moment want to miss the opportunity of seeing Mr. Chambers. I merely wanted the record to show that."

He then complained that parts of his testimony of the day before had been leaked to the press and implied that the Committee was responsible.

Finally, after about ten minutes of sparring on these collateral issues, I said to one of the staff members: "Mr. Russell, will you bring Mr. Chambers in?"

Russell went to the adjoining bedroom where Chambers was waiting. Minutes seemed to pass as we sat there in silence waiting for him to return. Actually, after only a few seconds, Russell opened the door and re-entered the room with Chambers.

They came through a door at the far end of the room, in back of Hiss, and then had to walk several steps to reach the davenport on his right. But during this period, Hiss did not once turn around to look at his accuser—the man he had said he was so anxious to see "in the flesh." He just sat in his chair staring straight ahead, looking out the window.

After Chambers reached the davenport, I asked both him and Hiss to stand. I then said, "Mr. Hiss, the man standing here is Mr. Whittaker Chambers. I ask you now if you have ever known that man before."

"May I ask him to speak?" said Hiss. "Will you ask him to say something?"

I asked Chambers to state his name and business.

Chambers responded: "My name is Whittaker Chambers."

Hiss walked toward Chambers until he was not more than a foot away and looked down into his mouth. He said, "Would you mind opening your mouth wider?"

Chambers repeated: "My name is Whittaker Chambers."

Hiss, speaking more loudly, demanded again: "I said, would you open your mouth? You know what I am referring to, Mr. Nixon. Will you go on talking?"

Chambers continued: "I am Senior Editor of *Time* magazine."

Hiss then turned to me. "May I ask whether his voice, when he testified before, was comparable to this?"

"His voice?" I asked.

"Or did he talk a little more in a lower key?" Hiss continued.

McDowell commented, "I would say it is about the same now as we have heard."

Hiss was not yet satisfied. "Would you ask him to talk a little more?"

I handed the *Time* editor a copy of *Newsweek* which was on the table and asked him to read from it.

Hiss said: "I think he is George Crosley, but I would like to hear him talk a little longer. Are you George Crosley?" he asked Chambers.

A quizzical smile came to Chambers' lips as he answered: "Not to my knowledge. You are Alger Hiss, I believe."

Hiss straightened up as if he had been slapped in the face. "I certainly am," he said defiantly.

Chambers answered quietly and with a smile, "That was my recollection," and continued to read from the copy of *Newsweek*—"since June, Harry S. Truman had been peddling the Labor Secretaryship left vacant by Lewis B. Schwellenbach's death in hope of gaining the maximum political advantage from the appointment."

Hiss interrupted: "The voice sounds a little less resonant than the voice that I recall of the man I knew as George Crosley. The teeth look to me as though either they have been improved upon or that there has been considerable dental work done since I knew George Crosley, which was some years ago. I believe I am not prepared without further checking to take an absolute oath that he must be George Crosley."

I asked Chambers if he had had any work done on his teeth since 1934. He replied that he had had some extractions and some bridgework in the front of his mouth.

Hiss then said, "Could you ask him the name of the dentist that performed these things?"

I could hardly keep a straight face, but I decided to play the game out.

"What is the name?" I asked Chambers.

He replied, "Dr. Hitchcock, Westminster, Maryland."

Hiss then said: "That testimony of Mr. Chambers, if it can be believed, would tend to substantiate my feeling that he represented [himself] to me in 1934 or 1935 or thereabouts as George Crosley, a freelance writer of articles for magazines. I would like to find out from Dr.

Hitchcock if what he has just said is true, because I am relying partly, one of my main recollections of Crosley was the poor condition of his teeth."

I thought the comedy had gone far enough and said, "Before we leave the teeth, Mr. Hiss, do you feel that you would have to have the dentist tell you just what he did to the teeth before you could tell anything about this man?"

Hiss realized he had overplayed the hand. After a long moment of silence, he changed the subject. "I would like a few more questions asked. . . . I feel very strongly that he is Crosley, but he looks very different in girth and in other appearances—hair, forehead, and so on, particularly the jowls."

Any of our last lingering doubts that Hiss had known Chambers were erased by this incredible, and in some ways almost pitiful, performance. All his poise was gone now. He knew that his daring maneuver of trying to deny that he had ever known Chambers had ended in disaster—but he was not finished. With a look of cold hatred in his eyes, he fought like a caged animal as we tried to get him to make a positive identification for the record.

But with his temper no longer under control, he did not fight as skillfully as he had before. When I asked him about the alleged rental agreement with Crosley, he said that he had not been paid "a single red cent in currency." He had forgotten that just twenty-four hours earlier he had testified that Crosley had paid him $15 or $20 in cash. He still insisted that he had given the car to Crosley as part of the rental agreement—just thrown it in because he had no use for it—without requiring Crosley, a man he knew so slightly, to pay anything extra.

He recalled now that Crosley, with his wife and child, had spent two or three days with him and Mrs. Hiss in their P Street house before moving into the Twenty-eighth Street apartment, and that on one occasion Crosley had ridden from Washington to New York with him and Mrs. Hiss in their car. He had made some small loans to Crosley, amounting in all to $35 or $40, some even after Crosley had failed to pay the rent. On several occasions, Crosley had stayed overnight in the Hiss home because "he couldn't get a hotel reservation."

The longer he testified, the more apparent it became that despite his original protestations, his acquaintance with Crosley was far from casual. On the basis of his own testimony, he had known him very well.

Stripling brought this point home most effectively. He said, "I certainly gathered the impression when Mr. Chambers walked in this room and you walked over and examined him and asked him to open his mouth, that you were basing your identification purely on what his upper teeth might have looked like. Now, here's a person that you knew for several months at least. You knew him so well that he was a guest in your home, that you gave him an old Ford automobile and permitted him to use, or you leased him, your apartment, and . . . the only thing you have to check on is this denture. . . . There is nothing else about this man's features which you could definitely say, 'this is the man I knew as George Crosley'—that you have to rely entirely on this denture. Is that your position?"

Forced into a corner, Hiss again made a damaging admission. "From the time on Wednesday, August 4, 1948, when I was able to get hold of newspapers containing photographs of one Whittaker Chambers, I was struck by a certain familiarity in features. When I . . . was shown a photograph by you, Mr. Stripling [on August fifth], there was again some familiarity [in] features."

Stripling reminded Hiss that in the public session on August 5, he had left the directly contrary impression with the members of the Committee and the press.

But Hiss still refused to take an oath that Chambers was Crosley. "He may have had his face lifted," he protested.

Finally, he requested permission to ask Chambers some questions. I told him to proceed.

He asked: "Did you ever sublet an apartment on Twenty-ninth Street from me?"

Chambers replied: "No, I did not."

"Did you ever spend any time with your wife and child in an apartment on Twenty-ninth Street in Washington when I was not there because I and my family were living on P Street?"[5]

This time Chambers answered: "I most certainly did."

Hiss then said: "Would you tell me how you reconcile your negative answers with this affirmative answer?"

Chambers replied quietly: "Very easily, Alger. I was a Communist and you were a Communist. . . . As I have testified before, I came to Washington as a Communist functionary, a functionary of the American Communist Party. I was connected with the underground group of which Mr. Hiss was a member. Mr. Hiss and I became friends.

[5] In both instances, this should have been "Twenty-eighth Street."

To the best of my knowledge, Mr. Hiss himself suggested that I go there, and I accepted gratefully."

Hiss finally gave up. "I don't need to ask Mr. Whittaker Chambers any more questions. I am now perfectly prepared to identify this man as George Crosley."

Once again, Hiss, not thinking with his usual clarity, had made a misstep. Chambers, according to his own testimony, was a consummate liar, a man who could not be believed on anything. Yet Hiss was identifying him on the basis of one of Chambers' own statements.

McDowell then asked Chambers, "Is this the man, Alger Hiss, who was also a member of the Communist Party, at whose home you stayed?"

"Positive identification," Chambers responded.

These words were hardly out of Chambers' mouth when Hiss arose from his chair and strode over to him, shaking his fist and exclaiming, "May I say for the record at this point that I would like to invite Mr. Whittaker Chambers to make those same statements out of the presence of this Committee, without their being privileged for suit for libel. I challenge you to do it, and I hope you will do it damned quickly."

Lou Russell, apparently thinking Hiss might strike Chambers, walked up to him and took him by the arm. Hiss recoiled as if he had been pricked with a hot needle and turned on Russell. His voice was shrill now. "I am not going to touch him. You are touching me."

"Please sit down, Mr. Hiss," Russell said.

Hiss shot back, "I will sit down when the Chairman asks me."

McDowell called for order and the questioning resumed. Hiss continued to deny vehemently the rest of Chambers' testimony. He denied that he was a Communist, that he knew Crosley as a Communist, or that there was anything unusual in giving his car away to a magazine writer he hardly knew.

Stripling again raised the point of his insisting on seeing Chambers' teeth before he could identify him. Hiss replied, "I wouldn't have been able to identify him for certain today without his own assistance."

"You are willing to waive the dentures?"

Hiss answered: "I am, on the basis of his own testimony. That is good enough for me."

The hearing came to an end with the feeling that a great hurdle had been surmounted: the two men had confronted one another and their pasts were linked. The inextricable chain of events that would ultimately send Alger Hiss to prison had been set in motion and Hiss must have sensed this. McDowell adjourned the hearing, saying, "That is all. Thank you very much."

"I don't reciprocate," Hiss snapped in response.

I should have been elated. The case was broken. The Committee would be vindicated and I personally would receive credit for the part I had played. We had succeeded in preventing injustice being done to a truthful man and were now on the way to bringing an untruthful man to justice. Politically, we would now be able to give the lie to Truman's contemptuous dismissal of our hearings as a "red herring."

However, I experienced a sense of letdown which is difficult to describe or even to understand. I had carried great responsibility in the two weeks since August 3, and the battle had been a hard one. Now I began to feel the fatigue of which I had not been aware while the crisis was at its peak. There was also a sense of shock and sadness that a man like Hiss could have fallen so low. I imagined myself in his place and wondered how he would feel when his family and friends learned the true story of his involvement with Chambers and the Communist conspiracy. It is not a pleasant picture to see a whole brilliant career destroyed before your eyes. I realized that Hiss stood before us completely unmasked—our hearing had saved one life, but had ruined another.

But this case involved far more than the personal fortunes of Hiss, Chambers, myself, or the members of our Committee. It involved the security of the whole nation and the cause of free men everywhere. When I thought of the lengths to which Hiss had been willing to go to destroy Chambers and the Committee as well, I knew that he was fighting his battle without regard to its effect on him or anybody else, individually or personally.

The next morning I learned a fundamental rule of conduct in crises. The point of greatest danger is not in preparing to meet the crisis or fighting the battle; it occurs after the crisis of battle is over, regardless of whether it has resulted in victory or defeat. The individual is spent physically, emotionally, and mentally. He lets down. Then if he is confronted with another battle, even a minor skirmish, he is prone to drop his guard and to err in his judgment.

Alger Hiss brought his wife, Priscilla, to the same room in the Commodore Hotel the next day to corroborate his story about Crosley.

Thomas and McDowell had returned to Washington, and I was the only member of the Committee present. As I read the record now, thirteen years later, I realize the opportunity I missed in failing to question her as thoroughly as I had Hiss.

There were several reasons for that failure. I was tired. I thought that after our major break-through with Hiss the night before, Mrs. Hiss's testimony was not too important. I felt, in other words, that the battle was won, that I could afford to relax. Undoubtedly, I subconsciously reacted to the fact that she was a woman, and that the simple rules of courtesy applied.

She played her part with superb skill. When I asked her to take the oath to tell the truth, she inquired demurely if she could "affirm" rather than "swear." Subtly, she was reminding me of our common Quaker background. When I asked her about Crosley, she said, "I don't think I can really be said to have been acquainted with him at all." She remembered hardly anything about Crosley or his wife. "It all seems very long ago and vague."

Offering her vague impression of Crosley, she said, "I think the polite word for it is probably I think he was a sponger. I don't know whether you have ever had guests, unwelcome guests, guests that weren't guests, you know."

She succeeded completely in convincing me that she was nervous and frightened, and I did not press her further. I should have remembered that Chambers had described her as, if anything, a more fanatical Communist than Hiss. I could have made a devastating record had I also remembered that even a woman who happens to be a Quaker and then turns to Communism must be a Communist first and a Quaker second. But I dropped the ball and was responsible for not exploiting what could have been a second break-through in the case.[6]

I was never to make that same error again. In the years ahead I would never forget that where the battle against Communism is concerned, victories are never final so long as the Communists are still able to fight. There is never a time when it is safe to relax or let down. When you have won one battle is the time you should step up your effort to win another—until final victory is achieved.

When I arrived back in Washington the afternoon of the eighteenth, the attitude in the Capital with regard to the Hiss-Chambers contro-

[6] Tom Murphy did not repeat my mistake. His disarmingly courteous but relentless questioning of Priscilla Hiss was to be a major factor in convincing the jury of Hiss's guilt in the perjury trials to come.

versy had changed perceptibly. Hiss's admission that he had known Chambers, even under another name, had restored some confidence in the Committee and in Chambers, and it had shaken those who had been completely taken in by Hiss's attempt to create the impression that he was being accused by a man he didn't even know.

But we were still not out of the woods. When we had taken the train to New York on the afternoon of the seventeenth we had been way behind. Now we were about even. But we still had to prove not simply that Hiss knew Chambers but to determine the truth of Chambers' charges that Hiss was a Communist. And on this specific issue, all we had was Hiss's word against Chambers'. In the week between August 18 and the public confrontation on August 25, we drove our staff at an even harder pace in an effort to find corroborative evidence that would prove either Chambers' or Hiss's version of their relationship.

We first tried to find witnesses who might be able to corroborate Hiss's version of the relationship. We tracked down everyone who might possibly have known or seen George Crosley—including the editors of the magazines for which he was supposed to have written; former Senator Gerald Nye; members of his old Committee staff; and three individuals who Hiss had told us on August 17 at the Commodore might have known Crosley at the same time he did. In every case, the answer was the same: they had never heard of a George Crosley. In the entire history of the case, both before the Committee on Un-American Activities and in Hiss's two trials for perjury, no one could be found who could remember George Crosley—except Priscilla Hiss.

We subpoenaed John Abt and Lee Pressman, whom Chambers had charged were also members of the same Communist group. Both men —like Henry Collins before them—refused to answer questions on grounds of self-incrimination.

The critical piece of evidence in the case, however, was Hiss's 1929 Ford roadster. Here our staff seemed to have reached a dead end. They searched the records of the Department of Motor Vehicles for all automobile transfers in the District for the year 1935 and came up with a blank. Finally I suggested that they might be checking the wrong year and that they extend their search to include both 1934 and 1936. On August 23, two days before the public confrontation, they hit pay dirt. We had found what we were looking for.

One of our investigators found a Motor Vehicle transfer certificate dated July 23, 1936. It covered a title transfer of a 1929 Ford automobile, signed by Alger Hiss as owner and notarized by a Marvin Smith. The car had been transferred, not to George Crosley or to Whittaker Chambers, but to one William Rosen. We also found a Certificate of Title dated September 7, 1935, assigning a new Plymouth sedan to Alger Hiss.

Now we put the pieces of the puzzle together. We subpoenaed Marvin Smith, the notary, and he swore that Alger Hiss had personally appeared before him and signed the Certificate of Title in his presence. We learned that William Rosen, to whom the car had been transferred that same day, had a long record of membership in the Communist Party. When we called him later to testify before the Committee, he refused to answer questions about his membership in the Communist Party and as to whether he had ever owned a 1929 Ford automobile—although he answered readily enough about his ownership of other automobiles.

We also found that the lease on Hiss's apartment, in which Chambers and his wife had stayed, had expired on August 1, 1935. Hiss's story had gaping holes in it. If he had "given" or "sold" the car to Crosley as he had testified, why did Crosley's name not appear on the Transfer of Title? The theory that Crosley might have taken the car from Hiss and delivered it to Rosen wouldn't stand up either: Hiss had stated emphatically that he had given away the car as "part of the rental transaction." Would he, a year after the supposed rental agreement had expired, still have given Crosley a car—and after they had parted "with strong words" because of Crosley's welshing on the rent?

From the day of the private confrontation on August 17 to the public confrontation on August 25, I put in longer hours and worked harder than I had at any time in my life. I tried to anticipate how Hiss might try to explain the mass of contradictions in his story and I sought to plug up each and every loophole with documentary proof.

As the day for the hearing approached I stepped up my activity until I was spending as much as eighteen to twenty hours a day at my office. I deliberately refused to take time off for relaxation or "a break," because my experience had been that in preparing to meet a crisis, the more I worked the sharper and quicker my mental reactions became.

I began to notice, however, the inevitable symptoms of tension. I was "mean" to live with at home and with my friends. I was quick-tempered with the members of my staff. I lost interest in eating and skipped meals without even being aware of it. Getting to sleep became more and more difficult.

I suppose some might say that I was "nervous," but I knew these were simply the evidences of preparing for battle. There is, of course, a fine line to be observed. One must always be keyed up for battle but he must not be jittery. He is jittery only when he worries about the natural symptoms of stress. He is keyed up when he recognizes those symptoms for what they are—the physical evidences that the mind, emotions, and body are ready for action.

There is naturally a physical limitation on how long an individual can sustain activity of this intensity. Age has something to do with it. I found, for example, that at thirty-five my capacity for intense mental work was greater than at any time before or since. But even while the body can take such punishment for days, it cannot do so indefi-nitely. I recall the afternoon before the big hearing on the twenty-fifth. Bert Andrews stopped by my office. He exclaimed, "You look like hell. You need some sleep." By that time my case had been prepared and, at Andrews' insistence and for the first time in my life, I took a sleeping pill before going to bed. I slept for twelve hours and woke up the next morning physically refreshed, ready for the most important test I had had up to that time.

The caucus room, where Hiss had appeared three weeks before, was again jammed. Klieg lights and television cameras were set up for the first major congressional hearing ever to be televised. It was unfortu-nate that, back in 1948, there were so few television sets in American homes. Had millions of Americans seen Hiss on the stand that day—as was the case, for example, when Estes Kefauver questioned Frank Costello in 1951—there would not have been the lingering doubts over the Hiss case which have continued for so many years.

The Committee pointed up through its questioning the scores of loopholes in the story about George Crosley. We produced source after source to show that George Crosley never existed except in Alger Hiss's mind. We spent three hours grilling him on his story about the car. He knew that we had found the records on the car and had pre-pared a line of defense. He changed his story. Now he said he had not "given" or "sold" the car to Crosley but had "given Crosley the use of the car." But he still insisted he had done so in connection with Crosley's rental of the apartment.

I asked him how he could have given Crosley the use of a car in 1935, before the lease on the apartment expired, when he himself did not acquire a new car until months later. I reminded him that he had testified that the reason he had given the car to Crosley was that he already had a new car and thus had no need of the old one. He tried to explain this inconsistency by saying that he might have given Crosley "the use of the car" only after he acquired his new one.

But why would he then even loan a car to a man who, as he himself had testified, had welshed on his rent, I persisted.

"These were housekeeping details which a busy government official with much more important things to consider couldn't possibly be expected to remember," Hiss responded.

I agreed that it was difficult to remember events which occurred so many years before. But was not this the only car he had ever given away? He had to reply in the affirmative.

Finally we showed him a photostatic copy of the Transfer of Title with his notarized signature on the back. We asked him to identify his signature. He hedged and indicated he would not want to do so until he had an opportunity to see the original document.

"Could you be sure if you saw the original?" asked Congressman Mundt.

"I could be surer," replied Hiss. He had played the delaying game too far. The hearing room broke into laughter. Even his friends sitting in the front row of the spectators' section shook their heads in disbelief.

But Hiss was far from finished. He knew that he had lost the battle as to the fictitious Crosley and on the issue of the car. So he proceeded to launch a desperate counterattack.

He declared the charges against him were more than personal—that they were being used "to discredit recent great achievements of this country in which I was privileged to participate." In doing this, he was attempting to wrap the cloak of President Franklin Roosevelt and the New Deal around himself, implying that any attack on him was, in effect, an attack against the foreign policy which he had helped to make and against the Administrations in which he had served.

Then, he again reviewed his fifteen years of public service and listed the names of thirty-four prominent living persons whom he said knew him, knew his work, and had never had any occasion to doubt his loyalty. The list included two Senators, two Congressmen, three former Secretaries of State, three Under Secretaries of State, four federal judges, and three former Senators. It was long and impressive. This was, in the highest degree, "innocence by association." Ed Hébert called him on this tactic, pointing out that if he could not say whether John Abt, Lee Pressman, Henry Collins, and others whom he had known and who had taken the Fifth Amendment were or were not Communists, then how could the persons he listed say whether or not he, Hiss, was a Communist?

Finally, Hiss repeated his challenge—this time publicly—to Chambers, "to make statements about me with respect to Communism in public that he has made under privilege to this Committee."

Very deftly he coupled the challenge with an unmistakable innuendo that Chambers was mentally unbalanced. He asked the Committee to pose a series of questions to Chambers—such as where he had lived, where he had worked, what he had written, and finally, whether he had ever been treated for a mental illness? Hébert again hit back hard on this one. He declared the Committee had already asked Chambers these questions because of the rumors following his first day of testimony. The answer was that Chambers had never been treated for a mental illness, had never been in a mental institution, and furthermore, was not an alcoholic.

After five hours, Hiss left the stand. Chambers followed him and again repeated his charges, denying that he had ever subleased his apartment or borrowed his car, and that he had ever been known as George Crosley. We asked Chambers the questions which Hiss had suggested in his statement. Chambers answered each one forthrightly and completely. In short, he said that Hiss's story was a complete fabrication.

For me, one of the most eloquent statements made in the history of the Committee on Un-American Activities was spoken by Chambers toward the end of that long seven-hour session when I questioned him about his motive for testifying against Hiss. The official transcript reads:

Mr. Nixon. You were very fond of Mr. Hiss?
Mr. Chambers. Indeed I was; perhaps my closest friend.
Mr. Nixon. Mr. Hiss was your closest friend?
Mr. Chambers. Mr. Hiss was certainly the closest friend I ever had in the Communist Party.

Mr. Nixon. Mr. Chambers, can you search your memory now to see
  what motive you can have for accusing Mr. Hiss of being a Communist at the present time?
Mr. Chambers. What motive I can have?
Mr. Nixon. Yes, do you, I mean, is there any grudge you have against
  Mr. Hiss over anything he has done to you?
Mr. Chambers. The story has spread that in testifying against Mr.
  Hiss I am working out some old grudge or motives of revenge or
  hatred. I do not hate Mr. Hiss. We were close friends, but we are
  caught in a tragedy of history. Mr. Hiss represents the concealed
  enemy against which we are all fighting, and I am fighting. I have
  testified against him with remorse and pity, but in a moment of
  history in which this nation now stands, so help me God, I could
  not do otherwise.

There was a long silence. Then we went ahead with the questions,
proceeding to play out our parts in this "tragedy of history."

The confrontation was over. The tide of public opinion which had
run so high in favor of Hiss just three weeks before had now turned
against him. Critics who had condemned the Committee for putting
Chambers on the stand now congratulated us for our perseverance in
digging out the truth. But while there could be no doubt as to the
outcome of the contest, many battles would have to be fought and
won before complete victory for the cause of justice and truth would be
achieved.

There was now no turning back in the struggle for Chambers, either.
Hiss had challenged him to make his charges beyond the halls of congressional privilege. Chambers could not side-step the challenge.

Two days after the public hearing he accepted an invitation from
Larry Spivak to appear on "Meet the Press." Ed Folliard, who had
covered the hearings for the Washington *Post,* posed the expected key
question: "Are you willing to repeat your charge that Alger Hiss was
a Communist?"

"Alger Hiss was a Communist and may still be one," said Chambers.
Those ten words set in motion a chain of circumstances which led
to revelations that neither Chambers nor Hiss desired nor expected.

It was ironic that Folliard's question was the one which served to
detonate these explosive developments. The Washington *Post,* which
was typical of a large segment of the national press and of public
opinion, had always taken a dim view of the Committee on Un-Ameri-

can Activities and had launched an all-out assault on its procedures after Hiss first testified.

It kept up a drumfire of comment and criticism throughout the weeks during which the case developed. Its editorials called on the Committee to drop its investigation and leave it to those with the proper "constitutional duty." It questioned the sense of believing "turncoats" rather than men of "unsullied reputation." It even termed the confrontation "inconclusive."

But a few weeks after Chambers had accused Hiss on "Meet the Press" and there had still been no response from Hiss, even the *Post* changed its tune: "Mr. Hiss had created a situation in which he is obliged to put up or shut up. Mr. Hiss has left himself no alternative." Hiss was learning what many people in politics had learned before him: those he thought were his best friends turned out to be the heaviest cross he had to bear.

Three weeks passed and then, at the end of September, Hiss filed a $50,000 libel suit—later increased to $75,000—against Chambers in the U. S. District Court in Baltimore. He charged that Chambers had damaged his reputation by publicly accusing him of having been a Communist. Chambers cross-filed the classic defense for libel: truth. You cannot libel anyone if you state only the truth about him, no matter how damaging.

With this, I felt that the Committee's work had come to an end. The issue was now in the courts, and any further investigation by us might interfere with judicial proceedings.

For the next six weeks, through October and into early November, I turned to other assignments. Nineteen forty-eight was an election year. I had no personal problems in that respect. My re-election to a second term had been assured when I won both the Democratic and Republican nominations in the June primaries, under California's cross-filing system. But I had accepted a number of invitations to speak in various parts of the country for the Dewey-Warren ticket and for other Republican candidates for the House and Senate.

Domestic Communism was not a significant issue in that campaign. Probably because of the uncertain status of the Hiss-Chambers case, Dewey felt it was not proper to give too much prominence to the issue of Communist infiltration in government during the Truman Administration. I found great interest in my audiences when I discussed the Bentley charges and our investigation of the Hiss case. But what I said, of course, received no more than local attention in the areas in which I spoke.

The result on Election Day, 1948, was an unpleasant surprise for me and all Republicans. It really jolted Whittaker Chambers. A few days after the election I stopped to see him and his wife in Westminster on my way to York County, Pennsylvania, for a visit with my parents. He was in a mood of deep depression. He was not concerned with the election results from a partisan standpoint—he had never mentioned his partisan affiliation with me in our many discussions. What worried him was that the whole investigation of Communist infiltration in the United States and particularly in our government might be allowed to die. President Truman had indicated during the campaign that he would push for abolition of the Committee on Un-American Activities if he were re-elected. Chambers feared that the investigations by the Committee and by the New York Grand Jury would be dropped and that, even if the Committee were to survive, its powers would be greatly weakened with the shift in the Eighty-first Congress from Republican to Democratic control.

Chambers did not seem to be concerned that he might lose his $25,000-a-year job with *Time* or that he might lose everything he owned if Hiss won a judgment against him in the libel suit which was still pending. He only mentioned in passing that he was to go to Baltimore in a day or two for the purpose of answering questions by Hiss's attorneys in a deposition hearing.

There was nothing at all I could do about the election results. My mind at that time turned to some purely personal matters. Pat and I had not had a vacation since coming to Washington in January of 1947. Our plans to take one in the summer of 1947 had been washed out when I was appointed a member of the Herter Committee and spent six weeks in Europe on that assignment. And then in 1948 the Hiss case intervened just as we were ready to take off for a few days of relaxation. Now, together with several of our friends in Congress, we had booked passage on the SS *Panama* for a ten-day cruise through the Canal Zone, sailing from New York on December 2.

"This time," I told Pat the day I brought the tickets home, "absolutely nothing is going to interfere with our vacation."

She smiled and said, "I hope you're right, but I still have to be shown."

The day before we were to sail I saw a brief United Press dispatch in the Washington papers: "The Justice Department is about ready to drop its investigation of the celebrated Alger Hiss-Whittaker Chambers controversy, it was learned today. Department officials still have under study the question of a possible perjury prosecution. But officials said privately that unless additional evidence is forthcoming they are inclined to forget the whole thing. One Department source said that on the basis of available evidence, officials in charge of the case believe it would be unwise to take it before a Grand Jury."

I immediately called Stripling on the phone. He had read the same story. He said he had also heard rumors that there was some new evidence in the case which might substantiate Chambers' charges.

Playing a long hunch, I suggested to Stripling that we drive to Westminster at once and talk to Chambers. We arrived late in the afternoon and I showed him a copy of the United Press dispatch. He put down the paper and looked out the window, shaking his head without saying a word for at least a minute. Then he turned to me and said: "This is what I have been afraid of."

"In a deposition hearing two weeks ago, I produced some new evidence in the case—documentary evidence. It was so important that Hiss's attorneys and mine called the Justice Department. Alex Campbell, Chief of the Criminal Division, came to Baltimore and took the documents back to Washington. Before he left he warned everybody present to say nothing whatever about these documents and that if we did divulge any information, we would be guilty of contempt of court. So, I can't tell you what was in the documents. I will only say that they were a real bombshell."

Stripling and I tried without success to get some inkling of the contents. Then I asked Chambers a pointed question: "Do you mean that Campbell has these documents in his possession and it is completely up to him if anything is done about them?"

He smiled and said, "No, I wouldn't be that foolish. My attorney has photostatic copies, and also I didn't turn over everything I had. I have another bombshell in case they try to suppress this one."

"You keep that second bombshell," I said. "Don't give it to anybody except the Committee." Chambers did not respond but I was sure that he got the point.

As we drove back to Washington that evening, Stripling and I tried to guess what the documents might contain. What intrigued us both was Chambers' use of the word "bombshell." In his testimony he seldom if ever used flamboyant language. I told Stripling I had an intuitive feeling that Chambers was trying to tell us something by his deliberate use of that word—not just once but twice.

Under these new circumstances I wondered whether I shouldn't postpone my vacation, scheduled to begin the next day. But I didn't have the heart to tell Pat the bad news. I explained my predicament to Stripling and told him that I would be in Panama within four days and, if necessary, could fly back to Washington if he felt I had to. Taking no chances, however, I stopped off at the Committee office and signed a *subpoena duces tecum* on Chambers for any and all documents in his possession relating to the Committee hearings on the charges he had made against Hiss. Stripling said he would have the subpoena served on Chambers the next day.

And so, the next morning, after taking the train from Washington to New York, Pat and I boarded the *Panama* for what we thought was going to be a pleasant week of cruising through the Canal Zone and back. At dinner the first night out, we remarked to the others that one of the reasons we had taken this cruise was that at sea we could be sure of no interruptions by telephone calls or by mail.

We had not reckoned with radiograms.

The first full day at sea, Friday, December 3, I received a wire that Bert Andrews had sent late Thursday night. It read: "Information here is that Hiss-Chambers case has produced new bombshell. Stop. Indications are that Chambers has offered new evidence. Stop. All concerned silent. Stop. However, Justice Department partially confirms by saying 'It is too hot for comment.' Stop."

That evening Pat and I were having dinner at the Captain's table with Congressman Mike Kirwan of Ohio, Chairman of the Democratic Congressional Campaign Committee; Congressman Sterling Cole, Republican of New York, who now heads the International Atomic Energy Agency; and their wives. The purser brought me another wire. This one was from Stripling. "Second bombshell obtained by subpoena 1 A.M. Friday. Case clinched. Information amazing. Heat is on from press and other places. Immediate action appears necessary. Can you possibly get back?"

I knew that Stripling would not have sent such a cable unless the evidence was really of great importance. I read the cable aloud at the table and Pat threw up her hands and said, "Here we go again!"

The following morning, Sunday, I received the clincher—a long cablegram from Andrews. It read, in part: "Documents incredibly hot. Stop. Link to Hiss seems certain. Stop. Link to others inevitable. Stop.

Results should restore faith in need for Committee if not in some members. Stop. New York Jury meets Wednesday. Stop. Could you arrive Tuesday and get day's jump on Grand Jury. Stop. If not, holding hearing early Wednesday. Stop. My liberal friends don't love me no more. Stop. Nor you. Stop. But facts are facts and these facts are dynamite. Stop. Hiss's writing identified on three documents. Stop. Not proof he gave them to Chambers but highly significant. Stop. Stripling says can prove who gave them to Chambers. Stop. Love to Pat. Stop. (Signed) Vacation-Wrecker Andrews."

I radioed Stripling to make arrangements, if possible, to get me off the ship. By that time we were in the Caribbean near Cuba and the Captain said that if a Coast Guard amphibian PBY would come get me, he could pilot the ship to a stretch of water calm enough for a landing.

In Washington, Stripling took the problem to the naval attaché assigned to Congress. He in turn took the matter up directly with Defense Secretary Forrestal, who issued a personal order to the Coast Guard station in Miami to meet the ship and fly me to the mainland. On Sunday morning the ship dropped anchor on the lee side of an island. A Coast Guard PBY landed on the water nearby. Members of the ship's crew lowered me to the water in a lifeboat and rowed over to the PBY. I climbed aboard and was on my way to Miami.

Reporters and photographers were on hand to meet me. They asked what comment I had on the "pumpkin papers"?

I didn't have the slightest idea what they were talking about and asked, "What is this, a joke?"

They explained that when he was served with our subpoena, Chambers had led the Committee investigators to his pumpkin patch at midnight, taken the top off one of the pumpkins, and produced five rolls of microfilm containing photographs of secret State Department documents.

I simply could not believe my ears. On the seven-hour flight from Miami to Washington, I began to have the same misgivings about Chambers I had had when he first told us his fantastic story. Now, I wondered if we really might have a crazy man on our hands.

Stripling met my plane and took me directly to the Committee office. I soon learned that Chambers was crazy—like a fox. Here is what had happened.

Shortly after I had seen Chambers in November he had gone to

Baltimore to give testimony in the pretrial deposition being taken by Hiss's attorneys. Hiss's chief counsel, William Marbury, a Washington attorney of outstanding reputation, had asked Chambers if he had any letters, documents, or any other communications from Alger Hiss which would prove their alleged relationship. It was obvious to Chambers, as he later told me, that Marbury did not have the slightest expectation that Chambers would produce anything. Hiss, a lawyer himself, had made the fatal mistake no client should ever make—he had not told his own lawyer the full truth about the facts at issue.

In answer to the question, Chambers had said that he would check his files to see if he had any such evidence. When he returned to his home in Westminster, he went through a long period of soul-searching. He knew he had documentary proof, but he didn't know if he should use it.

Not long before, Chambers had been called before the New York Grand Jury investigating Communist activities and had been asked if he had any information involving Soviet espionage. He had weighed the implications of that question and had answered, "No." This answer was untrue. In his book, *Witness*, Chambers explained that while he wanted to expose Communist underground activities in the United States, he did not want to destroy Hiss and others who had been his friends and associates with his evidence of espionage. He had hoped that, once he testified, they too would admit their former activities and join him in exposing Communist subversion.

But at the pretrial proceedings, Hiss's attorneys had been raking over every aspect of his life in an attempt to discredit and destroy him. Under the circumstances, Chambers wondered if he should not counterattack in kind. One day his wife, Esther, was cross-examined so unmercifully by Hiss's attorneys that she broke into tears. This incident made his decision for him. If this was to be, in effect, total war, he would use the ultimate weapons available to him.

The next Sunday, November 14, Chambers went to Brooklyn to reclaim a package he had left with his wife's nephew, Nathan Levine, after his break with the Communist Party in 1938. Because he feared assassination, he had told his nephew to hide the package and to make its contents public only if he, Chambers, met with a violent death. Now, ten years later, he and Levine went together to the hiding place —an unused dumb-waiter in the Brooklyn apartment of Levine's mother. There they found Chambers' large sealed envelope, covered now with ten years' accumulation of dust and cobwebs. Inside the envelope were sixty-five typed pages of copies and summaries of confidential State Department documents, three memoranda in Hiss's handwriting, two strips of developed microfilm, three cylinders of undeveloped microfilm, and an eight-page memo of confidential Treasury Department information in the handwriting of Harry Dexter White. These documents had been stolen not only from the State Department but also from the Communist Party. Rather than turning over this final haul to his Communist superiors, Chambers had kept them for "life insurance."

Three days later, Hiss's attorneys again made their demand for documentary evidence, and Chambers handed over the sixty-five pages of typewritten State Department papers—many of which were later identified as having been typed on Hiss's Woodstock machine—the memos in Hiss's own handwriting, and the old envelope which had contained the documents. This was Chambers' first "bombshell." The second was the microfilm—the so-called "pumpkin papers."

The story of the "pumpkin papers" was typical of how a seemingly fantastic incident in the life of Whittaker Chambers could have a simple explanation. The rolls of microfilm had not been kept in a pumpkin for ten years, as many people have been led to believe. They remained hidden in the unused dumb-waiter until Chambers recovered them and then kept them in his house. Only on the last day did he change the hiding place. Fearing that they might be found in his house by Hiss's investigators, whom he had seen near his farm, he stashed the rolls of microfilm away in a hollowed-out pumpkin and replaced the pumpkin in its original place in the patch. It was a fine hiding place—but it was used only for one day, not ten years!

When Stripling and I arrived at the Committee office, it was already past ten in the evening. And we stayed there until dawn, studying the photostats of typewritten and handwritten documents which Chambers had turned over to the Justice Department at the deposition hearing on November 17, and the hundreds of pages of photostats of State Department documents developed from the five rolls of microfilm.

Both Stripling and I had heard literally thousands of words of testimony before the Committee on Un-American Activities charging that Communist agents were guilty of espionage against the United States Government. But for the first time we had before us absolute proof of those charges. It was no longer a case of one man's word against another. Here was physical evidence that no words could deny.

Our major problem, on which we made a critical decision that night, was what role the Committee should now play in the case.

The Justice Department had finally begun to move on Chambers' charges as a result of the production of the "pumpkin papers." Chambers had been subpoenaed to appear before the Grand Jury in New York later that day—Monday, December 6. Should we turn over the microfilm to the Justice Department and leave the responsibility for further investigation completely in its hands? We decided not to do this. On the basis of the record to date, we simply did not have confidence that the Justice Department would resist the political pressures being brought to bear in behalf of Hiss and against Chambers. Several reasons led us to this conclusion.

In the two-week period between November 17—when Chambers turned over the typewritten and handwritten documents to Justice Department officials in Baltimore—and December 1, no one from the Department had appeared to follow up this disclosure or even to question Chambers.

And then a story had been leaked to the press that the Justice Department was "going to drop the Hiss-Chambers investigation for lack of evidence"—two weeks after the Justice Department had received documentary evidence pointing to Hiss's guilt.

Under the circumstances, we felt our lack of confidence was well justified.

We also faced an acute problem of time. The term of the blue-ribbon Grand Jury in New York was to expire in just nine days, on December 14. If it failed to return an indictment against Hiss, it would probably be months before the case could be presented to a new grand jury. By that time, the political pressures which Hiss would be able to summon to his aid would build up immensely.

And, as a result of the November elections, the Chairmanship of the Committee on Un-American Activities would change in January from the Republicans to the Democrats. Some Democrats, like Ed Hébert, might be just as vigilant in pursuing the investigation as the Republicans had been. But in view of Truman's campaign promise to seek the outright abolition of the Committee, we thought it was more likely that the Chairmanship would go to someone less independent of Administration pressures than Hébert. Consequently, we decided to hold public hearings beginning Monday, December 6. But even more important, we decided that under no circumstances would we turn over the microfilm which we had in our possession to the Justice Department until we had been given absolute assurance that the case would be vigorously prosecuted.

The week of December 6, the Committee's schedule was even heavier than it had been during the critical period before the decisive Hiss-Chambers confrontation on August 17. It became a tug of war between the Committee and the Hiss apologists.

"After all," their argument went, "even if these papers did come from the State Department, they didn't contain information which was too important and the security of the United States was not, therefore, endangered by their removal from the Department." We quickly and effectively laid that one to rest—and by the State Department's own witnesses. We requested permission to make all the documents public. This permission was refused on the ground that publication of some of the documents would be injurious to the national security, even though ten years had passed since they were taken from government files.

On the matter of the importance of the documents, John Peurifoy, the Assistant Secretary of State charged with security affairs, and Under-Secretary Sumner Welles testified that a foreign agent having in his possession even one of these documents would thus have been able to break the secret State Department code used at that time for the transmittal of messages. This meant that the Soviet agents who obtained these documents might have broken the State Department code and thereby could decipher all confidential communications transmitted in that code between the United States and other foreign governments during the critical period immediately preceding the Hitler-Stalin pact.

I later discussed the case with William C. Bullitt, who had been American Ambassador to both France and the Soviet Union during this period. Several of the secret messages appearing on the microfilm had been sent by him. He pointed out another reason why such documents would have been of tremendous value to the Soviet Government. "An Ambassador's reports to his government can only be as reliable as the sources from which he obtains information. These messages disclose the names of my best sources—representatives of other governments who were providing information to me on a confidential basis. Once their activities become known to others, the source immediately dries up."

Because of our hearings in this period and an aroused public opinion, attempts to dismiss the stolen documents as "not too important" failed to get off the ground. The St. Louis *Post-Dispatch,* which up to this point had editorially strongly supported Hiss, now said: "Whatever else President Truman may say in the future about the spy investigation, he cannot again call it a 'red herring.' It is no longer a 'red herring' after the release of more than two hundred documents which are out of their places in the confidential files of the State Department."

But the key witness in the case was still Chambers. And Chambers was testifying in New York before the Grand Jury. The Justice Department would not allow him to come to Washington to appear before the Committee. Consequently, we decided to go to New York that day (Monday) and to question him that night after he had completed his appearance before the Grand Jury.

But that morning, before taking the train to New York, a telephone call came in for Stripling. It was from Keith Lewis of the Eastman Kodak Company. We had asked Eastman to check the microfilm which Chambers had turned over to us and to determine when it had been manufactured. Rumors had been circulated that Chambers might have put the documents on film not ten years ago but only after the Committee hearings of the past summer, in order to manufacture evidence to prove his charges. A look of complete dismay came over Stripling's face as he took the call. I heard him say, "You mean this film couldn't have been manufactured before 1945?" Stripling hung up and turned to me. "Well, we've had it. Eastman did not manufacture the type of film Chambers turned over to us until 1945."

The news jolted us into almost complete shock. We sat looking at each other without saying a word. This meant that Chambers was, after all, a liar. All the work, the long hours we had put into the investigation had been useless. We had been taken in by a diabolically clever maniac who had finally made a fatal mistake.

I buzzed my secretary in the outer office and asked her to get Chambers on the phone in New York.

Before he had a chance to say anything, I asked him: "Am I correct in understanding that these papers were put on microfilm in 1938?"

He answered, "Yes"—obviously mystified by the question.

"We have just had a report from the Eastman Kodak Company that film of the type you turned over to us was not made by the company until after 1945," I retorted. "What is your answer to that?"

There was a long silence at the other end of the wire. For a moment, I thought he must have hung up.

Finally he answered in a voice full of despair and resignation: "I can't understand it. God must be against me."

Then I took out on him all of the fury and frustration that had built up within me. "You'd better have a better answer than that," I said. "The Sub-committee's coming to New York tonight and we want to see you at the Commodore Hotel at 9:00 and you'd better be there!"

I slammed the receiver down without giving him a chance to reply.

"What'll we do now?" Stripling asked.

"There's only one thing we can do," I answered. "I want you to have the staff call the reporters who cover the Committee and ask them to come to my office in thirty minutes for a statement I will make at that time."

I have made some decisions in my life more difficult than this one, but none could approach it in terms of personal embarrassment and chagrin. But there was no other choice. I reminded Stripling that it was the Committee's responsibility not to prove Hiss guilty but to find out who was telling the truth.

Stripling made several calls to the press from my office while his secretary was making the others. In the meantime, I tried to collect my thoughts and put down some notes for the statement I had to make. This would be the biggest crow-eating performance in the history of Capitol Hill, but I was ready to go through with it.

Five minutes before the time scheduled for the press conference, after some of the reporters had already arrived in the reception room of my office, the buzzer sounded on the intercom. I answered and my secretary said, "The man from Eastman Kodak is on the phone and wants to talk to Stripling again." He picked up the phone and I saw the expression on his face change to one of sheer joy. He shouted into the receiver, "You mean you were wrong? You did manufacture that film through 1938 but then discontinued it during the war?"

I had no need to hear the answer. Stripling put the receiver down, let out a Texas rebel yell, grabbed me by the arms, and danced me around the room.

"Chambers' story has stood up again," he exulted. "Every time we check into something which sounds questionable, he comes through."

After the rest of the reporters had arrived, I asked them to come into my office and informed them that we had checked with the Eastman

Kodak Company and had found that they had manufactured that type of film during the period Chambers claimed to have used it. I am sure they wondered why I had called them to make such a routine announcement; but I explained that the Committee was checking every aspect of Chambers' story and that they would be informed when we found holes in it as well as when it was corroborated.

But if the first inaccurate report on the microfilm had been disturbing to Stripling and me, it was almost fatal for Chambers. I immediately asked Dorothy Cox, my secretary, to reach Chambers on the phone in New York. I wanted to tell him of the new report and express my regrets for what I had said earlier. But she could not reach him before we boarded the train for New York. In *Witness*, Chambers recounts his reactions to my telephone call. He paced the streets for hours in utter despair. Even after he finally learned of the new report, as he relates it, this mood persisted. Chambers gave way momentarily to the inhuman pressures of his ordeal. He made an unsuccessful attempt at suicide late that same night.

Looking back, I think I can understand how he must have felt. His career was gone. His reputation was ruined. His wife and children had been humiliated. But all this would not have mattered to him if the cause for which he had taken these calculated risks had some chance to prevail. And now it did seem that "God was against him." From the time he testified on August 3, through the months of summer and fall, I had been the one public official who had stood by him and on whom he thought he could count. And now I was deserting him. Chambers was to go through many crises during Hiss's two trials, but this proved to be his most difficult moment. It seemed the height of irony that I was the one who found it necessary to put him through this ordeal—and all because of a mistaken first report.

When we arrived in New York at 7:30 that evening we were met by representatives of the Justice Department. They went with us to the Commodore Hotel where we were scheduled to meet Chambers at nine o'clock. There, we engaged in a violent verbal battle as to whether the Committee should continue its investigation of the case or should turn over the microfilm to the Justice Department and leave the entire responsibility to them. I made it clear that we had the greatest respect for lower echelon Justice Department officials who were just as interested in getting at the truth in this case as we were. But I also made it clear that I had no confidence in some of their superiors who were under great political pressures and who so far had made a record which, to put it politely, raised grave doubts. Did they intend to bring out any facts that might be embarrassing to the national Administration?

In short, we did not trust the Justice Department to prosecute the case with the vigor we thought it deserved. The five rolls of microfilm in our possession, plus the threat of a congressional public hearing, were our only weapons to assure such a prosecution. In retrospect, I imagine that some Justice Department officials suspected our motives were primarily political and that we were impeding the regular law-enforcement agencies by withholding evidence. We compromised the matter by agreeing to furnish the Department with full-sized copies of the documents which appeared on the microfilm, and the Department agreed to allow us to question Chambers, even though he was bound by their subpoena.

Our questioning of Chambers began at nine o'clock and went on until midnight. Finally the full story, which he had told in part in his first appearance before the Committee on August 3, unfolded. He admitted that Hiss and the other government officials with whom he worked were active participants in an espionage ring. Their procedure varied but generally followed this pattern: Alger Hiss would take documents home in his brief case at night. On some occasions he turned them over to Chambers, who had them microfilmed by a Communist photographer in Baltimore or Washington and then returned the documents that same night to Hiss, who replaced them in their proper files the following morning. On other occasions, Mrs. Hiss would type copies or summaries of the documents at home on the Woodstock typewriter. Chambers would then take the microfilms or the typewritten copies which Mrs. Hiss had made to New York where he gave them to Colonel Bykov, his superior and a Soviet intelligence agent. Bykov transmitted them to Moscow.

When Chambers made his decision to leave the Communist Party, he had systematically collected documents which had been given to him by Hiss, White, and other members of the espionage group so that he would have some physical evidence of their activities to hold over their heads in the event of threatened reprisals. These were the documents he had turned over at the deposition hearing in Baltimore and which appeared on the rolls of microfilm the Committee had subpoenaed.

It was in this hearing that Chambers also cleared up the mystery of the rug which Hiss had tried to explain away as a "payment on account" for the rent of the apartment in which Chambers had lived. We now were able to understand why the rug, like the car, had seemed to cause Hiss so much concern. Colonel Bykov had been greatly impressed by the volume and quality of documents produced by the Hiss-Chambers espionage ring. He wanted to express his appreciation and that of the Soviet Government. He had delivered to Chambers in Washington six Bokhara rugs which he directed Chambers to present as gifts from him and the Soviet Government to the members of the ring who had been most co-operative. One of these rugs Chambers delivered to Harry Dexter White. Another he gave to Hiss— but not as a routine "payment on rent." In the classic tradition of espionage operations, Hiss had parked his car on a street corner, and Chambers had driven to a point nearby. Chambers had taken the rug from the trunk of his own car and put it in Hiss's—but not while Hiss was in the car. Again, the story was almost too fantastic to believe. But by this time we had learned that where Communist espionage was concerned, we had to become accustomed to actions that stretched our credulity.

We returned to Washington the next day convinced that Chambers' case was so airtight that the Justice Department had no choice but to ask for an indictment of Hiss. And furthermore, we had great confidence in Tom Donegan, a former FBI agent who was the Justice Department attorney assigned to present the case to the Grand Jury. We knew that if he had his way there would be no question about the outcome.

But Hiss and his legion of supporters within the Administration still had an ace up their sleeves. They did not reckon, however, with some of the Justice Department employees in lower echelons who were so infuriated by their superiors' handling of the case that they apprised the Committee staff of every action that was being taken.

Thus, we learned on the morning of December 8 that some Justice Department officials were advocating that the Grand Jury be asked to indict not Hiss but Chambers for lying when he had denied under oath any knowledge of espionage. It would be a technically valid indictment. Chambers had lied before the Grand Jury on that point. But he also was the star witness in any case against Hiss. If Chambers were indicted, the case against Hiss would be destroyed.

This was shocking news to members of the Committee. The problem was whether or not to expose this Justice Department strategy publicly and risk the political consequences. I decided to take the risk of an open fight with the Justice Department, in the hope that public opinion on so clear an issue would force the Department's hand in seeking an indictment against Hiss.

That evening, at a public hearing of the Committee well attended by the press, I interrupted the testimony of a witness to declare: "We have learned from unimpeachable sources that the Justice Department now plans to indict Chambers for perjury before any of the other people named by Chambers in this conspiracy are indicted. It is clear that the Justice Department does not want this Committee to hear any witnesses scheduled to go before the Federal Grand Jury and is bringing pressure on the Committee to drop its investigation. Chambers has confessed. He is in the open. He is no longer a danger to our security. If Chambers is indicted first, Hiss and the others will go free because the witness against them will have been discredited as a perjurer. The Administration is trying to silence this Committee. But we will not entrust to the Justice Department and to the Administration the sole responsibility for protecting the national security in this case. We intend to do everything we can to see that the Department does not use the device of indicting Chambers as an excuse for not proceeding against Hiss who has continued to decline to tell any of the truth up to this time."

President Truman countered the next day, December 9, by again labeling the Hiss-Chambers investigation a "red herring" in his press conference. But by this time not even the immense power of a President who had just won re-election could stop the march of truth.

My gamble in exposing the Administration's plan to indict Chambers rather than Hiss paid off. On December 10, the Washington *Post* said: "The President's attitude suggests a desire to suppress the whole business and the indictment of Mr. Chambers at this time would certainly be a step in that direction. If this is the Administration's policy, it is incredibly shortsighted." This editorial coming from the *Post*, which was decidedly not an anti-Administration paper, represented the overwhelming opinion in the nation.

Only six days remained before the term of the Grand Jury would expire. But now the FBI finally was given the go-ahead signal to dig out the facts in the case. A massive search was initiated for the key "witness" in the case—the old Woodstock typewriter on which Chambers said Mrs. Hiss had typed the incriminating documents. On December 13, FBI agents found the typewriter. On that same day, I appeared before the Grand Jury with the microfilm. Justice Department officials demanded that I leave the microfilm with them. By this time, I believed that they would prosecute the case with diligence, but the full Committee had given me instructions that under no circumstances was I to surrender the microfilm without Committee approval. Alex Campbell threatened to ask the Judge to cite me for contempt. I, in turn, warned him of the constitutional question that would be raised if a member of Congress, appearing voluntarily before a Grand Jury, were so cited while carrying out a mandate of the Committee which he represented. After a few anxious moments, I was allowed to return to Washington with the microfilm still in my possession but with the understanding that, in the event Hiss was indicted, I would take the responsibility of seeing that the Committee would make the microfilm available as evidence in the trial.

It was still touch and go. Hiss and his lawyers fought down to the last hour of the life of the Grand Jury. On December 15, the critical last day, an expert from the FBI typed exact copies of the incriminating documents on the old Woodstock machine and had them flown up to New York as exhibits for the members of the Grand Jury to see. A typewriter has one characteristic in common with a fingerprint: every one is different, and it is impossible to make an exact duplicate unless the same machine is used. The evidence was unanswerable.

Grand Jury proceedings are, of course, secret. But reports leaked out as to what happened when the prosecutor asked Hiss for an explanation. He said: "Until the day I die, I shall wonder how Whittaker Chambers got into my house to use my typewriter." A ripple of laughter went through the jury room.

All nineteen members voted to indict Hiss on two counts of perjury: one, that he had lied when he testified that he had not unlawfully removed copies of numerous secret, confidential, and restricted documents from the State Department in February and March 1938, and given them to one David Whittaker Chambers; and two, that he had willfully and knowingly lied when he had testified that he had not seen Chambers after January 1, 1937.

I was in Washington in my office when my secretary brought the news which had just come in over the wire. I had a great sense of relief. Now, I thought, the fight was really over. But again I was to learn that where Communists are concerned, the battle is never over so long as they are still able to fight.

After six postponements, the case came to trial on May 31, 1949, before Federal Judge Samuel H. Kaufman in New York City. It ended July 8, with a hung jury, eight to four for conviction.

The second trial began November 17, 1949, and ended January 21, 1950. The jury found Hiss guilty on both counts. Judge Henry W. Goddard sentenced him to five years in prison. The verdict and sentence were appealed but they were upheld by the U. S. Circuit Court of Appeals on December 7 of that year. On March 12, 1951, the U. S. Supreme Court refused to review the case.

The libel suit in Baltimore was dismissed following the conviction. Alger Hiss served three years and eight months of his sentence, with time off for good behavior, in the Lewisburg, Pennsylvania, Federal Prison. He was released in November 1954, at the age of fifty, and drifted into obscurity, having found employment as a stationery salesman.

Whittaker Chambers, after leaving *Time,* retired to his Westminster farm where he wrote his autobiography, *Witness,* and lived out his remaining years. He died July 9, 1961, at the age of sixty.[7]

Now, I would like to attempt an answer to the question my daughter, Tricia, asked me.

"What was the Hiss case?"

Whittaker Chambers, with typical insight, perhaps came closest to the truth when he wrote in *Witness* that the situation which involved Alger Hiss and himself was not simply "human tragedy," not just "another fat folder in the sad files of the police," but rather was a "tragedy of history." Here, "the two irreconcilable faiths of our time, Communism and Freedom, came to grips in the persons of two conscious and resolute men."

In this sentence, he compressed whole chapters of world history: the

[7] This is not the time or place to tell the full story of the dramatic battle between Hiss and Chambers and their counsel at the two trials. But I would not want this opportunity to pass without paying a deserved tribute to the Federal prosecutor, Tom Murphy, now a Federal District Judge in New York, for his superb presentation of the case against Hiss, and to the agents of the FBI who added to the laurels of the world's finest investigative agency by tracking down bits of evidence going back over a period of ten to fifteen years with almost unbelievable efficiency. As Whittaker Chambers so accurately pointed out, without Murphy and the selfless devotion of the FBI agents, the successful prosecution of Alger Hiss would never have been possible.

rise, development, and—as some would argue—partial decay of the philosophy called "liberalism"; the parallel emergence of a liberal heresy called Communism; the assumption of world leadership by two superpowers, America and Russia, each wedded to a competing faith and each strengthened and yet limited thereby; and, finally, the present confrontation of these two faiths and these two superpowers at specific times and places in every part of the world. The issue at stake, to put it starkly, is this: whose hand will write the next several chapters of human history?

The Hiss case aroused the nation for the first time to the existence and character of the Communist conspiracy within the United States. It focused attention sharply on the conspiratorial aspects of the Party. The prevailing opinion in the country prior to the Hiss-Chambers case was probably that the Communists were nothing but a handful of noisy but relatively harmless left-wingers attempting to exercise their rights of free speech and political action. A substantial number of Americans believed the investigations of the House Committee on Un-American Activities were "Red-baiting" for partisan purposes only.

The unpopularity of the Committee, whatever the reasons, caused many political leaders and opinion-makers to dismiss without investigation anything the Committee might discover and disclose about Communism in the United States. Upon learning that Communists and fellow-travelers were holding important positions in government, in education, or in labor, many people simply responded—"so what! All they are doing is exercising their legitimate freedom of speech and political opinion." Some went even further and charged that the members of the Committee, and their allies, were really "Fascist agents," bent on denying free expression to "unpopular views."

The Hiss case, for the first time, forcibly demonstrated to the American people that domestic Communism was a real and present danger to the security of the nation.

As Herbert Hoover wrote me after Hiss's conviction, "At last the stream of treason that has existed in our government has been exposed in a fashion all may believe." Chambers testified that his espionage ring was only one of several that had infiltrated the American government. Yet he had turned over to the Committee and the Justice Department hundreds of pages of confidential and secret documents from the State Department and other government agencies. And he testified that on at least seventy different occasions, the members of his ring had obtained a like number of documents—all of which he had transmitted to Soviet agents.

Hiss was just one of the members of the group from which Chambers obtained government documents. Chambers' contacts included four men in the State Department, two in the Treasury Department, two in the Bureau of Standards, one in the Aberdeen and one in the Picatinny Arsenal, two in the Electric Boat Company, one in the Remington Rand Company, and one in the Illinois Steel Company. The individuals he named, almost without exception, held positions of influence where they had access to confidential and secret information.

But the purpose of the Hiss-Chambers group was not limited to stealing documents and passing information to Soviet agents like common spies. Some, like Hiss, reached positions so high in government that they could influence policy directly. As I said in a speech in the House of Representatives in 1950, this type of activity "permits the enemy to guide and shape our policy; it disarms and dooms our diplomats to defeat in advance, before they go to conferences; traitors in the high councils of our own government make sure that the deck is stacked on the Soviet side of the diplomatic table."

The Hiss case thus demonstrated the necessity of screening federal employees in sensitive positions for loyalty and security—rigorously, fairly, and with sophisticated insight into the many-sided Communist apparatus.

The Hiss case exposed the blindness of the Truman Administration and its predecessors to the problem of Communist subversion in government. It demonstrated the need for congressional investigatory bodies, like the Committee on Un-American Activities, which could expose such laxity and, with the help of a mobilized public opinion, could force the Executive branch to adopt policies adequate for dealing with the problem.

The record of negligence was almost too flagrant to believe. Chambers first made his charges in 1939 and he repeated them to government officials several times thereafter. Yet as far as the public record is concerned, the only action taken on his charges until the Committee started its investigation in 1948, was to promote each of the individuals he named to higher positions of power and influence within the government. The most damning proof of negligence on the part of the Executive branch was that Hiss himself had to be indicted and convicted not for espionage, the crime of which he was originally guilty, but for perjury—for lying when he denied committing espionage. The statute of limitations, requiring prosecution for espionage within three years after the crime had been committed, had already long expired.

The conduct of President Truman in this case was particularly hard to understand. No one would question the tough-minded anti-Communism of the man who had so boldly initiated the program of Greek-Turkish aid and the Marshall Plan. One can understand why he might have felt justified in terming the case a "red herring" when Hiss first testified before the Committee. But he did a disservice to the nation and to his own party by stubbornly maintaining that position as evidence to the contrary piled up. His error was sheer stubbornness in refusing to admit a mistake. He viewed the Hiss case only in its political implications and he chose to handle the crisis which faced his Administration with an outworn political rule of thumb: leave the political skeletons hidden in the closet and keep the door locked. He denied outright the evidence in front of him and he stumped the 1948 political trail flailing away at the "red herring," thus putting himself in a needlessly untenable position on an important issue and—of infinitely graver consequence—leading a large segment of the public away from a deeper understanding of the true threat of the Communist conspiracy in America.

I have no doubt that President Truman personally had just as much contempt for Alger Hiss as I had when the full import of his activities became known to him. An indication of his attitude was a report Bert Andrews gave me shortly after Hiss's indictment. He said Truman was shown copies of the stolen documents by a representative of the Justice Department. As he thumbed through page after page of the incriminating evidence, he muttered, over and over, "Why, the son of a bitch—he betrayed his country!" Yet when asked in his next press conference if he still thought the Committee's investigation of the Hiss case was a "red herring," he replied in the affirmative! When a friend asked him how he could possibly make such a statement in light of the new evidence, his reply was: "Of course Hiss is guilty. But that damn Committee isn't interested in that. All it cares about is politics, and as long as they try to make politics out of this Communist issue, I am going to label their activities for what they are—a 'red herring.'"

President Truman spoke quite properly and effectively of the need for bipartisanship in meeting the threat of Communism abroad. Along with a substantial number of the Republicans in both House and Senate, I responded to his pleas in this respect by voting for and supporting the Greek-Turkish Aid Program and the Marshall Plan. What he did not seem to understand—and here is the really crucial point—was that Communism in America is part and parcel of Communism abroad. The problem, like Communism itself, is indivisible. If, in other words, he had recognized the need for bipartisanship in fighting Communism at home as well as abroad, he would not have persisted in making his "red herring" statements with regard to the Committee investigations. And furthermore, there would have been no need for that investigation to be continued as it was, simply in order to force the Justice Department to take the action demanded by the facts.

Once the FBI was given the green light in its investigation of the Hiss case, it did a magnificent job. The blame for failing to act before that time rests not on the FBI but squarely on those officials of the Executive branch who had full access to FBI reports and who failed or refused to order a full investigation.

The Hiss case taught the nation some major lessons, too, about the most effective methods for fighting Communism in the United States. Communism cannot be fought successfully by brushing off or ignoring the danger because of the small number of Communist Party members, or by concentrating solely on "removing the causes of Communism by making democracy work." The nation finally saw that the magnitude of the threat of Communism in the United States is multiplied a thousandfold because of its direct connection with and support by the massive power of the world Communist conspiracy centered in Moscow.

But while we should not underestimate the danger, we also must not resort to Communist methods to fight Communism. We would then become little better than the Communists themselves—playing their game, by their rules. We must not be so blinded by the threat of Communism that we can no longer see the principles of freedom. The most effective weapon the Communists and their supporters use against their opponents is to complain of unfair play and abridgment of their civil liberties, in order to divert public attention from the charges being leveled against them. Even when the most impeccably correct procedures are used, they will cry "foul." When the investigators' conduct gives even a hint of unfair procedures, the Communists are able to make their accusers, rather than themselves, the issue.

There is nothing more irresponsible than for the radicals of the right to make a racket of anti-Communism. By exaggerating and making charges they can't prove, they raise doubts as to the very real danger that Communist agents in the United States in fact present. On the other hand, it is just as irresponsible for the radicals of the left to pooh-pooh the danger of Communism at home by denying it exists, even in the face of facts like the Hiss case—thereby adding fuel to the fire of the demagogues on the right.

We succeeded in the Hiss case for three basic reasons. First, we were on the right side. Second, we prepared our case thoroughly. Third, we followed methods with which few objective critics could find serious fault. This is not the easy way to conduct a congressional investigation and certainly not the best way to make sensational headlines. But it is the way which produces results. In dealing with Communists, any other procedure can play into their hands and usually does.

To give an extreme example. If we were to accuse X of having killed his mother, his two brothers, and five friends, X and his allies would shout back, "That's a lie! X never hurt a hair on his old mother's head and he only wounded *one* brother. Foul and unfair!" The counterattack would be on, with attention diverted from the five friends and the other brother whom X had, indeed, actually killed. Thus, if someone charges that there are fifty-eight Communists in the State Department, he is at once attacked on the exact number and on the fine distinction between Communists and security risks. The tactic of exaggeration and the deliberate "fishing expedition" does, to be sure, attract public attention to the problem. But it also tends to undermine the effort to develop an effective program for weeding out the actual security risks in the government bureaucracies. The best tactic in the face of suspicion from a large segment of the press and public is to be certain you can prove every statement you make about Communist activities.

These lessons from the Hiss case are important. But more vital still is that we understand why a man like Alger Hiss, with his education and background, joined the Communist Party in the first place.

The tendency too often is to try to find some convenient excuse for his conduct and thereby avoid facing up to the real reasons. But none of the typical excuses fit Alger Hiss. He did not join the Communist Party, accept its rigid discipline, and steal State Department secrets for money, position, or a desire for power, or for psychological reasons stemming from some obscure incident in his early life, or because he had been duped or led astray by his wife. He joined the Communist Party and became a Communist espionage agent because he deeply believed in Communist theory, Communist principles, and the Communist "vision" of the ideal society still to come. He believed in an absolutely materialistic view of the world, in principles of deliberate manipulation by a dedicated elite, and in an ideal world society in which "the party of the workers" replaces God as the prime mover and the sole judge of right and wrong. His morality could be reduced to one perverted rule: anything that advances the goals of Communism is good. Hiss followed his beliefs deliberately and consciously to the utmost logical extreme, and ended up in the area of espionage.

At a less rigorous level—somewhere in a vague area that goes by such names as "positivism" or "pragmatism" or "ethical neutralism"—Hiss was clearly the symbol of a considerable number of perfectly loyal citizens whose theaters of operation are the nation's mass media and universities, its scholarly foundations, and its government bureaucracies. This group likes to throw the cloak of liberalism around all its beliefs. Eric Sevareid's term "liberalists" probably describes them most accurately. They are not Communists; they are not even remotely disloyal; and, give or take a normal dose of human fallibility, they are neither dishonest nor dishonorable. But they are of a mind-set, as doctrinaire as those on the extreme right, which makes them singularly vulnerable to the Communist popular front appeal under the banner of social justice. In the time of the Hiss case they were "patsies" for the Communist line.

The "liberalists" now stand self-accused in all their vulnerability by a most damaging fact. As soon as the Hiss case broke and well before a full bill of particulars was even available, much less open to close critical analysis, they leaped to the defense of Alger Hiss—and to a counterattack of unparalleled venom and irrational fury on his accusers.

Some of the reasons may have been simply political. The New Deal had fallen hard for the popular front tactic and now it was going to be called to account for its past errors—or, perhaps, for its past "innocence." Some thought it had to be defended at any cost. Typical of this attitude was a conversation I had with a New Deal lawyer who had served in the Roosevelt Administration during World War II. The Hiss case was being discussed at a Washington dinner party shortly after the "pumpkin papers" came to public attention. He shouted at me, "I don't give a damn what the facts are. Even if Hiss admits he's guilty, these investigations are dangerous and will have a terrible and disastrous effect on the country—because the net result is to cast reflection on the United Nations and all the other progressive aspects of the Roosevelt-Truman foreign policy."

What then is the answer to the appeal Communism seems to have, not only in the so-called "underdeveloped" countries abroad and not just among the "downtrodden masses," but to those with excellent intellectual backgrounds and material security right here in the United States?

Certainly more is needed than a purely negative militant "anti-Communism."

Nor is it enough to answer Communism's constant claims of "we shall win—we represent the wave of the future" with a static position in which we say, "All we want is peace, and we will only defend what we have."

And we must never be put in the position of meeting the appeal of the Communists on their ground alone. A watered-down materialism of our own will be no match for the authentic article, with all its trappings, peddled by the Communists. If materialism is all we have to offer, then men like Hiss, impatient with compromise and anxious for faster progress, will turn to Communism as the simpler and swifter vehicle for the realization of purely materialistic goals.

Our goal cannot and must never be to force our way of life on others. But our fundamental belief that every nation has a right to be independent, that individual freedom and human rights are grounded in religious faith and because they come from God cannot be taken away by men, must be instilled in the new generation. And our beliefs must be combined with a crusading zeal, not just to hold our own but to change the world—including the Communist world—and to win the battle for freedom, individual dignity, and true economic progress without a hot war.

Foster Dulles, in commenting on Alger Hiss's conviction, said: "The conviction of Alger Hiss is human tragedy. It is tragic that so great promise should have come to so inglorious an end. But the greater tragedy is that seemingly our national ideals no longer inspire the loyal devotions needed for their defense." In these words, Dulles summed up the greatest lesson of the Hiss case for our generation, because the case so dramatically demonstrated the intellectual confusion of our time. Since 1917 Moscow had been successful in convincing all too many of our best educated citizens of the superiority of Communism and caused them to abandon Western ideals and values for the chimera of Soviet "idealism" which unconsciously became their moral standard. To this day, many "liberalists" are incapable of facing the brutal reality of Soviet totalitarianism and dealing with it accordingly.

The Hiss case was, of course, also a lesson for me. I learned first-hand about the true nature of the Communist conspiracy at home and abroad.

I learned, too, some valuable lessons in crisis conduct—the necessity for thorough preparation for battle; the need for handling a crisis with coolness, confidence, and decisiveness; the importance of guarding against a letdown in that most dangerous period of a crisis, after the battle is over.

The Hiss case brought me national fame. I received considerable credit for spearheading the investigation which led to Hiss's conviction. Two years later I was elected to the United States Senate and two years after that, General Eisenhower introduced me as his running mate to the Republican National Convention as "a man who has a special talent and an ability to ferret out any kind of subversive influence wherever it may be found, and the strength and persistence to get rid of it."

But in politics, victory is never total. The Hiss case brought me national fame. But it also left a residue of hatred and hostility toward me—not only among the Communists but also among substantial segments of the press and the intellectual community—a hostility which remains even today, ten years after Hiss's conviction was upheld by the United States Supreme Court. Bert Andrews once gave me his opinion about the primary motivating force for much of this attitude. "The surest way to make yourself unpopular with anyone who considers himself an intellectual," he said, "is to prove him wrong once he has gone out on a limb on an issue so charged with emotion as the Hiss case."

Ironically enough, I not only gained the deadly enmity of the Communists and others who, for a variety of reasons, defended Hiss; I was to receive, at best, lukewarm support and at times outright opposition from many of those who claimed to be the annointed apostles of anti-Communism in America. There were two reasons, I think, for this attitude. First, they deeply resented the fact that I would not go along with their extremes. The second reason is perhaps more controlling. Earlier in this section I pointed out the inexcusable attitude of some officials and apologists who could see the danger of Communism abroad but were blind to the threat at home. Strangely enough, many of those who speak up most vigorously about the threat of Communism at home simply reverse the blind spot: they oppose programs designed to deal with the same threat abroad. Because I have consistently supported what some of them consider to be "liberal" international policies—like foreign aid, reciprocal trade, collective security pacts, and adequate appropriations for our information and foreign service programs—the credentials I had gained as an anti-Communist because of my work in the Hiss case became somewhat tarnished with a tinge of "pink!"

And there were still others who were to mistrust me because of the Hiss case—without exactly knowing why. I remember one amusing incident demonstrating this attitude which occurred during the 1952 campaign. Bill Rogers, who was traveling on our campaign train at the time, used to make a practice of wandering among the audiences while I was speaking so that he could pick up reactions and pass them along to me. He heard one eminently respectable elderly lady say to another, "I like Eisenhower but I don't like Nixon." When she was asked why, she replied: "Oh, he was mixed up with that awful Alger Hiss!"

In any event, one of the personal aftermaths of the Hiss case was that for the next twelve years of my public service in Washington, I was to be subjected to an utterly unprincipled and vicious smear campaign. Bigamy, forgery, drunkenness, insanity, thievery, anti-Semitism, perjury, the whole gamut of misconduct in public office, ranging from unethical to downright criminal activities—all these were among the charges that were hurled against me, some publicly and others through whispering campaigns which were even more difficult to counteract.

And so, in retrospect, I suppose there may be a grain of truth in both of the observations I quoted at the very beginning of this section: had it not been for the Hiss case, I might have been President of the United States. But equally: had it not been for the Hiss case, I might never have been Vice President of the United States and thus a candidate for President.

But whichever of these propositions is "truer"—and neither of them is subject to proof—of this much I am sure: I shall always be grateful that at a period in my life when I had the requisite energy and drive to cope with it, I had the opportunity to meet the challenge which that case presented. Because through that case, a guilty man was sent to prison who otherwise would have remained free; a truthful man was vindicated who otherwise would have been condemned as a liar; and the nation acquired a better understanding, vital to its security, of the strategy and tactics of the Communist conspiracy at home and abroad.

The Fund

Going through the necessary soul-searching of deciding whether to fight a battle, or to run away from it, is far more difficult than the battle itself.

"SENATOR, what is this 'fund' we hear about? There is a rumor to the effect that you have a supplementary salary of $20,000 a year, contributed by a hundred California businessmen. What about it?"

When Peter Edson, a veteran Washington political columnist, asked me this question, I could not have been less concerned about his inquiry or more confident about what the future held for me. The day was Sunday, September 14, 1952. I was thirty-nine years old, the junior Senator from California, and the Republican candidate for Vice President of the United States. I had just finished a half-hour appearance on the nationally televised program, "Meet the Press," where I had been interviewed by Larry Spivak, Edson, and two other reporters. The program had gone well. Wires and phone calls congratulating me on my appearance had begun to arrive at the station even before the program ended. When we went off the air, I had stayed in the studio for a few minutes to express my appreciation to the technicians who had produced the show and to chat informally with the reporters who had questioned me.

When the other reporters drifted away, Edson took me aside and asked the question about the $20,000 "supplementary salary." He said he had not asked the question on the air because he had not had an opportunity to check the facts.

Any rumor that I had an extra salary was completely false, I explained to him. I suggested that the stories might be referring to a political fund which had been set up by my supporters in California. It was used to pay expenses for travel, printing and mailing of speeches, and extra clerical help—expenses which were strictly political in character and for which, therefore, I could not properly be reimbursed by the government. The fund had been set up after my election to the Senate in 1950. Dana Smith, my Finance Chairman in that campaign, handled the collections and disbursements as trustee. I described all this to Edson and gave him Smith's telephone number in Pasadena, California, so that he could call Smith directly if he wanted to get any further details. Edson thanked me and we left the television studio shortly afterwards. I did not give Edson's inquiry another thought. It never occurred to me that from such an innocent beginning would grow the most scarring personal crisis of my life.

The next morning Edson telephoned Dana Smith, who was the Southern California Chairman of Citizens for Eisenhower-Nixon, told him of our conversation, and asked him for the details. Smith welcomed the opportunity to tell him more about an idea which he had originated. He had started the fund after the 1950 election so that I, as a newly-elected Senator from California, could continue my political activities on a year-round basis—instead of my being restricted to campaign periods, when funds would be available.

The idea, Smith told Edson, was substantially this: if Republican Party supporters contributed to the election of Senator Nixon, why wouldn't they want to contribute funds between elections which would allow him to travel back to California more often to see his constituents, keep in touch with party workers by regular mailings, and carry on other political activities? The fund had been carefully established, limiting contributions to individuals, not corporations, and to a maximum of $500, so that no one could be accused of trying to buy special favors. The money was solicited from regular party contributors and it was administered by Smith as trustee. The funds were kept in a Pasadena bank and subject to regular audits. It was to be used for transportation, mailing, and office expenses connected with political activity, as distinguished from official government business.

Later that day, by coincidence, three more reporters came to see Dana Smith in Pasadena. Explaining that they were doing background stories on my life, they brought up the same subject as Edson had. The reporters were Leo Katcher of the New York *Post*, Richard Donovan of *The Reporter* magazine, and Ernest Brashear of the Los Angeles

Daily News. Smith, without hesitation, reviewed the fund's operation and purpose again, and these reporters left to prepare their news stories. Smith did not consider any of the inquiries of sufficient importance to contact me about them.

That same day, I flew to Denver to see General Eisenhower to discuss plans for the start of our campaign on Wednesday night.

As I thought of the campaign ahead, I could not have been more confident. All the public opinion polls and most of the expert political opinion predicted that Eisenhower would beat Adlai Stevenson decisively.

I thought that no one in the world could have been more fortunate than I. In July, when I went to Chicago for the Republican Convention, I knew that my name had been mentioned as one of a number of possible candidates for Vice President, but I did not think I had more than a remote chance to be nominated. I had not even bothered to pack a dark suit for the trip since I did not expect to have an opportunity to speak in Convention Hall.

Two days before Eisenhower's nomination, Jack Knight, publisher and editor of the Chicago *Daily News*, had carried a front-page column speculating that the ticket would be Eisenhower and Nixon. I sent a member of my staff down to the newsstand to buy a half-dozen copies because, as I told him, "That will probably be the last time we'll see that headline and I want to be able to show it to my grandchildren."

July 11, 1952, was the most exciting day of my life. I received a telephone call from Herbert Brownell (who later became Attorney General) informing me that General Eisenhower had selected me as his running mate. Nothing before or since was to exceed the excitement and emotion Pat and I both felt as we stood with General and Mrs. Eisenhower before the wildly cheering Convention audience. This was true not only because it marked the culmination of what many observers described as a phenomenally fast rise to national prominence, but even more because the event was so unexpected.

After the Convention, Pat and I experienced for the first time the spotlight of intense coverage which is accorded national candidates. Reporters and photographers covered everything that we did and said. Writers for magazines and newspapers interviewed us and members of our families for special stories. I keynoted the Ohio State Convention, was the speaker at Republican Day at the Illinois State Fair, and completed my "shakedown cruise" as a national candidate with four days of campaigning in Maine, which at that time still held its congressional and gubernatorial elections early. The mechanics and organization of my campaign staff had been worked out. In these early speeches, I had hammered hard at the three great issues of the '52 campaign—Corruption, Communism, and Korea. My speeches had been well received.

There had been a triumphal homecoming with a rally on the football field at Whittier, California, where I had attended college. I was able to point out in my remarks that one of the biggest thrills for me of being a candidate for Vice President was to return home and finally get a chance to stand in the middle of the field, after having warmed the bench for four years in college.

And now, as I went to see Eisenhower that September 15, the road ahead seemed full of promise and no pitfalls. No one should ever take anything for granted in a campaign, but this one seemed easy compared to the others I had been through. Historically, an election campaign is not too hard an assignment for the vice presidential candidate. The presidential candidate wins or loses the election. The number two man goes along for the ride, doing his best to stir up the party faithful but making no major pronouncements. The candidate for Vice President seldom, if ever, makes national news. In fact, a public opinion poll at about this time revealed that only 40 per cent of the voters could name the Republican nominee for Vice President. This might have dampened my high spirits except that the same poll disclosed that only 32 per cent could identify the Democratic nominee.

I saw General Eisenhower that evening in his headquarters at the Brown Palace Hotel in Denver. The place was swarming with aides, party workers, and visiting dignitaries. It had the aura of a command post. Eisenhower was not the ordinary run-of-the-mill candidate seeking friends and supporters. He had been Commander of all Allied troops in Europe during the Second World War; he was the General who won the war; and even as a candidate he was accorded the respect, honor, and awe that only a President usually receives. Despite his great capacity for friendliness, he also had a quality of reserve which, at least subconsciously, tended to make a visitor feel like a junior officer coming in to see the commanding General.

The first time I ever saw Eisenhower, he was in fact the victorious commanding General. It was shortly after V-E Day. I was thirty-two years old and a Lieutenant Commander in the Navy. After returning from service overseas in the South Pacific, I was assigned the task of negotiating settlements of terminated war contracts in the Bureau of Aeronautics Office at 50 Church Street, New York City. General Eisenhower, the returning hero, was riding through the streets of Manhattan in the greatest ticker-tape parade in the city's history. As I looked down from a twentieth floor window, I could see him standing in the back of his car with both arms raised high over his head. It was a gesture which was to become his political trademark in the years ahead.

I met him again five years later at the Bohemian Grove, near San Francisco, where we were both luncheon guests of former President Herbert Hoover. I had just won the Republican nomination for the United States Senate in California. We were introduced, but he met so many others during his stay there that I doubted then if he would remember me.

Less than a year later, in December of 1951, I met him again at the Headquarters of SHAPE in Paris, and this time we talked for almost forty-five minutes. He made a great impression on me with his grasp of international affairs. I came away from that meeting with my first personal understanding of the Eisenhower popularity: he had an incomparable ability to show a deep interest in a wide range of subjects, and he displayed as much interest when he listened as when he spoke. I recall that he was particularly interested in my role in the Hiss case. He had read accounts of it and pointed out that one of the reasons I had been successful where others in the Communist investigating field had failed was that I had insisted on scrupulously fair procedures in my handling of the case.

In Denver that Monday night we reviewed our campaign strategy. The plan was for General Eisenhower to stress the positive aspects of his "Crusade to Clean Up the Mess in Washington." I was to hammer away at our opponents on the record of the Truman Administration, with particular emphasis on Communist subversion because of my work in the Hiss case.

I left Denver early the next morning ready for battle and confident of victory. I had scheduled my campaign kickoff rally for Wednesday night in Pomona, California, fifteen miles east of Los Angeles. Pomona was the city where I had launched my successful campaigns for the House and for the Senate. It had spelled "good luck" for us in those campaigns, and we thought that a kickoff there would bring us good luck in the biggest campaign of all.

On our way from Denver to Los Angeles we made a sentimental stop at Ely, Nevada. That predominantly Democratic mining town gave a rousing welcome to its now famous native daughter, Pat Ryan Nixon. Then we flew on to Riverside, California, to spend Tuesday night at the Mission Inn where Pat and I had been married twelve years before, on June 21, 1940.

The next day, my Press Secretary, Jim Bassett, who was on leave from his job as political editor of the Los Angeles *Mirror,* told me that one of the reporters assigned to cover us had mentioned that his paper had a story scheduled for Thursday about a Nixon fund.

"That's probably the Pete Edson story. There's nothing to worry about," I told him.

We went ahead the next day with our plans for the rally at the railroad station in Pomona. It was to be televised nationally. It turned out to be colorful, exciting, and, by every political standard, completely successful. The crowd was big and enthusiastic, and the television cameras gave millions of people an opportunity to see a campaign train pull away from the station at the beginning of what was to be the shortest and most dramatic campaign trip in history. There was only one minor mishap. Governor Earl Warren said, in introducing me, "I now present to you the next President of the United States." But the crowd loved it and he, in high good humor, laughed at his slip of the tongue. Everyone was in fine spirits as the "Nixon Special" pulled out of Pomona on schedule, with the candidate waving good-by from the rear platform of his first campaign train. I had only one minor problem. I had caught a cold on the flight from Ely to Riverside and my throat was sore and my voice hoarse.

We had not reached our first stop in Bakersfield when word reached us from Republican headquarters in Los Angeles that a story with regard to a "Nixon fund" would be published the next day and that it might cause trouble. It still did not seem serious to me, but I decided to talk the matter over with four of my advisers in the lounge of my private car.

Those who joined me were Jack Drown, one of my oldest and closest friends, who was our train manager; Murray Chotiner, a Los Angeles attorney who had served as campaign manager to Earl Warren and William Knowland before managing my 1950 Senatorial campaign; Pat Hillings, who had succeeded me in the House of Representatives when I had been elected to the Senate; and William P. Rogers, a New York and Washington lawyer whom I had met in Washington during my work on the Hiss case when he was serving as Counsel for a Senate Investigations Committee. Drown, Chotiner, and Hillings, as Californians, knew about the fund. But Rogers was a newcomer. In fact, when I had asked him to come along on our campaign trip as one of my advisers, one of the selling points I had used was that it would be a pleasant experience and not too much of an ordeal because "nothing ever happens to a candidate for Vice President."

I now explained all the details of the fund to Rogers because I thought since he knew nothing of it he could give me a good objective opinion on the subject. I said that the fund had been set up at Dana Smith's suggestion and that we had been scrupulously careful to avoid any possible charges of improper collection or use of the contributions. For that reason, the fund was set up as a trust in which only Smith collected the contributions and disbursed the money according to vouchers and bills for political activities sent to him from my office. He had even arranged for an independent audit by a certified public accountant so that he could send reports to the contributors accounting for every dollar collected and spent. Rogers asked about the size of the fund and I told him that, as I remembered it, a total of between $15,-000 and $18,000 had been collected and disbursed over a two-year period.

Rogers observed that the only unusual feature of this fund, as distinguished from other political funds, was that it was so scrupulously accounted for, was openly solicited, the amount of any contribution was limited, and that none of the funds passed through my hands but were disbursed by a trustee.

I explained to him that there were two reasons for setting up such procedures. First, Smith himself was an impeccably honest man and had always insisted in the campaigns in which he had been finance chairman that the contributors deserved to have their money accounted for in a manner which would meet not only the legal requirements but the highest ethical standards as well. In addition, when Smith had suggested the idea of such a fund to me, I had told him that it would have to be handled in such a way that it would be completely above criticism, whether justified or unjustified.

I had recognized from the time I became a member of the Committee on Un-American Activities, and particularly after my participation in the Hiss case, that it was essential for me to maintain a standard of conduct which would not give my political opponents any solid grounds for attack. I have often told those who investigate in the field of Communist activities that they must always be sure that they are right on the issue, that their procedures are impeccably fair, and that their personal conduct is above criticism. "Even when you are right they will give you a rough time," I have said. "When you happen to be wrong they will kill you."

I knew that the standards which would be applied to the average Congressman and Senator as far as collection and disbursement of political funds were concerned might well not be applied to me, and I was determined not to give anyone even the slightest opening through which they might attack not only me, personally, but the work I was doing in investigating Communist subversion in the United States.

For example, I pointed out to Rogers, it is perfectly legal for a Congressman or Senator to have relatives on his payroll, provided they work for the salaries he pays them. It is also proper for a lawyer who happens to be a Congressman or Senator to remain a member of his law firm and to participate in the division of fees, except in cases where there is a conflict of interest. I had resigned from my law firm, however, and never received a fee from law practice after I was elected to Congress in 1946. My wife had spent many days working in my office, both while I was a Congressman and a Senator, but had never been on the government payroll.

After we had explored every facet of the fund, I asked Rogers for his honest opinion. He said, "I don't see anything to worry about. There is nothing illegal, unethical, or embarrassing about this fund. If your opponents try to make something out of it, they will never get anywhere on the merits." Chotiner was even more emphatic. He labeled the whole story as "ridiculous, a tempest in a teapot."

The consensus that night among our little strategy group was to ignore the attacks, on the theory that answering them would simply give them more publicity and would play into the hands of those making the attacks. This, I knew, was generally sound political strategy. "Let's wait and see what they do," I said.

We did not have long to wait. The next morning the attack began. But it was not in the Edson story, which as I had expected was a fair and objective account of the fund.

It was the New York *Post* which let me have it with both barrels.

Jim Bassett gave me the substance of the story between whistle-stops. The headline on the front page screamed, SECRET NIXON FUND. Inside the tabloid, the story by Leo Katcher, a Hollywood movie writer who also covered the Los Angeles area for the *Post*, was a masterpiece of distortion: "The existence of a 'millionaire's club' devoted exclusively to the financial comfort of Senator Nixon, GOP Vice Presidential candidate, was revealed today," said the opening paragraph. The story went on with substantially the same information that Dana Smith had told all the reporters. It was a clever example of the half-truth. In fact, more than half the story was true—but that was the bottom half. Nowhere did Katcher explain the "millionaire's club" and nowhere did he say or indicate that the fund was "secret." Only the headline said that. The subhead over the story declared: "Secret Rich Men's Trust Fund Keeps Nixon in Style Far Beyond His Salary."

The *Post* story did not worry me. It was to be expected. The *Post* was and still is the most partisan Democratic paper in the country. It had done an unusually neat smear job, but I did not expect anything to come of it. After all, I had come into this 1952 campaign well prepared, I thought, for any political smear that could be directed at me. After what my opponents had thrown at me in my campaigns for the House and Senate, and after the almost unbelievably vicious assaults I had survived during the Hiss case, I thought I had been through the worst.

In fact, that Thursday morning I was worried not about the campaign fund story but rather about the split-second timing we needed in order to make ten whistle-stops a day on our tour up the Central Valley of California and into Oregon and the state of Washington.

At our first stop, Bakersfield, I called to the crowd, "Who can clean up the mess in Washington?"

They knew the answer. They yelled back, "Ike can."

At Tulare, the next stop, the train started to pull out of the station before I finished my speech. I cut short my remarks by calling out, "Come along and join our crusade," and people ran down the tracks after the train. Like most candidates, I had an exaggerated idea about the importance of what I had planned to say if only a mistake hadn't been made in starting the train ahead of time.

I proceeded to chew out our staff and particularly Jack Drown, our train manager, for what I thought was a major error. Fortunately for everyone concerned, several members of our small staff combined an excellent intuition for politics with a sense of humor. As I was telling Jack, "never let that happen again," Bill Rogers walked up and said, "I thought you planned it that way. Just as soon as the train started to move you finished your sentence and then spontaneously said to the crowd, 'come along and join this crusade,' motioning for them to follow the train. It gave a sense of participation and excitement which could never be conveyed by ending a speech on time and then waiting for the engineer to get up steam." I laughed and recognized that I had just experienced another example of the truth of one of Eisenhower's favorite admonitions, "Always take your job, but never yourself, seriously."

But these light moments of relief from tension were now to be few and far between. As our "Nixon Special" moved up the Central Valley through Fresno, Madera, Merced, Stockton, and Sacramento, more and more reporters joined our campaign train and demanded that Jim Bassett get a reply from me to the charge that I had a "secret fund." Getting excerpts ready for the press, walking back through the lounge car to meet the political dignitaries who boarded the train at one stop and who were to get off at another, boning up on the local color and the local issues which I was trying to discuss at each of the stops, trying to use the microphone as much as possible so that I would not do any further damage to my already raw throat—thinking about these and other relatively minor problems left little time to prepare an answer on the fund. Finally, in midafternoon, Chotiner and Rogers prepared a brief statement of about two hundred words stating the facts with regard to the fund, which I approved and issued.

Our opponents had wasted no time in capitalizing on the *Post* story. By the time I issued my statement on Thursday afternoon, Democratic National Chairman Stephen Mitchell had called on Eisenhower to demand my resignation. Senator Karl Mundt, with whom I had fought so many battles against the Communists when we served together on the House Committee on Un-American Activities, countered for the Republicans. He asserted that the attack on me was a "left-wing smear" and a "filthy" maneuver by a pro-Stevenson newspaper. His statement, however, was lost in the back pages of most newspapers while Mitchell's demand that I resign made most of the front pages. But this is part of political warfare. An attack always makes more news than defense. When I turned off the light in my stateroom that night I was still convinced that because the attack was entirely partisan, it would not stand on its merits. I thought it would eventually run its course and be forgotten, provided I continued to play it down.

But I had not reckoned with the determination and skillful planning of our opponents. At nine o'clock the next morning I delivered my whistle-stop speech to a good-sized crowd in Marysville, a small mining and lumbering town in northern California. Just as the train started to pull out, a car screeched to a stop at the station and a group of men, who we later discovered were dispatched from Democratic headquarters in Sacramento, ran toward the train. "Tell us about the $16,000!" one of them yelled.

That did it. Despite all of our plans to ignore the attack, I could not see myself running away from a bunch of hecklers. I wheeled around and shouted, "Hold the train!" The train stopped a hundred yards down the track and the crowd pressed forward while I collected my thoughts. Instinctively I knew I had to counterattack. You cannot win a battle in any arena of life merely by defending yourself. I pointed my finger at the man who called out, directing the crowd's attention to him, and then I let him have it.

"You folks know the work that I did investigating Communists in the United States. Ever since I have done that work the Communists and the left-wingers have been fighting me with every possible smear. When I received the nomination for the vice presidency I was warned that if I continued to attack the Communists in this government they would continue to smear me. And believe me, you can expect that they will continue to do so. They started it yesterday. They have tried to say that I had taken $16,000 for my personal use.

"What they didn't point out is that rather than charging the American taxpayer with the expenses of my office, which were in excess of the amounts which were allowed under the law, what I did was to have those expenses paid by the people back home who were interested in seeing that information concerning what was going on in Washington was spread among the people of this state.

"I will tell you what some of the others do. They put their wives on the payroll, taking your money and using it for that purpose. Pat Nixon has worked in my office night after night, and I can say this proudly— she has never been on the government payroll since I have been in Washington.

"Do you want me to do what some others are doing? Take fat legal fees on the side? During the time I have been in Washington I have never taken a legal fee, although as a lawyer I could legally have done so, and I am never going to in the future."

The crowd was cheering thunderously as our train pulled away. I walked back into my private compartment feeling better. That had been my first public defense of the fund and I used it throughout the day, beating the hecklers to the punch at each of the whistle-stops. The crowds were now two and three times as big as they had been on Thursday, the first full day of the tour. And the overwhelming majority were with me.

The irony of campaigning, however, is that when a candidate is on a whistle-stop tour, meeting the people personally, he is usually out of touch with what is going on in the country at large. Such was my case. On our campaign train, we had contact with the outside world only for a few minutes at each stop. Then we would plug in our special train telephones and try to get the latest reports from our campaign headquarters in Washington or in California or from the Eisenhower train. While I was speaking, members of my staff made the telephone calls and then when the train was again under way they reported to me. Consequently, during the day we had little idea of the furor in Washington.

The fund issue was becoming a national sensation. Political panic had struck many Republicans. The National Committee in Washington was besieged with telephone calls, as was the Eisenhower train. Several of my office staff in Washington, I learned later, were in tears. The handwriting on the wall seemed to say: "Dick Nixon is through."

On our train, we went through northern California handling the fund issue as though it were an ordinary political attack. We decided to answer the attack with the plain, unvarnished truth. We telephoned Dana Smith to make public the list of donors. The list would show that the contributors were professional and business people who by no stretch of the imagination could accurately be described as a "millionaire's club." Smith was also told to prepare an audit of the money taken in and of how it was spent so that this data could be released publicly.

Toward the end of the day, we held another conference on the train. While by this time I must admit I was irritated, I was not in the least discouraged. Murray Chotiner insisted that in the end the issue would help more than hurt us because it was giving life to a campaign which had been described in the Scripps-Howard papers as "running like a dry creek."

He said, "Dick, all we've got to do is to get you before enough people talking about this fund, and we will win this election in a landslide." Bill Rogers predicted that the attack would boomerang on our opponents because it had come too early, was being overplayed, and could not stand up on its merits. But Jim Bassett sounded a pessimistic note. The reporters traveling with us, who had now been joined by some from the Eisenhower train, were getting reports from the East, and they considered the story far more serious than we had appraised it. They were demanding that I have a press conference to answer questions on the fund. But Chotiner, Rogers, and I believed that this would only give a bigger play to a story that was already receiving more attention than it deserved.

And so we continued on our way, speaking to the increasing crowds at each station stop, receiving scattered reports of the snowballing Democratic attack, and wondering why we had not heard from General Eisenhower during the almost two days since the New York *Post* article had been published. We did not realize that his staff had withheld the news of the attack from him all day Thursday because they did not want to interfere with his preparation of the major speeches he had scheduled that day. It was not until Friday that he was informed of the attack. Later that afternoon he issued a statement that "Dick Nixon is an honest man" and that "the facts will show that Nixon would not compromise with what is right."

It was ten o'clock Friday night when we finished our second full day of whistle-stopping after three stops at small towns in southern Oregon. The train had pulled off onto a siding for the night. It was then that I learned that my own staff was keeping some bad news from me. As I was walking through the corridor of the train, a reporter came up to me and asked, "Senator, do you have any comment on the Washington *Post* and the New York *Herald Tribune* editorials?"

"What editorials?" I asked.

"Both the *Post* and *Herald Tribune* have editorials tomorrow morning saying that you ought to offer your resignation to General Eisenhower!"

This one really hit me. I said something to the effect that I would not comment until I had an opportunity to read the editorials. Then I hurried back to my own compartment. I asked the porter to go into the next car and see if he could get Rogers and Chotiner to come to my compartment for a conference.

As I waited for them, I knew that if the reports with regard to the *Herald Tribune* were accurate, I had been hit by a real blockbuster. I had firmly believed up to this time that since the attack was strictly partisan and would not stand up on its merits, our strategy of continuing to play it down would pay off and it would be forgotten within a few days. I still believe this would have been the case had the attack continued to come only from Democrats and from newspapers which were opposed to Eisenhower as well as to me. But when Republicans as well as Democrats began to demand my scalp, the roof caved in. I could shrug off a demand for my resignation by a paper like the Washington *Post*. The *Post* had been consistently critical of me since the days of the Hiss case and had taken a dim view of my nomination. But the New York *Herald Tribune* was something else again. It was the most influential Republican newspaper in the East. Bert Andrews, the chief Washington correspondent for the *Tribune,* had worked with me on the Hiss case and had become one of my closest personal friends. I knew he was on the Eisenhower train. I also knew that the publishers and other top officials of the *Tribune* had very close relations with Eisenhower and with some of his most influential supporters. I assumed that the *Tribune* would not have taken this position editorially unless it also represented the thinking of the people around Eisenhower. And, as I thought more about it, it occurred to me that this might well be the view of Eisenhower himself, for I had not heard from him since the trouble began, two days before.

When Rogers and Chotiner arrived in my compartment, they admitted that they had received word of the *Tribune* editorial at about 8:30 that night but did not want to disturb me with it until the next morning. They felt I had had a hard day and needed a good night's sleep. They showed me a copy of the editorial. The last sentence read, "The proper course of Senator Nixon in the circumstances is to make a formal offer of withdrawal from the ticket. How this offer is acted on will be determined by an appraisal of all the facts in the light of General Eisenhower's unsurpassed fairness of mind." I knew now that the fat was in the fire. That sounded like the official word from Eisenhower himself.

Even Rogers was shaken this time. And Chotiner was furious. "Why do the Republicans have to play right into the hands of the enemy?" he said. "How stupid can they be? If those damned amateurs around Eisenhower just had the sense they were born with they would recognize that this is a purely political attack and they wouldn't pop off like this."

I was experiencing some of the same emotional reaction that Chotiner had put into words. But I had learned from my experience in the Hiss case that what determines success or failure in handling a crisis is the ability to keep coldly objective when emotions are running high. That experience stood me in good stead now. I found myself almost automatically thinking and making decisions quickly, rationally, and unemotionally. It was essential that we get firsthand information as to where the people around Eisenhower and he, himself, stood. And we had to get it fast. I asked Rogers to call Dewey. I asked Chotiner to talk with Fred Seaton (later named Secretary of the Interior), who was acting at that time as the unofficial liaison officer between the two trains. I told them that I would not talk to Sherman Adams or anyone else on the Eisenhower train except Eisenhower himself, since this was a matter in which he alone had the authority to make a decision. What none of us could understand was how any of those around Eisenhower could in fairness reach a judgment before they knew the facts. I knew I had done nothing wrong and had nothing to hide.

It was almost two o'clock Saturday morning when our meeting finally broke up. I had put on a reasonably good front with Rogers and Chotiner, but now I felt the full weight of fatigue and depression brought on by the day's events. I told Pat about the *Tribune* editorial. She was as shocked as I was and had somewhat the same reaction as Chotiner. But much of the fight had gone out of me by this time, and I was beginning to wonder how much more of this beating I was going to be able to take. I expressed some of my inner doubts to her. "Maybe I am looking at this too much from my own standpoint. If the judgment of more objective people around Eisenhower is that my resignation would help him to win, maybe I ought to resign."

Pat reacted with fire in her eyes. "You can't think of resigning. If you do Eisenhower will lose. He can put you off the ticket if he wants to but if you, in the face of attack, do not fight back but simply crawl away, you will destroy yourself. Your life will be marred forever and the same will be true of your family, and particularly, your daughters." I was never to receive any better advice, and at a time when I needed it most.

The next morning, the "Nixon Special" steamed on through Oregon, but the original thrill and anticipation with which we had started was gone. The train seemed like a prison with its inexorable schedule. The crowds grew even larger. Democrats as well as Republicans came out to get a look at the vice presidential candidate. The hecklers were more aggressive. I fought back harder.

In Eugene, Oregon, our second stop on Saturday, the Democrats picketed with their own campaign signs, one of which said: "No Mink Coats for Nixon, Just Cold Cash." This was a reference to the Republican campaign slogan of "A scandal a day" in the Truman Administration. We had hit hard at the numerous scandals, involving gifts accepted by various officials in the Truman Administration. A $9000 mink coat accepted by a White House secretary had become a symbol of all the corruption of the Truman Administration. My answer that day in Eugene to the pickets' sign was, "That's absolutely right. There are no mink coats for the Nixons. I am proud to say my wife, Pat, wears a good Republican cloth coat." This phrase came to mind simply because I had long been aware that I was unable to afford a fur coat for my wife and, at the same time, it struck back hard at the Democrats' mink coat scandal.

It was at Eugene, too, that I noted that the violence of the attacks was finally beginning to backfire. Those supporting me in the crowd were resentful of the hecklers. They were not only listening to what I had to say and believing it, but also they were willing to fight back, just as I was. The mink coat signs were torn to shreds before my speech was completed.

But reports reaching us from Washington and from the Eisenhower train indicated the situation was becoming worse and worse. Karl Mundt's defense was described in the newspapers as the "sole official reaction from Republican National Headquarters" in Washington. Rumors were flying thick and fast about "this friend" and "that friend" of Eisenhower who felt it was imperative that I be dropped from the ticket. Some of those who had supported other vice presidential candidates at the Republican Convention began to build up a dump-Nixon movement. Reports from the Eisenhower train indicated that his advisers were split into two groups—those who thought I should be dropped immediately, and those who wanted to wait and see how public reaction developed.

One report which created a particular stir among the newsmen was that Eisenhower had interrupted a speech to take a telephone call from his old friend, General Lucius Clay, and that Clay had urged him to find another running mate. Clay later denied this report.

Arthur Summerfield, the Republican National Chairman (and who later became Postmaster General), was the only major Republican official on the Eisenhower train who was arguing openly and strongly that I should be kept on the ticket, defended, and supported. Sherman Adams and Herb Brownell had telephoned William Knowland, the senior Senator from California who was then in Hawaii, to fly back immediately to join the Eisenhower campaign train. Knowland, it was reported, was meant to be the substitute candidate for Vice President if needed. Upon reaching the Eisenhower train, however, he immediately joined Summerfield in urging that I be kept on the ticket.

But the over-all impression from all the reports was that the people around Eisenhower were worried and angry that the fund controversy might cost the Republicans the election and that it was all my fault. Jim Hagerty told newsmen that the mail and telegrams reaching the campaign train was divided fifty-fifty. The press reported that an aura of gloom had settled over the Eisenhower train.

If that was so, it was nothing compared to the despair on the "Nixon Special" as we received reports from the East. What kept our morale up during the day was the overwhelmingly favorable reaction of the whistle-stop crowds to my speeches whenever I discussed the fund. And finally, early in the afternoon, I received the first bit of good news from the East since Karl Mundt's statement the day the story broke. Bill Rogers came back into my compartment as the train was pulling away from one of our whistle-stops to report, "I think the tide has finally begun to turn. Bob Taft has just made a strong statement in your behalf."

Taft, who was Mr. Integrity himself, had, with his typical fairness and objectivity, tried to put the whole affair in perspective: "I see no reason why a Senator or Representative should not accept gifts from members of his family or his friends or his constituents to help pay even personal expenses which are not paid by the government. The only possible criticism would arise if these donors asked for or received legislative or other favors. I know that no such motives inspired the expense payments in the case of Dick Nixon. Those who contributed to the fund probably agreed 100 per cent with his legislative position anyway."

It was ironical, but not surprising, that Taft, whose nomination I had opposed at the Convention, was one of the first major Republican leaders to speak up in my defense. First, he was a Senator himself. He knew that scores of Senators and Congressmen from the more populous states and districts had to have funds available for year-round campaigning. In addition, Taft was an experienced politician and party man. He knew exactly what the Democrats were up to. He knew they were aiming not at me but at Eisenhower and the big prize —the presidency. He was not so naïve as to think that I could be dropped from the ticket without creating a break in our ranks big enough for the Democratic campaign to drive through to victory. House Minority Leader Joe Martin, who was in California at the time, and Herbert Hoover also came to my defense before the day was over.

And while the attacks continued to increase in violence and volume, we all noted that one voice on the Democratic side was strangely muted. Adlai Stevenson had not joined enthusiastically in the chorus of attack. As Bill Rogers once put it, he was following his usual pattern of "considering the problem very carefully before making the wrong decision." I took at face value his statement that he wanted to be fair and wait until all the facts were in. But Chotiner was not so charitable. He smelled a rat. He said, "I will lay money against odds that Stevenson is afraid of something here. He does not want these attacks to continue." Chotiner was right, but neither he nor I dreamed that what Stevenson was afraid of was a disclosure of his own political fund which was, indeed, secret and which would never have been revealed had it not been for the attacks his supporters had made on me.

Meanwhile, Dana Smith made public the names of all seventy-six contributors to the fund, which totaled $18,235 (an average contribution of $240 a person) for a two-year period. His accounting showed that disbursements had been made for Christmas cards which had been sent to former campaign workers, for travel vouchers, for recordings of speeches, for postage, and for a few other smaller items—leaving a balance of $66.13.

Following Smith's report, I issued a formal explanation on Saturday afternoon of "The Basic Facts About This Fund":

(1) It was set up to pay for strictly political activities in which all public servants must take part, in which those who are not independently wealthy are financially unable to participate without assistance.

(2) It enabled me to keep my speaking and mailing schedule with-

out recourse to padding my Federal office payroll, free government transportation, misuse of the Senatorial franking privilege, or any subterfuge.

(3) I had never received one penny of this fund for my personal use.

(4) This fund has been a matter of public knowledge from its inception; no attempt has ever been made to conceal its existence or purpose. All its disbursements were made by Mr. Smith by check as Trustee.

(5) Contributors of this fund are longtime supporters of mine who sincerely wish to enable me to continue my active battle against Communism and corruption.

(6) None of them ever asked for or received any special consideration from me.

(7) This fund represents a normal, legitimate, open matter of permitting constituents actively to support the political activity of a candidate of their choice. Any other interpretation is a grave injustice to a fine group of public-spirited community leaders.

This statement on the "basic facts" was reported in the papers the next day. But somehow, along with the Taft, Martin, and Hoover statements, it got lost in the welter of news and speculation over whether General Eisenhower would or would not choose to find a new running mate. There were several reasons for this which our small group on the "Nixon Special" tried to analyze. The primary factor was that the answer to a charge is never considered as newsworthy as the original attack. Second, the big-name, influential Washington reporters cover the presidential candidates while the less well-known reporters are assigned to the vice presidential candidates. This meant that the stories from the Eisenhower train automatically tended to receive a bigger play than the stories from the Nixon train. Third, there was the physical factor that news traditionally travels from east to west because of the three-hour difference in time zones. And fourth, while most newspaper publishers are Republicans, the majority of working reporters are Democrats. As Bert Andrews once said to me, "Their natural bias has an effect, conscious or subconscious, on how they choose their words to tell their stories."

As our train pulled into Salem, Oregon, for the major stop of the day, we all wondered what Governor Douglas McKay would do. The political heat in Oregon was particularly strong for me to get off the ticket, and the Governor had been urged by some of his friends to avoid riding with me in the motorcade to the Capitol steps, where I was scheduled to speak. It was common knowledge that McKay was high on the list for an appointment to the Eisenhower Cabinet, and his advisers did not want him to appear on the wrong side of the fence.

I shall always be grateful for his reaction. He not only greeted me warmly but rode with me through crowds which included scores of sign-carrying hecklers. He introduced me at the Capitol in the warmest and friendliest possible terms. Years later, when he was Secretary of the Interior, I asked him why he had done this in view of the risks involved. He replied, "I didn't know whether Eisenhower was going to keep you on the ticket or not and, frankly, I hadn't had enough opportunity to study the facts to decide whether or not you should stay on the ticket. But I don't like to see anybody being kicked around when he is down and, particularly, before he has had a chance to state his side of the case. If you had the guts to fight it out, I certainly should have enough guts to introduce you."

My reception in Portland was altogether different. There the crowds were thin because of discouragement and lack of planning among local Republican leaders. But the pickets and hecklers were out in full force. They threw pennies into the car as we motorcaded to our hotel. Some of them were thrown so hard we were forced to duck. When we reached the Benson Hotel we were met by a jeering crowd blocking the entrance. Pat and I were shoved and jostled as we got out of the car, and only with the help of Bob Hamilton, who had taken leave from his job with the FBI in San Francisco to serve as my aide, were we able to force our way into the lobby.

When we reached our suite, I called Chotiner, Rogers, Hillings, and Bassett for a conference so that we could catch up on the latest news reports and determine our strategy for the next day. There still had not been any word from Eisenhower. Sherman Adams had left a call for me at the hotel switchboard, but I told Chotiner to call him back and inform him that I would not talk to anyone but the General. And there was a message from my mother, who was staying with the children in Washington. It was a simple one: "I will be thinking of you." This had been her Quaker way through the years of saying that she would be praying for me.

It was at this meeting that Jim Bassett informed me of the now-famous "hound's tooth" remark. The General had called reporters to his car for an informal, off-the-record talk. There he had repeated his personal conviction that although he did not know me well, he believed

I was honest and that I would not do anything crooked or unethical. But he had said that I would have to prove it and convince "fair-minded" people. Then he had gone on to say, "Of what avail is it for us to carry on this crusade against this business of what has been going on in Washington if we, ourselves, aren't clean as a hound's tooth?" Bassett reported that the press was reading into Eisenhower's statement the implication that Nixon would have to prove himself "clean as a hound's tooth" if he hoped to stay on the ticket with Eisenhower. Our little group was somewhat dismayed by reports of Eisenhower's attitude. I must admit that it made me feel like the little boy caught with jam on his face.

But by this time I was no longer interested in hearsay reports on what Eisenhower thought. I knew that now that we were off the train and were scheduled to be in a hotel for the next twenty-four hours, I would have an opportunity to talk to him directly.

In the meantime, some fundamental decisions could not wait. The first order of business was to get all the evidence in front of me. I asked Chotiner and Rogers to continue their efforts to get firsthand reports from Dewey, Seaton, Adams, Summerfield, and any others they could reach on the Eisenhower train. I asked Jim Bassett to check sentiment not only in our own press group but also among correspondents on the Eisenhower train. Hillings was to give me an appraisal of the wires and letters which were now arriving by the hundreds at the hotel, and was also to check sentiment among Congressmen and Senators.

I left for my evening speaking engagement in the Grant High School auditorium in a pessimistic mood. But there I was bucked up by the most wildly enthusiastic reception of the campaign to date. It was an overflow crowd which rose to its feet when Pat and I entered, and they cheered and applauded virtually everything I said. Our departure from the auditorium was delayed for over an hour while hundreds swarmed to the stage of the auditorium to shake my hands and say, "Don't quit."

When we arrived back at the hotel, I asked Chotiner, Rogers, Bassett, and Hillings to come to my room to give me their reports.

At times like this it is vitally important to look at the facts at their worst rather than at their best, and so I opened the conference by saying, "I don't want to hear any sugar-coated reports. I want to know who is for me and who is against me and then we can decide what to do."

The reports, to put it mildly, were not encouraging, and these men, each of whom was a colleague and a friend, gave it to me straight. Bassett reported that more than 90 per cent of the press on the Eisenhower train believed I was a liability to the ticket. They were predicting that if I did not resign of my own accord, I would be forced off the ticket. However, he added, some of our own press contingent were beginning to shift. At first they had thought I was through because of the scandal. But now some were beginning to blame Eisenhower for not making a decision one way or the other, thereby putting a stop to the mushrooming story. They had also been impressed by the enthusiastic reaction of the crowds when I had told my side of the fund story. But most of the television and radio commentators, as well as the newspaper columnists, were predicting that in the end I would be off the ticket.

Chotiner and Rogers reported that the sentiment among Eisenhower's staff, friends, and advisers was just as bad. Some of the staff members were withholding comment until Eisenhower himself made a decision, but privately they were saying that I should resign. And one of them had gone so far as to call some of the key members of the National Committee, urging them to demand my resignation.

The only relatively bright spot was Hillings' report to the effect that most of the Senators and Congressmen he had reached were advising me to stay on the ticket and fight it out.

After each had made his report, I put the key question to them. "All of us tend to see this story from my point of view. But we can't fly in the face of such overwhelming opinion against us unless we have some strong reasons to question the judgment of those who have reached the opposite conclusion. I want each of you to try to put yourself in the place of Eisenhower. Forget about me. If my staying on the ticket would lead to Eisenhower's defeat, I would never forgive myself. If my getting off the ticket is necessary to assure his victory, it would be worth it as far as any personal embarrassment to me is concerned. Looking at it this way—should I take the initiative and resign from the ticket at this time?"

Bassett replied that it would depend on whether I was able to get my story across more adequately to the press and to the country at large.

Rogers said that if Eisenhower asked for my resignation, "you would have no other course than to submit it. But unless and until he does, you should fight it out."

Hillings, who at twenty-nine was still young enough to have "fire in his belly," insisted vehemently that I should stay on the ticket regardless of what Eisenhower wanted me to do. "You simply can't let down the millions of people who have supported you through the years," he said. When I asked him how we were going to deal with the press and other opinion-makers who seemed to be so overwhelmingly against us, he replied, "You don't have to win them. The best way to answer them is to beat 'em."

Chotiner applied his keen political mind to the problem and came up with the same conclusion. "This is politics," he said. "The prize is the White House. The Democrats have attacked you and will continue to attack you because they are afraid to take on Eisenhower. You are the lightning rod. If they weren't taking you on this way, they would be taking you on on something else because they don't know how to get at Eisenhower and they are afraid he is too popular for a frontal assault. If you get off this ticket because Eisenhower forces you off, or if you do so on your own volition, Eisenhower won't have the chance of a snowball in hell to win in November. Your friends and those who supported Taft will never forgive him, and the Democrats will beat him over the head for his lack of judgment in selecting you in the first place. This whole story has been blown up out of all proportion because of the delay and indecision of the amateurs around Eisenhower. Every time you get before an audience, you win them. What we have to do is to get you before the biggest possible audience so that you can talk over the heads of the press to the people. The people, I am convinced, are for you but the press is killing you."

Chotiner, who had great respect for the working press, did not intend these remarks to be critical of the reporters covering us, but he pointed up hard realities as far as press coverage in general is concerned. Reporters temperamentally and traditionally are skeptical, and perhaps justifiably so, whenever the personal honesty of a public official is questioned.

Everyone present agreed that somehow I had to get an opportunity to tell my story to millions rather than to the thousands who were coming out to hear me at the whistle-stops. There was only one way to do this—through a national television broadcast. As our conference broke up after three in the morning, we agreed that the following day we would check out the possibilities for putting me on a nationwide TV hookup. The major question remaining unresolved was the type of program and the timing of the broadcast. Several commercially sponsored programs, including "Meet the Press," had offered me time for Sunday night. Chotiner thought that "Meet the Press" would be a bad format because he believed the program should give me an opportunity to state my case alone, without interruption by possibly unfriendly press questioners. Rogers objected on the ground that he thought Sunday was too early. "Let them shoot their wad first and then give it to them," he said.

After the four of them had left the room, I sat alone for another two hours and reviewed the entire situation. I realized that although others could help direct my thinking, the final decision in a crisis of this magnitude must not represent the lowest common denominator of a collective judgment; it must be made alone by the individual primarily involved.

The range and scope of this crisis began to fall into a pattern. It was, of course, an acute personal crisis. I realized that my decision affected not only me and my future but also that of my wife, my daughters, my parents, and other members of my family. They, as well as I, would have to live with the consequences of my action.

What I did would also affect Eisenhower and his personal future in the same way.

But more important, I knew that what I decided would affect the Republican Party and the millions of its members who had put their faith in me by nominating me as candidate for Vice President.

And most important of all, I believed that what I did would affect the future of my country and the cause of peace and freedom for the world.

Stripped of all personal and collateral considerations, the real issue was: who would win the election, Eisenhower or Stevenson?

To me, this was not a choice between two equally able men who happened to be members of different parties. I will admit that I was not an objective observer; but to me Eisenhower was a great leader who could provide the inspiration needed by the United States and the Free World in so critical a time. Stevenson, on the other hand, impressed me as being all veneer and no substance—a man plagued with indecision who could speak beautifully but could not act decisively. If my crisis over an $18,000 political fund was to affect who would lead the United States in the next four or eight years, it was a crisis of unbelievably massive proportions.

What had happened during the past week had not shaken my faith in Eisenhower. If, as some of my associates thought, he appeared to be indecisive, I put the blame not on him but on his lack of experience in political warfare and on the fact that he was relying on several equally inexperienced associates. I could see his dilemma. He had been a winner all his life and now his task as a candidate was to win again in a new arena where, as inexperienced as he was, he had to judge the voters' mood to decide whether or not I should be asked to stay on the ticket or resign. He had to win the election before he could lead the country. And his friends and associates, whom he trusted, were telling him that he might lose unless he got rid of me.

I recognized, however, that my personal decision had to be based on my own analysis of the facts as I saw them and politics as I knew it to be. If I were to resign from the ticket it would be an admission of guilt, Eisenhower might well lose the election, and I would forever afterwards be blamed for it. I decided that I had to do everything within my power to stay on the ticket—with honor. Having made that basic decision, I finally went to bed at about five in the morning and slept better than I had since the night the train pulled out of Pomona four days before.

Now the most difficult phase of the crisis was over—that agonizing period when I had to make the decision to fight the battle or to run away. Ahead of me were still three days of almost superhuman effort: preparing for the battle and then the battle itself, a half-hour broadcast in which the slightest mistake might spell disaster for me, my family, and my party.

But as I had learned in the Hiss case, the period of indecision, of necessary soul-searching was the hardest. Now the emotions, the drive, the intense desire to act and speak decisively which I had kept bottled up inside myself could be released and directed to the single target of winning a victory.

That Sunday was scheduled as a day of rest, with only one non-political speaking engagement on the calendar. However, it turned out to be another long day of ordeal, capped by another key decision. At about ten o'clock, Pat Hillings brought in the latest accumulation of wires and letters. The overwhelming majority urged me to stay on the ticket. But Harold Stassen, in a three-hundred-word telegram, advised me to offer my withdrawal from the race. He even spelled out a suggested text for my withdrawal message and stated that if my offer was accepted, Earl Warren should be named to step in. This, he said, "will also strengthen you and aid your career." As I read the wire, I realized how fickle fortune can be in politics. It was just eight months before, when Stassen had been seeking the presidential nomination himself, that he had called on me in my office in the Senate Office Building and urged me to support him for the nomination. He suggested that if I could swing part or all of the California delegation behind him, that that might start a bandwagon rolling and, under the circumstances, I would be "an ideal running mate" on his ticket.

Stassen's influence in the country at that time was still considerable. I realized his opposition was a severe blow. Yet, at times like this when my situation was desperate, little things can have as much effect as big ones. Tom Bewley, my former law partner, and John Reilly, who, as a former director of Rotary International, was one of our home town's most prominent citizens, flew up from Whittier to Portland to see me. They came into the suite for only a minute. "We just flew up to tell you," they said, "that all the folks back in Whittier are behind you 100 per cent."

When they left the room, I had a lump in my throat. Whittier at that time had no more than about ten thousand registered voters. What the people there thought didn't mean too much when the votes of sixty million in the country would determine the election. But acts of such thoughtfulness are so rare in political life that they have a meaning far beyond their significance in the ballot box.[1]

All afternoon, I talked with my staff about the alternatives we had for a television program. By this time, several commercial sponsors had offered to put me on for a half-hour without interruption, but we still felt that commercial sponsorship was not proper. Late in the afternoon I received a telephone call from Governor Dewey which was to have great influence on the format of the program.

"I think you ought to go on television," Dewey told me. "I don't think Eisenhower should make this decision. Make the American people do it. At the conclusion of the program, ask people to wire their verdict in to you in Los Angeles. You will probably get over a million replies, and that will give you three or four days to think it over. At the end of that time, if it is 60 per cent for you and 40 per cent against you, say you are getting out as that is not enough of a majority. If it

---

[1] Even from a political viewpoint, I should have recalled one of Jim Farley's favorite axioms: "The most important lesson for a politician to learn is that he must always be sure he can carry his own precinct."

is 90 to 10, stay on. If you stay on, it isn't blamed on Ike, and if you get off it isn't blamed on Ike. All the fellows here in New York agree with me."

The idea of leaving the decision to a vote of the television audience did not appeal to some of the members of my staff. They feared a concerted campaign might be put under way to "stack" the replies against me. But I had great respect for Dewey's political judgment, and I was trying to think of how his suggestion could be implemented when I left the hotel for my evening speaking engagement at the Portland Temple Club. There I put the fund furor out of mind and tried to lay to rest before a large and receptive audience one of the most malicious smears which had developed against me after my participation in the Hiss case: that I was anti-Semitic.

I arrived back at the hotel at around nine o'clock. We continued our discussion with regard to the broadcast. Chotiner insisted that the National Committee should sponsor the broadcast. He said, "They already have scheduled two nationwide broadcasts for the vice presidential candidate. What they have to realize is that this broadcast is just as important to the success of the campaign as the two they have regularly scheduled." This proved to be the understatement of the 1952 campaign!

While we were discussing the broadcast, Rose Mary Woods, my private secretary, came into the room and said, "General Eisenhower is on the phone." I was sitting on the couch with my legs propped up on the coffee table. I braced myself mentally for his decision and picked up the telephone. "Hello, General."

"Hello, Dick." His voice was warm and friendly. "You've been taking a lot of heat the last couple of days. I imagine it has been pretty rough."

I replied that the last four days had indeed been rugged.

"You know, this is an awfully hard thing for me to decide," he said. "I have come to the conclusion that you are the one who has to decide what to do. After all, you've got a big following in this country and if the impression got around that you got off the ticket because I forced you to get off, it is going to be very bad. On the other hand, if I issue a statement now backing you up, in effect people will accuse me of condoning wrongdoing." He said he had had dinner with some of his friends that night, and they were in disagreement as to whether I should stay on or get off. But they all agreed that I ought to have a chance to tell my story to the country.

46585

"I don't want to be in the position of condemning an innocent man," he said. "I think you ought to go on a nationwide television program and tell them everything there is to tell, everything you can remember since the day you entered public life. Tell them about any money you have ever received."

I asked him, "General, do you think after the television program that an announcement could then be made one way or the other?"

He replied, "I am hoping that no announcement would be necessary at all, but maybe after the program we could tell what ought to be done."

"General," I answered, "I just want you to know that I don't want you to give any consideration to my personal feelings. I know how difficult this problem is for you." Then I added: "But there comes a time in matters like this when you've either got to fish or cut bait. I will get off the ticket if you think my staying on it would be harmful. You let me know and I will get off and I will take the heat, but this thing has got to be decided at the earliest possible time. After the television program, if you think I should stay on or get off, I think you should say so either way. The great trouble here is the indecision."

But one of Eisenhower's most notable characteristics is that he is not a man to be rushed on important decisions. "We will have to wait three or four days after the television show to see what the effect of the program is," he insisted.

We talked on about the campaign and the crowd reactions and he ended the fifteen-minute conversation, our first since the fund episode began, by saying, "Well, Dick, go on the television show. Good luck and keep your chin up."

I informed the members of my staff who were in the room of the substance of the conversation and we went to work. In the next ninety minutes, we were in touch with Sherman Adams, Art Summerfield, and Bob Humphreys, of the National Committee staff. We finally got word that the National Committee and the Senatorial Congressional Campaign Committee had pledged the $75,000 necessary to buy a half-hour of prime evening time for Tuesday, just forty-eight hours away. We decided that the broadcast should originate from Los Angeles. While my staff worked out the broadcast arrangements, I sat alone in my room and, writing on the large lined yellow legal pads which I used for outlining my speeches, I reconstructed my conversation with Eisenhower and tried to evaluate it.

I could appreciate the terrible dilemma which confronted him. From a personal standpoint, he did not want to force me off the ticket. On the other hand, as the nominee of the party he had the responsibility to win the election. The way he had resolved the dilemma was to put the responsibility on me. I should go on television and present my side of the case, completely and accurately. But even then he might not make a decision one way or the other. It was up to me to decide whether I should stay on or get off the ticket.

I decided then and there to assume that responsibility completely and without any compromise. If I considered the broadcast a success, I would stay on the ticket. If I thought it was a failure, I would get off. Now everything was up to me, the challenge was clear, and I must prepare to meet it.

My first assignment was to inform the press of the decision. The newsmen covering my campaign were alerted at 11:00 P.M. to stand by for a press conference, my first since the fund crisis started. Jim Bassett, who had handled a very difficult assignment in those last four days, made several trips to the press room telling the reporters to stand by, while in my suite we made final arrangements to cancel my campaign tour so that I could fly to Los Angeles to prepare for the broadcast.

It was after 1:00 A.M. when I walked into the press room. I could sense the tension. The reporters must have expected a definite announcement—either that I was resigning or not resigning. I thought I might as well have a little fun on such a deadly serious occasion.

"I have come down to announce that I am breaking off—" I paused deliberately. There was an audible gasp in the room. Clint Mosher of the San Francisco *Examiner* almost jumped out of his skin. I laughed for perhaps the first time that day and began again. "I have come down to announce that I am breaking off my campaign trip tomorrow for the purpose of going to Los Angeles to make a nationwide television and radio broadcast." Mosher asked, "Senator, does this mean that you are going to stay on the ticket?" I replied, "This means I intend to continue the campaign tour. I have no further comment." This was a truthful answer because, whether I was on or off the ticket, I intended to continue to campaign for Eisenhower's election. But the result of this reply, which was not unexpected as far as I was concerned, was to create increasing suspense about what I would do on the TV broadcast.

Flying from Portland to Los Angeles, I hoped to catch up on some much-needed sleep. But I could doze only intermittently. My body needed rest but my brain was churning with ideas.

A new tension was now building up—the tension that precedes battle when all the plans have been drawn and one stands poised for action. This speech was to be the most important of my life. I felt now that it was my battle alone. I had been deserted by so many I had thought were friends but who had panicked in battle when the first shots were fired.

I realized I had to take my case to the people and convince them of my honesty and integrity. The public reaction to my speech would determine whether or not I was a liability to the Republican ticket. If I failed, I decided that I would get off the ticket and take all responsibility for doing so. And I went even further in my own thinking as to what I had to accomplish through the broadcast. I must not only remove any liability I might be to the ticket, I must become a positive asset. I had decided that unless I could attain both these objectives I would resign.

To attain these objectives, I knew I had to go for broke. This broadcast must not be just good. It had to be a smash hit—one that really moved people, one that was designed not simply to explain the complicated and dull facts about the fund to the people, but one that would inspire them to enthusiastic, positive support.

As far as content was concerned, I recognized that the speech had to meet three requirements.

First, I must answer the immediate attack that was being made on me by explaining and defending the fund.

Second, I must ward off future attacks along the same lines so that any further allegations that I had profited financially from my public service would fall on deaf ears.

Finally, I felt I had to launch a political counterattack to rally the millions of voters in my television audience to the support of the Eisenhower ticket. I knew this television audience would probably be the largest of the campaign and I was not going to allow this opportunity to pass without using it to full advantage to get across to millions of people who would never attend a political meeting the reasons why I felt the nation needed Eisenhower's leadership.

My only hope to win rested with millions of people I would never meet, sitting in groups of two or three or four in their living rooms, watching and listening to me on television. I determined as the plane took me to Los Angeles that I must do nothing which might reduce the size of that audience. And so I made up my mind that until after this broadcast, my only releases to the press would be for the purpose of building up the audience which would be tuning in. Under no circumstances, therefore, could I tell the press in advance what I was going to say or what my decision would be.

Unable to sleep on the plane, I took some of the picture post cards from the pocket of the seat in front of me and began to jot down my first notes for the speech. My remark in Eugene, Oregon, about Pat's cloth coat came to mind, and I marked it down as a good reminder of the mink coat scandals which were plaguing the Truman Administration.

I thought of General Eisenhower's suggestion that I disclose any gifts, financial or otherwise, I had received while I had been in public office. I remembered that right after the nomination, a Republican supporter in Texas had learned that our daughters wanted a puppy and had sent us a four-month-old, black and white pedigreed cocker spaniel—"born in Texas, from a long line of cocker spaniels that were particularly gentle and good with children." Thinking back to Franklin Roosevelt's devastating remark in the 1944 campaign—"and now they are attacking poor Fala"—I decided to mention my own dog Checkers. Using the same ploy as FDR would irritate my opponents and delight my friends, I thought.

The Democratic attack on my need for a political fund came to mind. "If a fellow can't afford to be a Senator, he shouldn't seek the office," Stephen Mitchell, the Democratic National Chairman, had said. The implication was that only rich men could afford to run for and serve in government. I thought of a Lincoln quote and jotted it down: "God must have loved the common people, he made so many of them."

For most of the flight I tried to think of a way I could carry out Eisenhower's suggestion, "Tell them about everything you have ever received from the time you entered public life." It was on this trip from Portland to Los Angeles that I decided the only way to blunt future attacks on my honesty was to lay out for everyone to see my entire personal financial history from the time I entered public life to the present. This was to prove to be the most difficult part of the broadcast, both to prepare and to deliver. It had to be absolutely accurate, and consequently, it entailed round-the-clock research of all my records, including income tax returns, bank accounts, and property transfers.

Even more difficult was the decision to discuss such purely private matters before millions of people who were complete strangers to Pat and to me. In the twelve years of our married life we had never acquired much in the way of the world's goods, but this had never concerned us. Our interests were in other directions. The fact that we might not have the latest model car, the most fashionable clothes, or the biggest house in the block, was never a source of embarrassment or envy. But both Pat and I had perhaps what some might describe as an overdeveloped sense of privacy. What we owned and what we owed was our own business and nobody else's. We had worked hard to earn what we had. We had bent over backwards since coming to Washington in 1947, paying our own way, refusing to accept favors we could not reciprocate, not just because we wanted to avoid any possibility of attack politically but because we both had a stubborn streak of independence and deeply disliked being under obligation to anyone. We had received no credit for this simply because we did not want any and had not asked for it.

"Why do you have to tell people how little we have and how much we owe?" Pat asked me as I was making my notes for the broadcast.

"People in political life have to live in a fish bowl," I replied.

"But aren't we entitled to have at least some privacy?"

I explained that under normal circumstances she would be right. But this situation was far from normal. I had no choice but to use every possible weapon to assure the success of the broadcast.

And so it went—thinking, dozing, scribbling, until the plane arrived at 2:45 P.M. on Monday at Los Angeles International Airport. As we stepped out on the ramp, we were heartened by a banner-waving, shouting crowd of several hundred Young Republicans who were there to greet us. "Don't Give Up," "Keep Fighting," "We're for you all the way," their placards read. No party bigwigs were there. Since there was no platform, I made an impromptu speech from the hood of a car and promised them, "We will not let you down."

An hour later we were in our suite at the Ambassador Hotel and I went to work in earnest preparing my notes for the broadcast. I had only twenty-four hours left in which to finish preparations for the most important speech I had ever made up to that time.

Some of my staff were worried for fear that I was working too hard and not getting enough sleep. They urged me to take Monday night off so that I would be fresh when I started to work again on the speech Tuesday morning.

I realize that in such situations, no two individuals react the same. But it has been my experience that once the final period of intense preparation for battle begins, it is not wise to break it. It always takes me a certain period of time to "warm up" to the point where my mind is working clearly and quickly in tackling a tough problem. This is especially true where creative activity like writing a speech is concerned. The natural tendency is to procrastinate, because the body and the mind rebel at being driven at a faster pace than usual over any long period of time. When one is working at this pace, it is always a temptation to take the pressure off—to leave the task for a while because the body needs rest. A man tries to rationalize such a course on the ground that "relaxation and change" will improve his efficiency when he gets back to the task.

This is true, of course, where the period of intense concentration and preparation stretches into months rather than days and, in the case of some individuals, it may be true at all times. But it has been my experience that, more often than not, "taking a break" is actually an escape from the tough, grinding discipline that is absolutely necessary for superior performance. Many times I have found that my best ideas have come when I thought I could not work for another minute and when I literally had to drive myself to finish the task before a deadline. Sleepless nights, to the extent the body can take them, can stimulate creative mental activity. For me, it is often harder to be away from the job than to be working at it.

Sometimes a brief change of pace—a brisk walk, a breath of fresh air—can recharge a mind that has become sluggish from overwork. I think perhaps the best analogy is that it may be necessary and helpful to take the machine out of gear once in a while, but it is never wise to turn the engine off and let the motor get completely cold.

This, incidentally, is one of the reasons I have never become a regular "twice a week" golfer. When I am in the middle of a period of intense study or work, leaving the problem for the five or six hours required for a pleasant day on the golf course simply means that I have to spend most of the next day getting myself charged up again—to the point of efficiency I had reached before leaving the task in the first place.

For most of Monday afternoon and all day Tuesday, I outlined the speech and gathered facts for it. The first section, explaining the fund, presented no difficulty. I already had it pretty well in mind, having covered the subject in my whistle-stops on my way to Portland. The second section, in which I was planning to disclose my financial status, could not be completed until all the facts were gathered together by my office staff in Washington and telephoned to Rose Mary Woods so that she could type up the information and have it available for me the day of the broadcast.

The problem of launching a counterattack solved itself that Monday when the Chicago *Tribune* reported a Stevenson fund which had been solicited from businessmen doing business with the state while he was Governor of Illinois. The national press gave the Stevenson fund relatively little play compared to the Nixon fund. But now we knew why Stevenson had been so reluctant to join in the attack on my fund. As Murray Chotiner put it: "He was hiding something—otherwise he would have been at your throat like the rest of them."

There were several differences between the two funds. Stevenson's had been secret while mine was not. The money had been paid directly to him and he had disbursed it, while mine had been disbursed by a trustee. There had been no accounting to the contributors to his fund, whereas mine had been fully accounted. The money in his fund had gone for the personal use of members of his Administration in Illinois, while the money in my fund had been used solely for mailing, printing, travel, and other political expenses and not for my personal use.

I decided to resist the temptation to attack Stevenson in my broadcast the way his associates had attacked me. But I thought I had the right to insist that there not be a double standard of conduct—one for a Republican candidate, and another for a Democratic candidate. Stevenson's fund might be absolutely proper and above suspicion. But he had an obligation to give an accounting of the fund and to indicate what favors, if any, had been accorded those who had contributed to it.

But the counterattack, I knew, must not stop there. What time I had left at the end of the broadcast I intended to use to set forth effectively and concisely the major reasons I thought Eisenhower, rather than Stevenson, should be elected President.

Late that night I took a long walk with Rogers up and down the side streets near the hotel to get some fresh air and exercise and to test out the first outline of my speech on him. He encouraged me to go forward with the plan I had adopted. I came back to the hotel and worked until after midnight and then, after four hours' sleep, got up early in the morning to continue my preparations.

Normally, I would have allotted a week's time for reflection and writing on a speech of far less importance. I was hoping that I would be able to get my thoughts well enough in mind that I would not have to use notes at all. This had been my usual technique over the years. My practice was to make a first general outline and throw it away; then make a second, tighter-reasoned outline without referring to the first one; and finally to make a third even shorter one which I would then read over several times. I then would be able to deliver the speech without any notes at all. Particularly on television, I always tried to avoid reading a speech. I never memorized a speech or practiced it before delivery. Only when I could deliver a speech without memorizing it, and if possible without notes, did it have the spark of spontaneity so essential for a television audience.

This does not mean that the speech would not be well prepared. More preparation and concentration is required to deliver a speech in this manner than in writing one out and reading it to the audience. But I had an acute problem in preparing this particular speech—there just were not enough hours in the day for me to get the ideas firmly enough in my mind so that I could deliver it entirely without notes.

From all reports, I knew that I would be speaking to the largest television and radio audience of the entire campaign. The suspense engendered by conflicting press reports over whether I would resign or be kept on the ticket had centered the attention of the entire nation on this one telecast.

One of my major problems was that a number of the "top name" reporters from the Eisenhower train had come to Los Angeles to cover the speech. "They are here so as to have front-row seats for the hanging," Bassett quipped. Broadcast time was 6:30 P.M., Los Angeles, or 9:30 P.M. on the East Coast. This coincided with the deadlines of most of the morning newspapers. Bassett reported the intense pressures on him as press secretary to give out something in advance. Most of my staff urged that I do so in order to assure better press coverage. But on this issue, I overruled them all. I knew that any advance notice of what I was going to say would cut down the size of my television audience. This time I was determined to tell my story directly to the people rather than to funnel it to them through a press account.

Consequently, Bassett made arrangements for the reporters to see my speech at television monitors in a separate room, with no advance text and with no notice of what I would say.

All day Tuesday I continued to work on my outline. By four o'clock, I had completed the second draft and had begun work on the third and final one. The loose ends had for the most part been filled in. Dr. Paul Smith, my history professor at Whittier College, had confirmed the accuracy of the Lincoln quote.

I had all the facts of my financial history—going back to 1945 when I came out of the Navy, with a net worth of $10,000 in government bonds, and became a candidate for Congress.

To make the case as airtight as possible, Price Waterhouse & Co. had audited my accounts in Washington, and Gibson, Dunn and Crutcher, one of the most respected of Los Angeles' law firms, had prepared a legal opinion stating that there was no law violation involved either in the collection of the fund or in its disbursement. Paul Hoffman, incidentally, had suggested both these reports because of his belief that they would have great weight, not only with the television audience but also with Eisenhower's associates from the world of finance and business on whose judgment the General placed such great reliance.

As I kept driving myself harder and harder with broadcast time approaching, my concern was not with my ability to speak at least fairly well. I had enough experience in speaking on television to be confident that with any reasonable amount of preparation I would not fall on my face. But I kept reminding myself, "It isn't enough for this just to be good. It must be the best you have ever done. It must be even better than you think you can possibly do. Because only a smashing success will win."

By this time, I was no longer thinking of the effect this broadcast might have on my own career. The attacks from my former Republican friends and from press and radio commentators had taken their toll. Personally, I now wanted to get the whole business over with as soon as possible, one way or the other.

This attitude served me well. Selflessness is by far the most helpful attribute an individual can have at such a time. A man is at his best in a crisis when he is thinking not of himself but of the problem at hand. Then he forgets, or at least is not bothered by, how he "feels" physically.

In such periods of intense preparation for battle, most individuals experience all the physical symptoms of tension—they become edgy and short-tempered, some can't eat, others can't sleep. I had experienced all these symptoms in the days since our train left Pomona. I had had a similar experience during the Hiss case. But what I had learned was that feeling this way before a battle was not something to worry about—on the contrary, failing to feel this way would mean that I was not adequately keyed up, mentally and emotionally, for the conflict ahead. It is only when the individual worries about how he feels that such physical factors become signs of self-destruction rather than of creativity. Two of the most important lessons I have learned from going through the fire of decision is that one must know himself, be able to recognize his physical reactions under stress for what they are, and that he must never worry about the necessary and even healthy symptoms incident to creative activity.

With personal considerations subordinated, I could concentrate on the issue which was far more important than my own political career. That was the election of Eisenhower. To me, Stevenson just wasn't in the same league and I had to do everything I could to see that Eisenhower was elected President. Eisenhower could not match Stevenson for elegance of language or eloquence of delivery. But Eisenhower was a man of decision. As General Walter Bedell Smith had pointed out in his book, *Eisenhower's Six Great Decisions,* he never did anything rashly. Sometimes he took more time to decide an issue than some of his eager lieutenants thought necessary, but invariably, when the line was drawn and the lonely responsibility for making the right decision rested solely with him, he came up with the right answer. The idea of putting Stevenson in the ring with a man like Stalin simply petrified me. On the other hand, I had faith that Eisenhower not only could hold his own but could gain the initiative for the cause of peace and freedom.

At four-thirty, with only a little over an hour left before I was scheduled to leave for the television studio, I asked Rogers and Chotiner to come in to discuss the one important section of the speech on which I had not made a decision. I had adopted Dewey's suggestion of asking the television audience to express their opinions by wire or letter. But to whom? To Eisenhower? To me? Or to the Republican National Committee?

We were still discussing this point when a call came through to my suite from "Mr. Chapman" in New York. That was the code name Tom

Dewey used when telephoning so as to confuse anyone who might be listening in. I knew that Dewey would not have called at this hour unless a matter of the highest urgency was involved. I left Rogers and Chotiner to continue their discussion and went into the next room and picked up the telephone.

From the tone of his voice, I could sense immediately that Dewey did not have his heart in what he had to tell me. "There has just been a meeting of all of Eisenhower's top advisers," he said. "They have asked me to tell you that it is their opinion that at the conclusion of the broadcast tonight you should submit your resignation to Eisenhower. As you know, I have not shared this point of view, but it is my responsibility to pass this recommendation on to you."

I was so shocked by what he said that I could not say a word for several seconds.

Dewey jiggled the receiver and said, "Hello, can you hear me?"

Finally I collected my thoughts and said, "What does Eisenhower want me to do?"

Dewey hedged at this point. He said he did not want to give the impression that he had spoken directly to Eisenhower or that this decision had been approved by Eisenhower. But he went on to say he was sure that, in view of the close relationship between those with whom he had talked and Eisenhower, they would not have asked him to call unless this represented Eisenhower's view as well as their own.

"It's kind of late for them to pass on this kind of recommendation to me now," I told him. I added that I had already prepared my remarks and it would be most difficult for me to change them.

He replied that he thought I should go ahead and explain the fund as I had originally planned. And then I should say that, although I felt I had done no wrong, I did not want my presence on the ticket to be in any way a liability to the Eisenhower Crusade and, therefore, was submitting my resignation to him and insisting that he accept it.

As he continued to talk along these lines, I looked at my watch and realized that I had only a half-hour left to get cleaned up and to read over my notes before I had to leave for the studio.

"What shall I tell them you are going to do?" he asked.

My nerves were frayed to a fine edge by this time and I exploded, "Just tell them that I haven't the slightest idea as to what I am going to do and if they want to find out they'd better listen to the broadcast. And tell them I know something about politics too!" I slammed the receiver down and went back into the next room to continue my conversation with Rogers and Chotiner.

They were as shocked as I was when I told them of the call. "You certainly aren't going to do what he suggests, are you?" demanded Chotiner.

"I just don't know," I replied. "You two had better get out of here and give me a chance to think." For the next half-hour, I moved around almost in a daze. I shaved, took a shower, put on the suit I was to wear for the telecast, and then went back to my notes. I had only had a chance to begin a third outline. I read the second one over again and decided to use it. I didn't have time to make another draft. Dewey's telephone call had not only shaken my equilibrium but had robbed me of time enough to get the whole outline in my head. I decided to speak from notes rather than from memory.

With only a few minutes remaining, I made the decision as to how I should conclude the broadcast. The more I thought of it, the more I became convinced that the wires should go to the Republican National Committee.

There were several reasons for my decision. Under the bylaws of the party, the National Committee selects the candidate in the event of resignation or death between nomination and election. If the broadcast were a success and the wires were to come to me, our opponents would inevitably charge that it was all a staged frame-up. If the wires were sent to Eisenhower and he decided to ask for my resignation, those who supported me might never forgive him, and his action could lead to loss of the election. If, on the other hand, the broadcast were not successful and a majority of listeners indicated their disapproval to the National Committee, it would be the politicians rather than Eisenhower who would take the responsibility for removing me from the ticket.

Then there was a fourth possibility. The broadcast might after all be a success and, if so, Eisenhower would need and welcome the backing of the National Committee for retaining me on the ticket. This would be much better than if he, personally, were to assume full responsibility for that decision.

I was just starting to write out what I intended to say with regard to the National Committee when Murray Chotiner stuck his head in the door. I looked up, irritated that even he would interrupt me at such a time.

Bluntly, he plunged right in: "Dick," he said, "a good campaign manager must never be seen or heard. But if you're kicked off this ticket, I'm going to break that rule. I'm going to call the biggest damn press conference that's ever been held. I'm going to have television present. And I'm going to tell everybody who called who, what was said—names and everything."

"Would you really do that?" I asked.

"Sure I'd do it," he answered. "Hell, we'd be through with politics anyway. It wouldn't make any difference then."

He ducked out and closed the door, without waiting for me to reply. I was glad that he had come in. His devil-may-care attitude, so uncharacteristic of him, had broken the tension and given me a needed lift.

I quickly jotted down the final notes, stuffed the five pages into my pocket, and went across the hall to pick up Pat. We walked down the hotel corridor to the elevator together. No one bothered us or spoke to us. It seemed like the last mile.

I rode in the front seat of the car on the way to the studio so that I could look over my notes again. No one spoke during the twenty-minute ride. We arrived at the stage of the El Capitan Theater in Hollywood just twenty-five minutes before broadcast time. Only the cameramen and electricians were onstage. As I had instructed, the 750-seat theater was empty. The newsmen were in another room with television sets and a battery of shorthand stenographers who would record the text as delivered. I even asked Chotiner, Bill Rogers, and Hillings to leave the studio so that I would have no possible distractions.

Ted Rogers, our television and radio producer, took me to a dressing room where a makeup man insisted on applying some beard-stick to cover my five-o'clock shadow even though I had shaved less than an hour before. Ted had wanted me to come to the studio earlier in the day for lighting tests but I told him that I simply couldn't spare the time from the preparation of my remarks. He consequently had taken full responsibility for selecting the set and preparing for the program. He used a salesman who resembled me as a camera stand-in when I had declined to come to the studio for rehearsal.

Ten minutes before air time he asked Pat and me to come to the set so that the lights could be adjusted. We sat onstage for less than five minutes while these last details were attended to. The director asked what movements I would be making and I told him, "I don't have the slightest idea, just keep the camera on me."

We moved back into the dressing room and Pat and I sat there alone for the six or seven minutes which remained before air time. I tried to read my notes again but by now the tension was too great. It had been a rugged six days since we left Pomona on September 17 and I think that if I had received one more jolt, like Dewey's phone call, in those few remaining minutes, I would have announced my resignation.

Three minutes before air time, Ted Rogers knocked on the door of the dressing room. I turned to Pat and said, "I just don't think I can go through with this one."

"Of course you can," she said, with the firmness and confidence in her voice that I so desperately needed.

We walked together with Ted Rogers to the set. Pat sat in one armchair and I sat behind a desk with the five pages of handwritten notes in front of me. The big clock alongside the camera showed less than two minutes to air time. I watched the second hand go round and then the director brought his hand down and pointed to me.

This was it.

I began to speak. "My fellow Americans, I come before you tonight as a candidate for the vice presidency and as a man whose honesty and integrity has been questioned." As I spoke, all the tension suddenly went out of me. I felt in complete control of myself and of my material. I was calm and confident. Despite the lack of sleep or even of rest over the past six days, despite the abuse to which I had subjected my nerves and body—some way, somehow in a moment of great crisis a man calls up resources of physical, mental, and emotional power he never realized he had. This I was now able to do, because the hours and days of preparation had been for this one moment and I put into it everything I had. I knew what I wanted to say, and I said it from the heart.

I am sure that you have read the charge, and you have heard it, that I, Senator Nixon, took $18,000 from a group of my supporters. Now, was that wrong? . . . It isn't a question of whether it was legal or illegal, that isn't enough. The question is, was it morally wrong? I say that it was morally wrong—if any of that $18,000 went to Senator Nixon, for my personal use. I say it was morally wrong if it was secretly given and secretly handled. And I say that it was morally wrong if any of the contributors got special favors for the contributions that they made.

And now to answer those questions, let me say this: not one cent of the $18,000 or any other money of that type ever went to my personal use. Every penny of it was used to pay for political expenses that I did not think should be charged to the taxpayers of the United States.

I went on to explain the fund and its uses as I had so many times before. After only a few minutes, I found that I was speaking without looking at my notes. I finished my direct defense of the fund by reading from the independent opinions of the auditing and legal firms:

It is our conclusion that Senator Nixon did not obtain any financial gain from the collection and disbursement of the funds by Dana Smith; that Senator Nixon did not violate any federal or State law by reason of the operation of the fund; and that neither the portion of the fund paid by Dana Smith directly to third persons, nor the portion paid to Senator Nixon, to reimburse him for office expenses, constituted income in a sense which was either reportable or taxable as income under income tax laws.

Then I turned to my second job—a disclosure of my entire financial history so as to discredit any future smears:

There are some that will say, "Well, maybe you were able, Senator, to fake this thing. How can we believe what you say—after all, is there a possibility that maybe you got some sums in cash? Is there a possibility that you might have feathered your own nest?" And so now what I am going to do—and, incidentally, this is unprecedented in the history of American politics—I am going at this time to give to this television and radio audience a complete financial history, everything I have earned, everything I have spent, everything I own.

I proceeded to do just that. I listed everything I owned:

—a 1950 Oldsmobile car;
—a $3000 equity in my house in California in which my parents were then living;
—a $20,000 equity in my house in Washington;
—$4000 in life insurance, plus a G. I. term policy which would expire in two years;
—no stocks or bonds; no interest in any other property or business.

I listed what I owed:

—$10,000 on the California house;
—$20,000 on the Washington house;

—$4500 to the Riggs National Bank of Washington;
—$3500 to my parents;
—$500 on my life insurance.

And then I wrapped up my financial accounting in this way:

Well, that's about it. That's what we have. And that's what we owe. It isn't very much. But Pat and I have the satisfaction that every dime that we have got is honestly ours.

I should say this, that Pat doesn't have a mink coat. But she does have a respectable Republican cloth coat, and I always tell her that she would look good in anything.

One other thing I probably should tell you, because if I don't they will probably be saying this about me, too. We did get something, a gift, after the nomination. A man down in Texas heard Pat on the radio mention the fact that our two youngsters would like to have a dog and, believe it or not, the day before we left on this campaign trip we got a message from Union Station in Baltimore, saying they had a package for us. We went down to get it. You know what it was?

It was a little cocker spaniel dog, in a crate that he had sent all the way from Texas—black and white, spotted, and our little girl Tricia, the six-year-old, named it Checkers. And you know, the kids, like all kids, loved the dog, and I just want to say this, right now, that regardless of what they say about it, we are going to keep it.

It isn't easy to come before a nationwide audience and bare your life, as I have done. But I want to say some things before I conclude, that I think most of you will agree on.

Mr. Mitchell, the Chairman of the Democratic National Committee, made the statement that if a man couldn't afford to be in the United States Senate, he shouldn't run for the Senate. And I just want to make my position clear.

I don't agree with Mr. Mitchell when he says that only a rich man should serve the Government, in the United States Senate or in the Congress. I don't think that represents the thinking of the Democratic Party, and I know it doesn't represent the thinking of the Republican Party.

I believe that it's fine that a man like Governor Stevenson, who inherited a fortune from his father, can run for President. But I also feel that it is essential in this country of ours that a man of modest means can also run for President, because, you know—remember Abraham Lincoln, remember what he said—"God must have loved the common people, he made so many of them."

And then I went over to the counterattack. I referred to Stevenson's fund and to the fact that Sparkman had his wife on the government payroll. And I issued this challenge:

I would suggest that under the circumstances both Mr. Sparkman and Mr. Stevenson should come before the American people, as I have, and make a complete financial statement as to their financial history. And if they don't it will be an admission that they have something to hide.

With Stevenson and Sparkman thus disposed of, I rose from my chair and walked to the front of the desk, leaving my notes behind, and for the last ten minutes talked directly into the camera and into the homes of millions of Americans.

I know that this is not the last of the smears. In spite of my explanation tonight, other smears will be made. Others have been made in the past. And the purpose of the smears, I know, is this: to silence me, to make me let up.

Well, they just don't know who they are dealing with . . . I intend to continue to fight.

Why do I feel so deeply? Why do I feel that in spite of the smears, the misunderstandings, the necessity for a man to come up here and bare his soul, as I have—why is it necessary for me to continue this fight?

. . . I think my country is in danger. And I think the only man who can save America at this time is the man that's running for President, on my ticket, Dwight Eisenhower.

You say, why do I think it is in danger? And I say, look at the record. Seven years of the Truman-Acheson Administration, and what's happened? Six hundred million people lost to the Communists.

And a war in Korea in which we have lost 117,000 American casualties, and I say to all of you that a policy that results in the loss of 600,-000,000 people to the Communists and a war which costs us 117,000 American casualties isn't good enough for America. And I say that those in the State Department who made the mistakes which caused that war and which resulted in those losses should be kicked out . . . just as fast as we can get them out of there.

And let me say that I know Mr. Stevenson won't do that, because he defends the Truman policy. But I know that Dwight Eisenhower *will* do that, and that he will give America the leadership that it needs.

Take the problem of corruption. You have read about the mess in Washington. Mr. Stevenson can't clean it up because he was picked by the man, Truman, under whose Administration the mess was made.

. . . And so I say, Eisenhower, who owes nothing to Truman, nothing to the big-city bosses—he is the man who can clean up the mess in Washington.

I had become so wrapped up in my subject that I did something I had never done before or since in making a television broadcast: I lost track of the time. The director began giving me the last-minute cutoff signal just as I was asking my listeners to send their telegrams and letters to the National Committee:

And now, finally, I know that you wonder whether or not I am going to stay on the Republican ticket or resign. Let me say this: I don't believe that I ought to quit, because I am not a quitter. And, incidentally, Pat is not a quitter. After all, her name was Patricia Ryan and she was born on Saint Patrick's Day, and you know the Irish never quit.

But the decision, my friends, is not mine. I would do nothing that would harm the possibilities of Dwight Eisenhower to become President of the United States. And for that reason I am submitting to the Republican National Committee tonight through this television broadcast the decision which it is theirs to make. Let them decide whether my position on the ticket will help or hurt. And I am going to ask you to help them decide. Wire and write the Republican National Committee whether you think I should stay on or whether I should get off. And whatever their decision is, I will abide by it.

But just let me say this last word. Regardless of what happens, I am going to continue this fight. I am going to campaign up and down America until we drive the crooks and the Communists and those that defend them out of Washington. And remember, folks, Eisenhower is a great man. Folks, he is a great man, and a vote for Eisenhower is a vote for what is good for America.

But now time had run out. I was cut off just as I intended to say where the National Committee was located and where the telegrams and letters should be sent. I was, in fact, still talking when the red camera light blinked off, leaving me in the middle of an unfinished thought. I stood there for another thirty seconds while the announcer took the program off the air. Finally, the ordeal was over.

I walked over to the camera crews to thank them for their work. There were tears in the eyes of many. Pat Hillings and Bill Rogers rushed onto the set. I said, "I'm sorry I had to rush at the last, I didn't give the National Committee address. I should have timed it better." But from what they said and the expressions on their faces, I knew

that at least as far as they were concerned, the broadcast had been a
success. Pat and I moved back into the dressing room. The makeup
man took off the beard-stick with a towel. As he did so, he commented,
"That ought to fix them. There has never been a broadcast like it
before." Ted Rogers came hurrying down from the control room. "The
telephone switchboard is lit up like a Christmas tree," he said. We went
out to our car and started out the driveway to the street. A dozen or
so Young Republicans who had been there to greet us as we came in
were shouting at the top of their voices as we left. As we turned the
corner into the street, a big Irish setter came bounding up to the car
wagging his tail. I turned to Pat and said, "Well at least we got the dog
vote tonight," and we had the first good laugh since leaving Pomona
six days before.

We talked about the broadcast as we rode back to the hotel. Pat was
particularly pleased that I had not stayed on the defensive but had
needled Stevenson and gotten in some good licks on the campaign
issues. Everyone in the car insisted that the broadcast had been successful beyond expectations. But I was not sure. I knew that the approval of my supporters was not what counted. I wondered about the
millions of listeners sitting in small groups in their living rooms across
the country.

In the hotel lobby, we began to get a partial answer to this question.
The long lobby which had been so quiet when we left for the broadcast an hour and a half before was now filled with people. Some I
knew, but the great majority were complete strangers. They literally
mobbed us, pounding Pat and me on the back, shaking our hands,
cheering, characterizing the broadcast as "great," "magnificent," and
with other superlatives. It took us almost a half-hour to make our way
through the crowds to our room. In my suite there was a whirlwind
of joyous activity as my staff moved about receiving telephone calls
and telling me of reactions to the speech.

Approximately sixty million Americans saw or heard that radio-
television speech, it was estimated, making it the largest audience in
television history. That record lasted until 1960, when I appeared on
radio-television again, in my "first debate" with John F. Kennedy.

Wires and calls came in from friends and strangers, Democrats as
well as Republicans. The hotel switchboard was jammed with incoming calls. When Jim Bassett reached the room, I asked him about the
press reaction. It had been mixed, he reported. Many of the reporters
felt put out because they did not have an advance text: some paid

little attention to the telecast, waiting for the copies of the text being made for them by the stenographers. But Bassett made a perceptive comment at this point. He said, "What the reporters think about the content of the speech is not important now. That's an old story anyway. The big story now is not the speech itself but the public reaction to it and on that one we can't help but win."

Because I had not given the address of the Republican National Committee in the telecast, there has never been an accurate count of the responses to it. Listeners wired and wrote to the Republican Committees in Washington and in their state capitals. They sent wires to me in Los Angeles, to Eisenhower in Cleveland (where he was that night), to his headquarters in Denver and New York, and to the stations to which they were listening. The response had been immediate. Thousands of people went out of their homes that night and lined up at Western Union offices. It was recorded as the greatest immediate response to any radio or television speech in history. The letters flowed in after the telegrams, and enough small contributions came in by letter and wire to more than cover the $75,000 cost of the telecast. The unofficial count was something between one and two million telegrams and letters containing more than three million names. The response overwhelmingly was "keep Nixon on the ticket." The effect was to lift my name to national prominence and to give me a national political following which helped in the years ahead to give new stature to the office of Vice President.

All this, of course, I did not know on the night of the broadcast. And as reactions poured in from Congressmen, Senators, and various Republican officials, it occurred to me that I now had heard everything except the verdict. There had been no word from Eisenhower. Jim Bassett brought the first word, a wire service report on Eisenhower's reaction in Cleveland where he had listened to the broadcast.

The General, Mrs. Eisenhower, and about thirty in his party watched the telecast from the manager's office of the Cleveland Public Auditorium where Eisenhower was scheduled to address a rally after the telecast. The reaction in the room was overwhelmingly in my favor, I was to learn later. As Eisenhower walked from the office to the auditorium he remarked to Allan Lowe, the manager of the Cleveland Hotel, who was walking with him, "I would rather go down in defeat fighting with a brave man than to win with a bunch of cowards."

Discarding his speech on inflation, he told the rally extemporaneously, "I happen to be one of those people who, when I get into a fight, would rather have a courageous and honest man by my side than a whole boxcar of pussyfooters. I have seen brave men in tough situations. I have never seen anyone come through in better fashion than Senator Nixon did tonight."

The crowd roared and then Eisenhower went on to say what his advisers before my telecast had recommended he do. A thirty-minute speech was too short a presentation to be complete, and so he was sending me a telegram to meet with him the next morning in Wheeling, West Virginia, so that he could talk to me and reach his personal decision, which he would then pass on to the National Committee.

But I knew nothing of this on Tuesday night in Los Angeles. His telegram got lost in the avalanche of wires which reached the hotel. My information came from the wire service bulletin which stressed only the "hot" news, and all the bulletin said was that Eisenhower had declared he could not make a personal decision until he saw me face-to-face—that a half-hour presentation was not enough.

For the first time in almost a week of tremendous tension, I really blew my stack. "What more can he possibly want from me?" I asked. Not yet having a full report of his Cleveland speech, my reaction was that he was being completely unreasonable. I had been prepared for a verdict. I was expecting a decisive answer. I didn't believe I could take any more of the suspense and tension of the past week.

I announced to everyone in the room that if the broadcast had not satisfied the General, there was nothing more I could or would do. I would simply resign, rather than go through the stress of explaining the whole thing again. To demonstrate that I meant exactly what I said, I called in Rose Woods and dictated a telegram of resignation to the Republican National Chairman. She, of course, did not send it, and Chotiner took the copy and tore it up. The next day when I learned the whole story—and the accurate one—of Eisenhower's reaction, it was quite clear to me that I should have waited for all the facts before going off half-cocked.

This was another demonstration of the lesson I had first learned in the Hiss case. The point of greatest danger for an individual confronted with a crisis is not during the period of preparation for battle, nor fighting the battle itself, but in the period immediately after the battle is over. Then, completely exhausted and drained emotionally, he must watch his decisions most carefully. Then there is an increased possibility of error because he may lack the necessary cushion of emotional and mental reserve which is essential for good judgment.

In any event, that night I decided that I had to go on with my campaign schedule until Eisenhower made a decision. Chotiner, particularly, insisted that I not allow myself to be put in the position of going to Eisenhower like a little boy to be taken to the woodshed, properly punished, and then restored to a place of dignity. We agreed that Eisenhower would have to make a decision before I went to see him. Consequently, we made plans to fly that night to Missoula, Montana, to pick up our campaign schedule at that point.

Finally, the first telephone call came through from the Eisenhower train. As irony would have it, the caller was Art Summerfield, the National Chairman, who had been my strongest supporter all along. Unfortunately, he had to take the brunt of my reaction. His conversation with Murray Chotiner went something like this:

"Well, Murray, how are things out there?"

"Not so good."

"What in hell do you mean, not so good?"

"Dick just wrote out a telegram of resignation to the General."

"What! My God, Murray, you tore it up, didn't you?"

"Yes, I tore it up, but I'm not so sure how long it's going to stay torn."

"Well, Dick is flying to Wheeling to see the General, isn't he?"

"No, we're flying tonight to Missoula."

"What? My God, Murray, you've got to persuade him to come to Wheeling."

"Arthur, we trust you. If you can give us your personal assurance direct from the General that Dick will stay on the ticket with the General's blessing, I think I can persuade him. I know I can't otherwise."

Had I not been through the stress of the broadcast and the long hard days before it, I am sure I would have reacted differently to the news story of Eisenhower's reaction.

Even before we took off for Missoula, I was able to appraise the situation more calmly and to appreciate the pressures under which Eisenhower had been operating. I think he had personal confidence in my integrity, but most of his knowledge of me was secondhand, not based on personal association. And, new as he was to politics, the overwhelmingly hostile reaction of the press must have raised some very grave questions in his mind. The further fact that the majority of his friends from the business, professional, and military worlds were urging him to put me off the ticket could not have had anything but a considerable effect on his thinking.

In addition, Eisenhower had developed a real crusader's zeal with regard to the necessity to clean up the mess in Washington, and to tolerate no corruption, either legal or ethical. He had been berating Truman for blindly condoning the actions of his friends and associates before checking the facts. Eisenhower felt strongly that he must not be guilty of the same error.

Still, at a time like this, I needed the calm, objective advice of an outsider to help me keep some sense of perspective. Normally the members of my campaign team would have provided such advice. But they, like myself, were too close to the situation and were deeply hurt by the first reports from Cleveland. It was Bert Andrews who provided the leaven needed at this critical juncture. He reached me by phone from Cleveland just before we left for the airport to take off for Missoula. He asked me what I intended to do. I told him bluntly that under no circumstances would I meet Eisenhower under the conditions he apparently had laid down.

Andrews then talked to me like a Dutch uncle. "You don't have to be concerned about what will happen when you meet Eisenhower," he said. "The broadcast decided that. Eisenhower knows it as well as anyone else. But you must remember who he is. He is the General who led the Allied armies to victory in Europe. He is the immensely popular candidate who is going to win this election. He is going to be President, and he is the boss of this outfit. He will make this decision, and he will make the right decision. But he has the right to make it in his own way, and you must come to Wheeling to meet with him and give him the opportunity to do exactly that."

Andrews' words had the ring of truth and of good common sense. After a few more telephone calls, arrangements were in order for us to fly to Wheeling after our stop in Missoula.

When we arrived in Missoula, we received scores of messages that had been forwarded to us from Los Angeles. And among them was the full text of the wire from Eisenhower in Cleveland. It read:

Your presentation was magnificent. While technically no decision rests with me, you and I know the realities of the situation require a pronouncement which the public considers decisive.

My personal decision is going to be based on personal conclusions. I would most appreciate it if you can fly to see me at once. Tomorrow I will be at Wheeling, W. Va. Whatever personal affection and admiration I had for you—and they are very great—are undiminished.

The staff of the Republican National Committee in Washington wired that 107 of its 138 members had been reached up to that time and they had all voted enthusiastically to keep me on the ticket. Even Harold Stassen had wired: "Congratulations on a superb presentation, Dick."

The flight from Missoula to Wheeling to see Eisenhower thus turned into a sort of victory ride. The various members of my staff and the reporters who had covered the fund story from the beginning were in rollicking spirits, singing songs with familiar tunes but with improvised and somewhat pungent words.

I fell asleep on the last leg of the flight. When the plane touched down, I had to rush to straighten my tie and put on my jacket. I was helping Pat put on her coat when Chotiner hurried up and exclaimed, "The General is coming up the steps." I was taken completely by surprise and hardly had time to turn around when I saw him walking toward me up the aisle of the plane, smiling, with his hand outstretched.

"General, you didn't need to come out to the airport," was all I could think to say.

"Why not?" he said with a broad grin, "you're my boy."

We walked to the head of the ramp, posed for photographers, and then rode together to the Wheeling stadium. I was still so surprised by his unexpected gesture of coming to meet me that I found myself riding on his right as the car pulled away from the airport. I apologized for what I, with my Navy training, knew was an inexcusable breach of political as well as military protocol, and tried to change places with him. He put his hand on my shoulder and said, "Forget it. No one will know the difference with all the excitement out there."

In the stadium, Eisenhower spoke first to the cheering crowd. He opened his remarks by reading a wire from the Chairman of the National Committee, Arthur Summerfield, indicating that the members of the Committee unanimously favored my retention on the ticket. Then, unexpectedly, he read another wire—one which my mother, completely without my knowledge, had sent him from Washington where she was staying with our two girls. It read:

Dear General: I am trusting that the absolute truth may come out concerning this attack on Richard, and when it does I am sure you will be guided right in your decision, to place implicit faith in his integrity and honesty. Best wishes from one who has known Richard longer than anyone else. His Mother.[2]

Then Eisenhower stated his own conclusion that I had completely vindicated my position and that he was proud to have me as his running mate.

After he concluded his talk, I told the crowd: "This is probably the greatest moment in my life." I praised Eisenhower for the way he had made the decision with regard to the charges against me. I contrasted his attitude of carefully investigating the facts before acting with Truman's policy of defending his cronies accused of wrongdoing without regard to the facts. We were back on the political campaign trail.

Finally, the rally was over and hundreds swarmed to the stage to shake hands with Pat and me and to congratulate us. I spoke to each of them almost mechanically until Bill Knowland came up to me, grasped my hand, and said, "That was a great speech, Dick." It was not so much what he said or the sincerity with which he said it, but at that moment I reached the point where I had exhausted all of my emotional reserve. Tears rushed into my eyes. Knowland put his arm around me and I hid my face on his shoulder. It was that scene that a news photographer caught in a picture which was forever to characterize the fund speech and my reaction to it.

At last the week-long crisis of the Nixon fund was over. But Pat and I were to live with its consequences for the rest of our lives.

In one sense it could be said that I was victorious in meeting the crisis of the fund. I emerged with far greater political and personal stature than I had before the New York *Post* launched its attack on September 18. For the balance of the 1952 campaign, the crowds that came out to see and hear me were far larger than any vice presidential candidate had drawn before. In several cities I even outdrew Stevenson. More important, the crowds were full of fight and confidence. There was that unmistakable sense of victory in the air which a candidate can feel.

At times the enthusiasm was so great that even the most seasoned political leaders presiding over our meetings were carried away by it.

[2] My father's comment after the broadcast, incidentally, which Pat remarked sounded just like him, was: "It looks to me as if the Democrats have given themselves a good kick in the seat of the pants."

Two days after my meeting with Eisenhower in Wheeling, a stamping, cheering crowd of over five thousand welcomed us in the jam-packed Rainbow Ballroom in Salt Lake City. Ivy Baker Priest, who later was to be appointed Treasurer of the United States, gave Pat a glowing introduction. When she came to the key line, she said: "And now it is my great honor and privilege to present to you the next wife of the Vice President of the United States." Senator Arthur Watkins introduced me as "Nick Dixon."

Going through the fire of crisis together had welded the members of my staff and several of the reporters who had covered the fund episode into a high-spirited, united team. Four days after we left Wheeling, Jim Bassett came up to me on a flight from Nashville to Washington and told me that the traveling press had a "profound proposal" to present to me. They suggested a new social organization—completely non-political: all of the press corps and my staff who had been with us on the long journey from Pomona to Portland and back to Los Angeles should be initiated as charter members of the Order of the Hound's Tooth. We formed the organization on the spot, fourteen thousand feet above sea level. Checkers was our mascot, Pat was president, and I was vice president. After the campaign, I sent out membership cards along with a watch charm to which was attached a sliver of ivory, as a fitting symbol of the immaculate hound's tooth.

Checkers emerged from the campaign the best-known dog in the nation since Fala. By Election Day we had acquired for her from dog-lovers around the country a vast collection of dog collars, hand-woven dog blankets, a dog kennel, and quantities of dog food—enough to last a year.

But there was a negative reaction to the fund broadcast, as well. As I had learned in the Hiss case, in politics there is never anything akin to "total victory."

The speech itself was smeared and labeled "a carefully rehearsed soap opera." Ted Rogers' statement of the truth—that there had been no rehearsal at all, and that I had not arrived at the studio until twenty-five minutes before broadcast time—received virtually no play in the press.

It was labeled as the "Checkers speech," as though the mention of my dog was the only thing that saved my career. Many of the critics glided over the fact that the fund was thoroughly explained, my personal finances laid bare, and an admittedly emotional but honest appeal made for public support.

But the other and more important consequence of the fund episode was that, like almost every smear, when enough mud is thrown at a man in public life, some of it sticks—justified or not.

For example, when I met General Eisenhower at Wheeling, he asked me in the privacy of his campaign train quarters about rumors that had been relayed to him by his staff—rumors that I had spent $10,000 with an interior decorator in furnishing our home in Washington. There was not a shred of truth to the charge and a very routine inquiry could have knocked it down before it was passed on to him.

I told him that I had put absolutely every fact about my personal finances into the broadcast. "This is just like a war, General," I said. "Our opponents are losing. They mounted a massive attack against me and have taken a bad beating. It will take them a little time to regroup, but when they start fighting back, they will be desperate and they will throw everything at us, including the kitchen sink. There will be other charges, but none of them will stand up. What we must avoid at all costs is to allow any of their attacks to get off the ground. The minute they start one of these rumors, we have to knock it down just as quickly as we can."

A week after the broadcast, the St. Louis *Post-Dispatch* printed a front-page story to the effect that I had been with Dana Smith, the trustee of the fund, in a gambling casino in Havana the previous April. The true story—that I was five thousand miles away from Havana at the time, making a series of speeches in Hawaii—was buried a few days later on the back pages of the papers that carried the original charge.

A few weeks later, a syndicated Washington gossip columnist printed a story which is an excellent example of how a half-truth can be distorted into a smear. He charged that I had "borrowed" money in 1945 from an engineering firm with which I was negotiating a settlement in terminating a war contract, so that I could fly back to California to run for Congress. The truth was that an officer of the company offered to pick up my ticket for me at the airline office in downtown Baltimore with his credit card so that I would not have to leave the negotiations which were in progress at the time. When he received the bill for the ticket, I paid him that same day and I had my cancelled check for $128.05 to prove it. But again, the same papers that considered the charge "news" showed no interest in the true story.

Five days *before* the election, the same writer sent out a syndicated column charging that Pat and I had made a sworn statement in California that our joint property did not exceed $10,000 in order to claim a State veterans' tax deduction of $50. This was so demonstrably false that I demanded a retraction and threatened to sue. Two weeks *after* the election, the retraction was printed—at the bottom of a column. It had been another Richard and Patricia Nixon, complete strangers to us, who had made the application. And again, even the most routine inquiry by a reporter interested in the truth would have established this fact before the charge was printed.

The smears did not stop on Election Day. Throughout my two terms as Vice President, I had to answer charges, some of which were printed, and many of which were not, reflecting on my personal integrity and honesty. In the 1956 campaign, for example, rumors spread like wildfire through the press corps that I had another "fund." This one supposedly amounted to $52,000 paid by the oil industry for my "services" and was fully "documented." I demanded that the rumor be investigated by a sub-committee of the Senate Elections Committee, which at that time was under the control of the Democrats. The subcommittee found that the rumor was based on a letter reputedly from a vice president of a large oil company to his public relations director, mentioning the $52,000 fund. The letter, when traced, turned out to be a complete forgery which had been instigated by some of my unscrupulous opponents on the far left.

Even when I left Washington in 1961 and returned to California, the attacks were to continue. Nasty rumors were circulated, asking with raised eyebrows how I could get the money to buy a new home in Beverly Hills. The implication was that I must have stashed away some money when I was Vice President and now was able to put out the full purchase price of the house. The rumormongers ignore the fact that when I applied the eighty-hour week, to which I had become accustomed during my fourteen years in Washington, to private pursuits, my income from law practice, from a syndicated newspaper column, from magazine articles, and from this book I am writing, in just one year will be greater than my entire government salary for the fourteen years I was in Washington. Under these circumstances, it should be obvious that my credit would be rather good and that I could easily afford the down payment on any house I might want to buy. But again, the truth is not nearly as newsworthy as the charge.

I recall, for example, a conversation with some of my friends in the press whom I had invited to a Christmas reception at my house in Washington after the 1960 election. I asked them if, in view of the charges that had been floating around through the years with regard to my financial affairs, they thought it would be worthwhile for me to take the unprecedented action of putting out a complete financial statement of all my assets and liabilities on leaving office. They indicated their personal understanding of my concern on this issue, but they doubted if the story would have enough news value for them to go to the trouble of writing it. If they had shown any interest, my statement would have shown that after fourteen years in Washington, including eight years as Vice President, all that Pat and I had in the way of an estate was the equity in our Washington house. After we deducted the cost of moving to California, that came to $48,000. We owned no stocks and bonds, and had no pension except for the Congressional Civil Service retirement plan to which I had contributed as a Congressman, Senator, and Vice President, and for which I would not qualify until I was sixty-two years of age.

I have been asked by friends, "How does a man in public life take the kind of attacks you have been subjected to over the years?"

A man who goes voluntarily into the political arena must expect some wounds in the battles in which he engages. Unwarranted attacks, particularly those involving personal integrity, do take their toll, of course. No matter how often you tell yourself that "this is part of the battle," or that "if you can't take the heat you ought to get out of the kitchen," or that "an attack is a compliment because your adversaries never bother taking on someone who amounts to nothing," there are times when you wonder if you shouldn't chuck the whole business. Many do. This is particularly true of businessmen. Many come to Washington, thinking they are going to tear the town apart and "show those politicians how a businessman can run the biggest business in the world," and then they are shocked, dismayed, and finally deeply hurt by what they call the "unfairness" of both politicians and the press in launching attacks which are not based on fact.

The crisis of the fund was the hardest, the sharpest, and the briefest of my public life. Because it was decided so quickly, it did not have the lingering effect which some of the more prolonged crises like the Hiss case had had, and were to have. Nevertheless, it left a deep scar which was never to heal completely. From that time on, Pat was to go through campaign after campaign as a good trouper, but never again with the same feeling toward political life. She had lost the zest for it. We had both become perhaps overly sensitive, even when we were subjected to the standard attacks which a public figure must expect with regard to his personal affairs.

Why then should an honest man enter public life and submit himself and his family to such risks? The answer, of course, is that if men with good and honest reputations do not take such risks, they leave the field of public service to the second-raters and chiselers who have no reputations to worry about. Every public figure, whose most important asset is his reputation, is at the mercy of the smear artists and the rumor-mongers. No one can keep pace with a concerted smear campaign. To deny a rumor publicly, to sue in a court for libel or slander, is generally a mistake, because it helps spread the smear. A charge is usually put on the first page of the newspaper; the defense is buried among the deodorant ads. The man in political life must come to expect the smear and to know that, generally, the best thing to do about it is ignore it—and hope that it will fade away. The 1952 fund smear was an exception to this general rule, but then it was an exceptional situation.

The over-all political effect of the crisis of the fund on my career was strikingly similar to that of the Hiss case. A distinguished political science professor, after making a thorough study of the 1960 election, stated his considered judgment that if it had not been for the fund broadcast I would have been elected President of the United States. It was a neat theory, brilliantly supported by facts and figures, but like most classroom theoreticians he had not faced up to the hard reality of the alternative. If it hadn't been for that broadcast, I would never have been around to run for the presidency.

The Heart Attack

Decisive action relieves the tension which builds up in a crisis. When the situation requires that an indivdual restrain himself from acting decisively over a long period, this can be the most wearing of all crises.

CHARLES G. DAWES once described the job of Vice President as "the easiest in the world." He said he had only two responsibilities—to sit and listen to United States Senators give speeches, and to check the morning's newspaper as to the President's health.

On Saturday, September 24, 1955, the United States Senate was not in session, and any concern about the state of the President's health was the furthest thing from my mind.

The day was unusual in one respect only: this was one of the few Saturday afternoons in my years in Washington that I had not spent in my office, catching up on the week's accumulated correspondence. Instead, Mrs. Nixon and I had attended the wedding of Drusilla Nelson, a pretty New Hampshire girl who had served as a secretary in my office for the past four years, and Henry Dworshak, son of the Senator from Idaho. By the time we returned home it was after five. I picked up the *Evening Star* from the sidewalk as we went into the house and sat down in the living room to scan the headlines. A brief item on the front page reported that President Eisenhower, out at the Summer White House in Denver, was suffering from a slight case of indigestion. I hardly gave the item a second thought.

Almost everyone close to the President knew he was susceptible to stomach upsets. I recall, for example, an incident on my first goodwill trip abroad as Vice President, a seventy-two-day round-the-world tour in 1953. The Governor General of Australia, Field Marshal William

Slim, who had served with Eisenhower during World War II, greeted me with a friendly, "How's Ike?"

I replied that, despite the rigors of his new job, he seemed to be in the best of health.

"How's his tummy?" he asked with a smile. "Ike always used to have trouble with his tummy."

I had practically forgotten the indigestion story and was checking the baseball averages in the sports section when the phone rang. I walked into the hall and picked up the receiver. "Dick," said a familiar voice, "this is Jim Hagerty—the President has had a coronary."

It is impossible to describe how I felt when I heard these words. The news was so unexpected, the shock so great that I could think of nothing to say for several seconds. The pause was so long that Hagerty thought we had been disconnected.

I slowly began to recover my equilibrium. "Are they sure? There are many times when people have indigestion and it is erroneously diagnosed as a heart attack. Doctors can make mistakes. I don't think we should announce it as a heart attack until we are absolutely sure," I told him.

"No," he replied slowly, "we are absolutely sure."

He went on to tell me that the press would be informed of the President's heart attack in about half an hour. His final words were, "Let me know where you can be reached at all times."

Later I discovered that Hagerty, who was in Washington at the time, had telephoned the news to me just after he had received word from his assistant, Murray Snyder, who was with the President in Denver.

I went back into the living room and sat down again. For fully ten minutes I sat alone in the room, and to this day I cannot remember the thoughts that flowed through my mind. The only accurate description is that I probably was in a momentary state of shock.

I had been completely unprepared for this turn of events. During the three years I had been Vice President, there had never been any reason to worry about the President's health. He had waged a vigorous campaign in 1952, and since his inauguration, despite newspaper criticism of his vacations and his golf, he had maintained a strict schedule of early rising and hard work at his desk. He was, in fact, a superb specimen of a man who believed in keeping himself physically fit. Golf was part of the regimen prescribed by his doctor as the best means of relieving the tremendous tension and strain of the presidency.

Yet now, he was the first of our thirty-four Presidents to have suffered a heart attack during his term of office. As I thought of this I realized what a tremendous responsibility had descended upon me. It was like a great physical weight holding me down in the chair. What I thought of, and what concerned me, was not the awesome problems I would have if I should become President, but how I could best handle my immediate responsibility as a Vice President who was now, more than any of his thirty-five predecessors, "one heartbeat from the presidency."

With the President of the United States gravely ill, the eyes of the nation and of the world would be focused upon me and what I did. Every word, every action of mine would be more important now than anything I had ever said or done before because of their effect upon the people of the United States, our allies, and our potential enemies. How I reacted to this crisis was infinitely more important to the nation and the world than the way I handled the Hiss case or my fight to stay on the ticket in 1952.

Because of my awareness of this responsibility, my first conscious decision at the time was that I should check everything I said and did in the next critical few hours with someone whose judgment I respected. My thoughts turned to Bill Rogers, who was then Acting Attorney General while Herbert Brownell was vacationing in southern Spain. I thought of Rogers, not because he was the ranking legal officer in the United States, but because he was a friend who had proved during the fund crisis that he was a cool man under pressure, had excellent judgment, a good sense of press relations, and was one to whom I could speak with complete freedom without any concern that what I might say would find its way into the Washington gossip mill.

I dialed his number and when he answered the phone I said, without any preliminary comment, "I wonder if you could come over."

"Yes, Dick, I'll be right over," he answered. I knew from the tone of his voice that he had the news; there was no need to spell it out.

As I hung up the receiver, I suddenly realized that Pat was unaware of what had happened and I went upstairs and told her the news. I then telephoned my secretary, Rose Mary Woods, who was still at the wedding reception, and asked her to go to her apartment so that she could handle the incoming telephone calls on an extension of my home phone located there. Pat in the meantime had tried to break the news, as quietly as possible, to the children. But just as I finished the call to Rose, Tricia, who was then nine years old, came running down the stairs crying.

"The President isn't going to die, is he, Daddy?" she asked.

"No," I tried to reassure her, "he's going to be all right."

Just then the doorbell rang. I asked her to look through the blind to see who it was because I knew newspapermen might be arriving on the scene at any moment.

"It's Mr. Rogers," she called back to me.

I went to the door and let Bill in. Before we sat down to talk we pulled the shades on the large picture windows which faced the street. We were just in time. Within minutes after Bill arrived, reporters and photographers were ringing the doorbell. Pat, with perfect poise developed over many years of handling similar situations, told them that I was not at home, that she did not know when to expect me, and while they were welcome to wait outside until I returned, they might be better advised to check with my office for further information. All of them, of course, decided to wait outside until I returned.

This was the first problem that Bill and I discussed. I knew the reporters had their job to do. But I believed that this was one of those rare occasions in which the public interest demanded no statement whatever be made to the press.

There were several reasons for this conclusion. Most important, I did not have the information at hand with which to answer the inevitable questions the reporters would ask. I knew nothing more about the President's condition than they did. In addition, I realized that my own position as Vice President had become extremely delicate; my every move during this period had to be made with caution, for even the slightest misstep could be interpreted as an attempt to assume power. I knew from my study of history how sensitive the members of the President's family, his staff, and for that matter the people throughout the nation, could be when the Chief Executive was gravely ill and his Vice President—or anyone else—did or said anything that smacked of exceeding his own authority.

I realized, too, that my position was even more difficult than that of some of my predecessors who had faced similar circumstances. Hundreds of thousands of words had been written in 1952 about my youth as a vice presidential nominee, questioning my ability to assume the duties and responsibilities of the presidency if required to do so. I had long been the whipping boy for those who chose not to direct their political attacks against Dwight D. Eisenhower, the most popular President in recent history. The nation's attention would be focused on the sickbed in Denver, but many eyes would be watching to see whether I became brash or timid in meeting the emergency. My job was to be neither.

As Bill and I discussed these problems we agreed that it was vitally important that I not only have no press conference that evening, but that I avoid being photographed if possible. Even a camera can misquote or misinterpret a man. An unconscious, unintentional upturning of the lips can appear in a picture as a smile at so grave a moment. On the other hand, too serious an expression could create an impression of fear and concern which would also be most unfortunate.

By this time the press corps outside the house had grown to the proportions of a street-corner political rally. Television cameras had been set up on the sidewalk. Floodlights were trained on the front of the house in the expectation that I might appear. I decided that the only thing I could do was to make myself literally unavailable for comment for the next few hours. I knew it would be impossible to be assured privacy in a hotel. Consequently, Bill and I decided to go to his house, which was well off the main road in Bethesda, Maryland.

Our next problem was getting there. I could not use my car because I would have to walk through the phalanx of reporters to open the garage. Bill had come by taxi. We finally telephoned his wife and asked her to come after us and to park Bill's car on the side street away from the front of the house. Just as she arrived, about fifteen minutes later, we had a bit of luck. Tricia had gone out the front door for a closer look at the TV cameras and had unintentionally drawn the attention of most of the reporters and photographers to herself. Bill and I went out the back door and walked quickly across my neighbor's yard to where Mrs. Rogers was parked in his Pontiac convertible, about a hundred yards down the street from our house.

Fifteen minutes later we were in the sanctuary of Bill Rogers' home, free from all unnecessary interruptions, while the press continued to maintain its vigil outside my house.

We kept in touch with the situation in Denver and Washington through the White House switchboard, making and receiving calls on the only downstairs telephone in the Rogers' home, a wall-type instrument in his kitchen which proved to be particularly uncomfortable for the amount of telephoning we had to do during the night.

I first called Denver to get the latest news on the President's condition. We learned that his personal physician, Major General Howard Snyder, had diagnosed a "mild" coronary thrombosis and that the President was resting comfortably under an oxygen tent in Fitzsimmons Army Hospital. The reports indicated that his chances of recovery were good, but that it was too early to tell for sure. We learned piecemeal that night what had happened that day in Denver, but it was not until some time later that the story of the President's heart attack became fully known. The events and particularly Dr. Snyder's actions are worth reflecting upon.

(Although on vacation, the President had put in one of his typically strenuous and full days. He worked hard and he played hard, too. He was that type of man, and nothing could change him—even after he had recovered from the heart attack. That morning, away on a fishing trip with friends 8600 feet up in the Rockies, he had arisen at 5:00, cooked breakfast for his companions, and then had gone by car eighty-two miles back to Denver, where he put in over two hours of concentrated paperwork at the Summer White House at Lowry Air Force Base.

Then he moved on to the Cherry Hills Country Club, where he played twenty-seven holes of golf. At lunch, after the eighteenth hole, he ate a hamburger with large slices of raw onion on the side (which later was blamed for his "indigestion"). Then he played out the final nine holes, conferred with Secretary of State Dulles by phone, and returned to the Doud home, where he plunged into three hours of work on a painting of a Rocky Mountain landscape. He ate a roast-lamb dinner with Mrs. Eisenhower, Mrs. Doud, and Mr. and Mrs. George E. Allen. Later, after the Allens had left, he complained to Mrs. Eisenhower of indigestion, but not seriously. He went to bed at about ten. Shortly after 2:30 Saturday morning, he awoke with a dull pain in his stomach and chest. Uncomfortable and unable to sleep, he got out of bed, turned on the light, and walked about his room, hoping the pain would pass. Mrs. Eisenhower heard him from the adjoining room and came in to find out what was wrong. When he complained of indigestion she gave him a dose of milk of magnesia and a glass of water, his usual medicine for an upset stomach. He went back to bed, and a few minutes later the full brunt of pain seared across his chest. He called out to Mrs. Eisenhower and told her she had better get the doctor. She telephoned Major General Snyder, his personal physician and a friend of many years. Dr. Snyder arrived a few minutes after 3 A.M. and he quickly realized that the President of the United States, just twenty days short of his sixty-fifth birthday, had been stricken with a heart attack, or, in medical terms, an acute coronary thrombosis —a blood clot in an artery of the heart.

The President, stretched out on his back in bed, was in great pain.

When I visited him in the hospital two weeks later he told me, "I got this pain in the middle of the night—boy, it sure hurt—I never told Mamie how much it hurt.")

Dr. Snyder administered immediate emergency treatment to counteract the blood clot before it was too late. He gave the President three injections: one to dilate the arteries in the heart, another to increase the liquidity of his blood to prevent clotting, and morphine to ease the pain and shock. This undoubtedly is standard medical procedure in such cases, but then Dr. Snyder faced the crisis of his career. There he was alone, the only person in the world who knew that the heart of the President had been damaged. It was somewhat after three in the morning in Denver, after six in the nation's capital. Should he call for help, summon the heart specialists of the nation, and thus spread the word of the President's bout with death around the world? That would be the easy, routine way—sharing the responsibility. But it would entail the risk of shocking Mrs. Eisenhower and her seventy-seven-year-old mother, and the excitement could even endanger the President's chances for recovery.

Deciding that complete, undisturbed rest was the best treatment for a coronary, Dr. Snyder chose to let the world wait while he did the best he could by himself. He gave the President a second injection of morphine at 3:45 A.M. to ease the pain. At 4:30 A.M. the President fell asleep. Dr. Snyder sat by the bedside and waited.

At 7 A.M., in line with his decision, he telephoned the press room of the Summer White House and left word for Assistant Press Secretary Snyder that the President had indigestion and would not keep his morning appointments. Thus the doctor allayed the suspicions of the press. The world was given the unexciting news that the President had indigestion. For twelve hours the truth was kept from the world for the President's benefit and at the risk of a career and reputation to his doctor. It was not until President Eisenhower awoke from his drugged sleep at 12:30 P.M. that Dr. Snyder called Fitzsimmons Army Hospital to have an electrocardiograph brought to the Doud home. It was not until 2 P.M. that Dr. Snyder's original diagnosis had been confirmed by an electrocardiogram which showed a lesion on the anterior wall of the heart. Only after the President had been moved to Fitzsimmons Hospital did Dr. Snyder telephone the shocking news to Murray Snyder.

In his report to the White House Dr. Snyder later wrote: "It was difficult for me to assume the responsibility of refraining from making public immediately the diagnosis of coronary thrombosis. I postponed public announcement because I wished the President to benefit from the rest and quiet induced by the sedation, incident to combatting the initial manifestations. This decision also spared him, his wife and mother-in-law emotional upset upon too precipitant announcement of such serious import. This action, I believe, limited the heart damage to a minimum and enabled us to confirm the diagnosis by cardiogram and make an unhurried transference from home to hospital."

I believe most would agree that Dr. Snyder met the crisis of his career with skill and courage and that he deserves the commendation of his medical colleagues in the country.

It was not because we lacked confidence in Dr. Snyder that for several hours that evening in Bill Rogers' home we discussed by telephone and in person the problem of providing the best possible medical care for the President. Not only must the care be the best to assure his recovery; it was vitally important that the people of the nation be convinced that every possible effort was being made to get the best doctors in America to the President's bedside.

We presented the problem to General Wilton B. Persons, Deputy Assistant to the President, who was in charge of the White House staff during the absence of Sherman Adams, when he arrived at the Rogers' house shortly after 7:30. Persons informed us that Colonel Thomas M. Mattingly, Chief of Cardiology at Walter Reed Army Hospital, was already on his way to Denver with a team of Army doctors. He said that Mattingly had a national reputation as an outstanding heart specialist and would provide the President with the best possible medical care.

I had already discussed this problem on the phone with Secretary of the Treasury George Humphrey and Foster Dulles before Persons arrived. They had both strongly recommended that a civilian specialist be brought into the case on a consulting basis. Rogers and I had reached the same conclusion. As I told Persons, we had nothing against military doctors, but we could not overlook the fact that many people in the country might have more confidence, however unwarranted, in a civilian heart specialist of national reputation. George Humphrey was among those who suggested that Dr. Paul Dudley White, heart specialist at Massachusetts General Hospital and a pioneer in cardiology, would be an excellent man for this assignment.

General Persons undertook the delicate and difficult task of informing Dr. Snyder of our views in a tactful manner. He made it clear that the suggestion that Dr. White be brought into the case was in no way intended to be a reflection on either his or Dr. Mattingly's competence, but that in view of the public relations aspects of the President's illness, adding a civilian consultant to the team of Army doctors would be reassuring and helpful. The fact that he and Snyder had been close personal friends for years made it possible for Persons to succeed where someone else might have failed in raising a quite understandably touchy subject. Dr. White flew out to Denver the next day on an Air Force plane to join the President's staff of physicians. As a pioneer in cardiology and a founder of the National Heart Association, he was in the best possible position to reassure the nation, as he did, that Colonel Mattingly, who headed the medical staff at the President's side, was "among the very best" of heart specialists in the country.

With this problem out of the way, Rogers, Persons, and I turned to a discussion of how the day-to-day operations of government were to be conducted during the President's incapacity. Neither the Constitution nor any law of the land provides for a situation in which a President is incapacitated for a temporary period. The President stands alone as the supreme authority of the Executive branch of government. The Cabinet and National Security Council can advise but cannot act for him. They cannot become a collective commander-in-chief of the armed forces, or sign legislation into law, or appoint judges, or decide high policies of government. Nor could I. Constitutionally, the Vice President is designated by the voters to take over only "in case of the removal of the President from office, or of his death, resignation or inability to discharge the powers and duties of said office. . . ." The Constitution does not make clear what it means by "inability to discharge the powers and duties of said office." It does not say who shall decide when a President is disabled, whether the Vice President assumes the "powers and duties" of the presidency or the "office" itself, and just how a President who recovers his health can then recover his office. However, this problem did not present itself seriously that first night or, for that matter, during the ensuing two critical weeks of the President's illness. President Eisenhower was fully conscious and presumably able to make the most important decisions affecting national security, if such were needed, during his stay at Fitzsimmons Hospital.

The problem for us was how to carry on in his absence without allowing the government to drift dangerously in foreign or domestic affairs. There is an old political axiom that where a vacuum exists, it will be filled by the nearest or strongest power. That had to be avoided at all costs.

The solution seemed clear to me, as it did to several of the key men in the Administration with whom I spoke over the Rogers' kitchen wall phone. The general policy was set that night and the details were worked out by ear through the following week: the "team" would carry on the Eisenhower policies and precepts in a confident atmosphere of "business as usual." Political comments and any semblance of a struggle for dominance on the team would be scrupulously avoided.

Eisenhower himself had established the concept of the "team" in one of his campaign speeches in 1952 when he declared: "When I speak of substituting good government for poor government, I do not mean electing one individual, one symbol, one person to typify the might and majesty of America—by no means. I mean to elect a team, to send to Washington the pick of our men and women chosen according to merit." This team concept was a part of our everyday life in Washington; everyone who worked with Eisenhower was aware of it. There was one other theme of the President's which always stood out in my mind, to the effect that he was not bringing to Washington a group of personalities but rather a set of principles which would guide his Administration in all its endeavors.

The President, who had spent his entire adult life in the Army, brought to Washington the "staff system" for conducting business in the White House. Each Cabinet member was given complete authority, along with the concomitant full responsibility, of his own section of operations. Where problems overlapped two or more departments, the President appointed a council. For a unique question, he formed an *ad hoc* group to handle it. Thus, he tried to get the best brains available to work on problems confronting the government. They did the groundwork. They put in the long hours of deliberation and argument. Then their report and recommended decision, or sometimes alternate choices, were sent up, always through channels, to him for final decision. Having chosen his Cabinet and staff on the basis of each man's ability to handle his job, he had confidence in the men working for him, trusted them, and delegated authority to them. Finally, though, in the staff system, he received the essence of the problem, the thinking that went into it, and the recommended solution. And then he either approved the decision, rejected it and substituted his own, or sent the problem back for further study.

There were some shortcomings to this system, particularly notable when there was an undetected failing in the complete gathering and study of the facts which should have been but were not presented to the President. But no one system can ever handle perfectly the multitude of problems which flow through the White House. The staff system did, however, keep to an absolute minimum the clashes of personalities, the bickerings, and scramble for power which characterized the two previous Administrations—and appear to be taking hold in the present one.

Of course, it has been argued that orderliness in government is not its prime objective, and that new ideas are more apt to flow amidst a clash of powerful personalities and an influence of tug-of-war which characterized the Administration of Franklin D. Roosevelt. The answer must be subjective, depending upon the personality of the Chief Executive, and yet it would seem a man could decide the complex problems which face a President better in tranquillity than from a puppet-master's perch, guiding a hundred strings with his ten fingers.

Eisenhower was by training a man with an orderly mind. He liked things in their proper place and order. Soon after he was established in the White House and the avalanche of paper, red tape, and ceremonial affairs descended upon him, he was heard to exclaim, "When does a man get some time to think around here!"

Despite whatever divided opinion there may have been before September 24, 1955, everyone saw clearly the wisdom of the staff system when the President was stricken. There were no jealousies and no struggle for power among the members of the Cabinet. Opinion was unanimous that the "team" must carry on. Only the details had to be worked out.

One question came up that evening to which we applied this principle. Secretary of the Treasury George Humphrey expressed his concern about leaving the next day for economic talks in Ottawa. Dulles, Humphrey, Secretary of Agriculture Ezra Taft Benson, and Secretary of Commerce Sinclair Weeks were scheduled to discuss trade and economic problems with their Canadian counterparts. I urged Humphrey that they all go to Canada as scheduled so as to avoid any impression that the business of government was grinding to a standstill with the President ill.

Rogers, Persons, and I talked until after midnight trying to anticipate the problems the Administration would face and the action which should be taken to deal with them. After Persons left for home, I telephoned Pat and found that the reporters were still waiting for me to return. In fact, they were in the playroom in our basement at her invitation, and she had just served coffee to the group. Under the circumstances, I decided it would be best to stay at Bill Rogers' house for the night.

Bill and I talked on for another hour, and then at about 2:30 I went up to the second-floor guest room where Mrs. Rogers had laid out for me a towel, toothbrush, and a pair of Bill's pajamas. Even had the President's illness not been on my mind I would not have slept well that night, and as it was I did not sleep at all. I have hay fever at that time of year and the pollen count must have been at an all-time high in the Washington area. On the floor above me, Bill's fifteen-year-old son, Tony, a ham radio operator, was engaged in some kind of all-night sending and receiving contest, and I could hear the high-pitched dots and dashes of the Morse code penetrating the ceiling overhead.

But in any event, it would have been impossible for me to go to sleep. My thoughts went back to the first time I met the President, when he was commander of the NATO forces in Europe, and of the great moments I had been privileged to share with him since then—highlighted by the unforgettable occasion when, with Pat and Mrs. Eisenhower, we had stood together on the stage in Chicago's Convention Hall after the Republican nomination in 1952. During the three years I had been Vice President, I had not consciously thought of the possibility of his becoming ill or dying. I doubt if any Vice President allows his mind to dwell on such a subject. Only once had the President himself remotely brought up the idea of succession. That had been about a year before when I had ridden to Denver with him at his invitation on the presidential plane, *Columbine*. Just after we had taken off, he said: "Dick, I've made a bad error here. I really don't think you and I should ever be on the same plane together." He saw to it that we never were after that.

I thought of Pete Carroll, a long-time friend and military aide to the President, one of the ablest and best-liked men in the White House, who had succumbed to a heart attack in September 1954. He had been only in his forties.

The whole range of affairs and potential problems discussed that evening went through my mind. Fortunately, this was vacation time in government when there was a lull in the usual rush of activities. Several long-range projects were underway, like preparation of the budget and the State of the Union message, but there seemed to be no pressing item that required immediate presidential action. Congress was in adjournment; there was no pending legislation. The cold war seemed frozen for the moment; the hammer and sickle was not poised to strike in any specific soft spot of the world. Everyone in government was exploring for anticipated problems and how they could be handled or delayed during this crisis.

It occurred to me that this was far different from any other crisis I had faced in my life and had to be handled differently. I had always believed in meeting a crisis head-on. The difficult period is reaching a decision, but once that has been done, the carrying-out of the decision is easier than the making of it. In meeting any crisis in life, one must either fight or run away. But one must do something. Not knowing how to act or not being able to act is what tears your insides out. Once I became convinced that Alger Hiss was guilty, the tension produced by doubt and soul-searching was relieved and I was able to pursue the investigation through to its conclusion with renewed effectiveness and decisiveness. Once I had decided to fight and not run away from the fund attack in 1952, I fought for my political life with every resource at my command.

But this crisis was different. My philosophy has always been: don't lean with the wind. Don't do what is politically expedient. Do what your instinct tells you is right. Public opinion polls are useful if a politician uses them only to learn approximately what the people are thinking, so that he can talk to them more intelligently. The politician who sways with the polls is not worth his pay. And I believe the people eventually catch up with the man who merely tells them what he thinks they want to hear.

But contrary to my usual instincts, I knew that the correct course in this crisis was precisely to lean with the wind. As long as the President was seriously ill, this would necessarily be a period of inaction, a period in which I could not act decisively. The crisis not only was different, but it probably would be long and difficult.

My own position as Vice President called for maintaining a balance of the utmost delicacy. On the one hand, aside from the President, I was the only person in government elected by all the people; they had a right to expect leadership, if it were needed, rather than a vacuum. But any move on my part which could be interpreted, even incorrectly, as an attempt to usurp the powers of the presidency would disrupt the Eisenhower team, cause dissension in the nation, and disturb the President and his family. Certainly I had no desire or intention to seize an iota of presidential power. I was the Vice President and could be nothing more. But the problem was to guard against what I knew would be easy misinterpretation of any mistake, no matter how slight, I might make in public or private. The crisis was how to walk on eggs and not break them. My problem, what I had to do, was to provide leadership without appearing to lead.

At 4:30 the telephone rang. It was Jim Hagerty on his final call of the night saying the situation was unchanged, the President was resting comfortably. I went back to bed and continued to lie awake for the rest of the night thinking of the problems I would face in the morning.

The next morning, I put into action a plan decided upon the night before. I returned home and drove with Pat and the girls to the Westmoreland Congregational Church, about a mile from our house. The newspapermen followed us and also attended the services. We heard the minister, Dr. Philip Gordon Scott, pray that the President be "restored to health and strength and to the power of full life." It was a somber service, similar to thousands upon thousands of others throughout the world. Eisenhower, the man who had led the Allied forces to victory in World War II, had become a symbol of the hope for peace for people everywhere.

After the services, the reporters crowded around and I invited them to return with me to the house. Eight or ten of them followed us home and we settled down in my living room for a talk. Few, if any, of them realized that this was precisely in line with my plan of action worked out the night before. This first meeting with the press, in which my words, my actions, even my mood, would be reported to the nation, for me was a crisis. I wanted to be prepared for it as best I could. Even the manner of my meeting the press, no matter what I said, could be subject to misinterpretation. If I called a press conference, attracting the whole Washington press and television corps, it would appear as though I were attempting to step center stage in the absence of the President. If I refused to see the press altogether, it might indicate a lack of confidence or even fear—and this would be a reflection upon the whole Administration. The answer was to have a casual meeting with the press, and that is just what this one seemed to be.

With this small group of newsmen, many of whom I knew personally, sitting with me in my own home, I was able to speak frankly and informally. Of course, they had their jobs to do and they fired questions at me, loaded with politics, in their quest for what they call hard news. But I knew perfectly well what I wanted to say and what I didn't. All questions on the President's condition and its political implications for the next year's presidential election, I declined to answer. "The only comment I can make," I told them, "is to express the concern that I share with all the American people for the early and complete recovery of the President. In comparison with this, all other questions and problems are not worthy of discussion."

This did not stop the reporters that day, and others thereafter, from questioning the political implications of every move I made. The Republican National Convention was less than a year away; Eisenhower was known to be reluctant, even before his heart attack, to run for a second term; virtually everyone was counting him out now; and the newspaper pundits seemed to be equally divided between a "wide-open race" for the Republican nomination and Richard Nixon being the "heir apparent." Somehow no one seemed to want to believe the truth, which was that the "team," myself included, was concerned exclusively with how to carry on through the present emergency. No one close to the President thought of jockeying for the nomination while he lay ill. It would have been in poor taste, ill-advised, and, as some who tried it discovered a short while later, political suicide. My concern was how to keep politics out of the picture. If a scramble for the Republican nomination broke out at this time it would be tantamount to desertion of the President personally and an irresponsible scuttling of the administration of government. Despite the millions of words written about the political implications at the time, no member of the "team" began to seek the nomination.

Our attention was directed on how to avoid the political maneuvers and how to maintain the balance of power in running a government without a Chief Executive. My first meeting with the press gave me the opportunity of making public the theme that the Administration would carry on the policies and practices of President Eisenhower until he himself was well enough to take over the reins. "The President has set up the Administration in such a way that it will continue its policies, which are well defined, during his temporary absence," I told the reporters. "The President has always made it clear that the business of government should go ahead. He set it up in such a way that it can go ahead despite the temporary absence of anyone."

Foster Dulles and George Humphrey, with whom I had conferred by telephone the night before, also told the press that the "team" could and would carry on, thus setting the interim policy in Washington.

Dulles, as the ranking senior member of the Cabinet, bolstered by his sense of history, long experience in government, and force of character, maintained a strong guiding hand behind the scenes upon all the actions of the team. It was he who strongly urged that Sherman Adams set up shop in Denver rather than Washington when Adams returned from overseas. He preferred Adams at the President's side, serving as a liaison between the Chief Executive and the Cabinet, rather than Hagerty, the press secretary, or anyone else who might try to fill that vacuum. Dulles, in one conversation with me, candidly recalled the difficult period when Woodrow Wilson was paralyzed with a stroke in 1919 and the only ones who had access to his sickroom in the White House had been his wife, his secretary, and his doctor. Neither the Vice President, the Cabinet, nor Congress could find out Wilson's state of health, and the only state papers he saw were those his wife and possibly his secretary chose to show him. For eight months, Wilson was unable to call a Cabinet meeting and when his Secretary of State, Robert Lansing, initiated Cabinet meetings in an attempt to carry on the drifting affairs of the Administration, Wilson flew into a rage and demanded (and got) his Secretary of State's resignation. That Secretary of State, Robert Lansing, was John Foster Dulles' uncle.

The word from Denver on Sunday, after Dr. White had consulted with the military doctors, was that the President had had "a moderate attack of coronary thrombosis without complications." Attention was focused on the word "moderate" because it differed from Dr. Snyder's original diagnosis of a "mild" heart attack. However, the really important words were that the heart attack was "without complications." The word from Denver, in short, was that the President had suffered a very ordinary coronary, one from which thousands of other men in his age-group had recovered. Barring complications, which could not yet be ruled out completely, the prognosis was that the President would be well enough in two weeks to take on limited duties and to resume normal activity in two months.

The news was heartening and, after spending most of the day on the telephone, I relaxed Sunday night with Bill Rogers and Jerry Persons, talking over the various details which would have to be tended to during the week. We were fairly certain by this time that there was nothing requiring the President's signature or attention which could not be delayed for two weeks. The significance of this was that it became apparent this early that we would not have to solve the thorny problem of a delegation of the President's constitutional powers. Despite all the speculation in the press, that possibility was never taken up seriously within the Administration, and as the President's health continued to improve, the constitutional question itself, aside from the practical considerations, faded into the background.

The next day, Monday, I reviewed matters pending at the White House during a luncheon meeting with the senior staff personnel and then stayed on for a private talk with Sherman Adams, who had just flown in from Scotland. My relationship with Adams was somewhat formal rather than friendly. But we worked well together, with a mutual respect for our abilities and positions in the government. Adams said little in this meeting, but for him that was not unusual or surprising. I stressed the importance of keeping all the Cabinet members informed and up-to-date on everything, and I emphasized the necessity of avoiding any impression that any one clique of Cabinet officers was running the government. Some of the members whom I had not reached by phone the night I had learned of the President's illness had raised this point with me, and I wanted to make sure that no jealousies arose within the Cabinet as a result of my having consulted that evening with Humphrey and Dulles and not with others.

On Monday night, Adams, Len Hall, who was then the Republican National Chairman, and his press aide Lou Guylay, along with Rogers, Persons, and myself, met at Rogers' home to discuss some of the political questions which were bound to arise during the President's illness. During this meeting, which lasted for over four hours, Adams volunteered nothing. As Len Hall later described his actions: "Every time we asked, 'Sherm, what do you think?' he would talk about fishing in Scotland." After three or four questions were put to him, we realized that Adams' sole loyalty was to Eisenhower and that he did not want to take part in any action before he knew his chief's inclinations.

The major subject of discussion that night was how to keep the lid on the political cauldron. Len Hall, a man who knew and loved his job, needed no instruction. He already had taken the first step. Caught by reporters that afternoon at a scheduled talk to the Union League Club in New York, Hall came out flatly with his prediction of the 1956 Republican ticket: Ike and Dick. That night I asked Hall to get word to all the Republican State Chairmen and political leaders throughout the country to say nothing which would set off a premature battle for the presidential nomination. I stated flatly that I would do nothing that could possibly be construed as political so long as we had a President who conceivably could run for a second term. No one at that time, it must be admitted, thought that Eisenhower would choose to run again even if he were physically able.

How to provide leadership to the party and to the nation during the President's illness came up as a problem of many facets. I refused to take any overt leadership, although I was equally determined that things must not be allowed to drift. My problem remained how to exert leadership without seeming to do so.

The next day and all through the next two weeks, I was careful to conduct all my business from my own office in the Senate Office Building. I made it a point to visit various Cabinet members in their offices rather than summon them to mine. I met with Allen Dulles, head of the Central Intelligence Agency, Herbert Hoover, Jr., Under-Secretary of State, and Dillon Anderson, Special Assistant to the President for National Security Affairs, to prepare for the regular Thursday meeting of the National Security Council. I put in several hours with the White House staff and, for the first time since the President was stricken, I signed some non-legal, ceremonial papers. I signed them, of course, with my own name, "in behalf of the President." My working day stretched from twelve to sixteen hours during the week, but that Wednesday was the opening day of the World Series and I managed to listen to the final three innings of the game.

At the two-and-a-half-hour meeting of the National Security Council on Thursday, attended by twenty-three ranking members of the Administration, we went through the regular agenda of reports and then spent considerable time reviewing and putting somewhat of an official stamp of approval on the course of action for the interim government. It was officially decided, for instance, that Sherman Adams should go to Denver to serve as liaison and administrative assistant to the President, while Jerry Persons would handle the paper work at the President's White House office, routing the documents which the President should see through Adams.

Presiding at the Security Council was not new to me. I had done this before when the President had been away from Washington. I was fully briefed for this meeting, but still there was an aura of tension in the air. I was mindful to preside as Vice President, not as acting President. My role was to see that the items up for discussion were handled effectively and efficiently. I was careful not to express my opinion on any decisions or to cut off the discussion until all the officials present, understandably sensitive about their prerogatives, had their say. Only at the end of the discussion of each subject did I express my own point of view and set forth what I thought was the sense of the meeting as to the decision which should be made.

Despite all my efforts, I was not completely successful in keeping harmony within the Cabinet group. I did my best during this period to avoid meeting the press, but it was virtually impossible to go in and out of the White House and my office in the Capitol without running into reporters who had the responsibility to cover me. Even though I tried to be completely noncommittal on such occasions, two Cabinet officers called me Thursday evening very upset because they thought I had sought out the press after the Security Council meeting, in violation of our general understanding to have no press conferences during this period.

Foster Dulles must have been aware of the great tension under which I had been working. The next morning, Friday, I presided over the meeting of the Cabinet. The Cabinet meeting went almost exactly like that of the National Security Council. I presided from my own chair opposite the empty seat of the President. The meeting was opened with a prayer for the recovery of the President, and I again took care to preside rather than to conduct the meeting. At the end of the two-and-a-half-hour session, Foster Dulles gave my morale a much needed boost when he said, "Mr. Vice President, I realize that you have been under a very heavy burden during these past few days, and I know I express the opinion of everybody here that you have conducted yourself superbly. And I want you to know we are proud to be on this team and proud to be serving in this Cabinet under your leadership."

As I had expected from the very first, my road continued to be straight and narrow. I had to move ahead, realizing that any misstep could bring disaster. While some Cabinet members feared I was doing too much, others told me I was not doing enough. Typical of the latter attitude was a wire I received from Styles Bridges, the senior Senator from New Hampshire: "You are the constitutional second-in-command and you ought to assume the leadership. Don't let the White House clique take command."

In Washington, there has always been a sort of continuous rating system, an intangible popularity poll, which fluctuates with the supposed importance and influence of each member of the government. In the Executive branch, the measure usually goes according to who has the ear of the President. In the absence of President Eisenhower, this rating system shifted gears in quest of someone who could be considered to be filling the huge gap left by the President's forced absence.

This even affected the Washington press corps. Some reporters who had known me since I had come to the Capital as a freshman Congressman changed their form of address from "Dick" to "Mr. Vice President."

The most noticeable effect was, of course, on the large group of sundry politicians, businessmen, and lobbyists who can always be counted on to "play the winner." Men who had hardly cloaked their antipathy before, now paid me courtesy calls or sought to give me sagacious advice about my brilliant future. A bandwagon of sorts had started the very first week, but I knew how fickle that sort of support could be. I was not surprised to note that as President Eisenhower's health improved, these new camp followers drifted off to different roads.

In Denver, the President regained his strength day by day. After a week in the hospital, he put his signature on two documents— primarily to reassure the nation of his recovery. A few days later he wrote me a letter, made public to put his stamp of approval on my activities: "Dear Dick, I hope you will continue to have meetings of the National Security Council and of the Cabinet, over which you will preside in accordance with the procedures which you have followed at my request in the past during my absence from Washington."

Pat and I were able to keep track of the pace of the President's recovery by the diminishing number of reporters who maintained a twenty-four-hour vigil at our home. The first two or three nights after the attack, when his condition was touch and go, this group numbered ten. As the reports got better during the week, one by one they drifted away to other assignments until ten days later only Bill Blair of the New York *Times* was on hand to greet me when I left my home for the office. He stayed on duty for three more days, and since he was the only one, I was able to give him a ride to the Capitol each morning.

But it was not until two weeks after the heart attack that the tension in Washington was eased. Although it was hardly mentioned, I am certain that many of us realized that our team-government would be inadequate to handle an international crisis, such as a brush-fire war or an internal uprising in a friendly nation or a financial crisis of an ally. The ever-present possibility of an attack on the United States was always hanging over us. Would the President be well enough to make a decision? If not, who had the authority to push the button? This two-week period was critical in the health of a heart patient, his doctors said. It was the period in which a recurrence or "complications" were most likely, and everyone in Washington was aware of the possibility. When that two-week period ended and the scar tissue in the President's heart had formed—for we had all started our course in becoming lay heart specialists—only then did we feel that the crisis had ended. Eisenhower would be well enough to handle the powers and duties which were vested by the Constitution in him alone.

I flew to Denver to see him for the first time since his attack with Dr. White and the President's son, John, on October 8, exactly two weeks after the heart attack; and Dr. White, an articulate and sophisticated physician, lectured me vigorously on his favorite theme: heart patients should not be treated as invalids. Once their recovery is complete, they should resume their previous normal activities. For President Eisenhower this would mean a renewal of his strenuous life, hard work, and plenty of exercise. One of the doctor's heart patients, I remember his telling me, was in his eighties and still played golf regularly.

I was the first of the visitors permitted to see the President after the "critical period." The Cabinet members followed according to rank. It was obvious that in Denver they were as mindful of protocol as I had been in Washington.

President Eisenhower looked startlingly thin and pale, but seemed in good spirits. His mind was agile and he roamed over various subjects, including his heart attack and problems of government. I told him he needn't rush to get back to his office, that the team was carrying on his policies without "one iota of jealousy" among us.

The President walked out of Fitzsimmons Army Hospital on Veterans Day, November 11, delivered a genial thank you and good-by to the people of Denver, and flew home to Washington, where he received a tumultuous welcome. The nation watched on television. He could have left the hospital a month earlier, his doctors said, but he preferred to walk out of the hospital rather than be carried out a month sooner.

The official family's welcome-home was given at a meeting of the National Security Council on November 21 and at a Cabinet meeting the next day at the presidential retreat at Camp David, high in the Maryland mountains some twenty-five miles from the President's Gettysburg farm, where he was continuing his recuperation. Fourteen of us were flown there from Washington in three separate helicopters after the Secret Service vetoed the idea of so many government officials flying in one craft.

The two days with the President at Camp David, so close to Thanksgiving 1955, passed quickly and pleasantly in an aura of warmth and good feelings among the "team" with the boss back at work again. At the Cabinet meeting he thanked us all for our "perfect" performance during his absence. But to my knowledge, he did not thank anyone personally. He felt that all of us, no matter how hard we worked, were merely doing our duty, what was expected of us under the circumstances.

This was characteristic of Eisenhower. Only when he believed someone had gone beyond what the job called for did he express personal appreciation to that individual. I remember him thanking me personally for representing him in defending the Administration's labor policy before a cold and hostile A.F.L. Convention in St. Louis in 1953, later after I campaigned cross-country in the congressional elections of 1954, and again after Secretary James Mitchell and I were successful in settling the steel strike in 1959. He had also spoken or written to me personally of his appreciation after each of my trips abroad. But after this most difficult assignment of all—treading the tightrope during his convalescence from the heart attack—there was no personal thank you. Nor was one needed or expected. After all, we both recognized that I had only done what a Vice President should do when the President is ill.

The personal crisis for Dwight D. Eisenhower was not the heart attack per se, because he had no control over that, but the decision of whether or not, after such a brush with death, to run for re-election in 1956. The basic considerations which went into this decision were the same before and after September 1955—with the exception of the heart attack—and I believe it was the heart attack itself which, more than anything else, helped convince him to become a candidate for re-election.

Eisenhower frequently had told his associates that he wanted to be a one-term President. He thought that in four years he could substitute his concept of a moderate federal government, a free economy, and a balanced budget for what he considered the Democratic Party's drift toward a welfare state. He wanted to build up the Republican Party into a moderate, responsible majority party, and then turn over the reins to a younger man. He intended to put this concept of a one-term President into his first inaugural address, but at the last minute he was talked out of that. However, this did not stop him from discussing the idea from time to time.

Despite his remarkable ability to present a public image of unfailing good cheer and optimism, Eisenhower in private can be a man of rapidly changing moods. He would go into a momentary tailspin of frustration, for instance, when a Republican he admired voted against one of his projects in Congress. The Eisenhower legislative record was as good if not better than that of any President. But that made little difference to him. His temperament was so volatile that those who knew him well often checked with Tom Stephens, his Appointments Secretary, on how the boss was feeling before they went in to see him. Tom, who knew him better than most, might say, "You'd better not see him on that today; he's wearing his brown suit," for Tom always insisted the President had a certain brown suit and one particular sports jacket he would wear when in a "Monday mood."

He was not in office much more than a year when he began to tell associates from time to time of his intention to retire at the end of his first term. Usually these outbursts were recognized as temporary sentiments of the moment, reflecting a recent setback of one kind or another. But as 1956 approached, they were regarded more and more seriously.

When he moved his office to Denver, August 14, 1955, the political pressures on the President to run again in 1956 had reached a crescendo. The Republican National Convention was just a year off. The respite from urgent government business at Denver was seen as a time when the President could reach the all-important political decision on a second term. At Denver, before the heart attack, Eisenhower seemed particularly testy, easily irritated, and on edge. He kept putting off those who wanted to talk politics with the exclamation that he was in Denver to fish and play golf.

Two weeks before the heart attack, following a meeting of Republican State Chairmen, Len Hall visited Eisenhower in Denver to press upon him the party's and the nation's need for him to run for re-election. The President listened and paced the floor, and told the party Chairman what he had told others: "What more do they want from me? . . . I've given all of my adult life to the country. . . . What more must I do? . . ." He then went on to list five or six names, mine included, of men he said were younger than he and just as able to carry on the Eisenhower mode of government.

Hall left that meeting discouraged, but not convinced that the chances of Eisenhower's running were hopeless. Hagerty, Adams, myself, and others in the Administration had heard the President speak of retirement, but we knew that the nature of the office always leaves important unfinished business at the end of a President's term of office, and that few real leaders can turn their backs on such a challenge. We knew that Eisenhower was not a quitter—that he liked to finish a job which he had started. Our arguments to him stressed that he was the best if not the only man who could accomplish the undone work which lay ahead.

If I had bet at that time, I would have wagered that he would seek a second term. Incidentally, my judgment of what Eisenhower would do was not based on any theory that a man in power loves power for its own sake. The office of President of the United States carries an aura of responsibility which transcends the personal power the office holds. It demands a dedication and devotion which is greater than any personal consideration of the man who occupies the office. No leader of men who has occupied that office and devoted his being to it can turn away when his work is still incomplete. To a lesser extent this holds true for leaders in other walks of life, who carry on despite great financial and physical problems.

After the heart attack, of course, there was a decided change in the odds on the question of the second term. The medical opinion was given by Dr. Paul Dudley White: "Many things are possible that may not seem advisable. It is up to him to make the decision. He may or may not have complete recovery. . . . If I were in his shoes, I wouldn't want to run again, having seen the strain." Later, he added: "If the President has a good recovery as he seems to be establishing, and if he desires to continue his career, which would of course be to the benefit of this country and the world at large, I would have no objections whatever to his running again. But that remains for the future to decide."

The Washington press corps was polled and 88 per cent said Eisenhower would not run. This fairly reflected the thinking in Washington at the time, and it set off the expected wave of political activity, despite all my efforts to avoid a scramble for the Republican nomination. On the very same day that the President's heart attack was reported, this typical story appeared on the front page of the New York *Times*: "Vice President Richard M. Nixon today fell heir to one of the greatest responsibilities and political opportunities ever presented to so young a man in the history of the Republic. The general feeling here (Washington) was that the 42-year-old Californian was in a better position than anyone else to get the Republican nomination, if, as seems almost certain, the stricken President retires at the end of his first term."

To the many suggestions that I step forward as the deputy or acting

President or as the heir apparent, I always answered: "We still have a President of the United States." Although aware of the future potentiality of my position, I knew that so long as the President lay ill or convalescing, my responsibility was to carry on with my own duties and responsibilities. Throughout the period of his illness and convalescence, I dedicated my thoughts, words, and actions to the crisis at hand: to help carry on the operations of government in the absence or partial absence of the Chief Executive. For any Vice President to politicize his activities during his President's term of office, particularly his first term of office, would be personally reprehensible, I believe, unless that Vice President disagreed fundamentally with the President's policies or truly believed that he could serve the country better. Neither of these conditions applied to me.

The first time that the Republican National Chairman saw President Eisenhower after the heart attack was at his Gettysburg farm on November 28. One of the known common aftereffects of a heart attack is frequent periods of depression, and it was in one of these moods that Len Hall found the President. Before he went in to see the President, he talked with Jim Hagerty and Sherman Adams. They, too, were despondent. "This man isn't going to go," they told Hall.

Hall, an astute politician, wisely did not ask the President the key question. He again expressed the hopes of the party and the nation for four more years of Eisenhower leadership. He informed the President that the latest polls showed he could be re-elected without a strenuous campaign. The President did not give any hint of an answer to the key question, but he described himself as "an old dodo," a man for whom the years had caught up. It was a gloomy discussion. But for Hall it brightened at the very end. "Okay," said Hall, "let's talk about what I'm going to say to the press when I walk out of here. Everyone else who visits you can say that they did not talk politics, but if I said that they'd call me a liar."

"Go out and say what you think you should say," replied the President. "I don't want to know what you are going to say."

Hall went out and said he believed Eisenhower would run again and that I would be his running mate.

For me, as well as the President, this period continued to be one which drained my emotional as well as physical energies, for it was, above all, a period of indecision. As Vice President, my role was to absorb some of the more routine duties of the President, relieving the burden on him, and yet not to appear to be stepping into his shoes.

To understand the President's inner turmoil during this period, it is necessary, I think, to understand the nature of convalescence from a heart attack. In the aftermath, for anyone, there is first the shock of having been stricken, followed by periods of deep depression when the patient doesn't want to do anything ever anymore—except take care of himself. Next, there comes a period of worrying about one's own condition and chances of another attack—so much so, I believe, that it inhibits a man from making completely rational decisions. Then, finally, when the disease has been fully arrested, there comes the natural human reaction for any active man to continue the battle and not, as he first contemplated, to retire from the arena.

On one of my visits to the White House, the Saturday before Christmas, I found the President in his apartment on the second floor, sitting alone on a bench against a wall, somewhat depressed. I came in with Jim Hagerty, Jerry Persons, and Ann Whitman to present the Cabinet's Christmas gift to him. He told us the doctor had just taken his blood pressure after exercise and found it quite high. Discussing generally the various symptoms of his recovery, he commented that quite possibly the doctors really did not know too much about the aspects of recovery. The uncertainty of it all was what troubled him, he said, for he did not have a high cholesterol count or any of the other usual explicable symptoms of the disease. As a result, he said, his fate was much more uncertain than that of other heart patients who knew what caused their attack and could rearrange their lives to avoid another.

He also told of having what he called "a little spell" after the Christmas party for the White House staff earlier that week. He had moved about the party shaking hands and exchanging greetings, he said, and had not realized how much strength it had taken out of him until he suddenly felt very, very tired. It was that same afternoon, I remembered, that Colonel A. J. Goodpaster, the President's Staff Secretary, had passed me a note that the President might have to leave the Security Council meeting early because he was very tired. But the President had called a recess of five minutes and had come back to finish the meeting.

The President, of course, was not always worried or depressed during this period. At that same White House visit, his expressive face glowed with pleasure when I presented him with a pair of gold candlesticks as his Christmas gift from the Cabinet and gold place settings for eight from the White House staff. And he roared with laughter when I commented that these gifts symbolized his Administration's attachment to the principle of the gold standard. David, the President's oldest and favorite grandchild, provided a pleasant interlude when he came into the room. Hagerty introduced me as "the Vice President of the United States." David took a second look and said, "The Vice President, wow!" Then he turned to his grandfather and said, "Ike, I didn't know there were two Presidents." The President explained that the Vice President had to be ready to step in whenever the President was too sick to perform his job. When David left the room, the President told us that the family tried to keep the children from being conscious of his rank. Only David, the eldest, was aware that he was President and that was one of the reasons they had insisted from the beginning that David continue to call his grandfather Ike, just as he always had.

The day after Christmas, Jerry Persons phoned me and asked if I would mind coming down to the White House to urge the President to take a needed vacation in Florida. His doctors had wanted him to convalesce in the warm climate of Florida when he left the hospital, but then the President had insisted on remaining close to Washington. That morning I found him in a talkative mood. When I explained that he certainly should go to Florida without any feeling that he had to be in Washington when Congress opened or for the State of the Union message, he indicated that he thought so too. But, he said, "my family is kind of sentimental about New Year's and other holidays" and they thought he should be at home for New Year's Eve.

However, one of the reasons he wanted to go to Florida, he said, was to have a chance to talk at length with his brother Milton and others about his plans for the future. He remarked that he wanted me to understand that it would be necessary for him in the next few days and weeks to have conferences from time to time on the political situation without my being present. This was necessary, he pointed out, because I would, of course, be one of those who would have to be talked about.

The President emphasized that the doctors could not say what caused his heart attack and so they probably would not be able to give him any assurance as to what the future would hold. That led up to the inevitable conclusion that, as he put it, he could not see how he could run in good conscience with that "sword of Damocles" hanging over his head.

I tried to convince him, as I had before, that the job need not be nearly so burdensome as it had been before and that many of the duties which were being taken away from him now should have been assumed by others in the Administration long before the heart attack. "As far as meetings are concerned," I told him, "no meeting should be over two hours." He laughed at this point and said that one thing he would never agree to was to get up and leave a meeting before it was over. It would be an affront to treat his "colleagues" in that way, he said.

I brought up this same point with Sherman Adams some time afterwards, arguing that despite the President's much heralded staff system, he sometimes listened to the same paper being read two or three times: once by members of his personal staff, later before the Security Council, and then sometimes again at a full Cabinet meeting. Surely he could excuse himself during the readings or rereadings of papers he had previously heard. But, Adams answered, if the President did not attend, the Cabinet members would not think it an important meeting and some of them might choose not to attend either. Then Cabinet meetings would lose their significance. The same problem arose over having the President's signature on some of the more politically important messages of greetings and proclamations. Every convention and conclave wants a message from the President of the United States, and only his signature will satisfy them.

At that December 26 meeting with the President, he seemed to be seeking some way of avoiding another campaign. He referred to the fact that when he had agreed to run in 1952 he had been told that he could serve for only four years and that by that time the Republican Party would be strong enough to elect another candidate. It was "most disappointing" to him, he said, to see that my popularity had not risen as high as he had hoped it would.

For that reason, he said, it might be better for me in a new Administration not to be Vice President but to be a Cabinet officer. He pointed out that I could hold any position in the Cabinet I wanted, with the possible exception of Attorney General, which he ruled out due to my lack of legal experience, and Secretary of State, which he thought I could handle but to which he thought Herbert Hoover, Jr., then Under Secretary of State, had an inside track. Secretary of Defense seemed to be the position he particularly favored for me in case I did not run again for Vice President.

The conversation was casual, the emphasis was on the possibility of his not running again, and, knowing how the President's mind worked, I did not take the suggestion seriously, just as I knew he was himself "trial-ballooning" the idea of his not running again. With people he knew well and trusted, Eisenhower liked to think out loud. He would sometimes make what would seem to be completely outlandish and politically naïve remarks, just to test them, perhaps even believing in some of them momentarily. He was very bold, imaginative, and uninhibited in suggesting and discussing new and completely unconventional approaches to problems. Yet he probably was one of the most deliberate and careful Presidents the country has ever had where action was concerned. Because of his military experience, he was always thinking in terms of alternatives, action and counteraction, attack and counterattack. This was true of every problem he handled. I cannot, for instance, imagine him countenancing the plan for the 1961 rebel attack on Cuba without air cover before asking: "What is our position if the landings fail?" He could be very enthusiastic about half-baked ideas in the discussion stage, but when it came to making a final decision, he was the coldest, most unemotional and analytical man in the world.

In his talk with me, the President also expressed great disappointment that Earl Warren had announced he would not leave the Supreme Court to be a candidate. "I don't see why he couldn't just have said nothing," he remarked, commenting that the Republican Party had dealt with Warren pretty well, and he certainly should have been willing to be a candidate in the event the party found it necessary to draft him. He pointed out that a recent Gallup Poll, asking Republican voters who they favored for the Republican nomination in the event that Eisenhower did not run, had shown Warren with 14 per cent to 11 per cent for me. He mentioned another poll in which I had run substantially behind Adlai Stevenson. He apparently had not seen a later poll, taken after his heart attack, in which I had run ahead of Warren and in which Stevenson's lead over me had been greatly cut down.

As we talked about polls, he said, "I want you to come in from time to time to discuss the situation with regard to yourself. We might have to initiate a crash program for building you up." It occurred to me that a pretty effective job had been done on him concerning my recent weak showing in the polls. I told him that in making his decision as to whether he should or should not run again, I did not want him to feel that I had to be the candidate for Vice President.

He shut off talk on that subject promptly, saying he would not hear of it because he felt it would hurt the ticket if he "jettisoned" me at this point. Besides, he said, we could win as handily as we had before.

He tried to reassure me of his satisfaction with my work as Vice President. "There has never been a job I have given you that you haven't done to perfection as far as I am concerned," he said. "The thing that concerns me is that the public does not realize adequately the job you have done. I just can't understand how any sane-minded person could choose Stevenson over you."

Leaving that meeting, the strongest impression I carried away was that the President was leaning toward not running, but had not closed his mind on the subject. The idea of accepting a Cabinet post I did not take seriously. I put it in the category of a typical Eisenhower trial balloon, something which someone had suggested to him and that he characteristically was testing out.

Two days later, the President and his brother Milton, accompanied by a small staff, flew to Key West, Florida, for a two-week vacation, and spent most of the time fishing and talking politics. Mrs. Eisenhower and her mother flew down on New Year's Eve to spend the holiday weekend with him. On his last day there, January 8, the President indicated to a press conference that he had reached a "subject-to-change" decision on the all-important political question. The fourteen reporters at the conference were polled for their opinion of the President's remarks. Twelve thought he would not run, two judged that he would.

Soon after his return to Washington, he again brought up the question of whether I could advance my own political career better by seeking an important Cabinet post instead of running for Vice President again, pointing out that no Vice President since Van Buren had ever been elected President. The subject came up at five or six of our private conversations, usually in a casual way, and I always gave the same answer: "If you believe your own candidacy and your Administration would be better served with me off the ticket, you tell me what you want me to do and I'll do it. I want to do what is best for you."

He always answered somewhat obliquely, praising my service to his Administration and saying, "No, I think we've got to do what's best for you."

This stalemate over what should have been a simple question arose, I believe, from our different attitudes on who should make the decision. I always believed, and still do, that no one should or could run for the vice presidency—the choice must be that of the presidential candidate. I considered it improper for me to indicate my desires until his plans, which were paramount, were made clear. I couldn't say: "Look, Mr. President, I want to run." He never put the question to me in quite the right way for that response. If he had said, "Dick, I want you to be the (vice presidential) candidate, if you want to be," I would have accepted, thanked him, and that would have been that.

But Eisenhower's mind did not work that way. He believed the Chief Executive should make only those decisions which could not be made by others. He preferred all other decisions to be made by his subordinates and then presented to him for his approval. Moreover, an Eisenhower characteristic was never to take direct action requiring his personal participation where indirect methods could accomplish the same result. That was why during the 1952 fund controversy he insisted that I should make the decision about resigning. And only if I had submitted my resignation would he have assumed the responsibility of determining whether my staying on the ticket would or would not be in the best interests of the party and his candidacy.

He was a far more complex and devious man than most people realized, and in the best sense of those words. Not shackled to a one-track mind, he always applied two, three, or four lines of reasoning to a single problem and he usually preferred the indirect approach where it would serve him better than the direct attack on a problem. His mind was quick and facile. His thoughts far outraced his speech and this gave rise to his frequent "scrambled syntax" which more perceptive critics should have recognized as the mark of a far-ranging and versatile mind rather than an indicaton of poor training in grammar.

So in the early months of 1956, before it became a public issue, I was thrown into another period of agonizing indecision, which more than any overt crisis takes a heavy toll mentally, physically, and emotionally. I could not be certain whether the President really preferred me off the ticket or sincerely believed a Cabinet post could better further my career. It probably was a little of both, for this was a period when, recovering from his heart attack, he could well have been confused to some extent by the multiplicity of advice. Some of his close advisers made little secret of their personal antipathy toward me and wanted to dump me in '56 as they had in '52; others probably thought that I would hurt the '56 ticket because of the attention which would be focused on the second spot in view of the President's health; still others felt an open race for the vice presidential nomination would create more public interest; and some honestly believed a Cabinet post would foster my own career.

John Foster Dulles, one of my warmest friends and supporters in government, might well have been in this last group of advisers. I do not know if he discussed this subject with the President, but he brought it up with me one morning at his home. He expressed his belief that I ought to be President one day and that the office was within my reach because of my age, ability, and experience. He advised me strongly to consider the history of Vice Presidents and suggested that I might better prepare myself by seeking an important Cabinet post.

He mentioned Defense and the possibility of Secretary of State when he resigned.

While I did consider the idea and did some private agonizing about what President Eisenhower had in mind, I soon reached the practical conclusion that I could not switch jobs without the disastrous appearance that "Nixon had been dumped." And I knew I was acquiring executive and administrative experience in the various assignments given me by the President. Considering all the practical political aspects, I also concluded that all this was largely a tempest in a teapot. If the President decided to run, I would almost certainly be his running mate. But he would have to make the decision!

Eisenhower himself, it must be understood, was going through an ordeal of anxiety over the second-term issue. All his advisers, myself included when called upon, were pressing on him the need of the nation, the world, and not least, the Republican Party, to have him at the helm of government for another four years. At times this challenge, this call to duty must have seemed paramount—and at other times, during the periods of despondency which were part of his convalescence, he wanted to quit, defeated by an imperfect heart. The heart attack itself forced an earlier decision on the question of the second term. If he had been well and had wanted to quit, he could have delayed the decision until the last moment and then given the nod to his choice as potential successor. But the heart attack, politically, had shifted the odds against his seeking re-election, and now, the longer he delayed, the more his control would slip. He had to make an earlier decision in order to stop speculation and a ruinous scramble for the Republican nomination.

Personal considerations, as always, played their role along with the political and public aspects of Eisenhower's decision. Several of his close friends and personal advisers became convinced that if he gave up his active life, he would never shake off the grip of despondency. General Lucius Clay, an intimate and long-time friend who could speak to him more frankly and bluntly than perhaps anyone else, observed a moody, depressed Eisenhower soon before he left Fitzsimmons Hospital, and from that day forward Clay worked all-out to get him to run for re-election. He called meetings and he rallied many of us privately to urge the President to run again for his own good. "I don't care what happens to the Republican Party, but if he quits, it'll kill him," was the way Clay, a Democrat, put it. The same opinion was held by Dr. Snyder, and, as time went on, others close to the President recognized the wisdom of Clay's attitude from Eisenhower's personal point of view.

My own view, which I expressed on several occasions in meetings with close associates and friends of the President, was that it was not possible to separate the problem into two questions—what is best for Eisenhower and what is best for the nation. The only problem, as I saw it, was to convince Eisenhower that his running was imperative in the interests of the nation and the cause of peace and freedom to which he was dedicated. Once he became convinced of that, he could not make any decision other than to run, both from the standpoint of the nation and of his personal well-being. His whole life had been dedicated to public service. While there would be some risk to his health if he undertook the exertions of continuing to serve as President, there would be even greater risk to him from a physical, emotional, and mental standpoint if he consciously turned his back on a clear call to national service.

While the Washington reporters, columnists, and gossipmongers thought, wrote, and spread stories that President Eisenhower most probably would not run for re-election, the inner circle began to believe otherwise. The difference was that while those on the outside were reporting their own opinions and political theories, we on the inside knew the man. We knew that Eisenhower, as a leader and activist, might say he wanted to quit and take it easy. But when the time came, he would not want to lay down the reins of leadership with his job not fully completed.

On January 13, the President held his now famous but then secret dinner meeting of his close political advisers. Seated in front of a roaring fire in the Trophy Room on the second floor, with Milton alongside him, and the others lined up on two couches facing one another, the President asked each one in turn to present his reasons why he should run for a second term "and Milton will be my lawyer." In turn, Dulles, Henry Cabot Lodge, Leonard Hall, Jerry Persons, George Humphrey, Arthur Summerfield, Jim Hagerty, Tom Stephens, Howard Pyle, and Sherman Adams presented their arguments. Milton made the summation. The President thanked them but held his counsel.

The questions and speculation continued for another month. On February 14, the team of doctors completed their tests, examinations, and analyses, and reported that there was no indication of any heart enlargement. Dr. White announced to the press that there was nothing to indicate that Eisenhower could not carry on "his present active life satisfactorily" for another five or ten years. The President then went to George Humphrey's Georgia plantation for golf and quail hunting. Ten days later he returned to Washington and told intimates that his answer was "positive."

The public announcement was made at his press conference of February 29 and when he had completed his statement, the first question was: would Richard Nixon be his running mate? The President evaded a direct reply, saying he could not properly speak out on the choice of a running mate until after the Republican National Convention itself had picked its presidential candidate. In politics, however, not speaking out can be another way of speaking out, and the President's words set off a wave of speculation by the public and a furor among my own friends and supporters. This, in turn, caused embarrassment to me because I still could say nothing before the President spoke.

At the next weekly press conference, on March 7, the President delivered his famous answer: "I told him (Nixon) he would have to chart his own course and tell me what he would like to do." His statement was telephoned to me soon after the press conference in a somewhat garbled version. The impression I got was that he was really trying to tell me that he wanted me off the ticket. I told Vic Johnston, Chief of Staff of the Senatorial Campaign Committee who was in my office at the time, that the only course I could properly take under the circumstances was to call a press conference the next day and announce that I would not be a candidate for Vice President so that Eisenhower would have a free hand to select his running mate. It seemed to me that it was like the fund controversy all over again. But *then* Eisenhower had not known me well and had every justification for not making a decision with regard to keeping me on the ticket until all the facts were in. *Now*, he had had an opportunity to evaluate my work over the past three years, and particularly during the period after the heart attack. If he still felt, under these circumstances, that he wanted me on the ticket only if I insisted on seeking the post, I concluded he should have someone else in whom he had more confidence as his running mate.

Later that day Len Hall and Jerry Persons, who had learned from Johnston of my intentions, cornered me at the Capitol and argued that if I issued such a statement it would split the Republican Party in two. I told them that everyone in politics knows a Vice President cannot chart his own course. "It's up to him if he wants me," I said. "I can only assume that if he puts it this way, this must be his way of saying he would prefer someone else."

"That's not what he meant at all," said Hall. He declared that I was judging Eisenhower's statement by standards which should be applied to a political sophisticate. Both he and Persons argued that the President was sincerely interested in my future and that I ought to consider the whole thing again and at least delay my decision.

I held off my decision and the speculation, the uncertainty, the tension dragged on. Perhaps the most difficult thing for me was placating my own close friends and associates. Letters and calls flooded my office charging that the President was being "ungrateful," particularly in view of my conduct during the period since his heart attack.

Then an unexpected event occurred which was to have a great impact on my decision as well as the President's. As the President pointed out to me much later in a letter he wrote while I was considering the possibility of becoming a candidate for Governor of California: "Over the years I have wrestled with many decisions. But somehow or other, when the chips were down, the decision seemed to come by itself and without a conscious thought process. Suddenly something seems inescapable or right, and any other course unthinkable. So I am sure the answer—whatever it is—will come to you."

Six days after the "chart his own course" press conference, Pat and I were dinner guests of Alice Roosevelt Longworth. She asked after dinner if we didn't want to tune in on the New Hampshire primary results. I told her not to bother because, since my name was not on the ballot, I did not believe anything of significance as far as I was concerned would happen. The following morning my phone was ringing off the hook. The New Hampshire primary, the first of the 1956 campaign, had returned a surprising, unsolicited write-in vote of 22,936 for me as the vice presidential candidate. It was a reassuring comment coming from the voters at a difficult time, and I reappraised the situation in the light of the result. If what had happened in New Hampshire was at all indicative of sentiment in the country, my refusing to run as Vice President might, as Len Hall had predicted, "split the Republican Party in two." As in the fund controversy, it was not just a question of what I personally wanted to do, but what was best for the party and the nation, as well, to the extent I thought Eisenhower's continued leadership was in the national interest. This was the core of the difference in the way Eisenhower and I looked at the question of whether I should again be a candidate for Vice President. He insisted that I should do what I wanted to do—what I thought was best for my

career. I had told him that I wanted to do what would best contribute
to his own re-election, and that he should be the judge on that issue.

Politicians in Washington had no difficulty reading the meaning of
the New Hampshire primary. After the vote was in, many Senators
and Congressmen and party stalwarts flocked to me with reassurances
of their support. The President, however, delayed a decision on the
question of my candidacy. He flatly denied wanting to "dump" me,
asserted again and again his affection for me, but insisted that it was
not his place to choose a running mate before he himself had been
nominated by the Republican Party. This continued for some seven
weeks until April 27, when Len Hall came to me and urged me to
unbend and put an end to the wrangling which was only hurting the
party. At his press conference that morning, the President had said
that I had not yet reported back to him on the charting of my own
course: "He hasn't given me any authority to quote him, any answer
that I would consider final and definite."

After Len Hall left my office, I did some intense soul-searching.
Would I hurt or help the party and the course of the Eisenhower
Administration by being on the ticket? I telephoned the White House
for an appointment and went to see the President that afternoon. I
told him I would be honored to continue as his Vice President and that
the only reason I had waited so long in saying so was that I did not
want to force my way onto the ticket against his wishes. The President
said he was delighted with my decision. He called in Jim Hagerty
and arranged for an announcement of the decision to be made from
the White House that afternoon.

And so ended the personal crisis involved in my decision to be a
candidate for Vice President in 1956. In retrospect, it was a minor
crisis, for the outcome really never was in doubt. Yet it was part of
the much more serious heart attack crisis for me—the aftermath when
my guard was down. I would otherwise not have been as sensitive
about Eisenhower's attitude toward my candidacy and would have
resolved the situation myself much sooner. The significance, at least
for me, once again was that the most dangerous period of a crisis is
not the preparation or the battle itself, but the aftermath when one's
normal reaction, after having mobilized all one's emotions and physical
resources to fight the battle, is to relax. If you cannot take the time off
to let your system relax and recharge normally, then you must be alert
to the fact that your temper will be short and your judgment less acute
than normally. During the trying months when the President had lain
ill, I had expended my energies not only in a heavier work schedule

but in treading a tightrope of political diplomacy. Then, before I could recover my equilibrium, I found myself on political tenterhooks and I reacted with less than my best judgment.

As if to prove the fickleness of political life in Washington, there was an aftermath to this crisis. Harold Stassen, the President's adviser on disarmament, came out with an open campaign to "dump Nixon." His maneuver was a comedy of errors too long to detail here, but it proved a nagging irritant right up to August 22, when the Eisenhower-Nixon ticket was renominated by the Republican National Convention in San Francisco.

Stassen, who had come to see me privately while Eisenhower lay ill in Denver to pledge me his support and efforts in winning the *presidential* nomination, went to Eisenhower on July 20 to report that according to a private poll he had had taken, I would detract from the ticket because I was a controversial figure—while someone else, like Christian Herter, then Governor of Massachusetts, would not. The President noncommittally replied, as he had said before, that he would not dictate the choice to the Convention. Stassen went ahead with his one-man campaign to substitute Herter for Nixon as the Republican candidate for Vice President. From this fracas, I could afford to remain aloof. Although some wishful thinkers lent erstwhile support to it for a brief time, it got nowhere. The upshot was that Chris Herter, who was embarrassed by the whole affair, placed my name in nomination—and Harold Stassen seconded it.

The President's ileitis attack on June 8, 1956, was divulged to me by telephone, once again with Jim Hagerty the bearer of bad news. But what stands out in my mind today is that the surgery focused the President's attention on the legal problems of the disability of a Chief Executive. It demonstrated that generally, where the crisis of physical illness is involved, fighting to get back in action is better for the patient than using the illness as an excuse for leaving the battle to others.

President Eisenhower was stricken late on the night of the seventh with severe stomach cramps, after attending a dinner of the White House Photographers Association. Mrs. Eisenhower called Dr. Snyder, who arrived at 1:15 A.M. and stayed through the night. The following afternoon the President was taken on a stretcher to Walter Reed Hospital. His case was diagnosed as ileitis, an obstruction in the lower intestines, an old complaint. But when it did not respond to medication through that day and that night, a team of doctors headed by Major General Leonard Heaton, commanding officer of Walter Reed Hospital, decided on immediate surgery. The President was on the operating table for two hours, from 2:30 to 4:35 A.M., while the nation slept.

The President realized the significance to the nation of that operation. On several occasions afterwards, he pointed out to me that for the two hours he was under anesthesia the country was without a Chief Executive, the armed forces without a Commander-in-Chief. In the event of a national emergency during those two hours, who would have had the undisputed authority to act for a completely disabled President?

The President recovered quickly and completely from the operation. Within a few days he began limited activity, which increased as the days stretched into weeks. Although his doctors told him the operation increased his life expectancy, I believe the President became more aware that age was creeping up on him, increasing the possibility of illness and a need to do something about it. He told some of those around him that if ever illness struck again and he felt he could not physically carry on the burdens of his office, he would resign.

His reaction to the ileitis was far different from that of the heart attack. The ileitis was not half as serious, but he suffered more pain over a longer period of time. He looked far worse than he had in 1955. He hobbled about, bent over, during his post-operation convalescence, but he was determined to carry out the responsibilities of his job as he saw them. His illness presented a perfectly valid reason for his not attending a meeting of American presidents in Panama, designed to counteract the increasing Communist activity in South America, but he saw an even better reason for going himself. His personal attendance, following his illness, would demonstrate to our Latin and South American friends the President's and the United States' concern and interest in inter-American affairs far better than if there had been no ileitis attack. For him not to go, on the other hand, would inevitably have caused at least some sentiment that Latin American affairs were not important enough for the President to discommode himself.

There was a sharp disagreement among the President's advisers and friends about the wisdom of his going on the trip so soon after his operation. Some thought it was an unnecessary strain and risk for him from a physical standpoint. But Dr. Snyder, who always saw a close relation between the President's physical condition and his mental outlook, insisted that the trip would do more good than harm. And the President followed his advice.

He sent a message to President Ricardo Manuel Arias Espinosa of Panama saying he would be happy to go if the other presidents would agree to postpone the meeting until his doctors allowed him to travel. The doctors said full recovery would take four to six weeks, and six weeks to the day, the President flew to Panama. His activities there were extraordinary, considering the fact that he was still recovering from major surgery. He left Washington at five minutes past midnight, Saturday, July 21, arrived in Panama City at 8 A.M., went directly to a meeting of eighteen presidents at the home of President Arias, then stood bareheaded at attention in a driving rainstorm at a wreath-laying ceremony at the grave of José Antonio Remón, the past President of Panama who had been assassinated a year before. Throughout the day he made some six automobile tours, standing in an open car and waving to enthusiastic crowds. That night he held four private conferences with Latin American presidents and then attended an evening affair at the Presidential Palace. On Sunday, he signed the Declaration of Panama, pledging all American nations to the principles of freedom and liberty, delivered his first speech since his illness, and then listened to other speakers for almost three hours. The next day, Monday, he held ten separate private talks with other presidents, each lasting about thirty minutes, took a sixty-eight-minute tour of the Canal Zone (again in a drenching rain) and then flew back to Washington—all, six weeks after major surgery!

This was a feat which would make any physician shudder, I am sure, but Dr. Snyder, who accompanied the President, was always an exponent of the President doing more instead of less after each illness. And the proof was in the result. When I met the President at the airport on his return to Washington, I saw a remarkably changed man. He had left looking like an invalid—sick, tired, and in pain—but he returned more the old leader, full of bounce and ready to plunge into work. The trip, despite all of its strain upon his weakened body, renewed his physical vigor as well as his mental well-being. Seeing him that day and observing the terrific pace of his work in the days which followed renewed for me my lifelong conviction that a man should give battle to his physical ailments, fight to stay out of the sickbed, and, except where his doctor otherwise prescribes, should learn to live with and be stimulated by tension, rather than numbing his spirit with tranquilizers. Eisenhower demonstrated a trait that I believe all great leaders have in common: they thrive on challenge; they are at their best when the going is hardest. When life is routine, they become bored; when they have no challenge, they tend to wither and die or to go to seed. While such men might think and often exclaim how nice it would be if they could play golf every day and take long vacations whenever they wished, in actual fact they need challenges, problems, and hard work to sustain the will to live.

More than anything else, the ileitis attack irritated President Eisenhower. For a man who loved to eat, he was forced to abide by a diet even more bland than the heart attack had required. But while it did cause him considerable pain and discomfort, it did not present any problems for the administration of the government. There never was any question of his ability to carry out the functions of the President. But his third serious illness in office did present a major crisis, not so much for me but for him and the nation—a greater crisis, in a way, than even that of the heart attack.

Seventeen months after the ileitis operation—on November 25, 1957 —Sherman Adams called my office in the Senate Office Building late one afternoon. He reached Rose Mary Woods, my secretary, on the direct White House line.

"Is Dick around?" he asked.

"Yes, would you like to speak to him?"

"No, I just need to be sure where he is," Adams replied. "I may need him in a minute or two."

Rose told me of the call and remarked that he sounded as though something serious was at hand. Ten or fifteen minutes later, his call came through. Adams, who considered "hello" and "good-by" a waste of time, was, as usual, laconic:

"Dick, could you come down to the White House right away?"

"Yes," I replied, "I'll be right down."

Ten minutes later I was in Adams' office in the West Wing of the White House. Speaking, as usual, without visible emotion, he related what at first seemed like a matter-of-fact chronology of what had happened: the President had stood for some time in a raw whipping wind at Washington National Airport that morning to greet King Mohammed V of Morocco, who arrived for a state visit. Upon his return to the White House, the President said he felt a chill coming on, and Dr. Snyder had put him to bed with an extra blanket and hot-water bottle. But later he had gotten up and gone to his office and begun dictating to his secretary, Ann Whitman. Then, suddenly, his words became jumbled and made no sense. Mrs. Whitman telephoned Dr. Snyder and urged the President to go back to bed. He refused. Then he tried to tell her something but could not express himself. Finally, he did go back up to his living quarters in the White House and Dr. Snyder again put him to bed.

Later, when Adams had gone up to discuss that night's scheduled state dinner for Mohammed V with Mrs. Eisenhower, the President had come out in his pajamas, looking for his dinner clothes. He insisted that he intended to go to the dinner. Both Adams and Dr. Snyder tried to convince him not to go. The President, then very distraught, declared: "If I cannot attend to my duties, I am simply going to give up this job. Now that is all there is to it." With that, he turned and stalked out of the room.

Adams told me all this in even greater detail, going over every important point in the story. Finally I asked him, "How serious is his condition?"

"We'll know more in the morning," he answered. And then, speaking with all the emotion he had bottled up within him, he said, "This is a terribly, terribly difficult thing to handle. You may be President in the next twenty-four hours."

He said that Dr. Snyder thought the President had suffered a stroke, and that Dr. Heaton and a neurologist had been called to the White House. He expressed his concern for Mrs. Eisenhower, who was deeply disturbed over the President's health.

Two immediate problems faced us: what to tell the press and what to do about the state dinner for the King of Morocco that night. The problems were intertwined, because the state dinner was set for eight and some explanation would have to be made for the President's absence. We decided first that we should announce only that the President had suffered a chill and that we should withhold any announcement of the stroke until we were certain that Dr. Snyder's original diagnosis was correct.

Then we weighed the factors involved in canceling the dinner against my substituting as host, and whether or not we should ask Mrs. Eisenhower to attend, in view of her distress. Realizing that to cancel the dinner and turn guests away at the door of the White House would alarm the press and therefore the nation, we decided the dinner must be held on schedule. We left the decision on Mrs. Eisenhower's attendance to her and she responded to what she saw as her duty as First Lady. It was perhaps the most difficult assignment she ever undertook in the White House.

At 6:20, a White House bulletin was issued stating that the President had suffered a chill, had taken to bed, and would be unable to attend the dinner or deliver a nationwide television speech scheduled for the following night in Cleveland. Just before I left the White House to change into white-tie and tails, the doctors sent down their diagnosis, which confirmed Dr. Snyder's opinion: the President had suffered an occlusion of a small branch of the middle cerebral artery on the left side, probably caused by a small blood clot or a vascular spasm. It was a stroke.

At the formal White House dinner that night, a very troubled First Lady greeted her guests with superb poise and charm. But talking with me during dinner about the heart attack, the ileitis, and now the stroke, her voice broke as she said, "This really is too much for any one man to bear." I tried to reassure her of his remarkable ability to recover. He always did better than the doctors' prognoses, I reminded her. We spoke quietly to one another, each of us knowing that no one else at the dinner except Pat realized what truly was going on upstairs.

Early the next morning I drove directly to the White House. The Secret Service man assigned to me was somewhat embarrassed waiting half through the morning at my office in the Senate Office Building, but only my personal secretary had been told where I was going. Foster Dulles, Bill Rogers, Jerry Persons, and some other key officials of the Administration also slipped past reporters to Sherman Adams' office. The tension seemed even greater than at the time of the heart attack.

In contrast to that period in 1955, this was the worst time possible, short of outright war, for the President to be incapacitated. It was a time of international tensions. Only a month before, the Soviet Union had put its first Sputnik in orbit, and the whole structure of America's military might and scientific technology was under suspicion here and throughout the world. The most immediate problem was a scheduled meeting of the North Atlantic Treaty Organization in Paris on December 16, only three weeks away—a meeting of the NATO heads of state at which President Eisenhower was being counted on to rally our allies. France and Britain were privately complaining of financial difficulties in maintaining their NATO force levels.

On the domestc front, the first signs of the 1958 economic recession were becoming obvious. At the same time, it was equally apparent that we would have to find more money to bolster our missile program. We were having serious budget problems: the fiscal 1958 budget was $71.8 billion, the highest in peacetime history, the government had borrowed up to its legal debt limit, and we had to prepare the fiscal 1959 budget with still higher defense spending. The Administration also had to complete its legislative program, the State of the Union message, the budget and economic messages for the opening days of Congress in January.

The medical report that morning, after the doctors had again examined the President, contained good news and bad. The President had suffered a "mild" stroke which affected only his ability to speak. His mind and reasoning powers were not involved. There were no symptoms of paralysis (such as struck down Woodrow Wilson). But the bad news was that the doctors said they could not tell whether this might be only the first in a series of more damaging strokes. The doctors prescribed sixty days of complete rest from the pressures of his job, if possible, or an extreme lightening of the work load. The idea, in simple terms, was to free him from any problems which might make his blood pressure rise dangerously.

I am sure that if the stroke had come before the heart attack, it would potentially have been a disaster as far as the orderly operation of the government was concerned. But following the first siege, everyone on the team was experienced in handling this type of crisis. For me, although my actual work load was far greater than it had been in 1955, the burden was easier. My responsibilities and prerogatives were more clearly defined and understood, and my actions more readily accepted. The eggs upon which I had to tread had harder shells.

The very first morning, there was general agreement that I should represent Eisenhower at the December 16 meeting of NATO. No one expected the President to be well enough for so arduous an undertaking. Dulles sent word to Paris asking if the NATO heads of state would agree to meet with America's No. 2 man. The answer was yes. Nor were any eyebrows raised when I participated in defense policy conferences throughout that day with Defense Secretary Neil McElroy, Deputy Defense Secretary Donald Quarles, Missile Director William Holaday, and Presidential Science Adviser James Killian. Nor were there any repercussions when I spoke to the press informally as I was leaving the White House at the end of the day. In fact, Sherman Adams and Jerry Persons urged me to see the press and help straighten out a mix-up in which some of the reporters had misinterpreted the White House announcement of the stroke as meaning the President had had another heart attack.

Jim Hagerty returned from Europe and, at the request of the reporters, arranged my first and the only formal White House press conference I was ever to have. In both meetings with the press, my task was to reassure the nation and the world that President Eisenhower was making a rapid recovery, had no intention of resigning, and that the Administration was carrying on business as usual.

The public reacted quite differently to the stroke than it had to the heart attack. A mental illness is somehow more terrifying than a physical one. During the heart attack, the nation worried if the President would live or die but not about his ability to carry on if he recovered. This was not the case during the stroke. The public seemed to say: okay, he may get well, but will he ever be the same again? I received hundreds of letters evoking the mythology of the dark ages on insanity, mental aberrations, and the like.

A considerable segment of the press, including a cross section of political persuasion, called on the President to resign. Even the New York *Post*, the most anti-Nixon of all newspapers, said editorially: "The issue is whether the U. S. is to have Richard Nixon as President or no President. We choose Nixon." The Washington *Post*, the Providence *Journal*, and columnist Walter Lippmann said the President should delegate his powers to me temporarily for the period of his convalescence.

The problem of maintaining public confidence was far greater in November 1957 than it had been back in 1955, probably because now the President was sixty-seven years old, had had three major illnesses, and his second term stretched out for three more years. Few newspapers failed to mention the fact that if the President survived he would be past seventy, the oldest President in history at the end of his term of office. Several newspapers, periodicals, and columnists recalled the President's own words on resigning, spoken at a press conference back on March 7, 1956: "I have said unless I felt absolutely up to the performance of the duties of the President, the second that I didn't, I would no longer be there in the job or I wouldn't be available for the job."

But the President reacted quite differently to the stroke than he had to the heart attack. In 1955 there had been great periods of indecision and despondency when he thought he really wanted to give up, retire, and rest. After the stroke, he fought back. He followed his doctors' advice and took it easy around his living quarters for three days, but on the fourth day, aware of the public doubts about his ability, he escorted Mrs. Eisenhower to church. It was Thanksgiving Day, and I remember it particularly because when I got home for my Thanksgiving meal after seeing Mohammed V off at the airport, I found that Julie, my younger daughter, who was then nine, had made separate place cards for each one in the family. Written on a page from one of my yellow pads, in red crayon, mine read: BE STRONG—BE WISE—BE THOUGHT-FUL—BE KIND.

Throughout the next two weeks, the President, rather than resting, pushed himself into ever-increasing activity, attended meetings, conferred with staff and, while many lesser chores were routed to subordinates, reacted belligerently when anyone tried to shield him from an important issue. "Either I run this damn show, or I'll resign," he said on more than one occasion. But the emphasis always was on his running the "damn show," not on resigning. Extremely sensitive to any suggestion that he was not able to do the job, the President brushed aside any expressions of sympathy and struggled to avoid giving any impression of weakness or disability.

Now he spoke of "dying with my boots on" and insisted on going to the NATO meeting in Paris. He wanted to hold a press conference before leaving to prove to the press that he was able to carry on, but I joined Hagerty and others in convincing him that the trip to NATO alone would reassure the nation of his health.

Actually the President went through a terribly agonizing period of frustration with his ailment. The problem was that the ideas produced by his ever-active mind were dammed up. He could not think of the words to express them. His cerebral occlusion affected the area of his brain which communicated his thoughts into words. The block scrambled the chain of communication and the words would not match the thoughts. However, the President's attack was mild. Within twenty-four hours there was a noticeable improvement in his speech, leaving only an occasional mix-up of words. For instance, the President might want to say "tomorrow," but instead, "yesterday" would come out, or he would become temporarily blocked on a particular word. To a man as high-strung as Eisenhower, this difficulty became at times extremely frustrating and irritating, and he had been warned by his doctors that such frustration might aggravate his injury or cause another stroke. This made it doubly frustrating.[1]

Among friends and intimates he could laugh off the occasional blooper, but he was very sensitive about it with others. Normally a fast talker, he was forced now to measure and choose his words.

During this period, those of us around him did our best to help him keep his spirits up. I recall one conversation we had after he had met with the congressional leaders for the first time since his stroke. The meeting had gone extremely well, but I could see that he had been distressed by minor slips in pronouncing words which others around the

---

[1] I thought that some of the press coverage of the President's difficulties in this period was unnecessarily savage and sadistic. Some reporters insisted on counting up and duly reporting the exact number of "fluffs"—actual or imagined—the President might make in a speech or press conference. Knowing what agony he was going through, I would become so infuriated on reading such reports that on more than one occasion I slammed the paper or magazine into the fireplace.

table had not even noticed. Consequently I called Ann Whitman and made an appointment to see him that afternoon. I reported to him that the unanimous opinion of the legislative leaders was that he had carried off the meeting with no difficulty. Lev Saltonstall who sat next to me at the Cabinet table at these meetings, I told him, had arrived late while the President was talking and had leaned over to me and whispered that he was unable to notice any word difficulty whatever.

The President was obviously relieved and pleased to get this report. He had attended this meeting before the doctors' schedule for recovery from the stroke indicated it would be wise for him to participate in such conferences. But he said he had to prove to himself that he was able to do the job. If he had been unable to come to this meeting, it would have been necessary for him to do some "very hard and tough thinking about the future."

I also pointed out that the columnists and editorial writers who were suggesting that he should delegate duties or should resign, and who were criticizing him on the ground that he could no longer be a full-time, vigorous President, were for the most part in the camp of those who never really had been for him. I said they had simply been waiting for some incident which would give them an excuse for expressing their opposition openly.

He smiled and said that he didn't pay any attention to the columnists because he didn't read what they wrote. But I knew that this was one of his stock statements which was not actually based on facts. Jim Hagerty had told me before I went in to see the President that he had been reading a considerable number of columns and editorials and had been disturbed by the tone they were taking.

I urged the President not to let his critics in the press force him into a course of action which was not in the best interests of his health or of the presidency. I pointed out that he was vitally needed—that the whole country realized how imperative it was for him to make the great decisions affecting our future, and that he owed a duty to keep himself in shape to make those decisions. I suggested that without any public announcement he could talk to his Cabinet and the intimate members of his staff and suggest that they should undertake to process some of the problems before they reached him for final decision. I noted that particularly in the domestic field there was no reason why a Cabinet officer had to come to him every time he had a decision to make.

He told me that he was going to Gettysburg over the weekend and that in his absence he did not feel it was necessary for me or others on the White House staff to undertake any of the responsibilities of holding meetings. He pointed out that this was in my best interests, too, because of the possible impression otherwise of my stepping in and exerting authority.

As distinguished from the situation during the heart attack, he now wanted no impression whatever to be left either that he was not running the show or was unable to run it. He told me for the first time that he was considering the advisability of writing a letter to me in which he would state expressly what he wanted the Vice President to do in the event of presidential illness. Finally he indicated that looking to the future he was going to watch carefully how he recovered his health and that if he did not progress beyond the point that he currently had reached, he would have to make a decision to relinquish some or all of his duties. The continued frustration of being unable to express himself would create too great a risk of another injury, which would leave the country in very bad shape. Before I left, I pointed out that in his conversation with me, which lasted almost an hour, he had hardly had any noticeable difficulty with his words. I said that he was a man who was greatly blessed in that—clearly apart from his present difficulty—he always had had a mind that worked much faster than his mouth, and that with most people the situation was reversed. He laughed and said that this reminded him of the joke about the politician who could always be counted on to have his mouth open and his mind closed.

The question of delegating authority during a President's temporary disability came up for discussion several times during this period. It had become apparent that the Democratic Congress would not go along with the Administration's or anyone's plan to allow the Vice President to become acting President during the President's disability. Eisenhower had put Herbert Brownell, then Attorney General, to work after the heart attack on a plan of delegating authority, but it got nowhere. After the stroke, Bill Rogers, who had by then succeeded Brownell, went into the problem; legislation was prepared by the Administration and had bipartisan support, but again Congress would do nothing on the subject. The reason was purely political and obvious. The Democratic congressional leaders would not approve any plan which might put Richard Nixon in the White House before the 1960 election. The press had already portrayed me as being on the "threshold" of the presidency; the Democratic politicians wanted no part in carrying me across that threshold.

The President's eye was on something far more important than the political implications: he wanted someone there with the authority to act in his behalf in a crisis or national emergency if he should again become incapacitated. The problem of presidential disability is complex, dating back to the Constitutional Convention in 1787 when Delaware's Delegate John Dickinson brought it up and got no answer.

Authorities and experts have written books on the subject, all dealing with the ambiguity of Article II, Section I, Clause 5 of the Constitution, which says:

In case of the removal of the President from office, or of his death, resignation, or inability to discharge the powers and duties of the said office, the same shall devolve on the Vice President, and the Congress may by law provide for the case of removal, death, resignation, or inability, both of the President and Vice President, declaring what officer shall then act as President, and such officer shall act accordingly, until the disability be removed, or a President shall be elected.

Simply stated, this clause does not make clear: who decides when the President is unable to discharge the powers and duties of his office? just what devolves upon the Vice President, the "powers and duties" or the "office" itself? can the President resume office once he has given it up? who decides if the President is well enough to resume his office, if he can at all?

Anyone, I think, can imagine two dozen troublesome contingencies which might become involved in passing the powers of a President to a Vice President, and constitutional lawyers, who have studied the question for more than a hundred years, can think of two hundred more. President Eisenhower, after studying the problem closely, was intent on solving the practical problem of giving his Vice President the authority to act immediately in a crisis, if necessary. He mentioned several alternatives, but kept coming back to the idea of writing a letter which would give the Vice President alone the authority to decide when the President was unable to carry on—that is, when the President himself was unable to make the decision.

In early February, the President called Rogers and me into his office, commented that he thought he had licked the problem, and handed each of us a copy of a letter. Then he leaned back in his chair and, while we followed on our copies, he read a four-page letter to us, beginning, "Dear Dick." We made some minor suggestions and he incorporated them into the letter and then sent it on to his secretary, Ann Whitman, for final typing. Marked PERSONAL AND SECRET, one copy went to me, one to Bill Rogers as Attorney General, and one to John

Foster Dulles, as Secretary of State and ranking member of the Cabinet.

With the exception of our very minor suggestions, the letter was wholly Eisenhower's in concept and drafting, and it was a masterpiece. Leaving the White House, Bill Rogers remarked that Eisenhower would have made an outstanding lawyer, for the letter handled the contingencies of a very complex problem from every angle and was as good a drafting job as any constitutional expert could have done.

The President made public the following key paragraphs:

The President and the Vice President have agreed that the following procedures are in accord with the purposes and provisions of Article 2, Section 1, of the Constitution, dealing with Presidential inability. They believe that these procedures, which are intended to apply to themselves only, are in no sense outside or contrary to the Constitution but are consistent with its present provisions and implement its clear intent.

(1) In the event of inability the President would—if possible—so inform the Vice President, and the Vice President would serve as Acting President, exercising the powers and duties of the office until the inability had ended.

(2) In the event of an inability which would prevent the President from so communicating with the Vice President, the Vice President, after such consultation as seems to him appropriate under the circumstances, would decide upon the devolution of the powers and duties of the Office and would serve as Acting President until the inability had ended.

(3) The President, in either event, would determine when the inability had ended and at that time would resume the full exercise of the powers and duties of the Office.

This letter established historical precedent. Eisenhower was the first President in American history to take cognizance of and act upon a serious gap in our Constitution. President Kennedy, even before his inauguration, drew up an identical list of procedures for his Vice President, Lyndon Johnson, to follow in exercising the rights and duties of the President in the event of Kennedy's incapacity. The new Administration adopted in its entirety the section of the Eisenhower letter which was made public, and it would be fair to assume that President Kennedy's successor will follow the precedent.

But what must be clearly understood is that the agreement President Eisenhower set forth in his letter to me, and the one President Kennedy has entered into with Vice President Johnson, are only as good as the will of the parties to keep them. Presidents and Vice Presidents have

not always had the mutual trust and the cordial relations President
Eisenhower had with me or that President Kennedy has had with Vice
President Johnson up to this time. Jealousies and rivalries can develop
within an Administration which could completely destroy such an
agreement.

Only a constitutional amendment can solve the problem on a permanent basis. President Eisenhower's agreement with me was personal
and had the force of his authority only during his term of office. President Kennedy's agreement is similarly limited. These agreements,
which are mere expressions of a President's desires, do not have the
force of law. Even a law passed by Congress might be subject to constitutional challenge. However, such a law would express the will of
Congress and should be passed while the incumbent President is in
good health and before a presidential election year drags politics into
an already complex problem. The experiences of Garfield, Wilson, and
Eisenhower should have taught us a lesson. Surely the time has come
for a truly bipartisan program to draw up a constitutional amendment
which would define the rights and duties of a Vice President during
any period when the President of the United States is incapacitated.

The urgent need for such an amendment becomes crystal clear when
a President is disabled, but that is precisely the time when politics bar
any reasonable agreement on the wording of such an amendment.
The time to begin solving this problem is now, when the incumbent
President is in good health and at a safe distance from the politics of a
presidential election year. It is hardly necessary to point out that these
perilous times in which we live will continue, and more than ever before our nation will need an able and healthy Chief Executive or acting
Chief Executive at all times.

Action on this problem will have important side effects as well. It
will assure the continued useful employment of the Vice President as a
deputy of the President rather than as a fifth wheel in the government,
another precedent established by Eisenhower. The Vice President
will thus become an integrated member of the incumbent Administration, able and ready to take over the rights and duties of the President
if it becomes necessary. This being true, it also will bolster the new
political trend of selecting capable men as vice presidential nominees,
men to whom the presidential nominee would be willing to turn over
his duties during a period of disability, rather than the selection of
men solely on geographical, factional, or party appeasement considerations.

The heart attack, the ileitis operation, and the stroke were terribly difficult personal crises for President Eisenhower. They were to a less and different extent personal crises for me. But even more, they were potential constitutional crises of the greatest magnitude for the nation. If such a crisis should arise in the future, its outcome should not be dependent upon the personal whims of whoever happens to hold the offices of President and Vice President, but on the law of the land, as approved by the Congress or as set forth in the Constitution.

Caracas

The classic crisis is one involving physical danger. What is essential in such situations is not so much "bravery" in the face of danger as the ability to think "selflessly"—to blank-out any thought of personal fear by concentrating completely on how to meet the danger.

OF all the trips I made abroad as Vice President the one I least wanted to take was my visit to South America in 1958—not because I thought it would be difficult but because I thought it would be relatively unimportant and uninteresting compared to the assignments I had in Washington at that time.

Early in March 1958, Roy R. Rubottom, Jr., the Assistant Secretary of State for Latin American Affairs, called on me in my office. He said that the State Department wanted me to represent the United States at the inauguration of Arturo Frondizi as President of Argentina. He said there were several reasons why they wanted someone of my rank to head the usual delegation of dignitaries for this event. South America needed recognition at the highest level. Argentina was a symbol of the new tides that were beginning to emerge throughout this hemisphere. Juan Peron had been the strongest of the dictators and had been overthrown. A responsible group of men forming a military junta had taken over and now after the first free election in twenty years, Frondizi was to be inaugurated.

It was essential, Rubottom pointed out, that the highest official available for such assignments from the United States attend the inauguration to help knock down the widespread impression in Latin America that the United States had sympathized with Peron.

I told Rubottom that I could see the merits of his arguments but I could not spare the time for a trip outside the country because of my current heavy work load in Washington. Nineteen fifty-eight was an election year. Despite President Eisenhower's landslide in 1956, we had not won the Congress and the prospects were that we would lose more seats in the fall. I thought I should stay in Washington to help make preparations for the campaign and to participate in the discussions going on within the Administration as to how to fight the deepening recession which was causing increasing concern throughout the country. Also, I did not believe that a "purely protocol" trip which Rubottom had described, where I would be one of sixty or seventy dignitaries from foreign countries, would afford enough of an opportunity for serious constructive conversations with the new government leaders to justify my leaving my duties in Washington. For these reasons, I told him flatly that I could not make the trip.

But Rubottom, a career foreign service officer, was not only persuasive, he was persistent. He also knew how to get things done in Washington. The day after his first visit to my office, I received a call from my long-time friend and original mentor in the foreign affairs field, Christian Herter, who was then Under Secretary of State. I had the highest regard and respect for Herter and I heard him out as he described the need for some dramatic gesture of recognition from the United States of the new government in Argentina. But I still said no.

A few days later, Foster Dulles dropped in on me one evening at my home and after discussing some other subjects he brought up the proposed trip. Like the master advocate he was, he analyzed my reasons for wanting to stay in Washington against the need for me to make the trip. He argued that it was essential for our foreign policy not only for me to appear at Frondizi's inauguration but also, if possible, to arrange to stop in several other South American countries.

The next day, after a Cabinet meeting at the White House, President Eisenhower asked me to step into his office. He mentioned that he had been speaking to his brother, Milton, and to Dulles and that they felt a tour of South America at this time would be of considerable long-range benefit to the nation. He said that while he understood my commitments in Washington were also of top importance he hoped I could somehow find time to fit in a brief assignment in the Southern Hemisphere.

This was the way, incidentally, Eisenhower always broached assignments he wanted me to undertake. He recognized that the Constitution had established the presidency and vice presidency as separate and independent offices. He never ordered me to do something. He would wonder aloud if I might like to take over this or that project, always couching his recommendations in terms which would cause no embarrassment to either of us if I preferred to say no. There was, of course, never an occasion when I did not willingly accept the assignments he suggested.

When I called Rubottom the next day I was somewhat irritated at him for boxing me in so neatly. But I had to admit to myself that he deserved considerable credit for his skill and follow-through in accomplishing an objective he thought was vital to the interests of his department and the nation. When I authorized him to make the preliminary arrangements I knew from my conversation with Dulles that the trip would be extended beyond the protocol visit to Argentina. Consequently I warned Rubottom, "Under no circumstances do I want to be away from Washington for more than one week—that is, from take-off to landing at National Airport, one week." He said that he would carry out my wishes in that respect. I figured that having given him a week, I had probably limited the trip to no more than ten days.

But even this was unrealistic. As word got out that I was going to Argentina, invitations poured into the State Department from other South American countries, accompanied by urgent requests from our own Ambassadors, that they be included on my trip. First Uruguay, Argentina's small but proud neighbor to the north, asked for "equal treatment." Then Rubottom came to me with invitations from Colombia and Venezuela. Both these countries had just rid themselves of dictators and they, too, felt entitled to a visit which would signify a United States salute of "well done."

As I looked into the information on Venezuela, I found that the provisional junta in Caracas was rather shaky and inexperienced and was having trouble dealing with the vigorous, well-financed, and meticulously organized Communist Party within its borders. I concluded that this well-motivated non-Communist junta needed all the encouragement and support from the United States it could get before the elections of a new permanent government later in the year.

I added Colombia to the list because after ten years of oppression and anarchy, its dictator, Gustavo Rojas Pinilla, had been overthrown and Alberto Lleras Camargo, an enlightened and dedicated statesman, had been elected President of a free representative government. I looked forward to the opportunity of helping demonstrate the United States' gratification over this turn of events in Colombia.

But I found after we had gone this far, we had to go all the way.

Rubottom persuaded me to visit all the nations in South America on a quick and intensive tour—excluding only Brazil, which I had visited on the occasion of the inauguration of President Kubitschek, and Chile, whose Chief of State would be in Washington at the time of my tour. Consequently, when the itinerary was finally settled, the "no more than one week, one country trip" had been stretched to a two-and-a-half week tour of eight countries with a short, informal stop in Trinidad, capital of the newly created West Indies Federation.

I plunged into an intensive program of predeparture briefings and research with the State Department, the Central Intelligence Agency, and other sources of information. I read volumes of memoranda and situation papers so that I would be up-to-date with the best available information on the political and economic problems of each of the countries I visited. This was the groundwork which I had found to be essential in other trips I had made overseas.

This was to be my seventh major trip abroad as Vice President and by this time I had convinced the career men in the State Department that I should use such visits not only to talk to government leaders but also to meet the opinion makers and people in all walks of life. I had long ago won my battle with those in the State Department who had taken a dim view of my practice of trying to make contact with the people as well as the leaders of foreign countries. Rubottom welcomed my suggestion to schedule representative meetings with groups of university students, labor leaders, editors, and other opinion makers.

I wanted to do more than simply mouth prepared platitudes designed to avoid trouble. I was determined to meet and answer head on some of the attacks which were currently being made against the United States in Latin America.

Allen Dulles informed me of intelligence estimates on the possibility of anti-American demonstrations in two or three of the capitals I was to visit. But there were no intimations of any possible violence.

Consequently when several newspapermen in Washington asked me if it would be worth their while to accompany me, I told them off the record that the trip had all the evidences of being routine and dull from a news standpoint and not worth their publishers' expense. Some of Washington's top newspaper and magazine reporters relied on my advice and stayed home. They probably will never stop needling me for that prediction. The trip produced one of the top news stories of the year.

No journey ever started out in a less exciting way and ended more dramatically than this one to South America. It was a bleak and drizzly day on April 27 when my wife and I said our formal good-bys at Washington's National Airport to the Ambassadors and Embassy representatives of the countries we were to visit. We reassured our two girls, Tricia, who was eleven, and Julie, who was two years younger, that this was going to be just like a short vacation and that we would be home in less than three weeks.

Trinidad was only a refueling stop for our special Air Force plane but it afforded me time for a friendly conversation with Sir Grantley Adams, Prime Minister of the new nation known as the West Indies Federation.

The first official stop on our eighteen-day journey was Montevideo, Uruguay. Uruguayan government leaders were out in full force and greeted me with the Latin *embraso*, which can best be described as a good-natured bear hug, which is much more expressive of friendship than our northern handshake. After making our informal arrival statements, we proceeded in a motorcade through the center of the city. Thousands of friendly, cheering people lined the streets. It was not until I reached the hotel that I learned that when we had passed Uruguay's University of the Republic there had been some students carrying placards reading FUERA NIXON which translated means "Go home, Nixon." I didn't consider the report at all significant. The number of pickets had been so small I hadn't even noticed them.

But the next morning, Bill Key, my administrative assistant, brought me the press reports. The carefully prepared statement I had made on arrival and the warm and friendly reception from thousands of Montevideans received only passing attention. The headlines and news stories in South America and in the United States featured the sign-carrying pickets. It was the old story I had learned long ago: the unusual or the controversial event always makes "news" over the expected or routine occurrences, even though the latter may be a more accurate picture of the true situation. I decided I should do something, if possible, to counteract these first press reports.

Robert Woodward, our Ambassador in Montevideo, urged me not to overestimate Communist activity in Uruguay. The Communists had made little headway in this pro-Western country, he said. The most active Communist network was centered in the University's law school, but even there a substantial majority of students were not Communists. I told the Ambassador that I felt I should point up that fact by making an unannounced stop at the University before leaving Uruguay the next day. We made plans to keep my unscheduled stop a secret so that the hard core of Communist agitators would have no advance notice of my coming.

The next morning as our motorcade was moving toward the airport we went by the University. I saw a few students on the grounds and ordered our cars stopped. Mrs. Nixon and I went up the steps of the University administration building and walked toward the law school wing with the Ambassador, Colonel Vernon Walters, my interpreter, and Jack Sherwood, my Secret Service escort. Events worked out as I had hoped they would. Word that I was there spread like wildfire through the school. Students swarmed around, asking for autographs, shaking hands as I moved into one of the law school classrooms. The room was soon jammed with students. I told them that I wanted to answer any questions they had with regard to United States policy toward Uruguay and other Latin American countries.

For almost an hour they questioned me about alleged U. S. imperialism, unfair trade practices, economic exploitation, and support of dictatorships in South America. No problem between the United States and Uruguay, real or imagined, was overlooked or bypassed, and because of my intensive briefing, I was able to answer each one directly and honestly.

The Communists, of course, could not take this lying down and toward the end of the session they got in some of their typical questions. But they had not had time to pack the audience. As we left the administration building, students crowded the staircases, the corridors, and the grounds. The Communist leaders regrouped their forces and tried to distribute some of their literature while shouting anti-United States slogans. But they ran into a hornet's nest of opposition. The students were so overwhelmingly on our side that they tore up the pamphlets, shouted down the hecklers and called out at the tops of their voices in Spanish, "Long live United States and Uruguayan friendship."

Back in the car, Woodward could not have been more pleased. A characteristic of Latin Americans, he told me, was their zest for controversy, admiration of courage, and contempt for fear or timidity. Nothing could have pleased and complimented them more than my unexpected visit. In the newspapers the next day the stories of my University visit and its reception canceled out the first day's reports of anti-American sentiment in Uruguay.

In Argentina, our next stop, my schedule was arranged so that I could attend all the inaugural functions and still undertake other activities.

I threw the switch that energized an Argentine atomic research reactor, powered with uranium provided by our government. This gave me an opportunity to speak of the promise that the peaceful development of atomic energy offered to the people of South America in helping to eliminate poverty and disease under a democratic way of life.

I spoke and answered questions at length before two labor groups and at the Buenos Aires University. The Communists are making massive efforts to infiltrate the labor unions and the universities in each nation of South America, and the United States programs directed toward these groups in South America, and in other parts of the world, are pitifully inadequate by comparison. I had long believed that we spend too much time concentrating on the elite groups who happen to be in power in government and too little time on those who represent the future in the Latin American countries. Our programs for labor and university groups are too heavily weighted on the side of impersonal propaganda. Communists are concentrating on organizing individual students, teachers, union leaders, and members into effective and powerful activist groups.

To the labor groups here, as in other countries I visited, I emphasized the incompatibility of free labor and dictatorships of either the right or the left. No Communist government will tolerate a free labor movement. I told the story of how the Communists, masquerading as champions of the legitimate aspirations of working men, tried to infiltrate the trade union movement in the United States and even succeeded to an extent. In time, true labor leaders saw the danger and threw the Communists out of American unions. From then on, organized labor moved ahead substantially, contributing both to the welfare of its members and the country as a whole.

My union audiences asked me some tough and provocative questions. But I was confronted with one of my most difficult problems not in the discussion period but at a mammoth *asado,* which can best be described as a South American barbecue party, given for Mrs. Nixon and me by one of the largest labor unions in Argentina. The main dish was beef barbecued over an open fire, Gaucho style, with the animal hair still on it. Sides of beef were cut out, placed against a vertical grill alongside the fire in such a way that the meat was cooked and the hair, on the side away from the fire, was not scorched. Pat and I found that trying to eat the beef without getting a mouthful of hair presented an even greater "crisis" than we had experienced in trying to eat a Chinese forty-course dinner with chopsticks in Hong Kong in 1953. The trick was to eat the beef like a melon, carefully cutting out squares of beef and leaving the skin and hair on the plate. The origin of the dish goes back to the days of the Gauchos who cooked enough beef for several days of riding the range, leaving the hair on to protect the cooked meat from dirt and insects.

On my visit to Buenos Aires University I learned that some Latin American students do not fit the definition of students as we know them in the United States. In Latin America, a young man may make a profession of being a student and more often than not that young man is a Communist functionary "studying" in order to indoctrinate younger students with the promises of Marxism.

Consequently, when I asked for questions at the University, Gregorio Selser, a well-known Communist newspaper writer who was thirty-four years old, shouted down other students and stood up to ask a question. His question was a twenty-minute tirade, a good part of which he read from a prepared text, straight out of the Communist line on every international controversy. I recognized him as the leader of the group which had handed out anti-American leaflets outside the University and I let him go on until he had finished. Then I remarked that he had forgotten to ask a question, and proceeded to answer his charges point by point, no matter how slanted, loaded, or ridiculous they seemed. This was a practice I followed in all discussions before student groups. My objective was not to convert the agitators, which I realized was impossible, but to convince those in the audience who might otherwise have been taken in by such persistent and shamefully false propaganda against the United States.

An important phase of my trip to Argentina was the conferences I held with business leaders and the officials of the new Frondizi government. In these meetings we discussed the severe economic problems facing the new government. The Peron dictatorship had plundered the country and left it at the brink of bankruptcy, torn politically by the extremists of the left and of the right. Controversy bordering on confusion enveloped the new government as it faced seemingly insoluble economic problems. Many observers privately were giving the Frondizi government only three months to live. But Frondizi courageously and firmly proceeded to steer a middle course between the extremists, and with the cooperation of the United States Government he has become one of the strongest and most respected leaders of the Western Hemisphere. One of his major achievements was to devise a formula for the development of Argentina's vast oil resources by privately owned companies while retaining "ownership" of the oil by the people—an absolute must from an Argentine political standpoint.

When I returned to Washington I recommended all-out cooperation with Frondizi and his government. As I flew from Argentina to Paraguay, I realized that Rubottom had been right. My four days in Argentina alone had been worth the trip.

Paraguay presented then and now a difficult problem in diplomacy for our State Department. It was, and still is at this writing, the last one-man dictatorship in continental South America. All of Latin America is sensitive to its long history of dictatorships, some of which were as oppressive as the Communist variety. The State Department added Paraguay to my trip agenda, knowing full well it was like throwing a bone to the American-hating elements elsewhere along my tour. But this was a country with a long history of friendship for the United States, one with which we had normal relations. There was no diplomatic reason to snub it pointedly.

United States policy toward all of Latin America was set with the Montevideo Pact of 1933, pledging non-intervention in the internal affairs of any country. The United States can and does show its true feelings when a country overthrows a dictator by coming to the aid of the succeeding regime if it is set up on democratic principles. This we had done in Argentina and Colombia. In order to indicate U. S. sentiments toward dictatorships, the State Department had limited my visit to Paraguay to a day. In each of the seven other nations I visited I spent two, three, or four days. This point, I am sure, was not missed in diplomatic circles where every nuance of protocol and procedure is studied. But it was not widely understood publicly. In my talks with General Alfredo Stroessner, President and strong man controlling the government since 1954, and in a speech to a special joint session of the Paraguayan National Congress, I noted with approval the strong opposition of the Paraguayan government to Communism. But I emphasized that the most effective way to fight Communism was not by setting up an opposing system of totalitarianism but by establishing a government based on political and economic freedom.

I do not know how much good, if any, my expressions had in Paraguay. They were not reported in the controlled Paraguayan press, for obvious reasons, and they got little play elsewhere because these sentiments are so familiar.

When I returned to Washington I proposed that the United States could abide by its non-intervention agreement and still indicate more strongly its preference for free governments over dictatorships in South and Central America by a policy of a "formal handshake for dictators; an *embraso* for leaders in freedom."

When we arrived at the airport in La Paz, the picturesque capital of Bolivia, we were still 13,000 feet above sea level, the highest altitude of any commercial airport in the world. Dave Ball, our airplane steward handling the baggage, fainted because of overexertion at high altitude. Despite the thin air, our reception throughout our two and a half days in Bolivia could not have been warmer or more friendly. A few Communist hecklers carrying anti-American signs were in evidence, but their efforts were literally snowed under by the thousands of cheering people who lined the streets as we traveled through the city and the surrounding countryside.

Yet Bolivia is the saddest example of abject poverty in continental South America. The country's economy is based on tin and, at the time of my visit, the world demand for tin was at an all-time low. Its mines were depleted, its mining methods outmoded, its agriculture poor and backward. Inflation was so fantastic that its standard piece of currency, the boliviano, was worth $\frac{1}{1000}$ of a U. S. penny.

Politically it was a free country but its leaders were so torn by ancient political and personal feuds and rivalries that its problems seemed to defy even a beginning to a solution. To help prevent mass starvation, the United States had provided over fifty million dollars' worth of surplus food and forty million dollars for special projects to bolster the economy during the four years preceding my visit.

While reviewing Bolivia's economic plight, President Hernan Siles pointed to the pictures of his two predecessors on the walls of his office. One, he said, had become despondent at the futility of his own efforts and had committed suicide. The other had been taken by a mob and hung from a lamppost in the street outside the window of the President's office. "I often wonder what my fate will be," he said with a wry smile.

From La Paz to Lima, the three-hour flight provided an opportunity for me to review the briefing papers on Peru prior to arrival. Peru is one of the most advanced nations of South America economically and culturally. No other country in Latin America has a longer history of friendship with the United States. Our economic ties have been close and mutually beneficial for many years. This had been particularly true during the administration of Peru's President, Manuel Prado, who had won power two years before in a free election, ending a long period of dictatorship in the land of the Incas.

However, the briefing papers also showed that Peru now was in the grip of several problems. There was evidence that the Prado regime was becoming shaky. For the past several months, Peru's economy had been sliding into a recession parallel to the situation in the United States at the time. This had caused several sore points in our relations with Peru. For example, copper, Peru's chief mineral export, had dropped in price in the world market from 46 to 25 cents. Lead and zinc posed similar problems, and the Peruvians feared their entire mineral industry, and particularly copper exports, would be ruined if the United States adopted certain import restrictions being advanced in Congress to protect our own depressed mineral industry.

The government of Peru objected even more strongly to the United States program of "dumping" our enormous surplus of cotton on the world market. Cotton was Peru's most important export and the Peruvians were complaining that we were crippling an important segment of their economy. In addition to economic troubles, Peru was involved at this time with another flare-up in their century-old dispute with Ecuador over the demarcation of the border between the two countries, which lay somewhere in the torrid Amazon Basin wilderness.

However, I was assured by Rubottom that from a social and diplomatic standpoint no capital in the hemisphere would provide a more gracious and friendly welcome. The briefing papers said that there were potential political troubles under the surface—that while the Communist Party was illegal, the laws against it were not enforced. But all in all I expected this visit to be a pleasant interlude after some rather difficult experiences on some of our previous stops.

At Lima Airport our reception could not have been more gracious and regal. But as we motorcaded into the center of the city, I sensed an air of suspense and uneasiness. There were not many people on the streets and most of those who were there did not seem to be aware of who we were. The few who recognized us greeted us with either indifference or a shrill whistle, which is the Latin American equivalent of the Bronx cheer. The Peruvian government official riding with me explained that the government had played down our arrival and had not published the motorcade route to avoid any "incidents." But, he assured me, my appearances the next day had been publicized and I would be welcomed by big, friendly crowds. His words were somewhat disquieting since I had not anticipated any "incidents" in friendly Peru.

In my suite at the elegant, old-world Grand Hotel Bolivar, in the center of the city, members of my staff reported that thousands of leaflets were being distributed throughout the city summoning all "students, workers, employees" to gather at San Marcos University the next morning to prevent me from speaking there. JOIN US—GATHER TO SHOUT WITH ALL YOUR FORCES—OUT NIXON—DEATH TO YANKEE IMPERIAL-ISM, said one leaflet, which referred to me as "the most insolent representative of monopolistic trusts." The leaflet was signed "The Communist Committee, Lima District."

Although the Constitution of Peru specifically outlawed the Communist Party, it was obvious that the government had done little to implement the law and that the Communist Party was operating openly throughout the country.

My two days' schedule in Peru was so tightly drawn that I had only time enough in the hotel to change clothes for my formal call on President Prado and for his state luncheon in honor of Mrs. Nixon and myself. But I asked Colonel Robert E. Cushman, Jr., my Assistant for National Security Affairs and chief of my personal staff, to check on the situation at San Marcos University. I had received invitations before leaving Washington to appear at the leading university in each of the countries I was to visit, and I did not want to bypass San Marcos. Established in 1551, it was the oldest seat of education and culture in the Western Hemisphere and one of the most revered.

The state luncheon was an example of Latin American cordiality and elegance at its best. Never have I attended a state luncheon or dinner in Washington or in any other capital which surpassed it. Conversation flowed with the finest vintage French wines, but no one brought up the Communist "incidents" which had been staged for my arrival.

After the three-hour luncheon, I had to rush to meet my schedule commitments for the afternoon. I placed a wreath at a monument, visited a cultural institute, had a private talk with the President of the Peruvian Senate, met with a group of labor leaders, and hurried back to my hotel to change into formal dress for a reception and dinner at the American Embassy.

In the sumptuous ballroom of the Embassy, Mrs. Nixon and I exchanged greetings with members of the diplomatic colony and with high-ranking Peruvian government, business, and church leaders. Miss Peru (Miss Gladys Zender), who had just won the 1958 Miss Universe beauty contest, was one of the centers of attraction among a group of exquisitely gowned women at the reception.

After the guests had passed through the receiving line and the reception was well under way, Don Hughes, my military aide, whispered that Ambassador Theodore Achilles had asked if I would step into the next room to discuss our next day's schedule. With Achilles were Rubottom; his deputy, Maurice Bernbaum, who was Director of South American Affairs; and three members of my own staff, Bob Cushman, Don Hughes, and Bill Key. Their reports added up to the fact that we had a crisis on our hands: should I go to San Marcos University as scheduled despite the threatened demonstrations? Or should I skip the visit and perhaps be pictured as running away from anti-American Peruvians? It was apparent that the Communists, after the failure of their efforts to disrupt my tour in Uruguay, Argentina, or Bolivia, had decided to make an all-out effort to embarrass me and the United States at San Marcos University, an institution so well known throughout Latin America that whatever happened there would be front-page news everywhere. Rubottom reported that the Communist agitators had been successful in sucking many non-Communist students at the University into their program for a mass demonstration. If I went to the University, he said, it would be difficult to avoid violence. The others joined in, adding that there would be an element of personal danger to me and that if anything happened to me, even a minor incident, it would be a news sensation throughout South America which might be detrimental to the United States.

As I listened to these reports, I could not help but think of the irony of this scene. Here we were discussing how to cope with a potential mob riot while in the next room the elite of Lima were dancing, talking, and imbibing in the great hall of the American Embassy. We could hear the laughter and the tinkle of champagne glasses as we sat discussing the deadly serious question of what we should do the next day.

I was told that the Rector of San Marcos had confided to an Embassy official the hope that I would cancel my scheduled visit and thus avoid possible personal danger. The Lima Chief of Police had expressed the same view to a member of my staff.

I told the group that I did not want to cancel my widely advertised visit to the University in the face of threats from Communist-led bullies, but that I did not want to put my judgment above that of those on the scene who knew more about the situation than I did.

I asked Ambassador Achilles to have a member of his staff call the Rector of the University and inform him that if he would publicly withdraw his invitation, I would abide by his wishes and cancel my visit. The call was made and within a matter of minutes we had the answer. The Rector was now more fearful than before of violent disturbances, but he would not publicly withdraw the official invitation. That would be an admission that he had lost control of his own institution, and it also might turn the agitators' wrath upon him.

In fairness to him, it should be pointed out that the rector of a Latin American university is in a far more vulnerable position than the head of a university in the United States. As a reaction to the authoritarian control which existed during the Spanish regime, many universities in Latin America went to the other extreme and adopted a system of so-called "democracy" which has led to virtual chaos in some institutions and a lack of discipline in others. In many Latin American universities, the students, rather than the board of trustees or the faculty, run the institutions. If the students don't approve the hours for classes, they go on strike. If they believe a professor grades too hard, they demand he be fired. If they disagree with his viewpoint, they condemn him and hold over him their power to get him discharged. Under these circumstances, I understood why the Rector did not want to handle the hot potato which I had tossed to him.

My next move was to ask that the Lima Chief of Police be informed that if he would say publicly what he had said privately—that he would prefer that I cancel the visit because of the danger of violence —I would do so. His answer came back promptly. He took the same tack as the Rector. He hoped I wouldn't go through with the visit. But he would not take the responsibility for publicly advising me to stay away from San Marcos, because he did not want to incur the wrath of the Communist-led students and also he did not want to create the impression that the Lima police force could not handle such a situation and provide protection for a high-ranking visiting official. By this time the reception was ending and later, as I rode with Mrs. Nixon to the state dinner given in our honor by the Vice President of Peru, I realized that the buck had been passed to me. I had to make this decision alone and take sole responsibility for the consequences.

Despite an undertone of uneasiness, the dinner was a gala affair. I informally put the question of my visit to San Marcos to various Cabinet officers and other high officials of the Peruvian Government at the dinner. Each expressed great concern but at the same time said, in effect: please don't quote me—publicly. It became apparent to me that as far as they were concerned I was a *visiting* dignitary and the Peruvian Communists were men they would have to contend and live with long after I had departed. It was clear also that the Communists exerted more power in Peru than my briefing officers in Washington had realized. My estimate of the brewing crisis sharpened accordingly. My decison on San Marcos now became critical.

It was after midnight when we arrived back at our hotel. I explained the situation to Mrs. Nixon and suggested that while I had not yet made up my mind about visiting San Marcos, she should plan not to accompany me to the events scheduled for the following morning.

I asked the same group with whom I had met at the American Embassy earlier in the evening to come to my room for a conference. Although I had to make the final decision, I wanted their recommendations on what I should do.

Rubottom and Bernbaum, the State Department officials primarily responsible for U. S. relations with Latin America, strongly opposed my going to the University. They were supported in this view by the second-level Embassy people who were now participating in the conference. Their reasoning was based on the element of personal danger to me plus the possible embarrassment to United States prestige and Peruvian sensitivity which a mob demonstration might cause, especially since the Communist Party was officially illegal in Peru.

Bill Key, my administrative assistant, suggested that I consider an alternative plan of action: if I were to change my schedule and visit Catholic University, near San Marcos, where I could expect a warm welcome, this would reflect discredit upon the San Marcos hecklers. I told Key and Jack Sherwood to work out the details of a visit to Catholic University in the event that I decided against San Marcos but stressed that the visit must be unscheduled and unannounced. Only the Rector of Catholic University was to be confidentially informed of the possibility that I might stop at his small but well-respected institution.

I asked each man in the room what he thought I should do and the opinion was unanimous that I should not go to San Marcos. I was to learn later that the members of my personal staff, particularly Cushman, Hughes, and Sherwood, were hoping that I would overrule them but felt that because their primary responsibility was for my personal safety, they had no alternative but to take a position against the visit.

Deliberately I waited until the others in the room had expressed their opinions and then I suggested that Ambassador Achilles and I discuss the matter alone.

Achilles, a mild-mannered, able career diplomat with a distinguished record in the Foreign Service, had joined in the gathering and assessing of the facts but, up to this time, had not expressed his own opinion. After the others had left the room, I requested his candid judgment as to the course of action that would best serve the interests of the United States. Perhaps unnecessarily I added that regardless of what he might advise I would assume full responsibility for the consequences of what I did the next day. He did not answer for what seemed like two or three minutes. Like most men of good judgment I have known, he wasted few words and he chose the best time to say what he had to say. This is approximately what he said: "From a personal standpoint you should not go. Latin American mobs often get out of hand and there is a risk not only of embarrassment but also of personal injury to you. On the other hand, when I consider the alternatives, I find none which would not give the Communists a propaganda victory. One characteristic common throughout this hemisphere is that the people admire courage. They have contempt for fear. That is why the bullfight is a favorite sport here. That is why the government officials, the university officials, and the police will not take responsibility for withdrawing the invitation. They would lose face. They know it is wrong for them to leave this responsibility to you, a distinguished guest in their country.

"However, if you do not go to San Marcos, the Communists will boast throughout Peru and all Latin America for weeks and months that the students of one of the oldest and greatest universities in the Western Hemisphere so disliked the United States that they refused to allow the Vice President of the United States to visit their campus and that he was afraid to go there because of the reception they had planned for him.

"In summary," Achilles concluded, "I believe from a personal standpoint you should make a decision not to go. But from the standpoint of the United States, I will have to say that your failing to go may lead to some very detrimental publicity reactions throughout the hemisphere."

It was past 2:00 A.M. when I finally turned out the light and tried to get some sleep. I had only eight hours in which to decide whether or not to keep the appointment at San Marcos. Whether, in effect, to fight or to run away from this crisis which had implications far beyond my personal safety. I slept very little that night. I could feel the tension building up. Outside the hotel, I could hear the chants of the mob, swirling around the hotel, *"Fuera Nixon, Fuera Nixon, Fuera Nixon."*

As I tossed in bed, I knew from previous experience that this necessary period of indecision was far more wearing than tomorrow's action would be, no matter which way I decided. This was part of the crisis syndrome as I knew it. I had discussed the decision-making process with President Eisenhower during the first year of his term on a long automobile ride from Quantico to Washington. He told me he had gone through hours and days of mental and physical tension before making the final decision for the time and place of the embarkation for the Normandy landing. But once the decision was made, his mind and body relaxed. He slept restfully and was in prime shape for the hundreds of subsequent decisions essential to the success of D-Day.

I carefully reviewed and analyzed all the factors of the decision I had to make, and I did this in the context of the objective I hoped to attain. The purpose of my tour was to present a symbol of the United States as a free, democratic, and powerful friend of our South American neighbors. In this context, my decision became clear. If I chose not to go to San Marcos, I would have failed at least in Peru. But if I did go, I would have a chance to demonstrate that the United States does not shrink from its responsibilities or flee in the face of threats. While I might not be able to break through a mob at the gates of San Marcos, there was a chance that I could face them down and possibly still win the day.

But the case for not going was also compelling. I would be risking injury, not only to myself but to others. If someone was hurt, I would be blamed. And if I took the easier and safer course of canceling the visit to San Marcos and going to Catholic University I might well be able to put the blame on both the Peruvian officials and the Communists.

But my intuition, backed by considerable experience, was that I should go. In doing so, I would be overruling a majority of my advisers. But a leader must do more than count noses of his advisers. He should consider their opinions, but he must always remember that it is his responsibility to make decisions—not theirs.

I gave little thought to the possibility of personal injury to myself not because I was "being brave" but because such considerations just were not important in view of the larger issues involved. A man is not afraid at a time like this because he blocks out any thought of fear by a conscious act of will. He concentrates entirely on the problem which faces him and forgets about himself. It would not be simply a case of Nixon being bluffed out by a group of students, but of the United States itself putting its tail between its legs and running away from a bunch of Communist thugs.

In a larger sense, this was another round in a contest which has been waged from the beginning of time between those who believe in the right of free expression and those who advocate and practice mob rule to deny that right. I did not believe that the feelings and opinions of the Peruvian officials who did not want me to go should play a part in my decision. I recognized that the United States, as a world power, should always take into consideration the sensitivities of smaller nations. While it is pleasant to be popular and liked, I have always thought that our country in its leadership should never lose sight of the goals, objectives, and aspirations of the United States itself. Thus, while I could understand why the Peruvian leaders shrank from this crisis, I thought that my actions should not be inhibited by their fears.

It was almost daylight when I reached a tentative decision to go, leaving open the possibility of changing my mind if events changed the situation. I had learned that in decision-making one should not commit himself irrevocably to a course of action until he absolutely has to do so. This leaves the least time possible between the time of decision and that of action in which changes may occur in the situation.

Leaving Mrs. Nixon behind in the hotel, I went downstairs the next morning for the scheduled ten o'clock wreath-laying ceremony at the tomb of General José de San Martín, the George Washington of Peru. The press, Peruvian officials, and members of my staff and the Embassy staff met me in the lobby and asked if the San Marcos visit was on or off. The press, I was told later, was split about 50–50 on the question of whether I would go. I told them I had not yet made a final decision. I wanted to retain my freedom of action until the last possible moment and I wanted to give the mob-leaders as little notice as possible of our plans.

The police cleared a path through an undemonstrative crowd as I walked to the San Martín monument, which was in the square directly in front of the hotel. About a thousand persons had been standing in the square for two or three hours, I was told, waiting to see how I would react to the Communist challenge which was the news of the day throughout Peru. Two American Marines from the Embassy helped me carry the wreath, a huge floral replica of the flags of the United States and Peru, to the base of the statue. Then I stepped back three paces and stood at attention in silence. The normal protocol is to stand in this position for approximately thirty seconds. But I stood there in silence for what must have been two minutes. It seemed much longer.

The time for decision had come. When I stepped away I would have to tell Sherwood whether we were going to San Marcos or to Catholic. Among the thoughts which ran through my head was that San Martín had led the fight against monarchist tyranny in South America. He would have fought just as fiercely against the Communist tyranny, represented by the mobs now gathered outside the gates of San Marcos. Finally I turned away, walked over to Sherwood, said "San Marcos," and then went on to my car. Sherwood knew what to do. The evening before, I had given instructions that if the decision were to go to San Marcos only he, Colonel Walters, and I would get out of the car, that the police were not to use any weapons of any kind, and that if violence occurred, under no circumstances were we to initiate it or, if we could avoid doing so, react to it.

Word of our coming was flashed ahead to the mob at San Marcos. I learned later that it came as an unpleasant surprise to the Communist leaders there. They had counted on a victory by default.

Our motorcade moved slowly through the virtually empty streets. Two blocks before we arrived at the University plaza, we began to hear ahead of us the frenzied howls of the mob. They were screeching, *"Fuera Nixon, Fuera Nixon,"* with an occasional *"Muera Nixon* [Death to Nixon]" dropped in. As my car moved slowly toward the plaza, I planned what I would do when I arrived on the scene. This was not my first experience in facing a Communist-led gang.[1] Among the tactics I had found effective in dealing with similar, although less hazardous, situations were these: take the offensive; show no fear; do the unexpected; but do nothing rash.

About fifty yards from the front gate of the University, I told the driver to stop. Walters, Sherwood, and I got out of the car and walked directly toward the crowd. There were more than two thousand of them against three of us, yet those in front backed away. Their surprise was unmistakable. The noise of the shouting and whistling

---

[1] It was in Pegu, Burma, on Thanksgiving Day 1953—during my first overseas mission as Vice President—that I had previously faced a crowd of Communist-led demonstrators. After a special civic luncheon, Mrs. Nixon and I were scheduled for a visit to a nearby Buddhist temple. An angry, sign-carrying crowd of hecklers had gathered just outside the City Hall, spurred on by a Communist agitator shouting anti-American slogans from a sound truck. The government officials and members of my own party urged that we drive but I insisted that we stick to our plans and walk to the temple. I also insisted that Mrs. Nixon and I walk first and alone —not surrounded by Burmese officials and guards. This is just what we did. When the first demonstrator accosted me, I asked him to point out the leader of the group. I retained the initiative I had gained, walked up to him, asked what his grievances were—and by this direct action put him completely on the defensive and, at the same time, swung the crowd to my side. We then went on our way, with a now overwhelmingly friendly crowd following along behind.

seemed to subside. I tried to get their attention, speaking in English with Walters shouting his interpretations in Spanish. "I would like to talk to you. If you have complaints against the United States, tell me what they are and I shall try to answer them. This is the free way, the democratic way to discuss the differences we have."

For a few moments, I thought I might get the situation under control. Those in front of me continued to give way and I walked directly into the mob. Some of the younger students started to quiet down. But the older ones in the rear, the ringleaders, saw what was happening. They tried to whip up a frenzy again, egging the younger students on, just as if they were driving them with whips. They shouted insults at those who shook hands with me. There were only a few leaders— the usual case-hardened, cold-eyed Communist operatives. The great majority were teenage students. And what struck me about them was not the hate in their eyes, but the fear. We had no weapons; the police, following my instructions, were not with me. And yet the very fact that we dared to walk toward them seemed to strike fear into their hearts.

Just as it seemed that the balance might be tipping in our favor, I felt something glance off my shoulder. Sherwood put his hand to his mouth. Walters whispered in my ear, "Mr. Vice President, they are throwing stones." I leaned toward Sherwood: "OK, all right, let's get out of here. But move back slowly, keep facing them."

We moved toward our car, continuing to face the mob and talking to those nearest us as though we were taking our leave but not retreating. As we got into the car, the rocks were flying around us but I could not resist the temptation to get in one other good lick. I stood up on the rear seat as the car moved slowly away and asked Sherwood to brace my legs so that I would not fall. I shouted, with Walters translating in rapid-fire Spanish, "You are cowards, you are afraid of the truth! You are the worst kind of cowards." I felt the excitement of battle as I spoke but I had full control of my temper as I lashed out at the mob. Those nearby us who heard me, quieted down but the rocks from the rear continued to fly.

As we moved out of range, I turned to Sherwood and said, "OK, now we're going to Catholic University." When he answered I could see why he had put his hand to his mouth; a rock had broken off one of his front teeth.

As we started to pick up speed, Tad Szulc, Latin American correspondent for the New York *Times,* ran alongside the car saying, "Good going, Mr. Vice President, good going." This, I learned later, was the verdict of virtually all the forty to fifty men in the press corps who were with me that day.

On the other hand, I was not sure who had won. I had hoped that I would be able to get through the mob so that I could keep my commitment to speak on the University campus. In this I had failed.

On the other hand, no one had been seriously injured and I was hopeful that people all over Latin America would see the lesson of what had happened—the Communists had had to stoop to violence to prevent a free discussion of ideas.

The Rector of Catholic University had kept his promise to say nothing about the possibility of our visit. Our arrival was a complete surprise. The Communist apparatus, which had only a few representatives in this institution, was taken unaware. By coincidence we walked into the administration building at the time the students were electing officers for the Student Council. When I entered the auditorium, bedlam broke loose. The students wanted me to speak immediately. But I said, "Nothing must interfere with a free election," and sat on the stage with the student officers for about five minutes while they completed the counting of the ballots.

Then I spoke for a few minutes and answered questions. I got off to a particularly good start when I compared the attitude of the students at Catholic University, who practiced as well as preached freedom of expression, with those of San Marcos, who had just denied it. I responded to questions for almost thirty minutes before some Communist hecklers tried to regain the initiative. They cut their own loudspeaker into the public address system and tried to drown me out. But the students were so overwhelmingly on my side that they tore out the wires of the loudspeaker, threw the hecklers out of the building, and asked me to continue.

A short time later, however, Sherwood walked up to the rostrum and whispered, "We'd better cut this off and get out of here; the gang from San Marcos is on its way." I quickly concluded my remarks and left the Assembly Hall with the students shouting *"Viva Nixon"* and slapping me on the back and shaking hands. We moved just in time. As our motorcade pulled away, we saw a hundred or so shouting, arm-waving men running down the street from San Marcos, but they were too late to intercept us.

Most of the mob, however, had moved on to San Martín Square in front of my hotel. At the square they had whipped up a frenzied reception for me. They had torn to shreds the floral wreath that I had placed at the monument to San Martín, the national hero of Peru. They had broken windows, torn down government welcome signs, and were leading the crowds like cheerleaders in stock slogans, "Yankee Warmonger," "Nixon, go home."

Again, as at San Marcos, I heard the crowd before I saw it. A block away from the hotel, I could see thousands of people milling around in the square in front of the hotel entrance and I ordered the motorcade to stop. I realized that if we drove up to the hotel, as they expected, the mob would have us trapped inside the car. Sherwood, Walters, Hughes, and I got out of the car and walked the block to the hotel entrance. Again, we caught the Communist leaders by surprise. They learned we were there only when others in the crowd began shouting "Viva America," "Viva Nixon." While the mob from San Marcos, swollen by the street bullies who had been in the square all night, made up a majority of the crowd, there were others who were spectators caught in the melee by their desire to see what would happen.

We were only about fifty feet away from the hotel entrance when the agitators first became aware of my presence. Then they began to push toward us from the fringes of the crowd. The whole mob began to sway. I was squeezed between Sherwood, Walters, and Hughes in a sort of three-layer club sandwich. The only sensation I can recall like it was when Pat and I were caught in the crush of the crowd celebrating V-E Day in Times Square in 1945. The hotel door was only a few steps away, but it took us several minutes to reach it. We succeeded only because Sherwood and Hughes had now become experts at using their elbows and knees to clear a path.

Just as I reached the hotel door I came face to face with a man I later learned was one of the most notorious Communist agitators in Lima. I saw before me a weird-looking character whose bulging eyes seemed to merge with his mouth and nose in one distorted blob. He let fly a wad of spit which caught me full in the face. I went through in that instant a terrible test of temper control. One must experience the sensation to realize why spitting in a person's face is the most infuriating insult ever conceived by man. I felt an almost uncontrollable urge to tear the face in front of me to pieces. Sherwood deserves the credit for keeping me from handling the man personally. He grabbed him by the arm and whirled him out of my path, but as I saw his legs go by, I at least had the satisfaction of planting a healthy kick on his shins. Nothing I did all day made me feel better.

Back in my hotel room, I peeled off my rumpled clothes, took a hot shower, and sank down into a comfortable arm chair for a few moments' rest. It was noon. I had been away only two hours, but I was completely worn out. I longed to relax, but I snapped myself out of that mood. My schedule for the day had hardly begun. Ahead was a twelve-hour agenda. I knew that if what had happened this morning were to have any meaning, it would depend on what I did and said during the balance of the day. While I was thinking of how I could present the incident in its proper context, Don Hughes came into the room. I looked up and saw that he was standing at attention in front of me. This seemed rather strange for there had never been such formalities between myself and my staff.

"Sir, could I say something personal?" he asked.

"Sure, go ahead," I said, still mystified.

"Sir," he said, "I have never been so proud to be an American as I was today. I am honored to be serving under you."

I couldn't think of anything to say in reply. I just nodded my head and smiled in appreciation and he turned and left the room. In my fourteen years of public life I had never been so moved as by this remark, coming as it did from a Purple Heart jet fighter pilot of the Korean War.

Everywhere I went that afternoon, I was hailed as a hero in Peru. Crowds lined our motorcade routes and shouted down the few hecklers who dared to show up. At a luncheon attended by Peru's leading businessmen, bankers, and industrialists I was able to speak with added force of the responsibilities of modern capitalism. I emphasized that it was the duty of a nation's business leaders to work positively to close the great gap between the very wealthy and the very poor in Peru and other South American countries. I told them it was not only wrong but dangerous to repeat today the mistakes some of the practitioners of free enterprise had been guilty of fifty years ago. Offering nothing more to the people than a defense of the status quo opens the way for Communist propaganda and infiltration. The business and political leaders of Latin America must demonstrate not only that they are against Communism because it denies freedom but also that they are for freedom because it provides a surer and better way to economic progress than Communism. In private conferences with government leaders, I was able to point out the fallacy of trying to appease Communists and of thinking of them as harmless radicals.

Later in the afternoon, I had the biggest press conference of my South American tour up to that time. I tried to spell out the true nature of the Communist conspiracy and the danger that even a few Communist agitators present to a free institution. My most telling point was that at San Marcos University probably no more than 200 trained agitators had led a demonstration of 2,000 students which had brought disgrace upon the whole of Peru. "I do not leave Peru with the idea that these demonstrators represent anything but a very small, though vocal, minority opinion," I said.

"The Communists who manipulated this outrage are not true Peruvians because like all who owe loyalty to that international conspiracy, they can never be loyal to this or any country. They proved this when they tore up the Peruvian as well as the American flag on the floral wreath I placed at the monument to San Martín.

"Their actions were not directed against me personally," I said. "When one of them spit in my face, he was spitting on the good name of Peru, he was spitting on the reputation of San Marcos, one of Latin America's greatest universities, and he was spitting on the memory of San Martín and all the men who through the ages have fought and died for freedom of expression." When the press conference ended, the Peruvian reporters stood and applauded.

The tide had so turned on the Communists that a scheduled anti-American demonstration against my appearance in the port area was canceled two hours before I spoke there. A large crowd of stevedores and other working men applauded and cheered as I emphasized again that the mob violence at San Marcos had unmasked the ugly face of Communism as it really was.

It was very late in the afternoon before I returned to my hotel room. By this time the emotional, physical, and mental stress under which I had been working during the day had really taken its toll. I was exhausted. I didn't think I had enough energy left to change clothes and get cleaned up for the formal dinner I was to attend that evening.

The major crisis of the day was over. But I was to learn again a lesson I should have borne in mind from my previous experience—not before or during but after the battle comes the period of greatest danger for an individual in a crisis situation. In battle an individual is able to mobilize emotional, mental, and physical resources far beyond his expectations. He does not feel tired no matter how great the stress. The layman's way of putting it is probably pretty close to the mark even from a scientific standpoint—"a man at such a time runs on his nerve." But once the battle is ended, a price is paid in emotional, mental, and physical fatigue.

I was feeling this kind of fatigue when I asked Bob Cushman to give me a rundown on the reaction to the San Marcos incident. He replied that all reports were favorable, except that Rubottom and Bernbaum had expressed concern that the episode had embarrassed the Peruvian Government and had compromised the good-will effect of the entire tour.

I blew my stack. I told Cushman to have Rubottom and Bernbaum come to my room immediately. He reported back that they were dressing for the state dinner that evening and would come when finished. I told him to have them come at once as they were. A few minutes later the two men appeared before me, half dressed. I ripped into them. I told them it was their right and obligation before a decision was made to advise me against the San Marcos visit. But once I had made my decision in a matter of this importance, it was incumbent upon them, as key members of my staff, to put aside their objections and to support me. I reminded them that I always expressed my viewpoints in Cabinet and National Security Council meetings, but if President Eisenhower's decision differed from my advice, as sometimes it did, I supported his decision fully. No loyal staff member could do otherwise.

This, in itself, might not have been too bad, but then I proceeded to deliver a tough lecture on some of my attitudes toward foreign service people in general: too many foreign service men, according to my experience, prefer to compromise, to avoid conflict, to play it safe. This may seem the safe way out when the Communists threaten, bully, or bluff, but this kind of conduct will, in the end, only lead to inevitable defeat for the forces of freedom. The Communists are out to win the world. They are probing at any weak spot they detect in the non-Communist world. They are willing to take chances to gain their objectives. It is essential, therefore, that those who represent the United States recognize that we will be doomed to defeat in the world struggle unless we are willing to risk as much to defend freedom as the Communists are willing to risk to destroy it.

"I am not suggesting that our representatives should be rash," I told them, "that they should go looking for trouble, that they should not exhaust every possible avenue for honorable compromise of differences. But I do know that we are up against opponents who are out to beat us, not just hold their own. We, too, must play to win. Too often what we try to do is to play not to lose. What we must do is to act like Americans and not put our tails between our legs and run every time some Communist bully tries to bluff us."

What I said in the heat of anger, I still believe to be basically true. But it was unfair for me to say it to either Rubottom or Bernbaum. Both were as dedicated to the national interest as I was. If we had conflicting views on any matters, I respected them for their honesty and integrity in presenting their differences of opinion. To their credit, neither man ever evidenced any resentment over my outburst of temper. They worked as hard during the remainder of our grueling trip and after it as they had before.

Our visits to Ecuador and Colombia during the next four days were a pleasant and welcome interlude after two action-packed days in Peru. It was evident in both countries that the Communist leaders had been knocked off balance by what had happened in Peru. They didn't know exactly how to handle my visit and now they were regrouping their forces looking for a good chance to counterattack. Everywhere I went large crowds of well-wishers shouted down the few hecklers who appeared.

In Quito, Galo Plaza, the former President of Ecuador, told me that I had made the right decision in going to the University not only in Peru but in other countries I had visited. "One of the great troubles with Americans who are stationed abroad," he said, "is that they talk only to themselves and to the few business and government leaders of the countries in which they are stationed. The great majority of them live in 'American ghettos.' I can understand their reluctance to move in circles which are different and foreign to their background. But American government officials, in particular, when in foreign countries should spend more time on a social as well as a formal basis with students, teachers, labor leaders and opinion makers who may not be members of the elite but who are the future leaders of the hemisphere."

In Colombia I was greatly impressed by the knowledge and understanding of Alberto Lleras who had just been elected President of the country. Here, as in Argentina, the members of the military junta who had overthrown the dictator, Rojas Pinilla, were men of outstanding quality. After my talk with them I realized why those who say we should withdraw all support of military forces in Latin America and concentrate our aid completely on economic projects would play right into the Communists' hands. It is true that the military assistance our Latin American allies could provide in the event of war would be nominal. At best such forces could maintain only internal security. But what we must realize is that the military of Latin America is a great stabilizing force and includes some of the ablest and most dedicated leaders in the hemisphere. While military leaders can be a threat to freedom, where they use their power to impose and support dictatorship, more and more of them are using their power and prestige to support free governments. A free government without strong military support would not last a month in a Latin American country against the highly-trained subversive cadres maintained by the Communists.

The aftermath of San Marcos also was gratifying. A flood of "well done" messages from officials and individuals came to us by cable, letter, and telephone. Chris Herter read President Eisenhower's wire to me over the plane's radio telephone on our flight from Peru to Ecuador. "Dear Dick. Your courage, patience, and calmness in the demonstration directed against you by radical agitators have brought you a new respect and admiration in our country." Clare Booth Luce summed up the general tenor of the messages in her one word wire, "Bully."

We tried to call our two girls at home by radio telephone on this flight but were unable to make connections. We learned later that they had heard of the Lima riots for the first time when Tricia turned on the radio when she and Julie had come home from school for lunch. She immediately called Loie Gaunt at my office in Washington and said, "What are they doing to Daddy and Mommy in South America?" This was the first news my office staff received of the incident.

In Lima, the government finally cracked down on the Communist operation there. The student federation at San Marcos University issued a formal communique condemning the violence and insisting that outsiders, not students, were responsible for the "barbaric acts." At a concert of the New York Philharmonic Orchestra in Lima four days after the incident, Leonard Bernstein told me later, the entire audience stood and applauded for several minutes the playing of the Star Spangled Banner.

In Ecuador and Colombia, we learned of several elaborate plans for Communist demonstrations but in each case they failed to materialize or fizzled like a wet firecracker.

As our plane took off from Bogota, it never occurred to me that the next day I would face death in the midst of a wild mob in Caracas, Venezuela, where Communist leaders had been preparing their revenge.

"The Central Intelligence Agency advises the Secret Service in Washington that information has been received relating to rumors of a plot to assassinate the VP in Venezuela." This message came from U. E. Baughman, Chief of the Secret Service, and was relayed to me by Sherwood two days before we were scheduled to reach Caracas, the capital of Venezuela.

Since the violence in Lima, Sherwood, as agent in charge of the detail of Secret Service escorting me, kept in constant radio-telephonic contact with his Washington headquarters. We had been alerted for possible disturbances in Ecuador and Colombia which had not materialized. Whenever any top-ranking government official visits a foreign country, there are the usual rumors and reports of assassination plots of the crackpot variety. While each one is investigated, such reports must be taken in stride. Since the cold war began, Moscow radio and the whole Soviet propaganda machine had blasted away at each and every good-will mission undertaken by President Eisenhower or myself. For days before I left Washington for my trip to South America and throughout the tour, Moscow radio joined Communist-controlled radio stations in South America in condemning the tour and trying to inflame public sentiment against me.

The report of an assassination plot in Venezuela came with a whole sheaf of background intelligence messages. But it was backed up with a report from Frank M. Berry, a former Secret Service agent who had become a principal adviser on security matters for Nicaragua. He sent word that his private intelligence sources had reported that a huge anti-American demonstration was being organized by a Communist-led student group in Caracas with an assassination attempt as the highlight of the plan. The day before we took off from Bogota for Caracas, I questioned Sherwood in detail with regard to these reports. Were these the regular run of rumors and threats? Or were they more serious? Sherwood's answer was that in either event we should and would take every precaution, especially in view of what had already happened in Lima.

He arranged to have the advance Secret Service agents, who had preceded us to Ecuador and Colombia to check security there, go on to Caracas rather than return to Washington as was customary. Thus we would have a twelve-man detail of Secret Service agents in Caracas while I was there instead of the usual three or four. At the same time, the U. S. Embassy in Caracas was told to prod the Venezuelan authorities into double-checking their security arrangements and to keep us posted. We received periodic reports from the Embassy up to the time we landed in Caracas and each one stated that the Venezuelan Government foresaw no serious trouble and was prepared to deal with any incidents which might arise.

On the eve of my departure for Caracas, the reporters traveling with me learned of the assassination reports and asked me for comment. I told them that such rumors were "just one of those things" which had occurred many times in the past and that I would not be frightened away by such obvious threats.

Actually, I had sent word that the Venezuelan Government should clearly understand that they were free to withdraw their invitation if they felt at all unable to handle the security arrangements incumbent upon the host country. The night before our departure for Caracas, our Embassy there sent me this message: "Venezuelan government security agencies are confident of their ability to handle the situation but are increasing security measures to such an extent that the advance representatives feel the Vice President might believe he is being overguarded."

My decision to go to Caracas as scheduled was not an act of "bravery." Security arrangements there were outside my domain and I relied upon Security Service and intelligence estimates. It was far more significant to me that the State Department considered Venezuela potentially the most important stop of the entire South American tour. In January, only five months earlier, the ten-year-old dictatorship of Perez Jimenez, second only to Peron in power and entrenchment, had been overthrown by revolution. Perez Jimenez, who was probably the most hated dictator in all of Latin America, had fled with his despised Chief of Secret Police, Pedro Estrada, to exile in the United States.

Our government, which does not believe that deposed rulers, no matter how despicable, should be put before firing squads without trial, granted the men sanctuary. This was meat for the Communist propaganda grinder and placed the United States in what is called a diplomatically delicate position. The Communist and nationalist elements in Caracas had been flatly equating the United States with the oppressions of the Perez Jimenez regime. We were in a position of having to explain how we could grant sanctuary to two men without approving of them or their actions, and to demonstrate that we believed in democracy and preferred the new ruling junta in Venezuela over the past regime. Even that is a simplification of why the State Department considered a good-will visit from the Vice President of the United States to Venezuela so important for establishing a new, abiding relationship with the ruling five-man junta.

The Junta Patriotica, a temporary coalition government pending the promised open and free elections, included representatives of the Communist Party. This accorded the Communists power and influence beyond their actual number in the country. They wielded their power through various student organizations and through the nation's press. According to my briefing papers, the Communists had infiltrated every daily newspaper in Caracas except one run by the Catholic Church and one English language paper. On the list of "distinguished personalities" invited by the Venezuelan Government to a luncheon in my honor, scheduled for my first day in Caracas, were six Communists and avid pro-Communists.

There was plenty of evidence that the Communists intended to demonstrate vociferously during my visit. But Charles R. Burroughs, the Minister-Counselor of our Embassy in Venezuela, reported to me on our flight from Bogota to Caracas that there would be tremendous numbers of friendly people who also would demonstrate their warm regard for the United States. He showed me various newspaper reports about my impending visit. One which I remember was the *Tribuna Popular*, the Communist Party daily. This paper contained a particularly vicious attack on the United States and a front-page photograph of me, doctored so that my teeth looked like fangs and my face like that of a war-mongering fiend. I was to see that retouched photograph on hundreds of placards during my two-day visit to Caracas.

Yet, at the time, neither our Embassy staff nor our intelligence people in Venezuela were able to discover that the Communist high command in South America had made a high-level decision to regain the ground they had lost in Lima by mounting a massive pay-off demonstration in Caracas. It was the scope of the effort which our people failed to assess properly.

Security arrangements in Caracas were checked and rechecked through the night prior to my arrival. At midnight, eleven hours before my plane was to put down at the Caracas airport, our Embassy advised that the government authority had "everything under control." A rumor of a plot to poison me had caused a switch in the caterer for the buffet reception in my honor. At 3 A.M. Sherwood got final word: the Caracas authorities had made still another check of security arrangements and they definitely wanted me to come.

As we flew from Bogota to Caracas that morning, I did not expect my visit to Venezuela to be a picnic. I knew there might be some incidents. But I didn't think anything could top what I had been through in Lima.

I felt, as a matter of fact, that I had had a pretty complete course in handling Communist hecklers at Pegu, Burma, on Thanksgiving Day in 1953, and at the University of Montevideo in Uruguay on this trip. By taking the offensive and making maximum use of the element of surprise, I had been able to turn potentially antagonistic crowds against the Communist agitators who were attempting to inflame them against me. At Lima, I thought I had had the graduate course on how to handle a mob. If I had written a thesis on mobs it would have set forth these conclusions:

A mob does not act intelligently. Those who make up a mob do not think independently. They do not think rationally. They are likely to do irrational things, including even turning on their leaders.

Individually, people in a mob are cowardly; only collectively, goaded on by a leader, will a mob appear to act courageously.

A mob is bloodthirsty. A taste of blood will whet its appetite for more violence and for more blood.

How then does one handle a mob?

Since a mob is unreasonable and irrational, nothing must be done which will tend to accentuate those characteristics. A mob has lost its temper collectively. An individual dealing with a mob must never lose his or he will be reduced to its level, and become easy prey for it. He must be as cold in his emotions as a mob is hot, as controlled as the mob is uncontrolled.

Since those who make up a mob are basically cowards, one must never show fear in the face of a mob. Since a mob is not intelligent, but stupid, it is important whenever possible to confront it with an unexpected maneuver. The leader of the mob may be able to cope with such tactics but by the time he gets the mob under control and changes its direction, the individual against whom the mob is demonstrating will have moved out of the path of danger.

I do not suggest that I consciously thought of these principles in those tense moments when I faced the mob at San Marcos University, but in retrospect, I can see the subconscious guidelines which influenced my conduct.

We landed at Maiquetia Airport, about twelve miles from the center of Caracas, Tuesday morning, May 13. As our plane stopped before the terminal building, we could hear the screeches and whistles of the crowd. When the steps were rolled up, Mrs. Nixon and I came out and stood at the top of the ramp for the traditional nineteen-gun salute and the playing of the national anthems of the United States and Venezuela. There was the usual group of visiting dignitaries at the foot of the ramp to greet us and one of the largest welcoming crowds that we had seen at an airport during our whole South American tour. They were standing outside the gate of the airfield and on the observation deck above the terminal building, waving banners and placards and shouting so loudly that we could hardly hear the sound of the music or of the salute.

Walters, standing beside me, whispered in my ear, "They aren't friendly, Mr. Vice President." Without being able to read the slogans on the placards or understand what they were saying, I could sense that this was the understatement of the trip. Most of those I could see appeared to be teenagers, but I could spot some tough-looking older men who obviously were the ringleaders. I learned later that the younger participants had been transported to the airport from Caracas in an organized caravan of buses and automobiles and, when one of our Embassy officials urged the Venezuelan Chief of Security before our arrival to make certain the mob did not get out of hand, he had replied: "Oh, they are just kids. They are harmless."

Pat and I walked down the steps of the ramp, greeted the welcoming committee, and I proceeded to inspect the military guard of honor. As I was doing so, I noticed twenty or thirty mechanics standing in a group nearby. They seemed friendly in contrast to the mob so I walked over and shook hands with them. This brief period gave me time to think. I decided then that I would dispense with the rest of the formalities at the airport. As I walked back to the official welcoming committee, the mob took out its wrath on the mechanics in particularly vicious and filthy language, which Walters interpreted to me.

"Let's dispense with the customary speeches here and go directly to our cars," I told the ranking member of the official host committee, Foreign Minister Oscar Garcia Velutini. "No one could possibly hear what we said over the noise of this mob." Before he had a chance to reply, I took Pat's arm and led the way down the plush red carpet leading from the plane to the terminal building. The Foreign Minister and his wife followed behind us. Our cars for some inexplicable reason were on the other side of the terminal building rather than on the airfield, which would have made far better sense. Just as we reached the terminal door, the band once again struck up the

Venezuelan National Anthem. We stopped and stood at attention. But the mob continued to scream so loudly that they almost drowned out the music. Then as we stood there I had the sensation that rain was falling—but it was an absolutely clear day, without a cloud in the sky. I looked up. The rain was coming down from the mob leaning over the rail of the observation deck above us. I had my first experience as a target for spit in Lima. But this was a real baptism. Not just one but hundreds of people were there on the balcony spitting down on us as we stood listening to their national anthem.

I saw Pat's new red suit, which she had purchased especially for this trip, being splotched, and what made it worse was that some of the spit was dirty brown, coming from a tobacco-chewing crowd. But we stuck it out until the anthem was completed. We preferred the indignity of spit to that of letting the mob see the Vice President of the United States duck and run away. And we also wanted to show them that we respected their national anthem even if they did not. As we started to move on into the airport lobby, an object hit my face. It was a whistle thrown or dropped by one of those on the balcony. I bent down, picked it up, thought for a moment of throwing it back and then dropped it. I realized that even if I were to toss back this little trinket I might lay myself open to charges that I was throwing things at the people of Venezuela.

The police did absolutely nothing, and this made those in the crowd all the more aggressive. Standing there for those few seconds was, from the standpoint of temper control, one of my most difficult experiences. Honoré de Balzac once wrote that politicians are "monsters of self-possession." Yet while we may show this veneer on the outside, inside the turmoil becomes almost unbearable.

Pat shared this trial at my side. In one sense, I was horrified that she should be subjected to it. In another sense, I was proud that she was with me. As we walked toward the car, she reached through a nearby barricade to pat a girl's shoulder and shake her hand. The girl, who had been one of those shouting and spitting, turned her head and wept in shame.

After we had passed through the terminal and came out the door in front, we were surrounded by a throng of people who had rushed down from the observation deck. There were no Venezuelan police in sight. Our own Secret Service men helped us push our way to the closed limousines awaiting us. Standard operating procedure was to have both an open and a closed car at the airport so that either one could be used. The determining factor usually was the weather. But in this case Sherwood wisely decided upon the closed car for obvious security reasons. As events turned out, if he had chosen otherwise, it probably would have cost us our lives.

It was a wild and weird ride along the Autopista from the airport to Caracas. The windows of the car were rolled up, the doors were locked, and it was hot and stuffy inside. Outside some of the mob who had automobiles "buzzed" the motorcade, zig-zagging between the official cars. In our car, the Foreign Minister sat at my left, Sherwood and Walters sat on the two jump seats in front of us, and Secret Service agent Wade Rodham sat up front with our Venezuelan driver. Mrs. Nixon was in the car behind us with the Foreign Minister's wife, Major Hughes, and two Secret Service agents.

The Foreign Minister, a gentle, well-intentioned man, was terribly upset. He kept wringing his hands, apologizing for what had happened. He took a neat white handkerchief from his pocket and tried to wipe the spit from my suit and shirt.

"Don't bother," I told him somewhat irritably. "I am going to burn these clothes as soon as I can get out of them." He tried to explain. "The Venezuelan people have been without freedom so long that they tend now to express themselves more vigorously perhaps than they should. In our new government we do not want to do anything which would be interpreted as a suppression of freedom."

I could see that he believed what he was saying and I dropped the diplomatic double-talk and let him have it with both barrels. "If your new government," I said, "doesn't have the guts and good sense to control a mob like the one at the airport, there soon will be no freedom for anyone in Venezuela. Freedom does not mean the right to engage in mob action. Don't you realize that that mob was Communist-led? Didn't the mob at the airport deny free speech to you and to me? Didn't they shout and spit during the playing of your own national anthem as well as mine?"

The Foreign Minister replied that he agreed with me. But then he went on, "I hope you won't say that publicly because our government is fearful of doing anything which might embarrass or anger the Venezuelan Communists. They helped us overthrow Perez Jimenez and we are trying to find a way to work with them."

This was too much. I sat back in silence and watched the cars of the mob buzz in and out of our motorcade like a swarm of angry bees. I realized that I had spoken to him rather brutally. But I felt that some shock treatment was necessary for one who was so naïve as to believe that the answer to the complex problem of government is simply to give the people freedom to do anything that they please, without any rules of conduct and order.

Then, just as we reached the city limits, I heard a dull thud and thought for a moment that we had hit a chuck hole in the road. But then another and another followed and I realized that rocks were hitting our car. A moment later our driver slammed on the brakes. We had come upon an ambush, which was one of four, we learned afterwards, which had been planned for us. A mass of people rushed into the street from their hiding places, spitting, throwing rocks, waving placards, and shouting obscenities.

Somehow the driver steered his way through this group and our motorcade sped on up Avenida Sucre, a six-lane highway, toward the Panteon Nacional in the center of Caracas where I was to lay a wreath at the tomb of Simon Bolivar, the great liberator of South America. As I looked out the window, I saw that the sidewalks were virtually empty, the stores locked and shuttered. The inside of the car, which was now stifling hot, made me think of a tank, battened down and ready for combat. But while there were no pedestrians in sight on the avenue itself, traffic seemed heavy despite the fact that I had been told the route would be cleared for the motorcade.

Then we hit our first real traffic jam, a roadblock of buses and automobiles backed up behind a huge dump truck which had been deliberately parked in the center of the street. We barely came to a stop when a crowd seemed to materialize out of nowhere. The Venezuelan and U. S. flags were ripped from the front of our car. Several men began kicking the fenders and doors of the car and one huge fat character threw himself over the hood. Then six Secret Service men jumped out of a car behind us and went to work on the men surrounding our limousine. Not one of the Venezuelan police officers got off his motorcycle to join in. I was told later that only one Caracas detective, who was a refugee from one of the Central European countries, worked with skill and effectiveness alongside our Secret Service men. After two or three minutes they had cleared away the obstructors and we moved on again.

We ran into our third blockade only four blocks from the Bolivar Tomb. Three banks of buses, trucks, and automobiles had been parked directly in the path of our motorcade. We could not cross the center island because of the traffic coming down the other side of the street. Looking ahead at the traffic jam, I could see that we were really stuck here. For a moment nothing happened and then Sherwood said, "Here they come." Out of the alleys and the side streets poured a screaming mob of two to three hundred, throwing rocks, brandishing sticks and pieces of steel pipe. They swarmed around our car. A large rock smashed against the shatterproof window and stuck there, spraying glass into the Foreign Minister's face.

"It's my eye, my eye," he moaned.

For twelve minutes, which seemed like twelve hours, we sat there, the crowd milling about, shouting, screaming, and attacking. The leaders were easy to identify because they rode piggy-back so that they could see and be seen by the mob they were directing. They hit the windows and doors of our car with pipes and sticks and those who had no weapons used their feet and bare fists to beat upon the car. The spit was flying so fast that the driver turned on his windshield wipers.

Again our Secret Service agents moved into action.[2] Never once using their weapons, they pushed and shoved the attackers from our doors but just as soon as one agent pushed someone away another would slip behind and attack again. As they beat upon the limousine and tried to open its doors, I could hear the shouts. "*Muera Nixon, Muera Nixon.*" Now it was Death to Nixon rather than Go Home Nixon.

This crowd was out for blood. I sat there as stoically as possible, knowing that the last thing I should do would be to show fear to a mob like this. Several times I glanced back at the car behind us. Pat appeared to be talking to the Foreign Minister's wife as calmly as though the trouble was no worse than an afternoon traffic jam on the Hollywood Freeway. Her driver had shown the good judgment to jam his front bumper against our car so that none of the mob could get at our back window. Looking ahead I could see the truck filled with reporters and cameramen in action. One man in the mob tried to scramble onto the truck and Hank Griffin, the Associated Press photographer, slugged him back to the street with his camera.

By this time the Foreign Minister was close to hysterics. He kept repeating, "This is terrible. This is terrible."

What does a man think of at a time like this? I can testify that he certainly does not think of the problems of the world; he thinks only

[2] The twelve Secret Service men were magnificent. They saved our lives and, just as important, not one of the attackers was killed or seriously injured. On my recommendation, each was later presented with an Exceptional Civilian Service Award (Gold Medal), with a special citation for his outstanding conduct in Caracas. One of my predecessors, incidentally, had declined the offer of Secret Service protection because "no one would ever bother to shoot a Vice President."

of what he can do to get out of the danger he is in. I knew that above all I had to control my emotions and think calmly: I must be as cold as the mob was hot. The test of leadership is whether one has the ability, as Kipling once said, to keep his head while others are losing theirs.

One thought flashed through my mind which was not related to the immediate danger. It made me almost physically ill to see the fanatical frenzy in the eyes of teenagers—boys and girls who were very little older than my twelve-year-old daughter, Tricia. My reaction was a feeling of absolute hatred for the tough Communist agitators who were driving children to this irrational state.

But there was little time for thoughts like this. One of the ringleaders —a typical tough thug started to bash in the window next to me with a big iron pipe. The shatterproof glass did not break but it splattered into the car. Walters got a mouthful and I thought for an instant, "There goes my interpreter." Sherwood was hit. Some of it nicked me in the face.

Then we heard the attacker shout a command and our car began to rock. I knew now what was happening. It was a common tactic for mobs throughout the world to rock a car, turn it over, set it afire. For an instant, the realization passed through my mind—we might be killed —and then it was gone.

Sherwood must have had the same thought. He pulled his revolver and said, "Let's get some of these sons-of-bitches." I could see Rodham in the front seat with the sweat pouring down his neck as he pulled his revolver and faced the attackers on my side of the car. "I figured we were goners and I was determined to get six of those bastards before they got us," he was to tell me later.

At this point I made a quick decision. I reached forward, put my hand on Sherwood's arm and told him to hold fire. Why I did this at the time, I cannot say, except that I knew intuitively that the firing of a gun would be the excuse for the mob to get completely out of hand. I also was aware of the Communist tactic of engaging in violence up to the point of forcing their opponents to react. Then when the victim tries to defend himself, the Communists blame him for starting the whole affair. I was determined that we not get caught in this position.

The mob rocked the car more and more vigorously and then suddenly our car began to move forward and we were off. The driver of the newsmen's truck in front of us somehow had edged his way into the oncoming lane of traffic, clearing a path for us like a football blocker leading a ball carrier. Our driver took off down the wrong side of the street with Mrs. Nixon's car following behind us.

As the remnants of our motorcade swung up the narrow street toward the Panteon Plaza for the scheduled wreath-laying, I made another spot decision which proved to be providential for our physical safety. If the Communists had prepared roadblocks on the Avenida Sucre, I assumed they certainly would have something planned for the ceremony at the Bolivar Tomb, I ordered the driver to turn down the next side street in the opposite direction from the Plaza. As he turned from the scheduled route, the Foreign Minister became hysterical. "We can't leave our protection," he cried, "we've got to follow the police escort."

"If that's the kind of protection we are going to get, we are better off going it alone," I told him.

Our Venezuelan driver, who had kept his head and done a superb job from the beginning, turned up an alley into another main boulevard and there we stopped to survey the damage and to determine what we should do next.

I went back to the car behind and found that Pat was probably the coolest person in the whole party. "She was as brave as any man I ever saw," Don Hughes later observed.

By this time the press truck had caught up with us and Herb Kaplow, the National Broadcasting Company correspondent, leaped off and ran up to us to ask if anyone had been hurt. I told him there were no casualties; it was only a coincidence that we had stopped across the street from a hospital.

By this time the other reporters gathered around and I informed them of our next move. Sherwood and I had agreed that we should under no circumstances go where our published schedules had indicated we were expected. So, instead of going to the Circulo Militar, the luxurious officers' club and government guesthouse built at a reputed cost of 35 million dollars, where we were supposed to be billeted, we headed for the American Embassy.

On the way to the Embassy, I felt as though I had come as close as anyone could get, and still remain alive, to a firsthand demonstration of the ruthlessness, fanaticism and determination of the enemy we face in the world struggle. I suppressed an urge to ask the Foreign Minister if he still believed that Latin American Communists were merely "harmless radicals."

As Pat and I walked into the Embassy residence, Don Hughes

put into words what we all felt. "This is American soil and a little bit of heaven."

I knew again that the aftermath of the crisis could be just as important as the handling of the crisis itself. I steeled myself for the balance of the afternoon and evening to guard against making any mistakes which were avoidable.

A few minutes after we arrived at the Embassy, we learned what happened at the Panteon Plaza. Bill Key, my administrative assistant, and a Secret Service agent had gone ahead to the Bolivar Tomb and there they saw several thousand people screaming for American blood. When two members of our Embassy staff arrived with the United States wreath for the Bolivar Tomb, they were surrounded, cursed, and manhandled before they could be extricated from the mob by a detachment of Venezuelan soldiers armed with fixed bayonets. The United States wreath was seized and torn to bits. Bill Key had sent back three separate warning messages in code through the Caracas Police Headquarters telling us to stay away. For some reason, none of these messages ever reached us. A subsequent investigation revealed that one group in the mob had a cache of homemade bombs which were to be used at the Panteon Plaza when I arrived with my party.

By this time I was beginning to feel the accumulated fatigue from my lack of sleep on the whole tour plus the stress of the morning's events. But I knew that, as in Lima, it was my responsibility to put these events in perspective in my meetings with Venezuelan officials and at the press conference which was scheduled for later. In view of the continuing threats of violence, I decided to cancel all scheduled visits and I invited those with whom I was to confer elsewhere to meet me in the Embassy.

That afternoon and evening in Caracas was to be one of the most difficult periods of my public life. My personal desire was to get away from people, from problems, from crises—to get some time alone by myself in which to think and even just to sack out. But now I had to go through a period of explaining the significance of what had happened which would require temper control, judgment, and hard mental concentration which could prove even more wearing than the events of the morning.

Outside, the Communist-directed crowds still were roaming the streets of Caracas. One band even tried to march on the Embassy shortly after I got there. The regular U. S. Marine Guard at the Embassy was supplemented by Navy, Army, and Air Force personnel, taken from our various military missions in Caracas, and the Embassy began to take on the appearance of a fortress.

My first callers were the members of the ruling military junta. Before they arrived, I made a minor decision which I have never regretted. Our battered limousine with its windows broken and fenders smashed was parked in front of the Embassy. One of the Embassy officials wanted to move it to the rear of the building so that the visiting Venezuelans would not be "embarrassed." Bill Key objected and put the question up to me. Without hesitation, I told him, "Leave it where it is. It's time that they see some graphic evidence of what Communism really is."

I received Admiral Wolfgang Larrazabal Ugueto, the Provisional President, and the five members of the junta with courtesy but with deliberate coolness. They had welcomed Communist support in the revolution against Perez Jimenez and now they did not know how to handle their Communist allies in the government. They would have to learn. I told them that freedom cannot survive in any coalition with Communists. My words apparently had very little effect on Larrazabal. The next year he ran for President with Communist support and was defeated.

I next met with the political leaders of all the major parties of Venezuela except the Communist Party. One of them protested that after ten years of ruthless dictatorship they all abhorred the idea of developing another strong police force.

This point, I discovered later, had been the major miscalculation of our own advisers in their estimate that Venezuelan security forces would be able to handle any demonstrations. They had failed to evaluate correctly the efficiency and state of mind of the Caracas police force: the country had just been through a bloody revolution and when the revolutionary forces won, their first targets for reprisals had been the brutal police of Perez Jimenez. Many of the Perez police were killed and tortured, probably with considerable justification. But, the result was that when the revolutionary junta took control, new inexperienced men had to be taken into the police and security forces. These men not only had relatively little experience, but they knew what happens to law enforcement men in Caracas when they oppose the people. Thus, when the mobs attacked my car, the police were reluctant to act. The explanation pointed up a lesson for all Latin American countries that there must be a balance between order and freedom. When there is an obsession for maintaining order, freedom suffers; but without some order there can be no freedom.

Sitting next to me in that conference was Romulo Betancourt, who now is the President of Venezuela. I pointed out that too few people understood that the dictators of the left could be just as absolute and brutal in their denial of freedom as the dictators of the right. The Communists joined in the revolution against Perez Jimenez, not because of any dislike of dictatorship but only because they wanted to become the dictators.[3]

I also met with a group of prominent American businessmen who had interests in Venezuela. To them I emphasized that while Communists had spearheaded the riots in Lima and Caracas, there were plenty of willing spear-carriers who were not Communists and that even if there were no Communists in South America, the problems of poverty, which lead to riot and revolution, still existed. It is essential, I told them, for American businessmen abroad to adopt practices which are above suspicion of any charges of exploitation of the workers.

At a press conference late that afternoon, I made these same points and others in answer to questions. I remarked that one Venezuelan political leader had suggested to me that the murderous mob action had been due simply to students tasting freedom for the first time and becoming intoxicated with it. I pointed out that some of the "students" that I had seen must have been pretty dumb because the ones leading the mob were old enough to have been in college for twenty years. They had used the same slogans, the same words, the same tactics that "student" demonstrators had used in every country in South America I had visited, which was absolute proof that they were directed and controlled by a central Communist conspiracy.

I again made in Caracas the point I had made in Lima—that those

[3] Betancourt learned the lesson well. Three policemen were killed during demonstrations which broke out as soon as President Kennedy's forthcoming visit to Venezuela was announced, early in December 1961. Starting two weeks before his scheduled arrival, Venezuelan government authorities began a systematic round-up of known Communists and left-wing agitators, shut down all Communist offices and several student organizations, and suspended publication of one newspaper, *Clarion*. Twelve hours before Kennedy's arrival, the highway from Maiquetia Airport to Caracas was closed to all normal traffic. Everyone at the Airport was checked and re-checked for concealed weapons. When the official party drove into the center of the city, 35,000 steel-helmeted troops were on duty, thousands of them standing three-feet apart with fixed bayonets, facing toward the crowds lining the highway. Helicopters hovered overhead. The U. S. cruiser Northampton stood just outside Caracas harbor, reportedly with a detachment of battle-ready U. S. Marines. At the time of my own arrival in Caracas in 1958, by contrast, no precautions had been taken. There were no troops on the parade route, and the handful of police on duty melted away at the first sign of demonstrators.

who led the riots had no claim to be loyal Venezuelans because they owed their loyalty only to the international Communist conspiracy. As proof of their attitude, I pointed out that they not only jeered and showed no respect for the American national anthem but that they had showed the same lack of respect when the Venezuelan national anthem was being played.

When one questioner charged that the United States was giving "sanctuary" to Perez Jimenez and Pedro Estrada, I pointed out that there was an extradition treaty between our two countries and that the United States would be more than glad to ship the two men back to Venezuela for trial whenever the present Venezuelan Government wanted to resort to the proper procedures.

I concluded the conference by emphasizing that despite the day's incidents "I came to Venezuela as a friend and I leave as a friend."

That evening Mrs. Nixon and I had dinner in the privacy of our room in the Embassy residence. Now at last I thought we could relax after a nerve-wracking day. But just after nine o'clock, Rubottom and Edward J. Sparks, our Ambassador in Venezuela, came to the door and asked to talk with me on an urgent matter. Rubottom reported that he had just received a news report from Washington that had put us in the middle of another crisis: President Eisenhower had just dispatched airborne troops to Caracas to insure our protection.

This took me completely by surprise. No one had consulted me or anybody in my party. We had heard nothing from the White House, State Department, or Pentagon. I asked Rubottom to check the story through official channels and a short time later he brought back a transcript of a statement issued by the Defense Department:

As a precautionary measure two companies of airborne infantry and two companies of Marines are being moved to certain U.S. bases in the Caribbean Area. The movement is being undertaken so these troops will be in a position to cooperate with the Venezuelan Government if assistance is requested. Orders for the troop movement were issued by the Chief of Staff, Army; and the Chief of Staff, Air Force; and the Chief of Naval Operations, Navy; after consultations between the Chairman, Joint Chiefs of Staff, and the Secretary of Defense with the President.

By this time, the Venezuelan radio was reporting that an enormous American troop movement was on its way to Venezuela. Realizing the propaganda impact of this development, Ambassador Sparks and I issued a joint statement to take the sting out of the next day's press stories. We said that a very limited troop movement was being made from one American base to another so that troops would be available to Venezuelan authorities if needed. But we added that we were sure the Venezuelan Government had the situation well in hand and neither the junta, the American Ambassador, nor I saw the necessity for outside assistance to keep order.

As expected, the announced troop movement caused a great outcry throughout Latin America. Yet from President Eisenhower's vantage point his decision was right. He recognized his responsibility to protect American citizens and American officials whose lives were endangered abroad and he acted decisively. What had happened, I learned later, was that about noon that day, immediately following the mob attacks, the Embassy had flashed word to the State Department indicating that the Caracas security system had disintegrated, that mobs were loose, that I was under attack, and that the situation appeared hazardous or at least unclear. The report was rushed to Christian Herter, then Under Secretary of State. He alerted the White House and the Pentagon.

At that point, communications between Washington and our Embassy in Caracas were cut. It was a complete breakdown, for some reason, and Washington could get no further word of what was happening here. As President Eisenhower, himself, explained, he ordered the troop movement as "the simplest precautionary type of measure in the world . . . we knew nothing of the facts. We could get no reports from the outside . . . and not knowing what was happening, and not knowing whether the Venezuelan Government might want some aid from us, we simply put it at places where it would be available." The next morning the President got through to me by telephone. We had a long conversation in which I reported on the day's events, assured him of our safety and of my belief that the Venezuelan Government had the situation in hand. He had been greatly concerned by the early reports and he was relieved to learn firsthand what had happened. Characteristically, he closed our talk saying, "Give my love to Pat."

The Caracas newspapers were covered with advertisements and formal messages from prominent officials and organizations expressing mortification and apologies over what had happened the day before. One advertisement appealed to me particularly because it indicated that my comparison between democracy and Communism in my talks of the day before had had some effect. The ad said bluntly: "What would happen to Poland if the Poles did to Khrushchev what we did to Nixon?" All morning long, scores of beautiful bouquets of flowers and hundreds of wires and personally delivered messages arrived from Venezuelans in all walks of life apologizing for the incidents of the day before.

Two important questions had to be decided on that morning. One was how and when to leave Caracas that day and the other was whether or not to attend a luncheon the provisional government wanted to give in my honor as a sort of face-saver. Behind these choices was the assumption that the Communist organizers might have re-grouped their forces and that the Venezuelan police could not deal with them any better this day than they had the day before. Major Hughes and our military people worked out a plan by which our party would use a helicopter and three C-47 planes to shuttle from a small airstrip near the Embassy residence to the Maiquetia Airport where my government DC6-B and a Panagra Airliner chartered by the press group were awaiting our arrival. I ruled out this plan because Am-bassador Sparks told me that Perez Jimenez had escaped from Caracas and the wrath of his countrymen by helicopter from that same small airstrip. I did not want any such odious comparisons made after my departure.

The ruling junta pleaded that we accept their luncheon invitation so they could make a public display of the cordiality the government felt toward me and my party. They gave us the strongest assurances that we could depend upon them to get us safely to the Maiquetia Airport. I accepted their invitation with some trepidation because I knew that the luncheon was to be held in the sumptuous Circulo Militar which was on the other side of Caracas from the Embassy.

Admiral Larrazabal and his colleagues came to the Embassy to es-cort us to the luncheon in a motorcade that looked like an invasion armada. Their black limousine was flanked by armored vehicles and twelve truckloads of battle-ready troops. We moved across town with-out incident. The luncheon was lavish and even by Latin American standards protracted far beyond my expectations. At three o'clock in the afternoon, I reminded my host that we were late for our scheduled departure. He nonetheless insisted on showing me through the plush military club. He guided me through every nook and cranny of the place, including the kitchens and quarters for the officers and the en-listed men. I kept looking at my watch and my patience was beginning to wear thin when finally at about 4:30 a Venezuelan Army colonel came up, saluted, and said, "All is ready." Then I realized why the luncheon had been extended so deliberately. The Venezuelan authorities intended to take us out of Caracas along the same streets by which we arrived so that they could show that they were capable of maintaining order.

If the government had been lax the day before, they were leaving nothing to chance on this day. Not only did we have the superabundant military escort but our own vehicles had become arsenals. On the floor of the car in which Admiral Larrazabal and I rode were submachine guns, revolvers, rifles, tear gas cannisters, and clips of spare ammunition. There was hardly room for our feet. As we sped through the streets, the city seemed deserted except for tanks or armored vehicles stationed at every intersection. I observed only four or five civilians during the entire ride and they were holding handkerchiefs to their noses. I thought at first that this might be another way of expressing an insult and then someone explained that at various points along the route tear gas had been used to clear the streets.

At the airport, Mrs. Nixon and I stood for a moment at the doorway of the plane waving the customary good-by. As I looked down on the empty terminal building, the Venezuelan government officials and the military force which had escorted us, I could not help but think, "When we had arrived, there had been no order and too much freedom in this capital of Venezuela; now when we leave, there is complete order and no freedom. Both situations are bad, and yet symbolic of the problems of so many of the Latin American nations."

The White House had asked us to delay our arrival until the next morning, May 15, so that a welcoming reception could be arranged. Consequently, instead of flying directly to Washington, we stopped over at San Juan, Puerto Rico for the night. It was dusk when we landed in San Juan. There had not been time to give any advance notice of our arrival but Governor Munoz-Marin, his wife, and a large group of Puerto Rican officials gave us an enthusiastic welcome. The Governor rushed up the steps of the plane and gave me an *embraso* with the words, "You were magnificent in Lima and Caracas." As his wife, Mrs. Munoz-Marin, kissed Mrs. Nixon, she said, "You are safe here. You are home now."

By this time the radio reports had flashed the word of our arrival throughout the city and as we proceeded to the Governor's residence, the streets were filled with cheering spectators. We enjoyed the relaxed atmosphere of Munoz-Marin's hospitality after our rugged experiences of the last forty-eight hours.

In his conversation with me he urged that the United States Govern-

ment be patient and understanding during this period of transition
for so many South American countries when they were throwing off the
yoke of dictatorships. "My people," he said, speaking of his Spanish
background, "have many fine qualities. But the art of government has
been one which at times has been most difficult for them to learn.
They find it hard to maintain that elusive, delicate but all-important
balance between order and freedom." On the other hand, he urged
that the United States Government, while following its traditional
policy of non-intervention, be wary of giving the appearance of fa-
voring dictatorships of the right or the left in Latin America. It all
came back to the policy of a formal handshake for dictators and
embraso for leaders of free countries which I was to propose thereafter
in Washington.

Fifteen thousand people greeted us when we arrived at the National
Airport the next morning. President Eisenhower put protocol aside to
meet Mrs. Nixon and me at the airport. He was accompanied by the
entire Cabinet. The Democratic as well as Republican leadership of
Congress was there. Several large groups of Latin American students
studying in the Washington area also were on hand, carrying placards
of a very different nature from those we had seen. In my airport remarks, I tried to bring home the theme that for every unfriendly face
we saw in Latin America we saw a thousand friendly ones.

After the welcoming ceremonies, Mrs. Nixon and I sat with the President in the back seat of his limousine and Tricia and Julie sat on the
jump seats for a ride to the White House and a visit with Mrs.
Eisenhower.

The ordeal of the trip was over, the trip I did not want to take because I thought it would be dull.

The story of the crisis of Caracas would not be complete without
describing at least briefly the impact those events had on the nation,
as well as on me personally.

This is not the place to discuss in detail the effect my trip had on
U. S. policy toward Latin America. But while no one in his right mind
would have "planned it that way," the net effect of the violent epi-
sodes in Lima and Caracas was probably more beneficial than harmful,
as far as long-range U. S. policy was concerned. The people and government of the United States have always had a tendency to take
Latin America for granted. Cabot Lodge has often said that if it were
not for the strong support we have had from the Latin American coun-

tries on key votes in the United Nations, the United States might not be able to stay in the United Nations. Yet, since we could count on the support of Latin American countries, we have tended to direct the emphasis in our exchange, information, and foreign aid programs to so-called "neutral" countries in other parts of the world, whose support we could not count on and whom we were trying to woo.

Caracas was a much-needed shock treatment which jolted us out of dangerous complacency. For years special missions have returned from Latin America with recommendations that the United States pay more attention to our neighbors to the South. These reports have been given wide publicity in the press—for one day—and then filed away in the archives of the State Department. The Caracas crisis was so sharp and so dramatic that it could not be brushed away so easily. After Caracas, when those charged with responsibility for our Latin American policy in the State Department tried to get proper treatment for their proposals, they could and usually did point to what happened in Caracas and Lima as a warning that we could no longer get by with fancy words and little action in dealing with the problems of our neighbors to the South.

The recommendations I made on this subject when I returned to Washington were:

(1.) American government personnel abroad must do a more effective job of reaching the opinion-makers of Latin America. It is no longer enough simply to know and talk to top government officials and the elite among the financial and business communities. Students, teachers, newspaper editors, reporters, labor leaders—these are the people who are exerting massive influence in the Latin American countries, and we must find a way to get our story across to them more adequately. Person-to-person contact is the most effective way to accomplish this. USIA broadcasts and giving publicity to public statements by U.S. officials, are generally ineffective.

(2.) We must develop an economic program for Latin America which is distinctively its own. Latin Americans do not like to be classed like the undeveloped countries of Asia and Africa. They believe they are in a special position and are therefore entitled to special consideration, because of their geographical proximity to the United States, and their long record of friendship for this nation. There must be a new program for economic progress for the hemisphere.

(3.) We should not appear to give dictators, of either the right or the left, the same moral approval that we gave to leaders who were trying to build free and democratic institutions. But we must not go overboard the other way. Dictators leave a legacy of revolution. When they are deposed, a vacuum is created. If this vacuum is not filled by strong government which can protect the newly-acquired freedoms of the people, another dictator will inevitably step in and take over.

(4.) We cannot expect that U.S.-style, democratic institutions will work without modifications in countries where the population has had no tradition or experience in self-government and is completely unprepared for such government in the form we have developed it in this country.

(5.) Economic progress is vitally important to Latin America. But economic progress alone will not stop Communist infiltration and takeover. Support of adequate military and security forces must continue so that free governments will have the strength to maintain stability and deal with subversive groups which may resort to force to overthrow the government.

(6.) The people of Latin America want to be on the right side, but they also want to be on the winning side. They respect courage, and they have nothing but contempt for policies which they consider too cautious or cowardly.

(7.) Above all, there must be a better recognition in the United States at all levels that it isn't how much aid we provide, but how we provide it that counts. The Latin Americans are a very proud people. We must show proper respect for their traditions, customs and culture.

Not all of these recommendations were implemented, and some of them found very little support in State Department circles. But I am confident they had a long-range effect which was beneficial.

But this is a story of crisis, primarily as it affects an individual, rather than government policy.

When a public figure becomes involved in a crisis of some magnitude, those around him rally to his support. If it is political, the diverse elements of his own political party coalesce behind him. When the crisis is of national or international significance, the people of the nation tend to rally behind him. This has been true throughout history of our wartime Presidents. It was demonstrated in the public support of President Truman when he unilaterally committed the United States to the police action in Korea, when President Eisenhower acknowledged responsibility for the U-2 reconnaissance planes over the Soviet Union, and even when President Kennedy assumed responsibility for the abortive invasion of Cuba, admittedly one of the worst U. S. fiascoes in recent history. It is the crisis, itself, more than the merits of the engagement which rallies people to a leader. Moreover when the leader handles the crisis with success, the public support he receives is even greater.

But the public official who believes this is enduring or "undying" support, will find himself embarrassingly mistaken. Because of the very nature of crisis, the reaction to it is primarily emotional. And emotions of loyalty and support engendered by crisis can cool off as fast as they can heat up, particularly where a political leader is concerned. I can think of no better illustration of this phenomenon than what happened to me in the period following my return from South America.

Thousands of congratulatory messages poured into my office. They came from a diverse cross section of the United States, from diplomats, from labor leaders, from university presidents, and from people in every walk of life, Democrats and Republicans alike. The newspaper columnists described me as a "hero" who had shown that "Mr. Nixon can dish it out . . . and he can take it too . . . a quality much admired in these United States." For the first two or three weeks after I returned, Mrs. Nixon and I found ourselves applauded by spectators in hotel lobbies, railroad stations, and other public places where we happened to be seen.

Walter Annenberg, publisher of the Philadelphia *Inquirer* remarked at a dinner he and his wife, Lee, were giving in our honor in Philadelphia one evening, "Dick, you now have the support of many Democrats, as well as Republicans, and I only hope you can find a way to keep it."

At this time, in June 1958, just one month after my return from South America, the Gallup Poll showed me leading Adlai Stevenson for the first time, and running neck-and-neck against John F. Kennedy. It was the high point of my political popularity up to that time.

This political picture was not lost upon the Democrats. The counterattack began late that summer. The Democratic National Chairman depicted what had happened in South America as a "Republican plot" to build me up politically. Then newspaper columnists, sitting at their desks in Washington, wrote their "interpretations" of what the South American trip meant. One wrote that the riots were directed against me as an individual, and that the attempts to stir up trouble against the United States could not be blamed on the Communists.[4] Another

[4] Not all the rioters, of course, were Communists. But this misses the major point: there can be no doubt that the riots were Communist-planned, Communist-led, and Communist-controlled. Fresh evidence of this fact keeps turning up. Just a few months ago, in December 1961, two Peruvian students—self-confessed former Communists—told of Communist organization of the San Marcos riots in Lima and also publicly apologized to me for their own part in these demonstrations.

said that I had planned the whole thing for publicity purposes, and implied that I had gone to Caracas in order to have rocks thrown at me. Another said it was undignified and unnecessarily dangerous for me to meet with students, labor leaders, and the like, on my trips abroad. These attacks, of course, had their effect in blurring the image the public had of my Caracas experience immediately after my return from South America.

But it was my participation in another crisis, this one not national but partisan in character, which was to virtually erase the public memory of my success in Caracas, and put in its place an image of failure with which my name was associated.

The crisis was the 1958 off-year elections. Personally, I had to decide whether or not to throw my efforts and my prestige into the campaign for the election of Republican candidates for Congress, the Senate, and twenty-one contested governorships. Whichever way I decided, it was generally conceded among political leaders and observers that the Republicans would lose; the only question was, "by how much?" Traditionally, the party in the White House loses seats in the House and Senate in the off-year elections. Beyond that, we were having some special troubles: President Eisenhower in his landslide victory of 1956 had not carried the Congress for the Republican Party; the party was torn from within over the President's second-term budget; the economic recession was hurting the voters' pocketbooks; the launching of the first Sputnik had cast doubts upon the Administration's defense and science programs; and the Adams-Goldfine investigation had shaken the party to its roots.

Scores of personal and political friends urged me to avoid the campaign, or, at most, to participate only in a limited way. Tom Dewey, for one, put the case against my campaigning most succinctly. Reminding me that my efforts in 1954 had not won the House or Senate for the party, he pointed out I had not been given credit for seats we did win, but was blamed for the ones we lost. "You have done enough for Republican candidates," he asserted. "Your conduct in South America finally has taken the blinders from the eyes of many Democrats and now you have wide support throughout the country. You are a national asset that should not be wasted. You are not a candidate this year. It will do the Republican Party no particular good for you to get into this campaign and could do you great harm. You owe it to yourself and the long-term interests of the party to keep and build on the support you now have among Democrats as well as Republicans."

His eyes, of course, were upon 1960. But those who were up for election and were facing defeat had their eyes on 1958 as well. As the individual campaigns shaped up, scores of candidates and local party leaders told me bluntly: "If you don't come in, Dick, it won't be just a defeat, it will be a disaster for the party." Some candidates who were personal friends of long standing called upon our friendship in asking my support.

President Eisenhower desperately wanted the Republican Party to win in the elections of 1958. He told me that summer, "I would give a year of my salary if we could win either the House or the Senate." But by personal and political inclination, he did not want to become enmeshed in political skirmishes which could destroy his ability to work constructively with any Congress, regardless of its political complexion. While almost all cabinets provide "big names" for political campaigning, the Eisenhower Cabinet was composed of men who were excellent administrators, but few of whom had any great interest or adeptness in the field of politics. If anyone was to carry the major load for political cross-country campaigning, I was the one who had to do it.

So weighing the alternatives and the pressures, I decided to do what I had to do. My responsibility was to the party. I could not stand aside and see fellow Republicans go down to disastrous defeat. I had to risk my political prestige to avoid a disaster, if possible, knowing full well, as in 1954, we would probably lose, and I would be the big-name target for the defeat.

I was weary after the stress of the South American trip and the long Congressional session, and I tried to limit my political appearances to the key states. That was impossible, of course. I ended up stumping more than 25,000 miles in twenty-five states. It was the most difficult campaign I've ever been through, harder even than my own presidential campaign. Because in 1958 there was a general feeling of discouragement which pervaded the Republican Party, and I, myself, could not completely fight off a feeling of futility in some of the states and districts I visited.

On election night I listened to the returns in my home in Washington, and almost all my fears came to pass. Internecine warfare among Republicans swept the Democrats to victory in my home state of California, in Indiana, and in several other states. The right-to-work issue sent Senator John Bricker, of Ohio, who had been considered unbeatable, down to defeat. Of the twenty-one contests for Governor, we won only eight. We lost a net of twelve seats in the Senate, and forty-eight seats in the House of Representatives. It was the worst defeat in history ever suffered by a party having control of the White House.

The only bright spots were Nelson Rockefeller's landslide victory in New York, the election of Mark Hatfield as Governor of Oregon and Chris del Sesto as Governor of Rhode Island, and the decisive re-election of Senator Barry Goldwater in Arizona.

One television commentator that night summed up the election results with this statement: "The big winner in this election is Nelson Rockefeller. The big loser—Richard Nixon." A few days later, on November 9, Governor-elect Rockefeller flew south for a vacation on his estate in Venezuela. When he landed at Maiquetia Airport in Caracas where I had been just six months before, reporters asked him, "What about Nixon?" He replied, according to press reports, "No tengo nada que ver con Nixon," which means, "I have nothing to do with Nixon."

Just six months before, following the San Marcos University episode in Lima, I had received a cable from Nelson Rockefeller which read, "Your courage and determination have inspired democratic forces throughout the hemisphere. We all feel a great sense of pride in your action. Congratulations. Nelson."

Khrushchev

---

*Communism creates and uses crisis as a weapon. Khru-
shchev, Communist man at his most dangerous best, has developed this technique to a highly sophisticated science.
Plans designed to meet his moves may prove useless because of the unpredictability of his conduct. But intensive
planning is absolutely essential, to avoid being knocked off
balance by what he does.*

"IN preparing for battle I have always found that plans are useless,
but planning is indispensable."

There could not have been a more dramatic demonstration of the
truth of this maxim—one of President Eisenhower's favorites—than my
meeting with Nikita Khrushchev in Moscow in July 1959.

I had never been better prepared for a meeting in which I was to
participate. During my previous thirteen years in government I had
had the opportunity to acquire more than a passing knowledge of
Communist strategy and tactics.

At home, as a member of the House Committee on Un-American
Activities I had met the Communist conspiracy face to face in the
Alger Hiss case.

Abroad, I had met and talked at length with Communist leaders in
Italy, England, Greece, and other countries, and in South America I
had seen Communism in action in all its violence and viciousness.

While I could not qualify as a so-called "expert" on Communism in
the popular sense of that term, I had studied the works of Marx, Lenin,
and Stalin, the Old Testament prophets of modern-day Communism,

as well as the statements of Khrushchev and the contemporary observers of Communist policies.

For months before the trip I spent every spare moment studying reports and recommendations from the State Department, the Central Intelligence Agency, the Joint Chiefs of Staff, and the White House staff.

I talked for hours with every person I could find in Washington who had met and knew Khrushchev. I was briefed on more than a hundred different issues which might arise in my conversations with him.

I gathered up and tried to absorb every bit of personal information about him which was available.

I even had the benefit of a preview of what I might expect from Khrushchev when Mikoyan and Kozlov, who occupy the next to the top rung on the ladder of the Soviet hierarchy, visited Washington in the period just before I left for Moscow. They threw some pretty fair fast balls and a few curves in the long conversations I had with each of them. But meeting Khrushchev, after talking with them, was like going from minor to major league pitching. He throws a bewildering assortment of stuff—blinding speed, a wicked curve, plus knucklers, spitters, sliders, fork balls—all delivered with a deceptive change of pace.

I had made hundreds of protocol calls on high government officials in nations around the world, but never before had a head of government met me with a tirade of four-letter words which made his interpreter blush as he translated them into English.

Khrushchev had insulted his visitors before, but this time he did it on TV. And not just ordinary TV but on a new, revolutionary type of color-television tape being shown for the first time in the Soviet Union.

He had threatened his adversaries with missiles, but never before while standing in front of a model American kitchen.

It was not unusual for him to have serious discussions at lunch, but it was unprecedented for the wives of the participants to be present as silent but tremendously interested observers through a five-and-a-half-hour debate covering the whole range of American-Soviet relations.

He sometimes takes his visitors for boat rides on the Moscow River, but this was the first time he arranged for an added attraction—"impromptu political rallies" of hundreds of happy bathers demonstrating their affection for him and for the Communist system.

It is obvious that no plans could possibly have been devised to cope with such unpredictable conduct. Yet, without the months of planning, I might have been completely dismayed and routed by his unexpected assaults.

The idea that I go to the Soviet Union was conceived and first suggested to me by Abbott Washburn, Deputy Director of USIA, who was working at that time on the cultural exchange program between the United States and the USSR. When I indicated my willingness to undertake the assignment, the proposed trip was presented to and approved by his chief, George Allen, head of the USIA; Chris Herter, then Under Secretary of State; Foster Dulles and the President.

The official purpose of my trip was to open the first United States Exhibition ever held in the Soviet Union, on July 24 in Sokolniki Park in Moscow. The national exhibition was part of a cultural exchange program which had been adopted in the "spirit of Geneva" as an attempt to thaw out the frozen relations between our two countries. The 1955 "spirit of Geneva" had not lasted long, but this exchange program had been one of the few positive results to flow from that meeting between Khrushchev and Eisenhower. A Soviet exhibition, which spotlighted recent scientific advances in the Soviet Union, including a model of the new Sputnik, had opened in New York the previous January. Frol Kozlov, Deputy Premier, represented the Soviet Union and I represented the United States in speaking at the opening ceremonies. The exhibition had had heavy overtones of Soviet military might. Our exhibition, under the direction of Chad McClellan, a Los Angeles businessman, stressed U. S. consumer goods. Its inevitable effect was to dramatize the difference in the standards of living here and in the Soviet Union.

Because Kozlov and Mikoyan had received wide television coverage on their visits to the United States, the Soviet Government had agreed to give me the unique opportunity of speaking directly to the Russian people on a nationwide television hookup.

My visit would also afford an opportunity for high-level talks with Khrushchev in which I could make clear the United States' position on world issues and, at the same time, obtain for President Eisenhower and our policy makers some firsthand information as to Khrushchev's attitudes and views on the points of difference between the United States and the USSR.

As soon as final arrangements for the trip had been approved in Moscow and Washington, I began the most intensive series of briefings I had had for any of my trips abroad. In addition to such issues as the Berlin problem, atomic testing, and East-West trade—which are still with us today—I was prepared to discuss with Khrushchev such specific items as the long-missing U. S. airmen who had been shot down in a C-130 transport plane by Soviet fighters, the possible lifting of travel restrictions, censorship, opening of consular establishments, the jamming of radio broadcasts, and permission for a list of over a hundred Soviet relatives of United States citizens to leave the USSR to live with their families here. Scores of subjects I had been briefed on did not come up in my conversations with Khrushchev of course. But to the credit of the State Department and other briefing teams, he did not raise a single issue on which I had not been briefed.

Beyond these briefings I tried to find, as many have before and after me, a new and fresh approach on how to talk to Nikita Khrushchev.

I sought out men who had studied Soviet affairs and men who had met Khrushchev. I saw Hubert Humphrey and Averell Harriman; I met with journalists who had interviewed him in Moscow, such as Bill Hearst, Bob Considine, Walter Lippmann, and Turner Catledge. Catledge gave me the kind of advice you might expect from the managing editor of the New York *Times*. In effect, he said: "The trouble with most meetings with Khrushchev is that he dominates the conversation, and the talk dwindles off into a maze of generalities going all over the lot. Be specific, have some definite questions in mind that you want to ask him, and keep after him until you get the answer one way or the other." This was to prove easier said than done, as I am sure he understood.

Some of those to whom I talked urged that I try to "reassure" Khrushchev of the peaceful intentions of the United States and try to find out "what he wanted" in the way of guarantees from us which would remove any fears he had that our power was a potential aggressive threat against the USSR.

William Yandell Elliott, professor of government at Harvard University, took an exactly opposite tack. In a detailed memorandum, he said: "Khrushchev doesn't need to be reassured that we are for peace, and that we do not threaten him with aggression. He knows this. It is he who is threatening aggression and advocating revolution around the world. He should be told that we are ready to negotiate on equal terms but will not be bullied; we are willing to enter into peaceful competition between our two economic systems; that we are confident that we will win, but that we are ready to fight to defend our rights if necessary."

One of our former Ambassadors to Moscow agreed substantially with this line. I remember his telling me that it had been a mistake for American officials after the Geneva Conference in 1955 to state that they believed Khrushchev was "sincere" in his desire for peace.

"Do you mean," I asked, "that Khrushchev does not want peace?"

"That isn't the question," he replied. "Khrushchev wants the world. But he knows the consequences of modern war as well as we do. He wants to accomplish his objective without war. In that sense, he wants peace. The mistake is saying he is sincere. We have to understand that a Communist approaches world problems from an entirely different frame of reference from those in the non-Communist world. We are idealists. They are materialists."

Then, pointing to a coffee table in front of us, he said, "You can no more describe Khrushchev or any other Communist as being sincere than you can describe that coffee table as being sincere. He is for peace not because he is sincere but because he believes that his objective—world conquest—can best be furthered without war—at this time."

Britain's Prime Minister Harold Macmillan and Chancellor Konrad Adenauer of Germany gave me their personal appraisals of the Soviet Premier. Khrushchev had fluctuated between warm and frigid with Macmillan, even to the point of snubbing him publicly. Macmillan had met the snub with the icy reserve and dignity which centuries of experience in top-drawer diplomacy have brought to England's leading statesmen. Then Khrushchev had reversed himself and once again played the gracious host. Macmillan came away from that visit to the Kremlin with an interesting insight into Khrushchev, one that is not often recognized. Khrushchev took a particular pride in showing off Russian state treasures to the British Prime Minister—the jewels and gold of the old Czarist Empire. Macmillan had sensed that Khrushchev desperately wanted to be "admitted into the club"—accepted and respected as a major world figure in his own right and not simply because he represented the great military and economic power of the Soviet Union.

Adenauer told me, "There's no question but that Khrushchev wants to rule the world. But he does not want war. He does not want to rule a world of ruined cities and dead bodies." Adenauer reported one exchange between the two men which is characteristic of each of them. When Adenauer had been adamant on one particular issue, Khrushchev had burst out, "I will see you in Hell before I will agree with you on that!" Whereupon the ageless German leader shot back, "If you see me in Hell, it will only be because you were there before I got there." The tone of the conversation changed perceptibly for the better after this interchange, Adenauer reported.

The most memorable briefing I received came from John Foster Dulles, the man I had sought out for advice throughout my career since the night in 1948 when I had gone to see him in connection with the Alger Hiss case. His advice on Khrushchev is particularly clear in my mind, because of its intrinsic wisdom and because it was the last time I saw him alive.

I believe the verdict of history will be that John Foster Dulles was one of the truly great men of our time. And he was never more heroic than during the tragic last months of his life.

I saw him shortly after he returned on February 10, 1959, from his last trip to Europe, which had included stops in London, Paris, and Bonn to shore up our allies in the face of the Soviet ultimatum on Berlin. He knew before he started on this journey, on February 2, that he was fatally ill with cancer. The aides who accompanied him on the trip said that during the eight days he was away from Washington he was never able to keep down a single meal. He suffered such intense pain that he could sleep at night only when given heavy sedation. But during the days he refused to take any sedatives to relieve the pain, for fear that his reasoning powers might be dulled as well.

I asked him how he was able to go through the conferences. He answered, matter-of-factly, that once the conferences began and controversial subjects came up which required his complete concentration, he never felt a bit of pain. State Department officials who had accompanied him to other conferences told me that Dulles was never better, never more effective in presenting the U. S. point of view than during these meetings. In his hour of crisis, his performance was eloquent evidence of the truth of the adage that adversity breaks the weak but makes the strong.

During this period, his thoughts were always of others and not of himself. He never dwelled on his own troubles. And under his austere exterior, Foster Dulles was one of the kindest and most thoughtful men I have ever known. Two personal incidents illustrate this little-known side of his character.

One day I had lunch with him in his office. He happened to have some fresh figs for lunch that day, and I remarked casually that Pat was particularly fond of fresh figs but that they were hard to get in Washington. Two days later, by air express from California, a carton of fresh figs was delivered at our house with a friendly handwritten note for Pat from the busiest man in Washington at the time—Foster Dulles.

After he resigned as Secretary of State, he returned to Washington from Florida to spend his last days at Walter Reed Hospital. I went to the airport to meet him, as I had on scores of previous occasions when he had returned from his diplomatic journeys abroad. I rode with him to the hospital and then returned to my office. A call was waiting for me on the White House line. It was Foster Dulles. When he came on the line he said that he just wanted to tell me how much he appreciated my coming to the airport. "You really didn't have to do it, you know," he added. After he hung up, I thought of how many times in his life Foster Dulles had done things "he really didn't have to do" which the world would never know about.

During the period he was at Walter Reed, I had several long talks with him. I always made it a point to have a subject on which I wanted his advice before asking for an appointment, because he wanted it that way. He wanted to lead a useful and constructive life at all times and this he succeeded in doing to the very day of his death. In our talks we often discussed my pending trip to Moscow. He had always taken a dim view of so-called "personal diplomacy" where the Communist leaders were concerned. He knew that more often than not these meetings were used by the Communists, not to settle differences but to exploit them and to gain propaganda advantage, but he had strongly supported the proposal that I make the trip to Moscow. He told me that we must always appear to be willing to do everything possible to settle the differences we had with the Soviet Union at the conference table rather than on the battlefield. He believed I could hold my own in conversations with Khrushchev and he thought the conversations might provide some additional insight into Khrushchev's tactics and strategy which could be helpful in any meeting he might have with the President at a later date. He also believed that I might be able to use the forum of the exhibition opening to expose at least some segment of the Russian people to the reasonableness and justice of the American position on world issues.

The last time I saw him, he was sitting propped up with pillows in a chair in the drawing room of the Presidential suite at Walter Reed. His body was wasted but his mind was as alert as ever. He sucked constantly on ice cubes to dull the burning in his throat. The doctors had told me that this might be the last time I would see him. I asked him the key question: "What above everything else should I try to get across to Khrushchev?" Dulles was never a man to give quick answers to important questions. This time he waited much longer than usual. Then he replied approximately like this:

"Khrushchev does not need to be convinced of our good intentions. He knows we are not aggressors and do not threaten the security of the Soviet Union. He understands us. But what he needs to know is that we also understand him. In saying that he is for peaceful competition, he really means competition between his system and ours only in our world, not in his. He says he is for peaceful co-existence. What he means, as he has shown in Hungary, is that while a revolution against a non-Communist government is proper and should be supported, a revolution against a Communist government is invariably wrong and must be suppressed. Thus, the peaceful co-existence which he advocates represents peace for the Communist world and constant strife and conflict for the non-Communist world.

"He must be made to understand that he cannot have it both ways. If we are to have peaceful competition of economic systems and political ideas, it must take place in the Communist world as well as ours. He will deny, of course, that he or his government are connected in any way with Communist activities in other countries—that those activities are simply spontaneous expressions of a people's resentment against capitalistic regimes. Point the record out to him, chapter and verse. Show him that we are not taken in at all by the mock innocence of Soviet leaders, that we have concrete proof of the Kremlin's activities around the world. He should be told that until he puts a stop to such activities, his call for reducing of tensions and for peaceful co-existence will have a completely false and hollow ring."

Dulles died four days later, on May 24, 1959. But his principles will live on after him through those of us who had the great fortune of knowing him and learning from him.

Preparations for my trip continued. Mrs. Nixon and I took a crash course in learning some common Russian expressions from Alexander Barmine. I completed my briefings and wrote the speech I was to deliver at the opening of the exhibition.

There was the usual haggling over arrangements with the Soviets. They insisted that my party use Soviet jet planes within their country. They tried to limit my travel to Moscow, but finally yielded to allow me to see Leningrad and two cities within central Siberia, Sverdlovsk and Novosibirsk. They refused to give me a travel carte blanche throughout their country, as we had extended to their two First Deputy Premiers, Mikoyan and Kozlov. They refused to permit me to travel across Siberia and leave the Soviet Union by way of Vladivostok. This decision boomeranged on them. Since I had to return to Moscow, I decided to accept a long-standing invitation to visit Poland after I left Russia, and this was to provide a memorable climax to the entire trip.

On the eve of my departure for the Soviet Union, I had a final session with President Eisenhower about the trip. After discussing my mission, he told me he had decided to invite Khrushchev to visit the United States and he authorized me to discuss the trip privately with the Soviet Premier. The pros and cons of inviting Khrushchev here had been discussed at length within the Administration and I understood the overriding reason behind the President's decision, which I agreed with wholeheartedly: while Khrushchev's tour of the United States would lend a certain degree of respectability to the Soviet leader and allow him to spread his propaganda among the American people, the United States stood to gain a great deal more by convincing Khrushchev of the size, the strength, and the spirit of the United States through the first-hand information he would gather while crossing the North American continent. Furthermore, I was convinced that a private talk with President Eisenhower would go far in dispelling from Khrushchev's mind any mistaken impression concerning the will and determination of the United States to stand up for its rights at the bargaining table of world affairs. I also believed that the President's return visit to the Soviet Union would have a far greater impact on the Russian people than Khrushchev could ever have here. The Soviet Premier apparently recognized this after my own trip to the Soviet Union, for he soon afterwards seized upon the U-2 incident as a pretext to withdraw his invitation to President Eisenhower.

We left the United States from Baltimore's Friendship International Airport at 9:06 on the night of July 22, aboard an Air Force jet transport. In my party were Milton Eisenhower, the President's brother; Admiral Hyman Rickover, father of the atomic submarine; State Department experts, members of my staff, and representatives of the President's Advisory Committee on the American National Exhibition. About seventy correspondents, columnists, and commentators flew from New York in their own chartered 707.

There was a surprisingly large crowd at the airport. Despite our attempts to keep the trip in perspective by emphasizing that it was primarily ceremonial in character, press and public interest was very high. Milton Eisenhower pointed out, as the plane was taking off, that people had come to the airport not just out of curiosity, but because this trip combined all the elements of hope, mystery, and even fear. I had received hundreds of letters before taking off, expressing concern for our safety in the Soviet Union. Some referred darkly to what had happened in Caracas the year before.

And there were some humorous sidelights. Just a week before I had been playing golf with Bill Rogers, the Attorney General. A Boeing

707 happened to fly overhead. Rogers told his caddy that that was the type of plane the Vice President would soon be flying to Russia in. The caddy stopped short, and asked, "You mean he is going to fly to Russia?" When Rogers replied in the affirmative, the boy, who was about twelve years old, said, "Won't they shoot him down?"

I had no concern whatever for our physical safety as our plane flew high over the Atlantic toward Moscow. My thoughts were on how I should conduct myself in my meeting with Khrushchev. As for information on issues that might arise, I was confident that I was better prepared than for any challenge I had faced in my entire life. But my problem was not what I knew: it was, how to use it. I fully realized that as Vice President I would be in no position to negotiate any issues with the Premier of the Soviet Union. But my talks could pave the way and set the tone for the exchange of visits between Khrushchev and Eisenhower. Khrushchev would have the advantage of being able to change the Soviet position on issues at any time. As Vice President I could only defend the publicly proclaimed American position. I decided that I should listen more than I should talk. Any additional insights into Khrushchev's thinking and his tactics would eventually be helpful to President Eisenhower. Because negotiations at Geneva on the Berlin situation were in a delicate stage—stalled at dead center—I knew that I would again be in a situation to which I had become somewhat accustomed—walking on eggs.

I expected, based on his previous conduct, that Khrushchev might take a belligerent, bullying attitude. I knew that I could not respond in kind, because under no circumstances could I run the risk of "rocking the boat" or giving him a pretext for breaking off the Geneva negotiations. I had also decided completely to reject the advice of those who had urged me to try and convince Khrushchev that we were "sincerely" for peace, that we believed his concern for the security of his country from attack was real, and that he should be reassured of our willingness to enter into any guarantees on that score. It was my belief that Khrushchev knew that our intentions were peaceful. It was he who was the aggressor in words and action, whose arrogantly admitted aim in life was to win the world so that our grandchildren would live under Communism. If the opportunity presented itself, then, I believed the most important single purpose of my talks with him would be to convince him that he could not hope to convert the United States to Communism, nor could he hope to "win" a nuclear war in the traditional sense of the word. In 1959 and since, Khrushchev had boasted that the Soviet Union could destroy and devastate all the nations of Europe, and the United States as well, without sustaining annihilation itself. Khrushchev must not come to believe his own propaganda, merely because of the Soviet Union's new advances in missile power.

While on a good-will trip of this type I must avoid the temptation to answer threat with threat and boast for boast. I should not miss an opportunity to get across to him that the United States did not believe his boasts about the operational capacity of Soviet intercontinental ballistic missiles and that such boasts were, in reality, threats which do not advance the cause of peace. He should understand that the United States is for peace, but that we would not be bluffed or pushed around.

Apart from my meetings with Khrushchev, I wanted to use every opportunity which arose on this trip to get through to the Russian people as distinguished from the Communist hierarchy. While Khrushchev and the Communist leaders did not really believe the United States threatened aggression against the Soviet Union, the 200 million people of Russia who are not Communists have been told for years that this was the case. My job was to convince them that the American Government and the American people were one in their dedication to peace and in their desire for friendly relations with the Russian people. In addition, I had to try to get across that it was their own Communist leaders who had deliberately created the tensions which might lead to war because of their insistence on spreading Communism by any means necessary, throughout the world.

I was keyed up and ready for battle as the flight neared Moscow. But I knew that this was not to be a single crisis in the classic sense. While my meeting with Khrushchev might be a personal crisis for me, I recognized that in perspective it was only one episode in the continuing crisis that Mr. Khrushchev and his Communist colleagues are determined to perpetuate through our lifetime. What I did in the Soviet Union would not in itself ensure peace, deter Communist aggression, or remove any one of the trouble spots in the world. I could not convince Nikita Khrushchev that individual freedom and liberty were better than dictatorial socialism, any more than he could convince me that my grandchildren would live under Communism. This crisis would not come to a head and be resolved during my two-week visit to the Soviet Union. It would continue most probably through my lifetime and certainly beyond that of Khrushchev himself. Yet, every move in this crisis-laden struggle was important. At stake was world peace and the survival of freedom. With my planning and preparation be-

hind me, I now intended to play my small part in this gigantic struggle
to the best of my ability.

Eleven hours after takeoff, with a one-hour refueling stop in Iceland,
our Air Force Boeing 707 came in for a smooth landing at Vnukova
Airport in Moscow—at 2:50 P.M. Thursday, July 23, 1959. The press
plane, which was a new long-range 707, had arrived before us, establishing two new records. It was the first commercial United States airliner to land in the Soviet Union since the end of World War II, and it
set a nonstop speed record between New York and Moscow: eight
hours and fifty-three minutes.

The day was warm but the reception was cool. I sensed immediately
that we were being given the "correct treatment" and nothing more.
Outwardly, the arrival procedure was scarcely different from what I
had experienced in scores of other world capitals. Yet, while listening
to the booming welcoming speech of First Deputy Premier Frol Kozlov,
who said all the correct things about peace and friendship, I could
sense a degree of coolness and oppression in the warm summer air.
Subconsciously it reminded me of the rather ominous unfriendliness
that I had experienced so consciously on our arrival at the airport at
Caracas.

There were the usual handshakes and words of greeting, but no
playing of national anthems, no band, no crowds. Approximately one
hundred diplomats and officials and perhaps an equal number of reporters and photographers were on hand. Otherwise, the airport area
was empty except for a few mechanics and passengers boarding other
planes. Our motorcade sped through empty streets, for the route had
been blocked off from other vehicles. The dozen or so people who
were on the streets scarcely turned their heads as we went by. They
had not the slightest idea who we were. When we arrived at the U. S.
Embassy residence, I felt the same sense of relief upon reaching a bit
of American soil in a foreign land that I had experienced when we
had finally reached the sanctuary of the American Embassy in Caracas
fourteen months before.

Ambassador Llewellyn Thompson, who with his wife, Jane, extended their usual warm and gracious hospitality, suggested an explanation for the cold reception: Khrushchev might be having some
second thoughts about the wisdom of his decision to allow an American
fair in Moscow and an American Vice President to speak to the Russian people. Khrushchev had returned from a ten-day tour of Poland,
where he had been coolly received, just ninety minutes before I

landed in Moscow. He had gone directly from the airport to the Moscow Sports Arena to address thousands of Moscovites. The timing worked out so that just when I was being greeted at the airport, Khrushchev was lambasting the United States generally and me personally for the Captive Nations Resolution passed by Congress a week before. The resolution called for prayers for those behind the Iron Curtain. It was difficult for me to imagine that the resolution truly disturbed the Soviet Premier because it was simply the expression of a well-known opinion in the United States, and not a call to action.

Ambassador Thompson informed me that news of my visit had been buried in the back pages of the Moscow newspapers. The U. S. Exhibition had been ridiculed by the Communist press for the past four days as not representative of life in America. But it must actually have impressed them, because just recently the Soviet Government had decided to open a competing exhibition of Soviet-produced consumer goods.

Late that afternoon, Mrs. Nixon and I went out for our first stroll on Russian soil. It was with a somewhat strange feeling that we walked along Chaikovsky Street, one of Moscow's main thoroughfares, to Smolensky Square. We looked in the shop windows, observed the men and women on the street going about their normal everyday business, and with my rudimentary Russian and the help of our interpreter introduced ourselves to several shopkeepers, customers, and occasional pedestrians. Each time we saw surprise and then delight upon the faces of those we met. We were greeted with sincere words of welcome. As we returned from this pleasant walk, I was encouraged at the prospects of my visit.

That evening we dined with the Thompsons, and I received a first-hand briefing on the latest in Soviet policies and thinking from the Ambassador and members of the Embassy staff.

I also received my first indoctrination in how to conduct confidential conferences in a police state. We did not have our meeting in the spacious drawing room on the first floor of Spaso House. Instead, we used a small sitting room on the second floor, adjacent to the Thompsons' bedroom. This was the only room in the entire Embassy residence which the small technical crew assigned to the Ambassador's staff could guarantee was free from "bugging" devices. And this was accomplished only by keeping it under constant surveillance and by checking it daily with electronic instruments. Everywhere we went in the Soviet Union we were confronted with the same problem. When we stayed in Soviet guesthouses, we conducted any confidential conversations in walks we would take around the grounds, and even then we were careful: we always talked in open spaces, never near trees or bushes large enough to conceal a listening device.

Tommy Thompson, a career man in the foreign service since 1929, had served in Moscow off and on since 1939. In October 1941, when the diplomatic corps had fled in fear of the Nazi panzer thrusts deep into Soviet territory, Thompson had stayed behind to guard our Embassy and United States interests in Moscow. I first met him late in 1956 while checking into the Hungarian refugee situation in Austria, where he was then representing the United States in the negotiations which led to a treaty of independence for Austria. He became our first Ambassador to the new government there, and then in 1957, President Eisenhower appointed him Ambassador to the Soviet Union, one of the most important diplomatic posts in the world. He has served so well, and his judgment on Soviet affairs has proved to be so acute, that the Kennedy Administration wisely persuaded him to remain on in that post.

I turned in early that night in anticipation of the next day's schedule: a meeting with Khrushchev, a preview tour with him of the American Exhibition, and a major speech officially opening the exhibit to the Soviet public. But as usual before any major crisis, I found I was too keyed up to sleep except intermittently. Finally, at 5:30 A.M., I gave up trying and decided to go out for a walk again, to get a feel of the city before starting my official calls.

I woke up Jack Sherwood and, together with a Russian security policeman who acted as our driver and interpreter, we drove to the Danilovsky Market. As a boy, working in my father's store, I used to drive a pickup truck to the produce markets in Los Angeles in the early morning hours so that I could get the fresh fruits and vegetables back in the store ready for sale when we opened at 8:00. I thought it would be interesting to compare the Soviet market, which was primarily a retail rather than a wholesale establishment, with the one I had known as a boy in the United States.

As I moved through the market, testing my few Russian phrases, the people greeted me with genuine warmness. The venders plied me with gifts of fruit, vegetables, and anything at hand, refusing to let us buy anything. As word of my identity spread, the crowd grew. Question after question was put to me about life in the United States and the people hung on my every answer. It was obvious they were starved for information about the outside world. For almost an hour I moved around that market in an atmosphere of warm friendliness. I was struck by one detail which was different from our own markets back home. At each stall or counter, there were two sets of scales: one used by the stallkeeper, and the other by the customer to reweigh his purchase as a check against any cheating!

While most of those around me apparently had not heard of my visit, they all knew about the American Exhibition. As we were about to leave, several asked me if I had any tickets to the exhibition. Distribution of the tickets, which cost one ruble, or twenty-five cents, each, was left to the Soviet authorities. Explaining to them that I did not have any tickets, I said that I would be very happy to buy tickets for those in the market who had been so kind to me. At my suggestion, Jack Sherwood handed the spokesman for the group a 100-ruble note, but he handed the bill back with a laugh, explaining it was not the cost but rather the unavailability of tickets that prevented them from attending the exhibition. I laughed with them at the difficulty of prying tickets loose from authorities, and then shook hands all around to take my leave.

But before I could go, one stallkeeper presented me with a huge bouquet of flowers which he said had been purchased with contributions he had hurriedly collected from the people at the market who wished to demonstrate their friendship for the United States and the American people. I walked away from the market with the same impression that most American tourists get in Moscow: the Russian people want to live in peace, they are friendly to Americans, appreciative of U. S. aid during World War II, and they are starved for knowledge about the non-Communist world. But I learned a lesson the next day when the Communist newspapers were read for me: never confuse the desires of the Russian people with the aims of their Communist leaders.

Pravda, Izvestia, and *Trud,* the three largest and most influential government and Party newspapers, accused me of trying to "bribe" and "degrade" a Soviet citizen. One account said that I had pulled a capitalistic trick of handing money to a "poor Soviet citizen" while my capitalistic photographers recorded the scene for the "Wall Street press." The Communist newspapers made a *cause célèbre* out of the incident, even though there had been no photographers at the market at the time.

Later that morning, accompanied by Milton Eisenhower and Ambassador Thompson, I paid my first courtesy call in the Kremlin, a walled city within a city, housing the government and Communist Party of the Soviet Union. Marshal Kliment Y. Voroshilov, President of the Supreme Soviet, a figurehead in the Communist hierarchy little-known outside Russia, greeted me "as a dear guest of the Soviet Union" and wished me "health and success" on my trip through his country. After the usual courtesies and protocol of the visit, we left his office and were escorted down the hall to the office of the real boss—the First Secretary of the Communist Party.

This was the moment for which I had been preparing myself for many months. I was on edge with suspense as I entered Khrushchev's office shortly after 10:00. He was toying with a model of Lunik, the satellite which the Russians had shot off toward the moon several months before. It looked like an oversized baseball in Khrushchev's chubby hands. I have no clear recollection of his office, except that it was large and luxurious. But I remember vividly that while Khrushchev was somewhat shorter than I expected, he somehow conveyed the unmistakable impression of great physical strength and vitality.

The reporters and photographers recorded our first handshake and his accepting from me the personal letter of greetings which President Eisenhower had asked me to deliver. Then he abruptly asked them to leave the room.

This was supposed to be a pure protocol courtesy visit at which serious business was not to be discussed. Our talks on substantive issues were scheduled for Sunday in the Soviet Government guesthouse about twenty miles outside Moscow. But as soon as the newspapermen had left the office Khrushchev motioned us to sit around the conference table. I could sense that he was in a testy mood. He kept looking me up and down from head to toe, as a tailor might estimate a customer's size for a suit of clothes, or perhaps more as an undertaker might view a prospective corpse with a coffin in mind. There was nothing about Khrushchev to match the jovial bombast of Kozlov or the suave courtesy of Mikoyan. I expected him to take me on, but I had thought that since today's events were primarily protocol in nature he would wait until we had our private talks the next day. But Khrushchev never plays by the rules. He delights in doing the unexpected. Just as soon as we sat down at the conference table, he started in on a bone of contention that was to be the major Soviet irritant throughout my tour. It was the Captive Nations Resolution, passed by Congress on July 6, calling on the President to issue a proclamation designating the third week in July as Captive Nations Week, during which free people would rededicate themselves and pray for the liberation of "enslaved peoples" behind the Iron Curtain. President Eisenhower had issued the proclamation on July 17, five days before my departure for Russia.

In a long harangue, speaking in a high-pitched voice and frequently pounding the table, Khrushchev declared that the Soviet Government regarded the resolution as a very serious "provocation."

Why did President Eisenhower issue such a proclamation just before my trip if he wanted me to have a good reception, he asked. And this resolution would certainly not improve the chances for any agreement at the Geneva Conference on a peace treaty for Germany or for a general improvement in relations between our two countries, he added.

As he talked and the translation was made, I had to make a quick decision on how to react to his attack. I did not feel that this was the time to debate with him on the merits of the resolution, on which I had some strong feelings. I was sure that he was going through an act—that he was using the resolution as a pretext for taking the offensive against me, and that had it not been for this resolution, he would have found some other excuse for doing so. But I could not tell whether he was trying to get me to lose my temper and respond in kind so that he could make an incident out of my conduct, or whether he simply was trying to put me on the defensive at the very outset of my visit.

Consequently, I decided at this time to try to finesse his attack by answering him collaterally. I pointed out that this was a decision made by the Congress over which Eisenhower had no control. And the resolution was not a provocation, but an expression of opinion widely held in the United States.

Khrushchev expressed bewilderment. "Any action by an authoritative body like Congress must have a purpose," he exclaimed, "and I wonder what the purpose of this particular action can be?" He asserted that the resolution could not change anything in the USSR or in any other country, adding that if the United States meant to bring about any change it would mean war. Then he recalled how the Russian people had repulsed what he called United States intervention at the time of the birth of the Soviet regime, during 1919–21, and certainly would do so now.

I tried again to explain to him the operation of our constitutional system—how our Congressmen and Senators represent all segments of our population, how millions of U. S. citizens emigrated from or had their relatives in Eastern European countries, and how the resolution represented the strongly-held views of those citizens, as well as many other Americans. I also pointed out that the resolution did not call for our intervention, or even for our support of a revolution in the satellite nations, but only expressed moral support and asked for prayers for those who want freedom in those nations.

But Khrushchev chose not to understand. He belabored the point. I listened carefully and responded each time he allowed me to make a point. Now I could see what Khrushchev was trying to do. He was on the offensive, trying to throw me off balance and to force me to debate him on the ground he selected. Each time I tried to reason with him or even to change the subject, he brushed my answer aside. He did this not because he thought my arguments were unreasonable but because he wanted to create and maintain all the tension he could on this point.

Toward the end of the conversation, he shook his finger at me and warned that I would be hearing about this Captive Nations Resolution throughout my stay in the Soviet Union. I told him I welcomed free discussion on any point. He warned me that I might even hear cat-calls. I responded that I had had some experience as far as catcalls were concerned. We went round and round in this fashion until I reminded the Premier of the American expression, "We have beaten this horse to death; let's change to another." But Khrushchev insisted that he wanted to tell us once more what he thought of that resolution.

"This resolution stinks!" he shouted, pounding the table. Then he spelled out what he meant in some earthy four-letter words, so beyond the pale of diplomacy that Troyanovsky, his interpreter, blushed bright red and hesitated before finally translating his words.

It was on that "peasant" note that my courtesy call on the leader of the world Communist movement came to an end. His attack at this early stage of my visit had been a surprise. His vehemence and choice of language had been a shock. But my intense preparation for this visit and my study of his past tactics helped me to meet his attack without losing my temper or my sense of balance.

From the Kremlin, we drove to Sokolniki Park for a preview of the American Exhibition. I expressed concern to Thompson about the meeting we had just had. I had done my best to turn away Khrushchev's wrath with soft answers, but with very little apparent success. Thompson advised me, however, that I should continue to follow the same tactics. He said that Khrushchev's purpose was to goad me into some rash and impulsive statements and that I should avoid falling into this trap.

As we arrived at the exhibition grounds, I had no idea what to expect, except to be on guard for almost anything. Since Khrushchev had blown off so much steam at our private meeting, however, I thought he might put on the air of the proper host for the benefit of the hundred or so newsmen who were now observing every move he made. But when God created Khrushchev (something Khrushchev would deny), He broke the mold.

No sooner had we started to walk around the exhibition grounds with more than a hundred newsmen gathered around us than Khrushchev let loose with a jibe. "Americans have lost their ability to trade. Now you have grown older and you don't trade the way you used to. You need to be invigorated."

"But *you* need to have goods to trade," I responded.

He quickly dropped that subject and moved to another one. And then through a combination of circumstances neither of us could anticipate, we found ourselves by accident, rather than design, standing on a stage with literally millions of potential viewers and listeners watching every action and listening to every word we were saying. We had come upon a model television studio featuring a new type of color-television tape. A young Ampex Company executive steered us to a stage in front of a camera and asked each of us to say something which later could be played as a form of greeting to visitors to the fair.

Khrushchev at first seemed reluctant to say anything. He apparently thought he was being tricked. But then he saw a large crowd of Soviet workmen in a gallery overhead, and the corps of newspapermen around us, and the temptation was too much for him. He seized the opportunity as eagerly as an American politician accepts free television time. Instead of greeting the visitors to the exhibition, he took out after me.

First, he said the Soviet Union wanted to live in peace and friendship—but was fully prepared to protect itself in war. Then, boasting that the Soviet Union would be on the same economic level with the United States in another seven years, he twitted me by saying, "When we catch up with you, in passing you by, we will wave to you. Then if you wish, we can stop and say: 'Please follow up. . . .'" Then he denounced the Captive Nations Resolution again. Wrapping his arms around a Soviet workman nearby, he declared, "Does this man look like a slave laborer? With men of such spirit how can we lose?"

As Akalovsky, my interpreter, whispered what he was saying into my ear I again had to do some quick thinking. Should I try to answer his outlandish and sometimes even insulting charges on the spot, or should I take a conciliatory line as I had at our first meeting? Again, I had to remind myself that I was the host at the exhibition with the obligation to treat a guest with courtesy. I was his inferior in rank, a Vice President speaking to a head of government. And again, I could not be sure what his motive was. Was he trying to goad me into giving him an excuse to break off the current Geneva negotiations? Or was he attacking me for propaganda purposes to display Soviet superiority over "soft" Western negotiators and leaders?

As at our previous conference, I decided this was not the time to take him on. I tried to change the subject to color television, and the other consumer items which were on display at the American Exhibition. I urged that we needed a free exchange of ideas between our two countries. "You must not be afraid of ideas," I said. "After all, you don't know everything . . ."

"If I don't know everything," he interrupted, "you don't know anything about Communism—except fear of it."

Still determined not to be provoked or goaded into saying anything which could be misinterpreted, I tried again to change the tone of the conversation, but he would have none of it. Constantly interrupting me, he insisted that I was a lawyer and he was a coal miner, but that he still could outargue me on Communism vs. capitalism.

As we watched the playback of the conversation, I could see that he had been aggressive, rude, and forceful. He had gone after me with no holds barred. And I had had to counter him like a fighter with one hand tied behind his back. It was this television tape which was later played before millions of viewers in the United States and in other countries. Khrushchev's obvious rudeness made an unfavorable impression and my keeping my temper despite considerable provocation met with public approval. But his attack had shaken me right to my toes. He had been on the offensive and I on the defensive throughout. I knew that he had scored heavily and I felt it was imperative that I find an opportunity to strike back so that the record could be set straight publicly. Bob Considine later compared the episode to the first round of the Dempsey-Firpo fight. Khrushchev had started the encounter by knocking me out of the ring. At the end, I had climbed back in to fight again. And the second round was still coming up.

As we continued to walk through the exhibition grounds he kept up his needling. Once he believes he has gained an advantage over an opponent, he never lets up. He kept making references to me as a smart lawyer with the innuendo that I was a slick and dishonest manipulator of words in contrast with his own "honest" background as a miner and a worker.

Consequently, as we walked by a model American grocery store, I commented, "You may be interested to know that my father owned a small general store in California, and all the Nixon boys worked there while going to school." Khrushchev with a wave of his arms snorted, "Oh, all shopkeepers are thieves." But this one I did not let pass. "Thieving happens everywhere," I responded. "Even in the store I visited this morning, I saw people weighing food after they had bought it from the State." This time it was Khrushchev who changed the subject.

Then we came to the center attraction of the exhibition, a model American home, fully furnished and equipped with all our modern conveniences. The Soviet press had focused their ridicule on this model home during the past week, saying that it was no more typical of a worker's home in the United States than the Taj Mahal was typical in India or Buckingham Palace in Great Britain. Khrushchev and I walked up the center hall of the model home, looking into the exposed rooms, and we stopped at the kitchen.

And here we had our famous "kitchen conference" or, as some reporters put it, the "Sokolniki Summit." This conversation, incidentally, was not carried on television in the United States but was reported in the newspapers.

The conversation began innocently enough. We discussed the relative merits of washing machines. Then I decided that this was as good a place as any to answer the charges that had been made in the Soviet press, that only "the rich" in the United States could afford such a house as this.

I made the point that this was a typical house in the United States, costing $14,000, which could be paid over twenty-five or thirty years. Most U. S. veterans of World War II have bought houses like this, in the $10,000 to $15,000 range, I told him, adding that most any steelworker could buy one.

"We too can find steelworkers and peasants who can pay $14,000 cash for a flat," he retorted. Then he went into a harangue on how American capitalists build houses to last only twenty years and the Soviets build for their children and grandchildren. He went on and on, obviously determined to deny the American know-how he saw so plainly in front of him:

"You think the Russians will be dumbfounded by this exhibit. But the fact is that all newly built Russian houses will have this equipment. You need dollars in the United States to get this house, but here all you need is to be born a citizen. If an American citizen does not have dollars he has the right to buy this house or sleep on the pavement at night. And you say we are slaves of Communism!"

I finally interrupted him. "In our Senate we would call you a filibusterer," I said. "You do all the talking and you do not let anyone else talk. I want to make one point. We don't think this fair will astound the Russian people, but it will interest them just as yours interested us. To us, diversity, the right to choose, the fact that we have a thousand different builders, that's the spice of life. We don't want to have a decision made at the top by one government official saying that we will have one type of house. That's the difference . . ."

"On political differences, we will never agree," Khrushchev said, again cutting in on me. "If I follow you, I will be led astray from Mikoyan. He likes spicy soups and I don't. But that doesn't mean we differ."

I tried again to point up our belief in freedom of choice, and I put in a plea for more exchanges between our two countries to bring about a better understanding. But Khrushchev did not want to debate me on my grounds. He changed the subject back to washing machines, arguing that it was better to have one model than many. I listened to his long harangue on washing machines, realizing full well that he was not switching arguments by chance or accident; he was trying to throw me off balance.

"Isn't it better to be talking about the relative merits of our washing machines than the relative strength of our rockets?" I said at the end of his long speech. "Isn't this the kind of competition you want?"

At this he gave the appearance of turning angry and, jamming his thumb into my chest, he shouted: "Yes, that's the kind of competition we want, but your generals say we must compete in rockets. Your generals say they are so powerful they can destroy us. We can also show you something so that you will know the Russian spirit. We are strong, we can beat you. But in this respect we can also show you something."

As Akalovsky translated what he was saying into my ear, I knew that now was the time to strike back. Otherwise I would leave the impression to the press and through them to the world that I, the second-highest official of the United States, and the government I represented were dealing with Khrushchev from a position of weakness —militarily, economically, and ideologically. I had to be firm without being belligerent, a most difficult posture to preserve. With this in mind, I pointed my finger at him and said:

"To me, you are strong and we are strong. In some ways, you are stronger than we are. In others, we are stronger. But to me it seems that in this day and age to argue who is the stronger completely misses the point. . . . No one should ever use his strength to put another in the position where he in effect has an ultimatum. For us to argue who is the stronger misses the point. If war comes we both lose."

Now Khrushchev changed the pace. He tried to laugh off what I had said by exclaiming: "For the fourth time I have to say I cannot recognize my friend Mr. Nixon. If all Americans agree with you, then who don't we agree with? That is what we want."

This time I was determined not to let him get off the hook. I pressed on: "I hope the Prime Minister understands all the implications of what I have just said. When you place either one of our powerful nations in such a position that it has no choice but to accept dictation or fight, then you are playing with the most destructive thing in the world. This is very important in the present world context," I went on before he could interrupt. "It is very dangerous. When we sit down at a conference table it cannot all be one way. One side cannot put an ultimatum to another. It is impossible."

Now we were going at it toe-to-toe. To some, it may have looked as though we had both lost our tempers. But exactly the opposite was true. I had full and complete control of my temper and was aware of it. I knew the value of keeping cool in a crisis, and what I said and how I said it was done with as much calm deliberation as I could muster in a running, impromptu debate with an expert. I never doubted, either, whether Khrushchev had lost control of his emotions. In situations before the kitchen debate and after it, according to my observations, Khrushchev never loses his temper—he uses it.

Now, using his temper, Khrushchev struck back. He accused me of issuing an ultimatum, he vehemently denied that the Soviet Union ever used dictation, and he warned me not to threaten him. "It sounds to me like a threat," he declared, poking his finger at me. "We, too, are giants. You want to threaten—we will answer threats with threats."

"That's not my point," I retorted. "We will never engage in threats."

"You wanted indirectly to threaten me," he shouted back. "But we have the means to threaten, too."

"Who wants to threaten?" I asked.

"You are talking about implications," he went on, apparently getting more and more excited. "I have not been. We have the means at our disposal. Ours are better than yours. It is you who want to compete. Da, da, da . . ."

"We are well aware that you have the means. To me, who is best is not material."

"You raised the point," he went on. "We want peace and friendship with all nations, especially with America."

I could sense now that he wanted to call an end to the argument. And I certainly did not want to take the responsibility for continuing it publicly. We both had had enough. I said, "We want peace too."

He answered, "Yes, I believe that."

And so we ended our discussion on the underlying question of the whole debate—the possibility of easing Cold War tensions at the then current Four Power Conference in Geneva.

"It would be a great mistake and a blow to peace if that conference should fail," I said.

"That is our understanding as well," he said.

Then, returning to my responsibilities as his host, I put my hand on his shoulder and said with a smile, "I'm afraid I haven't been a good host." Khrushchev turned to the American guide in the model kitchen and said, "Thank the housewife for letting us use her kitchen for our argument."

As we walked away from the model house, to view the rest of the exhibition, I began to feel the effects of the tremendous tension of the past two hours. Holding back when you have something you want to say is far more wearing on the system than letting yourself go. I felt like a fighter wearing sixteen-ounce gloves and bound by Marquis of Queensberry rules, up against a bare-knuckle slugger who had gouged, kneed, and kicked. I was not sure whether I had held my own. But two widely differing sources of opinion buoyed me up on this score. Ernie Barcella, the correspondent for United Press International, came alongside and whispered in my ear, "Good going, Mr. Vice President." A moment or so later, Mikoyan took me aside and through my interpreter paid me an unexpected compliment. "I reported to Mr. Khrushchev when I came back from Washington that you were very skillful in debate and you proved it again today . . ."[1]

[1] Even Khrushchev got into the spirit of the occasion again. As we continued our stroll, it happened that Voroshilov and I walked on ahead and Khrushchev fell

Khrushchev now engaged in a bit of personal public relations. He shook hands with Soviet workmen, and then, spotting one old woman who had been cheering him, he gave her a tremendous hug in which they both rocked back and forth for several seconds while photographers took pictures.

As we approached one exhibit I saw Bill Hearst in the crowd and beckoned to him. Khrushchev recognized him immediately, for Hearst had interviewed the Soviet Premier on several occasions. He grabbed both of Hearst's hands and shook them emphatically, shouting goodnaturedly, "Hello, my capitalistic, monopolist, journalist friend. Do you ever publish anything in your papers that you disagree with?"

"Oh, boy, do I!" said the publisher of the Hearst chain.

"You should see what some papers print about me," I remarked. Khrushchev looked surprised, as though he didn't believe either of us. A moment later, I saw Westbrook Pegler and called him over. As I introduced them, I thought that probably never before had two men who thought less of each other shaken hands.

That evening I officially opened the American National Exhibition and delivered a major speech which I had prepared before I left Washington. The Soviet authorities had promised the speech would be carried in *Pravda* and *Izvestia*, a pledge they honored, so that it reached millions of Russian people. *Time* magazine characterized the speech as "a ringing retort to Soviet internal propaganda that the exhibition was not typical of U. S. life." More than that, however, I used the exhibition as a means of describing our way of life, our standard of living, and our aspirations to the Russian people. It was my chance, a unique one in Soviet-American relations, to tell the Russian people that "the 67 million American wage earners are not the downtrodden masses depicted by the critics of capitalism in the latter part of the nineteenth and early part of the twentieth centuries." That caricature of capitalism was as out-of-date as a "wooden plow," I said.

I cited figures to show that the 44 million families in America own 56 million cars, 50 million television sets, 143 million radio sets, and that 31 million of those families own their own homes. Then I made the point that so many people overlook. "What these statistics dramatically demonstrate is this: that the United States, the world's largest capitalist country, has from the standpoint of distribution of wealth

---

behind. When I turned around and asked if he did not want to walk with us, he replied with a somewhat sardonic smile, "No, you walk with the President. I know my place!"

come closest to the ideal of prosperity for all in a classless society."

At this point, Khrushchev, who had spoken just before me and was sitting on the stage next to me, tried to interrupt, rising and shouting "nyet, nyet." I stopped him firmly but pleasantly by saying, "I have the floor now, it's my turn to speak." He was easy to handle compared with some of the Senate sessions over which I had presided!

I described the personal and political freedoms we enjoy and take for granted in the United States, over and above our material progress. "There is nothing we want from any other people except the right to live in peace and friendship with them. The peace we want and the peace the world needs is not the peace of surrender but the peace of justice; not peace by ultimatum but peace by negotiation." And finally, warning of the grave risk of nuclear war, I concluded, "The last half of the twentieth century can be the darkest or the brightest page in the history of civilization. The decision is in our hands to make."

After the official opening of the exhibition, I led Khrushchev to a table of California wines (which he praised) and he proposed a toast. I understood his first Russian word to mean "peace," but I waited until the translation was completed before raising my glass. Khrushchev, up to one of his usual tricks, had proposed that I drink "To peace and the elimination of all military bases on foreign lands."

Without raising my glass to his toast I countered by proposing, "Let us just drink a toast to peace."

Then Khrushchev began an argument about foreign bases until a bystander interrupted by proposing another toast: "One hundred years to Premier Khrushchev!"

"I will drink to that," I said. "We may disagree with your policy, but we want you to be of good health. May you live to be a hundred years old."

Khrushchev accepted the toast, and after we had drunk, he quipped, "At ninety-nine years of age we shall discuss these questions further. Why should we be in haste?" To that, I responded, "You mean that at ninety-nine, you will still be in power with no free elections?"

I then escorted him to his limousine. Following his usual custom he got into the front seat with the driver and drove off to the Kremlin, where we had first met just eight hours before.

That evening Ambassador and Mrs. Thompson gave a reception for the Americans who were visiting the exhibition and the American members of the press. The opinion was unanimous that the day, after a shaky start, had turned into a smashing success.

"No matter what happens now," one American businessman told me, "your trip to the Soviet Union will go down as a major diplomatic triumph."

It had been a long, tense day and I would have welcomed the chance to relax and enjoy some of the sense of accomplishment which comes from a degree of success after so many hard months of preparation. But one thing I had learned through my years of conflict with Communism, going clear back to the Hiss case, is that there is never a period when it is safe to let up in the battle with our Communist opponents. They are out to win, and one of the tactics they use is to keep the pressure on. They try to wear us out. To keep them from winning and to win ourselves, we must have more stamina and more determination than they have.

I knew that my most important meeting with Khrushchev was yet to come—on Sunday when we were to have a private conversation. That is why, after the reception, I spent most of the night going over again my voluminous briefing notes on issues that might arise in those discussions.

The next day I paid official calls on Deputy Premiers Mikoyan and Kozlov, visited the Soviet Agricultural Exhibition, lunched with Soviet officials at the sumptuous Golden Sheaf Restaurant, and in the evening attended the dinner tendered by Ambassador Thompson at Spaso House for Khrushchev and the Soviet top hierarchy.

The dinner was a culinary and social success except for one incident. Khrushchev had always shown a great interest in American corn production. Mrs. Thompson thought she would surprise him by having some fresh corn flown to Moscow in our plane and served at the dinner in his honor. Her cook, however, had never prepared corn on the cob before and, despite Mrs. Thompson's most careful instructions, boiled it for over an hour until it was nothing but an unpalatable, soggy mass of kernels hanging on the cobs. Mrs. Thompson could not have been more chagrined, but the Premier and Mrs. Khrushchev dutifully went through the motions of nibbling at it and proclaiming it a fine dish. I could sympathize with them because I could recall the many occasions when Pat and I had been confronted with some very strange concoctions on our trips abroad, which we would gulp down in complete ignorance of what we were eating and with dire forebodings of how our systems might react the following day.

Khrushchev, who was in an expansive mood, insisted that we all spend the night at his *dacha,* or summer home, so that we could have the entire day there on Sunday. When Ambassador Thompson's dinner ended, shortly after 10:00, our American party drove the twenty-two miles to Khrushchev's beautiful summer mansion overlooking the Moscow River.

On Sunday morning, Mrs. Nixon and I, Ambassador Thompson, Milton Eisenhower, and others in our party walked over the grounds of the dacha, as luxurious an estate as any I had ever visited. I could not help but think that the old Bolsheviks had come a long way since the days of their revolution. Mikoyan, Kozlov, Deputy Foreign Minister Vasily Kuznetsov, and several aides arrived later in the morning, and then at about noon Mr. and Mrs. Khrushchev drove up in their limousine. Khrushchev, dressed for the summer Sunday in a dazzling embroidered sports shirt, posed for photographers with me and then seeing the one pool reporter allowed on the grounds, he made a point to correct any unfavorable impression he might have left at the kitchen debate. "Some newsmen described our talk at the fair as if we were quarreling and offending each other," he said. "Were you offended?" he asked me. "Never," I replied. Then turning to the reporter, Ernie Barcella, Khrushchev told him, "You can write down a refutation by Vice President Nixon on some reports that our kitchen talk was so quarrelsome that we insulted each other, while in fact we had a really friendly talk. . . ." I managed to keep the record straight by giving my own characterization of the talks as "direct, frank, and nonbelligerent," lest Khrushchev shape the interpretation entirely to his own liking.

Here again was an example of Khrushchev, the persistent Communist tactician: every little propaganda point was important to him in the Cold War. He obviously had received the same reactions to the kitchen debate as I had, and now he was trying to use me to correct any unfavorable impression he may have made.

After the news pictures were taken, he proposed that we take a boat ride on the Moscow River "to see how the slaves live." For two hours I rode down the Moscow River in a twenty-five-foot motor launch with Khrushchev, the others following in boats behind us, and I was treated to probably the most novel boat ride ever taken by two representatives of government. I saw a brand of politicking which would be envied by any man running for office in the United States. On eight separate occasions, Khrushchev had the boat stopped so he could stoop down to shake hands with bathers in the water. "Are you captives? Are you slaves?" he would shout out to them. "Nyet, nyet!" the swimmers would shout back, treading water and waving at us. Then he would nudge me in the ribs and shout, "See how our slaves live!" The Soviet newsmen in the nearby boats took down every word.

On the way back to the dacha, the boat in which Khrushchev and I were riding struck a sand bar and we were left high and dry while the other boats raced on down the river. Khrushchev looked as if he were going to shoot the pilot of the boat on the spot. I tried to break the tension by pointing out that just a few months before I had been in Florida with a friend who was a very experienced boatman and who had had the same kind of accident. But as we climbed out of our boat into another one and continued our trip, I looked back at the pilot and saw the most forlorn, hopeless-looking individual I was to see in my visit in the Soviet Union. He was at least fortunate that things apparently have changed in the "worker's paradise" so that a worker who now makes a mistake generally loses only his job, not his head.

When we returned to the boat landing at the dacha, Mikoyan commented with great enjoyment about the "fine river rallies." I told the beaming Khrushchev, "You know, I really must admire you; you never miss a chance to make propaganda."

"No, no," he retorted, "I don't make propaganda, I tell the truth." Thompson told me later in the afternoon that the only bathers who were allowed to use the beaches on the Moscow River were the elite of Communist society.

We sat down to lunch with our wives at a long table set up on the lawn of the dacha, beneath stately birches and pines planted originally in the time of Catherine the Great. It was then that I got some further insight into Khrushchev's habits—and his essential nature as a cold, calculating, self-controlled tactician. The table was laden with all sorts of food, delicacies, and liquor, but I noticed that Khrushchev, despite his world-wide reputation for imbibing, hardly touched the array of vodka and wine bottles. He likes both his food and his drink. But just as his famed temper is always his servant and not his master, his drinking is strictly for pleasure and is never permitted to interfere with business. He was stone sober throughout our long afternoon of talks.

Khrushchev played the role of jovial and gallant host as the first course was served. When Mikoyan tried to start a conversation across the table with Pat, who was seated on Khrushchev's right, the Premier cut in and said: "Now look here, you crafty Armenian. Mrs. Nixon belongs to me. You stay on your side of the table." He then drew a line with his finger down the middle of the table and added: "This is an iron curtain. And don't you step over it!"

Then came an unusual course. It was a frozen white fish from Siberia, sliced thin and served raw, spiced with salt, pepper, and garlic. "It was Stalin's favorite dish. He said it put steel in his backbone," remarked Khrushchev, urging me to try some. Since Khrushchev had taken a double portion, I did likewise. I knew that I needed as much fortification as he before the afternoon's talks.

As we ate the raw fish, Mikoyan, who often served as the straight man for Khrushchev's jokes, commented that Stalin had some peculiar work habits. He would often summon his subordinates in the middle of the night to work on a particular project, said Mikoyan—commenting, "We sleep much better now since Comrade Khrushchev is our Premier." Then Mikoyan did a double take at what he had said. Smiling, he added, "I guess you can take that in more ways than one."

It was right after the fish course, whether by coincidence or otherwise, that Khrushchev suddenly dispensed with the diplomatic small talk and started to act like a Stalinist. In a cold, matter-of-fact tone, he launched into a long discussion designed to impress me with the missile power of the Soviet Union. He told of plans for shooting a Soviet rocket into orbit around the earth with a pay load of 100 tons, enough to carry a man and equipment into outer space and bring him back safely. He reported that just the week before the Soviets had launched an ICBM over a 7000-kilometer course with final deviation off target of only 1.7 kilometers to the right.

And then, leaning across the table toward me, he said that he wanted to tell me a "secret." Just a month ago the Soviet Government had been very concerned because the engine cut-off system in an ICBM had failed and the rocket had overshot its course and headed toward Alaska. Though the missile had not contained a warhead, Khrushchev said he had feared a "fuss" if the missile had landed in Alaska; fortunately, it had fallen in the Atlantic, well short of the continental United States.

For the next four hours he went on to tell me several "secrets" of the Soviet Union. He said the Soviet Union was in possession of the "United States operational plans for war," and that he suspected American spies probably had obtained Soviet operational plans as well. He said the USSR was building submarines to carry missiles which could destroy ports, coastal areas, and an enemy's navy. He told us he planned to build missile bases in Albania, if and when the United States constructed missile bases in Italy. He said the Soviet Union had on hand at that time intermediate and long-range missiles in sufficient quantity to destroy all of its enemies in Europe and the major cities in the United States. He had no doubt that he could destroy Germany, France, England, and other European countries on the first day of a war. While the Soviet Union would, of course, suffer losses too, the other countries would become deserts. He spelled out in specific detail the massive military power which he had described in general terms in our "kitchen debate."

But in this discussion the rules were different, as far as I was concerned. This was a private conversation. I could answer him and counterattack, point by point, and I proceeded to do so. It was cold steel between us all afternoon.

I asked why he had refused to let me see his missile plants, when we had invited Kozlov to observe missile launchings at Vandenberg and Cape Canaveral on his visit to the United States.

He replied that the time for such exchanges would come only when U. S. bases abroad had been liquidated.

I retorted that this was a two-way street and referred to Averell Harriman's report that Khrushchev had told him that he had given the Communist Chinese missiles for use against Quemoy.

Khrushchev denied that he had said this, and contended that all he said was that he would supply China with missiles if it were attacked by the United States.

I asked him why, in view of the confidence he had expressed in the number and accuracy of his missiles, he was continuing to build bombers. He replied that bomber production had almost been stopped, because missiles were much more accurate and because humans were sometimes incapable of dropping bombs on targets because of emotional revulsion, a factor which was not present where missiles were concerned.

He then said that the military service he really felt sorry for was the Navy; except for submarines it was completely obsolete and could only provide "fodder for sharks." Cruisers and aircraft carriers, because of their slow speed, were "sitting ducks" for missiles and he had stopped building them.

I knew that we were ahead of him in the development of Polaris-type submarines which could launch missiles from underwater. But

when I asked him what progress he had made in this respect, he replied that the Soviets believed that launching from land was better
than from the sea.

I also knew that we were ahead in the development of solid fuels
which greatly facilitate missile mobility. He said that he did not want
to discuss this question because it was a technical subject and he, as a
politician rather than a technician, was not qualified to discuss it.

This was the only point in the five-and-a-half-hour discussion at
which one of the six ladies present put in a word. Pat laughingly expressed surprise that there was any subject Khrushchev was not prepared to discuss. She had thought up to this time that in his one-man
government he had everything in his own hands and knew everything.
Everybody laughed, and Mikoyan stepped in with the remark that not
even Khrushchev had enough hands to handle everything and needed
others to help him.

I asked him if the real reason he was considering putting bases in
Albania was that if missiles were launched from there, there would be
no danger in the Soviet Union from fallout. He denied this was the
case.

I then took him on frontally on his practice of constantly bragging
in public statements about the superiority of his power over that of
the United States and other countries. I suggested that such tactics,
whether he intended to or not, created the impression that he was
threatening other countries and the peace of the world. I returned to
my theme that each of our two countries should recognize and respect
the military power of the other without creating tension and fear by
constantly debating which was the stronger.

Khrushchev now in private agreed with my thesis, claiming that he
had never engaged in such talk. But he charged that "U. S. generals"
had done so. Then he proceeded, on the spot, to do what he had just
denied. He referred to Marshal Vershinin's interview of the year before
with regard to Soviet destructive capabilities. He said the Soviet Union
was superior to the United States in rockets, that there was no defense against rockets, and that there was no need for pin-point accuracy
since a 100-kilometer tolerance would be adequate. He laughingly
referred to a joke he said was current in England about pessimists
and optimists. The pessimist said only six atomic bombs would be
needed to wipe out the United Kingdom, while the optimist said nine
or ten would be required.

Khrushchev moved now to another line of attack and said that his
agents had obtained copies of a secret U.S.-Iranian agreement which

provided for United States assistance to Iran in the event of "indirect aggression." This meant, he charged, that the United States would be against the Iranian people when they arose against the government.

I had been waiting for an opportunity to counterattack on his charges with regard to the Captive Nations Resolution and American "imperialism," and this gave me an opening.

I told him that I hoped he did not think that the Soviets could hold a meeting of Communist representatives from fifty-one countries in Moscow without the United States knowing what went on. We knew, I said, that those attending that January meeting had been instructed to conduct subversive activities throughout the world. And I asked how he could reconcile his words about peace with his public statement, on his recent visit to Poland, that the USSR would openly support revolution anywhere in the world.

Khrushchev tried to side-step. In addition to taking the usual Soviet line that uprisings spearheaded by Communists are "simply peoples' revolutions" and are not assisted or directed from the Soviet Union, he said the trouble was that the United States did not understand Communist ideas. Communists had always been against subversion and terror, and true Marxists had always been against "individual terror." But mass uprisings, where the bourgeois do not surrender their power peacefully, are a different thing altogether and are favored by Marxists.

Did he then mean that the people in bourgeois countries were "captives" whose liberation was justified, I asked?

Now Khrushchev changed his tune. "Captives" was a vulgar term, not "scientific."

I pressed the point. If it was true that the Soviet Union did not support revolutions in non-Communist countries, how could he account for the uprising the previous week in northern Iraq, or for the *coup d'état* in Czechoslovakia? And if Communists were against individual terror, how could he justify the Soviet radio broadcasts to Latin America which had incited and approved the use of terrorism against Mrs. Nixon and me in Caracas?

This point struck home. Khrushchev replied that he never evaded tough questions and quoted the Russian proverb, "You are my guest, but truth is my mother." He admitted that the sympathy of the people of the USSR was with the people who had been against me on my trip to South America, but their indignation was not directed against me and Mrs. Nixon personally—only against the "imperialistic" policies of the United States. And here he appeared to be addressing Mrs.

Nixon—for whom he seemed to have genuine admiration—as much as me. The trouble was that the United States was trying to control Venezuela because of its strategic importance. This was imperialism and the people could never tolerate that.

I asked him what then, if he thought our policies were imperialistic, he would call his policy toward Hungary, Poland, and East Germany, where Communist governments were kept in power because of the presence of thousands of Soviet troops.

He brushed aside my question on the ground that that was a different matter.

He turned the discussion to Vietnam and charged that Ho Chi Minh, the leader of Communist North Vietnam, wants elections for the whole country, while the United States opposes them, contrary to the agreement that had been reached three years before. Why did we do this, he asked? While it was true that the refusal to have elections had been announced officially by President Diem of South Vietnam, everybody knew, he said, that we pulled the strings on him.

I countered by asking him who pulled the strings in North Vietnam. I pointed out that the reason Diem had opposed elections was that Communist North Vietnam would not permit the International Control Commission to supervise the elections in its territory. And I added that I was glad to hear that he agreed with the principle of free elections but I could not understand why, if he was for free elections in Vietnam, he was against free elections in East and West Germany as a method of unifying Germany and settling the German problem once and for all. Khrushchev's response was that free elections as proposed by the West would engulf East Germany and make all of Germany an ally of the West. In effect, while he did not say this directly, he was simply stating the proposition that he was for elections only when he was sure that the Communists would win.

For the last two hours of our discussion we went around and around on the German problem, with him restating the Soviet position and me setting forth again the American position. I pointed out that it was the Soviet proposal to sign a separate peace treaty with East Germany that was creating the present (1959) crisis which threatened peace. I emphasized repeatedly that the vital interests of both our countries were involved in the Berlin and German problems and that neither side should confront the other with an impossible situation.

Ambassador Thompson, upon my suggestion that he outline the details of the Western proposals for a Berlin solution, declared that if the

Soviets pushed the situation to a crisis, it would be hard to reconcile this with their words about peace. For the first and only time that afternoon, Khrushchev seemed to have a burst of temper and raised his voice. The Ambassador should be careful when using the word peace, he warned; what he had said sounded like a threat. The Soviet Union would sign a peace treaty and the West could declare war if it wished. Thompson countered by pointing out that all he had wanted to say was that forcing a crisis was not a step toward peace.

Khrushchev now switched his ground again. He demanded that I state what was incompatible with Western interests in the Soviet proposals on Berlin and Germany. In other words, he was insisting that we negotiate on his demands rather than on ours.

I could not in any event change our government's position. I could only try to see where his position might be flexible. But even had my hands not been tied in this way, I would not have fallen into his trap. I side-stepped his invitation to debate on his own ground. Instead, I said that in order for agreement to be reached on that problem and on others such as disarmament, nuclear testing, and trade, both sides must be willing to agree to changes in their positions and that progress in these areas could be made only in a climate of calm, not of crisis.

Khrushchev agreed that a calm atmosphere was desirable but said that the United States should not threaten the Soviet Union with war. He charged that apparently I did not want to use that sort of language, so I had asked my Ambassador to do so. I responded that I had listened carefully to Ambassador Thompson's statement and that under no circumstances could it be described as a threat.

We moved to the subject of an atomic test ban. I pointed out that the major problem as far as inspection was concerned involved underground tests. Why, then, should he not accept President Eisenhower's proposal for discontinuing tests in the atmosphere as a first step, since such tests can be detected without an elaborate inspection system, and since this would solve the fallout problem. I asked him whether his position, as far as a test ban was concerned, was "all or nothing."

Khrushchev replied bluntly that that was precisely the Soviet position, and that he couldn't understand why the United States wanted to continue tests since we had more bombs anyway. He wondered whether they were inferior to those the Soviet had.

I asked whether he had considered the possibility of testing underground for the purpose of developing so-called "atomic dynamite" for peaceful purposes, such as building canals and harbors. He said that such development was completely unnecessary and that TNT was sufficient for construction purposes.

We had been talking for over four hours when I put a key question to Khrushchev. "I want to ask one question—do you think there is any room for negotiation in the Soviet position on Berlin and Germany?" Certainly Khrushchev would not want to come to a meeting if President Eisenhower were not prepared to negotiate. If President Eisenhower were sitting across the table from him, would Khrushchev have anything that he would be willing to negotiate?

Khrushchev said that this was a "fair" question. But then he said it would be easier for him to reply in terms of what the Soviet Union could *not* accept. After in this way avoiding negotiating on my grounds, he then proceeded again to spell out the Soviet position: the Soviet Union would never accept a perpetuation of the occupation regime in West Berlin, with or without a summit meeting.

We had ended up, in effect, where we had started. On each controversial point, Khrushchev had insisted that he was right and that we were wrong. He did not give an inch.

He yielded perhaps a half inch on only one point I made: that he could not expect President Eisenhower to go to a summit conference merely to sign his name to Soviet proposals. But he added that the same was true for him: he would not go to a summit to sign U. S. proposals.

"I would much rather go hunting and shoot ducks," he said.

At this point I asked Dr. Milton Eisenhower to express any further views he might have on the subjects we had been discussing, and he made a most eloquent statement. He said that it was a privilege to attend this historic meeting, a meeting that offered real hope for peace. He emphasized that never in history had the people of the United States started a war. All that our people wanted was that the people of the world might live in peace, choose their own governments, and select their own methods of progress. He observed that in another eighteen months his brother, President Eisenhower, would have completed fifty years of service to his country. He expressed the hope that by some miracle, within the time before the Eisenhower Administration ended, something would be done to ensure that no war should occur.

I watched Khrushchev closely as Dr. Eisenhower's statement was translated for him. His expression never changed. His eyes were as cold as they had been all afternoon.

At 8:50, over five hours after we had sat down for lunch, we got up from the table. I decided that I would try to make one more effort to get through to Khrushchev. I asked to speak to him alone. Walking over the grounds of the dacha with only Troyanovsky, his interpreter, with us, I brought up the invitation President Eisenhower had extended to him to come and visit the United States, which we had not discussed before. I explained that his visit would be met with mixed reactions in the United States. I urged him to do everything possible to create the proper atmosphere for constructive talks. Then I suggested that the eyes of the world were on the Geneva Foreign Ministers Conference and that some action on his part to break the impasse on the Berlin question could be a dramatic event which would make his visit to the United States not only successful but also historical in making progress toward a peaceful settlement of our differences.

It was the most persuasive plea I could make. He listened without interruption and then answered, noncommittally, that he would keep in touch with Andrei Gromyko in Geneva. I sensed that my plea had not moved him any more than had the eloquent statement of our hopes for peace which Milton Eisenhower had made at the luncheon table.

For over seven hours, beginning on our ride down the river and continuing through the long luncheon, I had been engaged in virtual hand-to-hand combat with Khrushchev on the outstanding differences between the United States and the USSR. But I was not nearly as tired physically and emotionally after this session as I had been two days earlier after our much shorter "kitchen debate." The reason lies in one of the most common characteristics of the effect a crisis has on an individual. At the long, five-hour conference I had been able to express my views without restraint—to go all out in defending the United States' position and in attacking vulnerable points in the Soviet position. In the "kitchen debate," I had had to restrain myself time and time again from expressing views I deeply felt and wanted to get across. There is nothing more wearing than to suppress the natural impulse to meet a crisis head-on, using every possible resource to achieve victory.

Now my talks with Khrushchev were over. When I returned to the Embassy residence that night I tried to evaluate not only what he had said but even more what kind of a man he was. I recalled a conversation I had had with an Ambassador from a European country shortly after Khrushchev came to power, when, with Bulganin, he had made his first trip outside Russia to visit Prague. He had been crude, appeared to be drunk, and, in his first brush with the international social set, seemed to be uncomfortably out of place. Many of the press observers who covered that visit spoke of him contemptuously. They wrote that "he was a lightweight compared to Stalin"; "he was crude and out of his class"; "he would not last long." And the general conclusion was that he would not be nearly as difficult to handle as Stalin because of lack of sophistication and knowledge in international affairs.

"These observations could not be more superficial or wrong," my diplomat friend had told me. "Those who write this way are making the usual mistake of many who move in international society. Fine manners and appreciation of culture, elegant language and fashionable clothing, are given too much weight as they evaluate an individual. No man could have fought his way up through the jungle of Communist intrigue, through purges, exile, and disgrace, during the period of Lenin, Trotsky, Stalin, and Malenkov, without having not only iron determination and unlimited stamina, but also intelligence and extraordinary all-round ability. These observers, as is too often the case, are looking at the veneer, rather than what is underneath."

As I look back over my conversations with Khrushchev, I could see how right my friend had been. A picture of Khrushchev, the man, began to form in my mind. Intelligence, a quick-hitting sense of humor, always on the offensive, colorful in action and words, a tendency to be a show-off, particularly where he has any kind of a gallery to play to, a steel-like determination coupled with an almost compulsive tendency to press an advantage—to take a mile where his opponent gives an inch—to run over anyone who shows any sign of timidity or weakness—this was Khrushchev. A man who does his homework, prides himself on knowing as much about his opponent's position as he does his own, particularly effective in debate because of his resourcefulness, his ability to twist and turn, to change the subject when he is forced into a corner or an untenable position.

In one respect the world is fortunate that, with the incredible power he has at his disposal, Khrushchev is the kind of man he is. Because the danger of war would be infinitely greater if Khrushchev, like Hitler, acted rashly and impulsively during fits of anger, verging on insanity. Despite giving the public impression of being a highly emotional man who might start war in a moment of anger, or when he had had too much to drink, Khrushchev had just demonstrated to me that when anything of importance was being discussed he is sober, cold, unemotional, and analytical. He will be influenced in his conduct only by the hard realities of the power balance, and to that extent we can exert some control over his actions and our own destiny.

Khrushchev has often been called a chess player in conducting his international policies—I suppose because chess is a favorite Russian game. I do not know chess, but I do know poker; and there is no doubt but that Khrushchev would have been a superb poker player. First, he is out to win. Second, like any good poker player, he plans ahead so that he can win the big pots. He likes to bluff, but he knows that if you bluff on small pots and fail consistently to produce the cards, you must expect your opponent to call your bluff on the big pots.

That, in effect, is what happened in Laos and in Cuba. The United States talked big and did not back up its talk with action: we bluffed, and, when called, we did not produce the cards. The effect of this on Khrushchev is obvious: he has caught us bluffing on some small pots. He assumes, therefore, that we may be bluffing on Berlin—the big pot —and he may be tempted to call us on that one. There is nothing more dangerous in dealing with a man like Khrushchev than to talk bigger than we are prepared to act. It is this kind of conduct that could lead to the miscalculation on his part which would bring war. Khrushchev probably would have probed the Berlin situation and created a crisis, in any event. But what happened in Laos and Cuba tended to make him more cocky and far more belligerent than he would otherwise have been.

The Eisenhower-Dulles foreign policy was formulated on the principle that we should stand ready to call international Communism's bluff on any pot, large or small. If we let them know that we will defend freedom when the stakes are small, the Soviets are not encouraged to threaten freedom where the stakes are higher. That is why the two small islands of Quemoy and Matsu, and all the other peripheral areas, are so important in the poker game of world politics.

Finally, I had seen a striking example of Khrushchev's diplomatic tactics.

First, he demands something to which he is not entitled. Second, he threatens war if he does not get what he demands. Third, he charges that we will be endangering the peace unless we negotiate on his demands. And fourth, the price of peace is giving him half or more of what he was not entitled to in the first place.

This, in essence, was what he was trying to do in 1959, and what he is trying to do today, on the question of Berlin. If we are not constantly to be in the position of simply negotiating the rate of our retreat, we must counter his demands—which are designed to extend slavery—with our own, which have the objective of extending freedom. That is our best course for avoiding both retreat and war. At the core, we must remember, Khrushchev is a cold, hardheaded Marxist, as undeviating as Stalin, and far more sophisticated.

The next morning we received an interesting message from Khrushchev. He said that he had just learned that we would like to take our own plane to Leningrad and that he had no objection to our doing so. (It was too late, of course, for us to change the arrangements we had made to use the Soviet jet transports.) The night before, he had urged us to stay at the dacha, rather than return to the Embassy residence, because he thought we would be far more comfortable there.

The pattern was clear. In discussions on matters of substance, he conceded nothing and demanded everything. He could not have been more unreasonable. But he also was determined to do his best to see that his public image was one of sweet reasonableness. He knew that inconsequential gestures of courtesy cost him nothing as far as his major objectives were concerned and served to convince some people that he was a fair and reasonable man.

I left Moscow early that morning with a sense of relief, thinking that I would now have a respite from the tension and crisis-laden atmosphere of dealing with Khrushchev. This was wishful thinking. The "spirit of Khrushchev," or the line he laid down for my visit, followed me constantly, without letup, on my four-day tour of Leningrad and the Siberian cities of Novosibirsk and Sverdlovsk.

The American party and the press traveled in a convoy of three twin-engined Soviet jet planes, TU-104s, because Soviet officials had initially refused to allow us to use our own planes for travel within the Soviet Union. Presumably they feared we might photograph their country from our own planes.

I had looked forward to spreading the good word, *mir i druzhba,* peace and friendship, to the people of Russia, and I believe I was partially successful in this for it seemed that the farther away from Moscow I got, the friendlier the people were. Large crowds in Leningrad, in the Ural manufacturing city of Sverdlovsk, and in the Siberian frontier city of Novosibirsk, came out to greet us. Thousands upon thousands answered my words of greeting with the cry, *druzhba*—friendship. The masses of the Russian people, as distinguished from the elite few who make up the Communist hierarchy, are truly friendly toward the United States. They remember our help in World War II, they know at firsthand the terrible destruction of war and desperately want peace.

Nevertheless, everywhere I went there were planted hecklers who asked obvious, rehearsed political questions. As I toured hydroelectric projects, factories, schoolrooms, or mines, a familiar routine developed. Someone would step out of the crowd, describe himself as a worker or "just a plain Soviet citizen," and request permission to ask me a question. I would always reply in the affirmative. Then he would recite a question almost by rote. Why is the United States blocking agreement on stopping atomic testing? Why does America want war? Why does America threaten us with military bases on foreign soil? Why won't America agree to a solution of the Berlin question? The questions were obviously designed to embarrass me, and through me the foreign policy of the United States. With the swarm of newsmen around, I would answer each and every question rationally, explaining with pointed patience the position of the Western Allies on each question and the opposing Soviet position.

The routine became so repetitious that the traveling press corps began to make bets among themselves about the time and place of the next "little kitchen debate." These "debates" occurred in all kinds of places, every day—on a factory assembly line, at an electric plant, at the ballet, in a hotel lobby. The most amusing encounter occurred deep within a copper mine in Petrolyarsk, near Sverdlovsk in the Urals. Dressed in long johns, a wool shirt and breeches, knee-length rubber boots, a miner's coat, and a miner's hat with a lamp on it, I was slogging my way through the muck and slime, accompanied by four newspapermen and several Soviet officials, when two miners shut off their clattering air drills and presented themselves to me.

"Mr. Vice President," said one, "may I ask a question? The Soviet Union has proposed suspension of atomic tests but the United States refuses. Why?" The setting for such a question was so incongruous that everyone, including the Russians, burst out laughing. Even the two miners recognized the ridiculous circumstances of their assignment and joined in the laughter. But I did not miss an opportunity to answer the question. "You couldn't have asked such a question in a better place," I said. "An agreement must have inspection provisions which will assure the detection of underground tests."

Harrison E. Salisbury, dean of the American correspondents in Russia, summarized the heckling situation for the New York *Times* this way:

Vice President Richard M. Nixon preached the virtues of free speech to several hecklers . . . today. It was one of the rarest of experiences in Soviet life—a free and easy interchange between a leading personality and challengers who appeared from the crowd. The similarity of the questions directed at Mr. Nixon and the tactics of the questioners suggested a central source of inspiration. That the agitation and propaganda department of the Communist Party Central Committee is increasingly nervous over the impact of Mr. Nixon's man-to-man approach was indicated by several pin pricking reports in the press. . . .

It must be understood that this heckling campaign provided the only unpleasant incidents in four full days of touring in which I observed a great deal of the Soviet Union and its people and spoke out repeatedly for friendship and peace. These were sixteen-hour, tiring days, beginning early in the morning and often stretching to midnight. I recognized the obvious strategy of the Soviets to probe for any weakness that might be within me, not unlike their international strategy of probing for soft spots around the world. But I was determined to maintain my equilibrium and composure. My objective was to turn the hecklers' questions into an opportunity for presenting United States policy to the Russian people. Only once did I lose my temper. That occurred near the end of the tour and with considerable provocation.

It came after a grueling four-hour tour of the huge Uralmash machine plant near Sverdlovsk. The factory was still using some of the huge lathes and drill presses which the United States had sent to Russia under the Lend-Lease program during World War II. It was now manufacturing textile machinery for Red China. At least twenty times, as I started down each new assembly line, a heckler would stop me and put me through the now familiar inquisition. At the end of the tour of the plant, the factory manager insisted that we come to his office, and there, sitting around a table, he and his associates hammered away at me on U. S. policy toward Red China. Finally, realizing that I was two hours behind schedule, I rose and cut short the conversation. The press corps by this time had gone ahead to the next scheduled stop.

When I walked out of the factory, with only Georgi Zhukov, the Soviet Minister of Information, and Akalovsky, my interpreter, with me, it was almost dark. But there outside the gate, patiently waiting for me since the change of work shifts, were more than 2000 factory employees. They had been standing there for over an hour. When I waved to them, they sent up a rousing cheer with intermittent shouts of "Welcome!" The Soviet authorities had become increasingly irritated by the warmth of my reception. I had noticed that on several previous stops the police had been trying to discourage the crowds from expressing their enthusiasm. On this occasion, I just happened to see one burly character roughly seize a woman by the shoulder to stop her from applauding. Leaving Zhukov behind without any explanation, I turned and walked quickly over to the police officer, grabbed him by the shoulders, and shook him as hard as I could. "Don't ever do that again," I said sharply. "When the people are happy and want to express themselves, you leave them alone." Akalovsky, standing beside me, caught the spirit, and translated what I had said as angrily in Russian as I had in English.

"I didn't do anything," the policeman protested.

"Yes, you did," I said. "I saw you push this woman. Don't ever do that again."

The crowd swarmed around, apparently delighted that someone dared take on the Soviet police. Akalovsky told me later that he heard several workers say to the officer, "Now you've caught it. You'd better leave us alone."

By this time, Zhukov walked up and asked what was the matter. "Let's get in the car and we'll discuss this later," I told him. Zhukov, who was my official escort on the entire tour, was a confidant of Khrushchev and chief propagandist for the government. He was a suave, well-educated man of about fifty who had traveled extensively in Europe and the United States as a correspondent and editor of *Pravda*. As we drove away from the factory, I was in no mood for polite explanations and I laid it on the line to Zhukov, whose official title, ironically, was Chairman of the State Committee for Cultural Relations with Foreign Countries.

"Mr. Zhukov," I said, "this little game you've been playing with me through your planted hecklers for the past few days has not been going well with the press, and in my opinion it is backfiring even among your own people. You underestimate their intelligence. They aren't dumb. They know when somebody is acting and when it is the real thing—particularly when the acts have been so amateurish. Now, I just want to put you on notice that I will continue to answer your hecklers without protest. But the next time I see one of your policemen trying to keep a crowd from indicating its friendship for the United States, I am going to blast the whole bunch of you publicly in a way you'll never forget. We have our differences, and I believe in discussing them honestly and candidly. But we don't have to make a joke out of the whole business."

Zhukov tried to deny that he or Khrushchev were responsible for the hecklers or the police control of the crowds. "The police were just trying to protect you," he said.

"The police don't have to protect me from friendly people," I answered, and then sat in silence for the balance of our drive to the next stop on the schedule. I do not know if my talk with Zhukov did any good, but it helped me personally: I had let off some of the steam which had been building up to the exploding point.

I wound up my ten-day tour of the Soviet Union back in Moscow with an unprecedented thirty-minute speech to the Russian people on a nationwide radio-TV hookup.

The preparation of this broadcast was a crisis in itself. Thompson kept emphasizing to me how important it was. This would be the first time in history that a Russian television audience would hear a top American official defend United States foreign policy.

I knew the broadcast was important, but my schedule was so full that I had no time whatever during the day to prepare my remarks. For four days before the broadcast I used every free moment to jot down notes. For the two nights before the broadcast, I did not go to bed at all, using the time to write my final draft. I tried to get what sleep I needed by dozing on long automobile or plane rides.

As I worked on the broadcast, I thought back on a week of crisis, of unrelenting pressure created and controlled by the Communist authorities. The discipline and the cohesive line of attack of the Communist functionaries, big and small, which had extended from Moscow to Leningrad and into Siberia, had been both impressive to me and discouraging. Yet, there was one encouraging factor that I had noted in every city I visited: the unrestrained expressions of friendship on the part of the Russian people. This was evident particularly in those areas where the people were less under the eye of Communist authorities. Shipyard workers in Leningrad had cheered references to Eisenhower in my speech. In the heart of Siberia, people had leaned out of windows and from jam-packed streetcars to cheer and to applaud our party of Americans. Thousands had gathered on the streets outside of each building we entered and they had cheered when we came out. School children in the Urals threw bouquets of flowers into our cars and had shouted in English, "Friendship . . . friendship," for that was one of the first words they had been taught in their English classes. A workman in a construction project in the Urals had thrown his arms around me and had said, "I met many Americans during the war and I never want to fight against them."

Working on my speech at a desk in Spaso House, I thought of the contrast between the warm, friendly, gracious, and good people I had met—and the tough, cold, ruthless Communist leaders. It was the same here in the heartland of the Communist empire as in all the countries I had visited. The Communists are a class apart. They are a minority with enormous power. This did not mean, of course, that the Russian people are ready to rebel against their government. But it did point up the fact, which any observant visitor can see, that the Communists gain and retain their power through an iron discipline in an elite class of leaders and organizers, not through any development of true mass support. While this is the strength behind Communist tactics, it also is potentially a fatal weakness in the international Communist movement.

These and many other thoughts flowed through my mind as I selected what I wanted to say to the Russian people. One basic decision I had to make was whether to aim my speech primarily at the Russian people or at the American people, for I realized that this speech would be heard by the Russian people but also read in the press by the American people. With the 1960 presidential election not far off, a tough blasting speech would be politically expedient for me and, with some justification, I was tempted to deliver my own thoughts about the obvious evils of a Communist police state which I had seen firsthand.

However, with all things considered, I chose to speak out solely with the Russian people in mind. The best use I could make of my historic opportunity was to cite some facts for the Russian people which they never got in the Communist press. I tried to present these facts in such a way that the Russian people would recognize that I was not being belligerent or bellicose or discourteous to my hosts. For one thing, I intended to give the Kremlin hierarchy no excuse for preventing other American visitors, particularly President Eisenhower, from also addressing the Russian people. I was the first high American official to have this opportunity. I did not want to be the last.

Ambassador Thompson, whose intimate knowledge of the Soviet Government and people proved invaluable, advised and guided me through this task. At his suggestion, I included the whole story of the incident at the vegetable market, when the Soviets had accused me of trying to bribe a citizen. While on the surface this seemed a minor incident, it proved to be one of the most effective parts of my speech: it was the first time in recent Soviet history that anyone had publicly challenged the veracity of *Pravda.* According to reports I received later, it stimulated quite a bit of debate among the Russian people about the accuracy of the news they were receiving. In fact, the speech itself set off a wave of new discussions within the Soviet Union, for never before had the Russian people been given so fully the Western side of the East-West conflict.[2]

I spelled out in detail that the United States had fought in two great world wars and had never exacted any territorial gains or reparations and that the United States had no designs on world conquest. Our armaments, our bases were for defense. Following Foster Dulles' advice, I firmly placed the responsibility for peace upon Khrushchev's shoulders and told the Russian people:

I would not be so presumptuous to give [Mr. Khrushchev] advice on how he should fulfill that responsibility. But could I relate something that I noted on the trip I have just completed? In every factory and on hundreds of billboards, I saw this slogan, "Let Us Work for the Victory of Communism."

If Mr. Khrushchev means by this slogan working for a better life for the people within the Soviet Union, that is one thing. If, on the other hand, he means the victory of Communism over the United States and other countries, this is a horse of a different color. For we have our own ideas as to what system is best for us.

If he devotes his immense energies and talents to building a better life for the people of his own country, Mr. Khrushchev can go down in history as one of the greatest leaders the Soviet people have ever produced. But if he diverts the resources and talents of his people to the objective of promoting the Communization of countries outside the Soviet Union, he will only assure that both he and his people will continue to live in an era of fear, suspicion and tension. . . .

The next day, Sunday, August 2, was my last in the Soviet Union. I attended a pleasant reception for our American personnel at the Embassy. Then I went through a long press conference with the newsmen who had covered my trip. I tried to be scrupulously fair in recognizing alternately Soviet and American reporters. But one of the *Pravda* reporters proceeded to launch into a long harangue, charging I was discriminating against the Soviet newsmen. James Reston of the New York *Times* came to my defense and set the record straight, something for which I was most grateful at the end of what had been a long and trying ordeal.

I had a final talk with Ambassador Thompson and confided to him my sense of frustration over my visit. I felt that my personal contacts with the Russian people on my tour outside of Moscow would have

[2] See Appendix for text of this speech.

some lasting effect for good and might in turn affect Khrushchev, for no dictator can totally ignore the deep-seated desires of his people. I felt I must have convinced some of the Russian people of our desire for peace, which matched theirs. But I knew that I had had no success whatever in getting through to Khrushchev and the Soviet leaders.

In thinking of the little progress I had made against the enormity of the task, I was left with a sense of depression. Even the way the Soviets had carried my television speech was typical. They complied with their technical agreement to give me similar exposure to that of Mikoyan and Kozlov in the United States, but they did so on the smallest possible network and with no advance notice of my appearance.

Thompson, however, reassured me. "Five years ago," he said, "it woud have been absolutely unthinkable for anyone to say the things you did to the Russian people. Those of us who have lived with this problem know what a momentous thing this was for them [the Soviet leaders] to do."

I was reminded of a similar comment about the course of progress made by Prime Minister Macmillan—to the effect that one hundred years elapsed between the reign of Queen Elizabeth I, who beheaded her councilors who fell out of favor, and Queen Anne, who because of the pressure of public opinion, could only send hers into exile. And now, only five years had elapsed between Stalin, who had executed his real or imagined rivals, and Khrushchev, who had demoted Malenkov from Premier to manager of a small power plant, and Molotov from Foreign Minister to an Embassy post in Outer Mongolia. Perhaps even in the Communist empire there is a ray of hope for peaceful change.

On the two-hour flight from Moscow to Warsaw, I looked back on my trip to the Soviet Union with little satisfaction, and on my impending visit to Poland with even less hope. And the reason had nothing whatever to do with material power. After seeing the Soviet Union, I was not concerned about the ability of the United States to stay well ahead of the Communists militarily and economically. But what had most impressed me was the ruthless efficiency of the whole Communist operation.

None of the Communist functionaries who had challenged me were as able as Khrushchev. Some were obviously limited in their educational background for the assignments they were undertaking. But whether it was Khrushchev, Mikoyan, or Kozlov, a lesser Communist functionary running a factory in the Urals, a shop steward on an assembly line, or a miner, there was a steel-like quality, a cold determination, a tough, amoral ruthlessness which somehow had been instilled into every one of them. I knew that whereas many of the Russian people might not realize what kind of a victory they were working for, the Russian leaders had no doubt on that score. Their goal was not just victory over the poverty, inequality, and misery which is still the lot of millions of Russians, but victory for Communism in every non-Communist nation. They would never be satisfied until they had achieved their ultimate objective of a world completely Communist-controlled.

It was not a question of who was on the right side, at least not in the short run. History is full of examples of civilizations with superior ideas which have gone down to defeat because their adversaries had more will to win, more raw strength physically, mentally, and emotionally, to throw into the critical battles. It was not Khrushchev's shameless bragging about his ability to overtake the United States economically, or about his superiority in the field of science and missiles, that concerned me. The primitive condition of the Soviet transportation network alone is enough to keep them from even starting to close the gap between their production and ours for years to come. Nor was it the comparative productivity of our factories, the strength of our arms, or of our abilities in the field of scientific research.

I thought of our people, our leaders, and those who represented us at home and abroad, in private enterprise as well as in government. And here my concern was not with educational background or basic intelligence. The question was one of determination, of will, of stamina, of willingness to risk all for victory. How did we stack up against the kind of fanatically dedicated men I had seen in the past ten days?

I thought how ironical it was that the Communist leaders were getting more production out of their people by special incentives. In a nation which supposedly is guided by the philosophy of "everyone receives according to his needs and produces according to his ability," the disparity between the amounts paid more efficient workers and those who are less efficient is far greater than in the United States. Yet at a time when they have found it necessary to turn our way in order to get more production from workers and to encourage their more talented people, we seem to be turning their way with economic policies which increasingly tend to penalize rather than to reward our more creative people.

Why do men like Alger Hiss, from our best families, educated in our finest schools, become conscious agents of the Communist conspiracy? Not because they want money or power, but because they become convinced that Communism as a way of life is superior—even more, that it is the wave of the future.

And worse still, there are other Americans, with the same advantages of background and education, who have so immersed themselves in competition for material gain that they deliberately stay above the great battle of the generation in which they live. They will not take the time to learn what this world struggle is all about. And because they lack knowledge, they fail to develop the intelligence and the will to act, to think and speak effectively for our cause, as the Communists do for theirs.

I thought of others who do care enough about the outcome of this struggle to participate in it, but who are always insisting on trying to find an easy way out.

"There can be no answer to Castro until we raise the economic standards of all of Latin America," they proclaim.

When there are riots in Caracas or Lima, all we have to do is spend more money for radio broadcasts to Latin America, so that our neighbors to the South will "understand us and like us better."

Or, at the other extreme, when the Communists probe some area of the Free World, all we have to do is to increase our military budget to demonstrate our determination to resist them—we need not bother with trying to meet them in the economic and political areas on which the Communists are concentrating.

As one who had supported all programs of this type in government, I recognized their importance. But I knew they were only part of the answer. If we relied on any one of them alone, we would go down to certain defeat. We need all the weapons—military, economic, and ideological—to fight the most complex battle in world history.

The Communists have developed a completely new concept of conquest—one in which they go under borders, rather than over them, to dominate a non-Communist country. They not only have developed new tactics, but they have brought to the battle an iron will which could only stem from faith and convictions deeply held.

How can we instill in our children not only a faith greater than theirs but the physical, mental, and moral stamina to outlast the enemies of freedom in this century of crisis?

These questions were running through my mind as our plane put down at Babice Airport near Warsaw. As Pat and I stepped out on the ramp and looked over the airport area, I said to myself, "Here we go again—it's Moscow all over." The only people there to greet us were members of the official government party, personnel from the American Embassy, and a few other diplomats—and the inevitable red roses for Mrs. Nixon.

I had been briefed before leaving Moscow not to expect any crowds in Poland—first because I was arriving on Sunday, the only day Polish workers were allowed off, and more importantly, because the Polish Government had not announced the time of my arrival or the route of my motorcade. Khrushchev had been given a cool reception in Poland only three weeks before, and the government did not want to be embarrassed by having the people greet an American more warmly than they had the Soviet Premier himself. In explaining this to me, Frank Siscoe, Counselor at our Embassy in Poland, said I should not interpret the absence of friendly crowds as a lack of warmth of the Polish people toward Americans. It was just that it was Sunday and that Russia was a great threatening giant on the border of Poland.

We went through the usual airport ceremonies and then got into open cars for the motorcade into the city. As we drove toward the airport exit, I saw the first indication that things might be different in Warsaw than they had been in Moscow. The crack Polish Honor Guard, which had used the Russian goose step as it marched in review, now did an astonishingly unmilitary thing—the men applauded and cheered us as we drove by. The thought occurred to me that Khrushchev would have real problems in getting these men to fight on his side in the event of a war between the Soviet Union and the United States.

As we turned into the highway, I noticed small clusters of people shouting at us from the side of the road. Then something hit me in the face. But it was not a rock: it was a bouquet of roses.

I turned to Dr. Oskar Lange, the Vice Premier, and asked him what the people were shouting. "Niech Zyje America," he replied, "Long live America."

As we drove through the suburbs, approaching the heart of the city, the crowds grew larger and larger. They were clapping and cheering and hundreds threw bouquets of flowers into my car, into Mrs. Nixon's car behind us, and into the press buses which followed. As we reached the downtown area, the situation got completely out of hand. The crowds overflowed the sidewalks and pressed into the street, stopping the motorcade altogether. The government had tried to discourage crowds and consequently had not anticipated any.[3] Very few police

---

[3] The official blackout of all news concerning my visit and the time of my arrival in Warsaw was rendered a failure because the Polish Government had not taken

were on hand, and those we could see were busy trying to clear a single lane for our motorcade through this avenue of humanity.

We moved at a snail's pace, stopping time and time again because of the throng of people who surged around us. I stood in the back of the car and waved back my greetings and appreciation. Whenever our car was stopped I had a chance to look closely into the faces around me. Some were shouting, others were singing, and many were crying —with tears running down their cheeks. It was the most moving experience of all my trips abroad.

I knew this welcome was not for me personally. It was an expression, a spontaneous outpouring of warm feeling, toward the country I represented.

"Niech Zyje America."

"Niech Zyje Eisenhower."

"Niech Zyje Nixon."

"Sto lat!"—"May you live a thousand years!"

Two-hundred-and-fifty thousand people lined the streets of downtown Warsaw, according to the official and unofficial estimates. It was unprecedented and unexpected. So many flowers and bouquets were thrown at us that our driver had to stop the car several times to clear the windshield. Dr. Lange could not believe what he saw. I could not believe it. The press corps could not believe it. But there it was before us—a crowd almost twice as large as that which had greeted Khrushchev only three weeks before.

Several newspapermen ventured into the crowd and they were told, "This time we bought our own flowers." Upon Khrushchev's arrival, the people explained, the Polish Government had declared a school holiday, had transported children and government workers to his motorcade route, and had even provided the flowers for the people to throw in a "spontaneous" welcome. Many had kept the flowers and had not thrown them to Khrushchev. And now they proudly exclaimed, "This time we bought our own flowers!"

It took us more than two hours to inch our way through the crowds. When we reached Myslewicki Palace, the government guesthouse where we were staying, the newsmen asked me for a comment on our reception. I said "tremendous" and "wonderful" and at the same time knew that words were completely inadequate to express what was in my heart.

Radio Free Europe into consideration. RFE had flooded the airwaves with announcements—and so the word was spread throughout the population of Warsaw and its suburbs.

Only later, when I had collected my thoughts, did it occur to me what I should have said. My reception in Warsaw was a message to free people and to those throughout the world who yearn for freedom, telling them that the torch of freedom still burns in the hearts of millions of Poles despite fourteen years of Soviet occupation and Communist rule. And it was an unmistakable message to Khrushchev, a warning more pointed and eloquent than a thousand speeches or state papers, that he was sitting on a powder keg.

This warm reception from the Polish people followed me wherever I went in Poland and it posed an unexpected and strange problem. Wherever I spoke—at the Tomb of the Unknown Soldier, at the Warsaw University, at the cathedral—I had to be particularly careful of what I said. I could speak of friendship and peace but I had to steer clear of such words as "independence" or "freedom" for fear of sparking a demonstration which might bring dire consequences on an unarmed people.

At one gathering, for instance, I mentioned that "we must all work for a better life for our children." A woman in the crowd shouted back: "Yes, freedom for our children!" Others took up the chant and in a few seconds it appeared there might be a riot. Then several quick-thinking Polish Government officials in our party struck up "May he live a thousand years" and the force of the crowd was diverted back to a "safe," nonpolitical display of affection. But the combustible potential was always just below the surface.

One of the most effective ways of subtly getting across to the Polish people the way of life in America was simply to introduce to them Vice Admiral Rickover and to explain that he had been born in a small town near Warsaw, that he had migrated to the United States, a land of opportunity, and that now he was an admired and respected hero in our country for his outstanding career in our Navy and for his leadership in the planning and building of the world's first atomic submarine. Admiral Rickover, an outwardly unemotional man, was greatly moved by the reception given him in Poland. He was a hero there as well as in the United States.[4]

As I traveled through Poland, the character of its proud people became clear to me. And I could better understand the tremendous problems the Communists were encountering in trying to impose the drab dullness of socialist conformity upon the rich cultural heritage of

[4] He had turned in a particularly outstanding job the week before in Leningrad, where he demanded to see a new Soviet atomic icebreaker—just as we had shown U. S. atomic ships to visiting Soviet officials earlier.

an independent people. The Polish farmer loves his land and his horses, as his father did before him. He refuses to be moved into co-operative farms on the inflexible Communist design. The religious instincts, the abiding faith of the Polish people are so strong that the Communist Government has not dared to make a frontal assault on the Catholic Church there. Family ties are so respected that the government has been unable to brainwash the new Polish generation and win its deep-rooted loyalty.

There were many incidents which revealed for me the innate strength of the Polish man on the street and the wide gap between that average citizen, with his inherent strength, warmth, and heritage, and the Communist leaders and functionaries I met. It can best be summed up in one sentence spoken by my Polish interpreter, who did not happen to be a Communist Party member. A young Communist factory manager had conducted us on a guided tour of a new steel plant. He had insisted on showing off every detail of the machinery, but he had shown no interest at all in the workers on the assembly line. As we left the plant, my interpreter said, "The trouble with him and all Communist factory managers is that they know all about machines and nothing about people." In that sentence he captured a vital truth concerning Communist leaders I had seen in Poland, in the Soviet Union, and throughout the world. He had put his finger on a great potential weakness of all materialistic, Marxist regimes.

As our plane took off for the long flight back to Washington, I looked down on the flat Polish countryside and realized that these people, and millions like them in the other satellite countries, represent Khrushchev's greatest danger and the Free World's greatest hope in the struggle for the future.

My encounter with Khrushchev was one of the major personal crises of my life. But, far more important, it was a fascinating case study of the continuing crisis of our time—a crisis deliberately created and maintained by World Communism. In the person of Nikita Khrushchev, "Communist man" at his most dangerous best, I had seen Communism in action—not just in theory.

I would not be so presumptuous even to try, here in a few pages, to suggest a program to "solve" the crisis of Communism. Because I do not presume to be an expert; and only the experts on Communism, who are sprouting up all over the landscape these days, have single, simple solutions for the problem.

Their formulas are as diverse as they are well-intentioned. To list only a few of the one-shot panaceas:

—Take care of the Communists at home and you won't need to worry about them abroad.
—Everyone knows the danger of Communism is from without and not from within.
—We should concentrate on the "important" areas like Europe, and not devote so much attention to the "peripheral" areas in Southeast Asia, Africa, and Latin America.
—The danger is primarily military: keep America strong at home and stop the give-away programs to undeserving foreigners abroad.
—The danger is primarily economic: if we would only "give every Asian another bowl of rice" there would be no Communism in Asia, and so on around the world.
—The danger is primarily ideological: what we have to do is spend billions of dollars more on Voice of America and other propaganda programs so that "people will like us better."
—We should submit more of our differences with Communism to the U.N. for decision.
—We should get out of the U.N.
—The major problem is one of "understanding and communicating" with Khrushchev. Rather than being more tough, we must be more flexible.
—If our diplomats will only be tougher at the conference table, the Communists will back down. But economic and mutual security programs (which our diplomats say they must have as weapons if we are going to be "tough") are a waste of money and tinged with "pink."

There is no question about the loyalty of those who hold these differing views. It is not a question of one being "more patriotic" than the other. The question is not too much or too little patriotism, but too little knowledge—knowledge about the Communists and, perhaps more important, about ourselves.

The Communist threat is indivisible. It confronts us both at home and abroad, and those who emphasize one to the exclusion of the other do a disservice to the cause of freedom.

The Communist threat is universal. There could be no more dangerous fallacy than to assume that there are some peripheral areas which "do not matter." Our failure to meet a Communist probe in Asia or Africa or Latin America only increases the probability that we will be forced to meet such a probe in Europe.

The Communist threat is total. And so must be the arsenal of weapons we must have at our disposal to meet it. Those who would build a "fortress America" and concentrate exclusively on military strength have forgotten that Communism made its greatest gains immediately after World War II when the United States had a monopoly on the atomic bomb and massive military superiority over the Soviet Union. Military strength is vital—but unless supplemented with economic, political, and propaganda programs, it is completely inadequate.

On the other hand, those who downgrade the importance of military strength and claim that all we need to stop Communism are economic aid programs to raise living standards in underdeveloped countries, have only to look at the Czechoslovakian experience to realize that the Communists can take over countries with no serious economic problems.

Mr. Khrushchev and his colleagues are fighting the battle for the world with all weapons—military, economic, political, propaganda— using each at the time and place, and in the quantity, the situation may require. We must do the same if we are going to battle them on equal terms.

But, not only must we know the nature and complexity of the Communist threat, we must know ourselves. We must objectively assess our strengths and our weaknesses, and particularly those areas in which we have something to offer that the Communists cannot match.

Khrushchev has challenged us to peaceful competition. We should not only accept his challenge—we should extend the area of competition.

I have no doubt if the competition were limited merely to military and economic strength that we would win. But we are sure to win only if we play the game our way and not his. The answer to those who believe in an all-powerful government as the primary instrument of progress is not more power in government, but more power and responsibility in individuals. Communism provides an opportunity for maximum creative activity, at best, for thousands in an exclusive elite class. Our advantage is that our system, at its best, provides this opportunity for millions. But the system succeeds or fails to the extent that individuals respond to the challenge and seize the opportunity. Our potentially creative people must not stay on the side lines. They must play their part in the greatest drama of human history—the culmination of man's fight through the centuries for human dignity and freedom, and against reaction and slavery.

But even more important, we must not make the mistake of competing with the Communists only on the grounds and in the areas they select. We must extend the competition beyond the race to space, the power of our arms, the productivity of our factories—the areas, in other words of sheer materialism. Our spiritual and moral heritage, our dedication to individual liberties, our belief in the right of all people to choose the kind of economic, social, and political system they want —these are the truly great strengths of free government, and the correspondingly fatal weakness of dictatorial regimes. We must extend the competition—to both sides of the Iron Curtain—and deepen it.

But our major need is to match and surpass the Communists in still another area. The greatest strength of Communism is not its military power, its exaggerated claims of economic progress, or the appeal of its ideology. It is, rather, its sense of mission, the will to win which its adherents carry into every battle. It is this spirit which can prove decisive in the outcome of any crisis—particularly the type of continuing crisis the Communists have created. They use crisis as a weapon, as a tactic in their all-front, all-out struggle against free peoples. They keep the pot boiling, they shift from burner to burner. They are implacable, relentless, and tireless.

We must learn to live with this continuing crisis, to keep our guard up constantly, but without stretching our resources to the breaking point at all times, which would in the end destroy us. We must bring to this battle the maturity and serenity which will see us through periods of temporary setbacks. We must have that indispensable ingredient for success in times of crisis: a selfless concentration on the problem which confronts us. We must, as leaders in this struggle, decide what is right. And then we must lead, rather than restrict our action to what the weak and the timid will approve. Because, as in the case of an individual, a nation will be confident, cool, and decisive in battle to the extent its people have decided that its cause is just, that they must fight the battle rather than run away from it, and then make the preparations necessary for victory.

History tells us we are on the right side. Despite the temporary successes of dictators, it is the ultimate destiny of men to be free. The great Indian statesman-scholar, Rajagopalachari, in 1953 put it this way to me: "Communism is doomed to failure because its principles are contrary to the nature of man." Man needs God, and Communism is atheistic. Man wants to be free, and Communism enslaves him. Man cherishes his individual dignity, and Communism collectivizes him.

And if we needed any further proof that freedom rather than Communism will prevail, we could point to what has happened on all the borders between Communism and freedom. In Korea, in China, in Vietnam, in Hungary, and in Germany, millions chose freedom when they had the choice.

Foster Dulles summed up the case a year before his death when he said: ". . . The Communist rulers have shown an immense capacity to extend their rule. But nowhere have they developed a capacity to make their rule genuinely and freely acceptable to the ruled." He spoke, as always, with the voice not of complacency but of abiding faith.

Nikita Khrushchev brings to the great crisis of this century all the elements necessary for success—except one. He is a man of decision; he is superbly prepared; he fights with coolness, confidence, and courage; he has unlimited stamina. But in the very area where he claims supreme confidence, he has a fatal weakness. Despite all his boasts, it is freedom rather than Communism that is the wave of the future.

The Campaign of 1960

The most dangerous period in a crisis is not in the preparation or in the fighting of a battle, but in its aftermath. This is true even when the battle ends in victory. When it ends in defeat, in a contest where an individual has carried on his shoulders the hopes of millions, he then faces his greatest test.

ON November 9, 1960, I joined a select group of four living Americans—Herbert Hoover, Alfred M. Landon, Thomas E. Dewey, and Adlai E. Stevenson—who have sought the Presidency of the United States, as the nominee of one of the two major parties, and who have lost.

I will not try here to tell the complete story of the campaign of 1960. This entire book, and even more, would be required to do that. And I would be the first to admit that the candidate himself is least able to treat the subject objectively.

What were the major decisions that affected the outcome? How and why were these decisions made? What are the reactions of the candidate, his wife, his children, his friends, as they realize that the longest, hardest, most intensive campaign in American history has ended not in victory but in defeat—and by the closest margin in this century?

Years of effort go into the planning and execution of a presidential campaign. But in the end, only a few hours prove really to have mattered. Millions of words are written and spoken, but only a few phrases —usually unpredictable at the time—affect the result.

So often is the candidate confronted with crises and decisions that they become almost routine. Preparing a major speech, approving a key platform provision, holding an important press conference, debating with his opponent—any one of these events may prove to be crucial in a close election.

So I will try here merely to highlight those few hours, words, and decisions that from my vantage point, as the losing candidate for President in 1960, had the greatest effect on the result.

I admit at the outset to some understandable bias. Some of the flash output that was rushed into print immediately after the campaign made me wonder if the writers were reporting the same campaign I had just lived through. I am also aware that many of my friends and supporters sincerely (and in many cases even angrily) believe that if only I had followed their advice in the campaign, the infinitesimal margin by which Kennedy was declared the winner would have been overcome and I would have been elected.

Several weeks after the election, Len Hall summed it all up with one of his half-humorous, half-ironic quips. After analyzing the returns state-by-state, he said, "You know, Dick, a switch of only 14,000 votes and we would have been the heroes and they would have been the bums."

As I review in retrospect those significant events twelve months later, I am the first to recognize that if the year 1960 could be relived, I would revise some decisions and would do some things I did not do. But as I view this vast mural, with all the big and little factors that supposedly caused voters to cast their ballots one way or another, I must admit that I look back with a certain degree of pride on the campaign my associates and I waged. I have set forth this opinion at the outset only so that those who read these pages will take this factor into account as they try to evaluate for themselves the events I shall describe.

One other preliminary comment. Anyone who reads this section, looking for others than myself to blame for decisions that may have contributed to defeat, will be disappointed. For those who practice the art of politics, there are two unbreakable rules. In a winning campaign, the candidate (if he wants a future in politics) must not only allow but encourage each one of literally hordes of advisers and associates to take credit for the tactics that led to victory. In a losing campaign, only the candidate is responsible for the tactics that led to defeat.

When does a presidential campaign really begin?

I suppose this would make a better story if I could fit the facts of my life into the Great American Legend as to how presidential candidates are born and made.

The legend goes something like this. A mother takes a child on her knee. She senses by looking into his eyes that there is something truly extraordinary about him. She says to herself and perhaps even to him, "You, son, are going to be President some day." From that time on, he is tapped for greatness. He talks before he walks. He reads a thousand words a minute. He is bored by school because he is so much smarter than his teachers. He prepares himself for leadership by taking courses in public speaking and political science. He drives ever upward, calculating every step of the way until he reaches his and—less importantly—the nation's destiny by becoming President of the United States.

So goes the legend. The truth in my case is not stranger than fiction perhaps—but it may be more believable.

The last thing my mother, a devout Quaker, wanted me to do was go into the warfare of politics. I recall she once expressed the hope that I might become a missionary to our Quaker mission fields in Central America. But true to her Quaker tradition, she never tried to force me in the direction she herself might have preferred.

As far as I was concerned, my first ambition as a child was to become a railroad engineer—not because of any interest in engines (I have no mechanical aptitude whatever)—but because I wanted to travel and see the United States and the world. Only one train a day went through the town of Yorba Linda (population then of less than 300) and hearing its whistle as it slowed down at the crossing never failed to start me to daydreaming about the places I would visit when I grew up.

I won my share of scholarships, and of speaking and debating prizes in school, not because I was smarter but because I worked longer and harder than some of my more gifted colleagues.[1]

---

[1] I recall a pungent comment which illustrates this point. During my first year at Duke Law School, I was concerned about my ability to keep my scholarship in competition in a class that numbered over twenty Phi Beta Kappas out of a total enrollment of fifty. I had expressed this concern to Bill Adelson, a third-year man who ranked near the top of his class. Adelson, who had noted the long hours I spent studying in the law library, reassured me: "You don't have to worry," he said. "You know what it takes to learn the law? An iron butt."

There were perhaps two major reasons for my competitive drive during these years. One was economic, the other personal.

From an economic standpoint, I knew that I could not go on to college and to law school unless I was able to earn scholarships. It was as simple as that.

The personal factor was contributed by my father. Because of illness in his family he had had to leave school after only six years of formal education. Never a day went by when he did not tell me and my four brothers how fortunate we were to be able to go to school. I was determined not to let him down. My biggest thrill in those years was to see the light in his eyes when I brought home a good report card. He loved the excitement and the battles of political life. During the two years he was bedridden before his death (which came just at the start of the 1956 campaign) his one request of me was that I send him the *Congressional Record.* He used to read it daily, cover-to-cover, something I never had the patience to do. I have often thought that with his fierce competitive drive and his intense interest in political issues, he might have been more successful than I in political life had he had the opportunity to continue his education.

My college education fits into the traditional pattern of training for prospective presidential candidates no better than my early family background. The small Quaker college I attended—Whittier, in the pioneer Quaker community of that name just east of Los Angeles—did not offer a course in political science in the years I spent there. But looking back, I think the limited quantity of courses offered was offset by the high quality of the group of dedicated teachers under whom it was my privilege to study. History, literature, philosophy, and the classics—taught by inspirational men—is the best foundation for a career in politics. There will be plenty of time later to learn firsthand the intricacies of political strategy and tactics by working in the precincts. There will be too little time later for gaining indispensable knowledge in depth about the nature of man and the institutions he has created—an understanding which, from my experience, can better be acquired from the classics than from the more "practical" courses in politics.

I hasten to add that this is not a case against courses in political science. After all, had I been exposed to one, I might have won the last election rather than losing it! I only express my opinion that if a choice has to be made, the college years—when the mind is quicker, more receptive, and more retentive than it will ever be again—can best be used to develop the whole man rather than the specialist. I would say that this is important whatever the field an individual may plan to enter. In the field of politics, it is an absolute must. It is not that people do not "grow" after they finish their formal education and enter public life. But the capacity to grow will be determined by the breadth and depth of the intellectual base which is acquired during the college years. If a man comes out of college with only the narrow and thin background of the highly trained political specialist, he may win elections—but he will serve neither his country nor himself as well as he should. He will be a sitting duck for every half-baked idea or time-worn cliché that comes along.

In one respect, my education does fit the prescribed pattern for those planning to embark on a political career. I studied law, and approximately half of all the members of Congress are lawyers by background. To the extent that the study of law disciplines the mind, it can be most helpful in politics as well as in other fields. But as a lawyer I should add a *caveat* at this point: lawyers tend to be "nit-pickers." Too often, when confronted with a problem, they approach it from the standpoint of "how not to do it" rather than "how to do it." Lawyers in politics need non-lawyers around them to keep them from being too legalistic, too unimaginative. Looking back on my own years in law school (at Duke University in Durham, North Carolina), the most valuable course I had from the standpoint of preparing for political life was one in jurisprudence, the philosophy of law, from Dr. Lon Fuller, now at Harvard and during the '60 campaign the head of my Scholars' Committee. It was not a required course for the degree. But it would be, in my opinion, an essential course for any law student who is planning to enter public life. Because the public man must not only know what the law is: he must know how and why it got that way. And again, the time to acquire this background is during the college and university years when a man has the time to indulge in the luxury of reading and thinking. Later on, he may well find himself too busy acting and speaking; and if he does not acquire this perspective and background in his college years he may never acquire it.

The balance of the period prior to my entrance into the political arena can be quickly covered. I practiced law for five years in my home town of Whittier; then came ten months in Washington, in 1942, writing rationing regulations for the OPA, followed by three-

and-a-half years in the Navy during World War II. Nothing occurred in this period to indicate a possible future political career—except that, as President Eisenhower put it, "Like all successful politicians I married above myself."

I ran for public office for the first time in 1946. Here again, I did not fit into the pattern usually attributed to successful political practitioners. I have always liked to meet and talk to people, but the back-slapping, baby-kissing, exhibitionist activities expected of the average candidate were missing from this campaign and all the others in which I was to participate. I have always felt that above everything else a man must be himself in a political campaign. He must never try to be or to do something which is not natural for him. Whenever he does, he gets out of character and loses the quality that is essential for political success—sincerity and credibility. My success in the '46 campaign was probably the result of three factors: intensive campaigning; doing my homework; and participating in debates with my better-known opponent, the veteran incumbent Congressman, Jerry Voorhis.

When I went to Congress in 1947, a national newspaper syndicate chose me as the subject for a feature piece entitled, "The Greenest Congressman in Washington." The consequences of my appointment to the Committee on Un-American Activities are recounted in the first section of this book.

My major committee assignment was Education and Labor and it was here, thirteen years before the election of 1960, that I met for the first time the man who was my opponent in that campaign and is now President of the United States. Jack Kennedy and I shared one distinction on the Education and Labor Committee: we were the low men on the totem pole. I was the most junior member on the Republican side and he on the Democratic side. This was probably a challenge and incentive to both of us. The custom in committee hearings is for the questioning to start with the chairman and then to alternate between Democrats and Republicans until the last man finally has his chance. This meant that before Kennedy or I could ask a question, both the witness and the subject had been pretty well worked over. Each of us had plenty of opportunity to do a lot of thinking as our senior colleagues fired away, and each of us, I believe, usually managed to come up with some pretty good questions at the end of the hearing.

In fact, it was in our capacity as members of that committee that we had our first "debate." In the spring of 1947, at the request of Congressman Frank Buchanan, we went to McKeesport, Pennsylvania, a suburb of Pittsburgh, to debate the merits of what was then the "hot" issue under committee consideration, the Taft-Hartley Act. I doubt if either of us, or those who were in the audience of 150 to 200 that night, will recall much of what was said during the course of the evening. I was for the bill. Kennedy was against it. And we both presented our points of view as vigorously as we could. As far as the audience was concerned, I probably had the better of the argument because most of those present, as employers, tended to be on my side in the first place. After the meeting, we rode a sleeper from Pittsburgh back to the capital. I remember that our discussions during the long, rocky ride related primarily to foreign affairs and the handling of the Communist threat at home and abroad, rather than the Taft-Hartley Act. I do not recall the details of our talk but of one thing I am absolutely sure: neither he nor I had even the vaguest notion at that time that either of us would be a candidate for President thirteen years later.

It was not until the spring of 1952 that the thought first seriously occurred to me that I might be a possible candidate for national office. As a result of the Hiss case and my election to the Senate in 1950, speaking invitations came into my office from all over the nation. One of these, the principal speech at a fund-raising dinner of the New York State Republican Committee, May 8, 1952, at the Waldorf-Astoria, turned out to be one of the most important speeches I had made up to that time. I devoted a full week to preparing it. I knew I faced a major test before a highly sophisticated audience and was keyed up for the occasion. It turned out to be one of my more successful efforts. When I concluded, the audience gave me a standing ovation. As I sat down, Governor Dewey grasped my hand and said: "That was a terrific speech. Make me a promise: don't get fat; don't lose your zeal. And you can be President some day."

I was somewhat embarrassed by the generosity of his remarks. It was not the first time that someone had suggested that I might be presidential timber. Every public figure, at one time or another, and particularly after he has made an effective speech, has had someone say—"you have what it takes to be President," or words to that effect. It is a way some people have to pay their highest compliment to a speech they may have liked.

I thought at first that this was all Governor Dewey meant to convey. I assumed that he was simply indulging in the usual practice of trying to say something nice to a fellow political practitioner after a major effort. However, as I was to learn when I came to know him better, he is not addicted to that kind of political puffing. Through the years I served as Vice President, I was to find him one of my most objective critics. If he thought one of my speeches was good he would say so. But he would never hesitate to tell me that another one had not been up to par, or was even "lousy," if he thought that to be the case. This candor on Dewey's part probably lost him some friends in the political world, but I respected and admired him for it. I thought that his failure to win the presidency in 1948, at a time when I did not know him personally, was a great loss to the nation. As I got to know him well through the years after 1952, I came to believe this even more deeply. At his best, Dewey is one of the most brilliant, tough-minded, resourceful men of this era. He would have been more than a match for Khrushchev or any other world leader. It is America's and the Free World's loss that his great talents were never utilized on the world scene.

Despite the success of my New York speech and Dewey's unex-pected reaction to it, I did not consider myself a serious contender for the vice presidential nomination when I attended the Chicago Convention in July 1952. And this is perhaps as good a place as any to lay to rest one of the many myths regarding my selection as General Eisenhower's running mate in 1952. It has been alleged that there was a "deal" beween Dewey and myself under which I was to receive the vice presidential nomination in return for "delivering" the California delegation to Eisenhower. There are two facts which completely de-molish this allegation. In the first place, I was for Eisenhower long be-fore I met Dewey at the New York dinner in May. And in the second place, the California delegation was pledged to Governor Earl War-ren and stayed with him to the finish. It did not shift to Eisenhower until after he had already been assured the nomination by reason of the switch to him, over Harold Stassen's objection, of the Minnesota delegation.

From the time I became the Republican nominee for Vice President, everything I was to do or say inevitably was appraised in light of the possibility that I might eventually become a candidate for President, but it was not until November of 1958 that the story of my candidacy really begins.

Friday, November 7, was a bleak day at the start of a long, cold Washington winter. It was a particularly cold day in the fortunes of the Republican Party and of Richard Nixon. My political career had been one of very sharp ups and downs since my nomination and election as Vice President in 1952. My stock soared after the success of my first round-the-world trip in the fall and winter of 1953. It went down just as sharply when, in 1954, my back-breaking campaign for a Republican House and Senate fell short. It went up again in 1955 because of the general approval, even from my most severe critics, of my conduct during the period of the President's heart attack. It went down again in 1956 when Harold Stassen made his abortive attempt to dump me from the ticket. My renomination and re-election in 1956 more than compensated for the losses sustained during the Stassen attack. But in 1957 and 1958 my support drifted downward again as the recession began to be felt throughout the country. Then the crisis of Caracas, in May 1958, carried me to an all-time high. But just six months later, the shattering Republican defeat in the '58 Congressional elections drove my stock down to an all-time low.

It was at this time that I received a telephone call from Len Hall. Len had been a long-time personal and political friend. We had served together in the House. He had been Chairman of the Republican National Committee during the period of the President's heart attack and the successful campaign of 1956. He told me—this Friday in November—that Clifford Folger, who had been National Republican Finance Chairman during Hall's tenure as Party Chairman, was on leave in Washington from his post as U. S. Ambassador to Belgium and that they would like to drop by to discuss the political situation. I invited them to dinner at my home.

After dinner Len quickly got down to essentials. "It is time for you to decide what you are going to do in 1960," he said. "If you are going to be a candidate, you must start now."

The thought that I might be a candidate in 1960 had, of course, occurred to me before. But for the first time, I now had to face up to the problems I would be confronted with if I made the decision to run.

First we discussed the odds against us. They were formidable indeed.

At the beginning of the 1952 campaign, by way of contrast, there were 199 Republicans in the House of Representatives (out of a total of 435 members) and 47 Republican Senators against 49 Democrats. There were Republican Governors in twenty-five states and the Republican Party controlled both houses of twenty-six state legislatures. The Republican candidate in 1960 would find that there were only

153 Republicans in the House (out of a total of 437), 35 Republican Senators out of 100, 14 Republican Governors, and that the Republicans controlled both houses of the state legislatures in only seven states. As a further indication of party weakness, a Gallup Poll as to party preferences (in February 1960) showed that 47 per cent of American voters considered themselves Democrats, 30 per cent Republicans, and 23 per cent independents. To win in 1960, the Republican candidate would have to get practically all the Republican votes, more than half of the independents—and, in addition, the votes of between five and six million Democrats.

My personal stock was no higher than that of the party because I had campaigned throughout the country for our Republican candidates in the 1958 elections. As a result of that massive national defeat and Nelson Rockefeller's victory in New York, columnists and commentators were freely predicting that I was on the way down and Rockefeller was on the way up as the potential Republican candidate in 1960.

One major winner in the '58 campaign was Jack Kennedy. He had won an overwhelming re-election victory in Massachusetts and his presidential bandwagon, which had started to roll immediately after his narrow defeat for the vice presidential nomination in 1956, was now moving at high speed. In a trial heat between Kennedy and me which Gallup took at this time, it was Kennedy by 59 to 41 per cent. This would have meant a Kennedy landslide of the same proportions as Eisenhower's decisive victory over Stevenson in 1956.

I asked Len Hall, in light of all these discouraging facts, to give me his honest appraisal of the odds against me on winning the nomination and the election. He replied that he was confident we could win the nomination—even though the odds at the moment were probably in Rockefeller's favor. As far as the election was concerned, he estimated the odds against any Republican winning in 1960 at about five-to-one. But speaking from his wealth of political experience, he refused to concede that the situation might not change drastically before Election Day 1960, particularly if we mounted an effective campaign.

Before our evening's conversation was over, Len Hall agreed to assume the responsibility for directing the campaign to line up delegates to the 1960 National Convention. Cliff Folger said that he would undertake the role of Finance Chairman as soon as he completed his assignment in Belgium.

As we entered the year 1959, some breaks began to come our way. President Eisenhower sent me to London late in November 1958 to represent him at the dedication of the chapel in St. Paul's Cathedral honoring the American dead of World War II. The trip was rated a success by most observers. My speech at the historic London Guildhall received a particularly favorable reaction, both in Britain and in this country.[2] The effect of these events in the United States was not massive. But it did tend to erase the memories of the unsuccessful '58 campaign and started me on the way back from the low point I had reached.

Another factor that worked in my favor was one over which I had no control. After a good beginning as New York's Governor, Nelson Rockefeller had fallen on lean days. Because his predecessor, Averell Harriman, had left the state's fiscal affairs in such bad shape, Rockefeller had to ask for new taxes in order to put the state budget on a pay-as-you-go basis. This step was, in my opinion, necessary—and I publicly said so. But raising taxes is never popular, even when it is right, and Rockefeller's standing in the public opinion polls began to fall off.

And as the national economy began to turn upward in the winter and spring of 1959, the Administration's standing rose accordingly— and along with it, the personal stock of all of us associated with it.

Then came a decisive break—my meeting with Khrushchev in July 1959. Until that meeting, polls indicated my support was no greater nationwide than that of the Republican Party. After my return from the Soviet Union, my personal standing rose the critical five to six points above Republican strength in general—a margin I had to maintain if I were to have a chance to win in 1960. The trial heats between Kennedy and myself provided further dramatic evidence of this increase in my public support. Before the trip, a Gallup Poll showed Kennedy's strength at 61 per cent and mine at 39 per cent—a margin even greater than Eisenhower's over Stevenson in 1956. After the trip, the gap closed to 52 per cent for Kennedy, 48 per cent for Nixon. In November 1959, I moved ahead of him in the polls for the first time: Nixon 53 per cent—Kennedy 47 per cent.

I had no illusions, however, that this margin could be maintained without an extraordinary effort. Kennedy's problem was simply to get the Democrats to stay in their own party and vote for him. My prob-

[2] The full text of this speech may be found in the Appendix.

lem was to hold virtually all the Republicans and then persuade five to six million Democrats to leave their own candidate and vote Republican. I recognized that I could accomplish this only as President Eisenhower had—by acting and speaking not just as a Republican partisan but as a representative of all the people. My trips to Caracas and Moscow had provided an opportunity for me to appear in this role. And it was only àfter these trips that my strength rose the necessary level above that of my party.

One more opportunity to demonstrate "national" leadership occurred before the campaign year of 1960. A crippling 116-day steel strike—running from July 15 through November 7, 1959—had been suspended by a Taft-Hartley injunction which was due to expire on January 26, 1960. President Eisenhower, on December 3, began a trip which would take him to Europe, the Middle East, and South Asia and would continue until December 22. Before he left the country, Secretary of Labor James Mitchell and I discussed the strike with him and he approved a plan for us to attempt to mediate the dispute in his absence. After numerous preliminary "feeler" sessions and then eight days and nights of the most intensive discussions I have ever participated in, we were able to work out a settlement—on January 4, 1960—acceptable to both sides. The settlement, which would run until July 1962, was attacked in some quarters as being inflationary, but the critics overlooked the fact that this was the first steel labor contract since World War II which was not accompanied by a price boost. And whereas the postwar pattern of annual wage increases had averaged out to about 8 per cent, this new contract provided for an average of less than 3 per cent—almost exactly in line with the annual "productivity" factor. At any rate, the political effect of the settlement was to sustain my narrow lead over Kennedy in the trial polls into the early months of 1960, and to project Jim Mitchell into the foreground as a potential vice presidential candidate.

Len Hall had proved to be a good prophet. As a result of two events none of us could foresee in the discouraging winter of 1958–59—my Russian trip and the steel settlement—the almost prohibitive odds against me a year before had now shifted. As the campaign year began, I was a strong favorite to win the Republican nomination and was running practically a dead-heat in the public opinion polls against the strongest Democratic candidate—Jack Kennedy.

But now both Kennedy and Rockefeller were beginning to make

their moves and the decisive battles would shortly be under way. Early in January, I invited some of the key men in my campaign—Len Hall, Cliff Folger, Bob Finch, Herb Klein, Fred Scribner, Jim Shepley, Fred Seaton, and Claude Robinson—to lunch in my Capitol office to discuss our strategy for the period up to the Republican Convention in July.

We foresaw no serious difficulty in winning the Republican nomination. The problem was to win it in such a way as to strengthen rather than weaken our chances to win the November election. And this was the only real threat that Rockefeller's candidacy posed to us. His stock had dropped considerably since his victory in New York in 1958. His political advisers had shown appallingly bad judgment on several occasions. Most recently, for example, he had made the error of publicly suggesting that I should settle the steel dispute—at the very time that Jim Mitchell and I were in the process of negotiating a settlement. To become a serious contender for the nomination, he had only one course of action open to him—to enter and win one of the earlier primary contests. When he failed to take this step, what little chance he had to win the nomination was lost. When he finally made his move, through a late spring attack on me, it was too little and too late.

However, with mounting belligerence, Rockefeller was taking a line very similar to that of the Democratic critics of the Eisenhower Administration. He favored, for example, putting the "senior citizen" medical care program under Social Security, and he attacked the President's defense policies even more strongly than some of the Democratic candidates. Anti-Administration columnists and commentators, as well as Democratic candidates, gleefully seized on every statement he made and used them effectively against the Administration and, thus, against me. But while these attacks were irritating, we all recognized that they would not be decisive. In the end, once the Convention choice was made, I had every confidence that Rockefeller would campaign for the Republican nominee.

Our primary subject for conversation that afternoon in January was the problem we would confront in winning the election itself. I insisted from the outset that Kennedy was most likely to be nominated and would be the hardest to beat. While some of those present dissented from this view, Len Hall agreed with me.

I listed Kennedy's assets as I saw them at the time. From a personal standpoint, he had high intelligence, great energy, and a particularly effective television personality. He also had unlimited money which already had enabled him to employ a large, skilled staff of organizers, speech-writers, pollsters, and others essential for a successful campaign. He had a head start with a personal staff who had begun their drive back in 1956, soon after he had come so close to winning the Democratic nomination for Vice President.

But Kennedy's most decisive asset, as far as getting nominated was concerned, was the weakness of his opponents.

Adlai Stevenson had strong emotional support but he was a two-time loser and none of the Democratic professionals, who control the votes at national conventions, gave him any serious chance.

Hubert Humphrey was a tireless campaigner, a good speaker, and had strong support among the liberal elements of the Democratic Party in the North and West. But while he had become more restrained and moderate in recent years, some of his more radical and irresponsible positions of the early days in Washington could not be lived down. The Southerners and the big city bosses of the party would never take him.

Stuart Symington had never been able to recover from what many observers had considered a rather mediocre performance during the Army-McCarthy hearings.

Lyndon Johnson was the strongest and ablest of Kennedy's prospective opponents for the nomination but, despite his efforts to portray himself as a Westerner rather than a Southerner, the Southern tag would inevitably deny him the support of the big delegations from the Northern states and of organized labor.

In summary, Kennedy had going for him, therefore, not only his own affirmative assets but also the powerful negative factor which is as true in politics as in any other field: you can't beat somebody with nobody.

Claude Robinson, a polling and public opinion expert, summarized Kennedy's potential liabilities in this order: youth, inexperience, wealth, and religion. I responded that each of these potential liabilities could be turned into an asset by an intelligent candidate, and that no one should ever underestimate the intelligence of Kennedy or of his corps of close associates and advisers.

As far as youth was concerned, I pointed out that he was only four years younger than I, and had begun his career in Washington the same year.

As for his inexperience, I recognized that one of my major assets was my experience as Vice President. But experience, itself, can be a liability and inexperience an asset in a political campaign. To gain experience, a man must make decisions. And when he makes decisions, he makes enemies. Then too, he must assume responsibility for the consequences of those decisions. As long as the peace and prosperity issues held up, my experience would be a decided advantage; but to the extent that public confidence in the Administration on either score was shaken, I would also lose support. The advantage of Kennedy's inexperience was the very fact that he had not participated in the making of critical decisions—and thus there was very little for his opponent to shoot at. All that the voter could judge him on was what he said, rather than what he had done, and voters quickly forget what a man says. They remember much longer what he has done.

Turning to Kennedy's wealth, I admitted that there was a time when great wealth might have been a liability in a presidential campaign. But that time has long since passed. Indeed, the time may have come in America, in view of the length and tremendous cost of presidential campaigns, when far from being a liability, personal wealth is actually a necessity for a candidate.

Kennedy's religion was obviously going to be a major factor in the election, and there was sharp disagreement in our group as to its probable effect. From the outset, though, I had no doubts whatever on this score: I believed that Kennedy's religion would hurt him in states he could afford to lose anyway, and that it would help him in states he needed to win. There were several reasons why I reached this conclusion.

First, I knew that I, personally, would never raise the question and would not tolerate any use of the religious issue by anyone connected with my campaign, directly or indirectly. I did not believe it to be a legitimate issue. There were several questions as to Kennedy's qualifications for the presidency, but I never at any time considered his religion in this category.

A second reason for my conclusion was this: although there were groups and individuals in different parts of the country who had undeniably launched an anti-Kennedy campaign based solely on his religion, I felt that the nation had come a long way in terms both of political sophistication and religious tolerance since the election of 1928—which Al Smith probably would have lost in any event but in which the margin of his defeat was increased because of the effect of the religious issue.

The most convincing argument in support of the view that Kennedy's religion would probably be helpful rather than harmful to him came from his own campaign organization. During the 1956 Democratic Convention, Kennedy's staff prepared and circulated a memorandum filled with past election statistics to show that a Catholic candidate on the national ticket could assure a Democratic victory—not despite but rather because of his religion. This memorandum—later printed verbatim in *U. S. News & World Report* on August 1, 1960—predicted the final 1960 results with great accuracy. It stated in part:

There is, or can be, such a thing as a 'Catholic vote,' whereby a high proportion of Catholics of all ages, residences, occupations and economic status vote for a well-known Catholic or a ticket with special Catholic appeal . . .

But the Catholic vote is far more important than its numbers—about one out of every four voters who turn out—because of its concentration in the key states and cities of the North. These are the pivotal states with large electoral votes, which vary as to their party support and several of which are inevitably necessary for a victory in the Electoral College . . .

His campaign would be largely concentrated in the key states and cities . . . If he brought into the Democratic fold only those normally Democratic Catholics who voted for Ike, he would probably swing New York, Massachusetts, Rhode Island, Connecticut, Pennsylvania and Illinois—for 132 electoral votes. If he also wins the votes of Catholics who shifted to the Republicans in 1948 or earlier, he could also swing New Jersey, Minnesota, Michigan, California, Wisconsin, Ohio, Maryland, Montana, and maybe even New Hampshire—for a total of 265 electoral votes (needed to win: 269) . . .

Claude Robinson produced perhaps the most convincing evidence of all of Kennedy's potential strength. Every poll since late in 1958 showed him running stronger than any other Democratic candidate against me and the other potential Republican candidates.

We made one important decision at the conclusion of our meeting: to enter my name in all the primary contests. This was, in many respects, a risky maneuver. I would be unable to campaign extensively in the primary states while Congress was still in session. I had broken more tie votes since becoming Vice President than any other Vice President in history, and I knew that if I were away campaigning at the time such a vote occurred in the Senate, this fact could be used devastatingly against me. This meant that an opponent for the Republican nomination could select one primary state, concentrate his efforts there, and conceivably pull off a victory due to my inability to campaign on the scene. The state in which we feared this the most was New Hampshire, in view of Nelson Rockefeller's many close ties and considerable strength there. When he failed to file in New Hampshire, we concluded that we were pretty much out of the woods as far as this danger was concerned.

There were several reasons behind our decision to enter all the primaries. First, we wanted to give Republicans an opportunity to vote for their candidate at the time the Democrats would be flocking to the polls because of the sharp contest in their party. Second, we wanted to show confidence and, at the same time, make it clear we were taking nothing for granted. And third, we wanted to give our campaign organization an opportunity to try out some of its tactics before the election itself—provide it with a "shake down cruise" in effect.

The primary campaigns made a great deal of news at the time but, in retrospect, they were relatively unimportant except that they made Kennedy's nomination at Los Angeles inevitable. The fact, however, that in each of the primary states Kennedy was beating somebody and I was running unopposed naturally gave him more attention in press, television, and radio than I received. This was reflected in the polls. Before the first primary—in New Hampshire in April—Gallup showed the race Nixon 53 per cent—Kennedy 47 per cent. After all the primaries and immediately prior to the Democratic Convention, Kennedy had pulled ahead, with Gallup showing a 52 to 48 per cent margin. In view of the much greater exposure he had had in this period, I was not greatly concerned by this shift. I was convinced that once the conventions were over and I was no longer tied down by the Senate session, I would be able to devote my entire time to campaigning, regain the lost ground, and move into the lead again.

Two other developments occurred before the conventions, however, which were to have far more effect on the election outcome than all our carefully considered strategy decisions put together.

Early in March, Dr. Arthur E. Burns, the former chairman of the President's Council of Economic Advisers and probably the nation's top authority on the economic cycle, called on me in my office in the Capitol. In January, virtually all the economists in the country had been bullish about the prospects for the economy throughout 1960. But when Burns came to see me in March, he expressed great concern about the way the economy was then acting. Steel, in particular, was in trouble—new orders were lagging after the strike. Production was barely over half of rated capacity. Burns' conclusion was that unless some decisive governmental action were taken, and taken soon, we were heading for another economic dip which would hit its low point in October, just before the elections. He urged strongly that everything possible be done to avert this development. He urgently recommended that two steps be taken immediately: by loosening up on credit and, where justifiable, by increasing spending for national security. The next time I saw the President, I discussed Burns' proposals with him, and he in turn put the subject on the agenda for the next Cabinet meeting.

The matter was thoroughly discussed by the Cabinet but, for two reasons, Burns' recommendation that immediate action be taken along the lines he had suggested did not prevail. First, several of the Administration's economic experts who attended the meeting did not share his bearish prognosis of the economic prospects. Second, even assuming his predictions might be right, there was strong sentiment against using the spending and credit powers of the Federal Government to affect the economy, unless and until conditions clearly indicated a major recession in prospect.

In supporting Burns' point of view, I must admit that I was more sensitive politically than some of the others around the cabinet table. I knew from bitter experience how, in both 1954 and 1958, slumps which hit bottom early in October contributed to substantial Republican losses in the House and Senate. The power of the "pocketbook" issue was shown more clearly perhaps in 1958 than in any off-year election in history. On the international front, the Administration had had one of its best years. My own experience in Caracas in May had won bipartisan acclaim. That fall, President Eisenhower made what were, in my opinion, two of the most courageous and wise decisions of his entire Administration—the landing in Lebanon, and holding the line on Quemoy-Matsu. In both instances, his firm, decisive leadership avoided war and kept the peace without surrender of principle or territory. Yet, the economic dip in October was obviously uppermost in the people's minds when they went to the polls. They completely rejected the President's appeal for the election of Republicans to the House and Senate.

Unfortunately, Arthur Burns turned out to be a good prophet. The bottom of the 1960 dip did come in October and the economy started to move up again in November—after it was too late to affect the election returns. In October, usually a month of rising employment, the jobless rolls increased by 452,000. All the speeches, television broadcasts, and precinct work in the world could not counteract that one hard fact.

The second development, which was to have its effect during the election, was the shooting down of the U-2 reconnaissance plane over the Soviet Union, just before the Summit Conference slated for Paris in early May. Khrushchev used this incident as an excuse for breaking up the Conference. I am confident that it was only an excuse—that he undoubtedly would have found some other reason for torpedoing the Conference had the U-2 incident never occurred. But great as was the effect of the incident in Paris, it was even greater in the United States. Adlai Stevenson and Kennedy launched an all-out and, in my opinion, irresponsible attack on the President.

In a speech before the Democrats of Cook County, on May 19, Stevenson said:

We handed Khrushchev the crowbar and the sledgehammer to wreck the meeting. Without our series of blunders, Mr. Khrushchev would not have had a pretext for making his impossible demands and wild charges . . .

Kennedy went further at a press conference held May 19 in Portland, Oregon. Because there was some question of exactly what he said on that occasion, Kennedy made the following explanation in the *Congressional Record* on May 23:

I do not think that the timing of the U-2 incident is defensible. I think it was obviously the wrong time . . . It was a risk you would not want to take at that particular time.

Once the summit had broken up . . . Mr. Khrushchev indicated . . . there were two conditions for continuing. One, that we apologize. I think that that might have been possible to do—and that second, we try those responsible for the flight. We could not do that . . . If he had merely asked that the United States should express regret, then that would have been a reasonable term . . .

The initial reaction of the American people was not one for which either of these critics had bargained. People invariably rally around a President in a period of international crisis. And the dignity with which Eisenhower took Khrushchev's crude insults in Paris gained him support in the United States from members of both parties. But the long-range effect was something else again. The "peace issue" was tarnished. Democratic orators were to hammer away on this theme throughout the campaign.

A third event prior to the National Conventions which affected the conduct of the campaign and possibly even the result of the election was the special session of Congress. Instead of adjourning Congress *sine die* before the Democratic Convention, Lyndon Johnson asked for a recess and set a date for Congress to reconvene following the Republican Convention. This was one of the shrewdest maneuvers of the 1960 campaign. It meant that while the Senate was in session, I would again be held down in Washington because of the possibility of a tie vote. Kennedy and Johnson, on the other hand, would not be so inhibited. As Senators they could arrange a "live pair" to protect their position in the event that they were away campaigning: their votes would be recorded anyway. The session itself was to turn out to be singularly non-productive. But if one of its purposes was to delay the start of my campaign, it could not have been a more complete success.

As the Democratic National Convention opened in Los Angeles, I was at Camp David already working on the first draft of my acceptance speech. I did not believe there was any question as to Kennedy's winning the nomination. In fact, I did not listen to any of the preliminary convention proceedings except for a portion of Senator Frank Church's inept keynote address.

The only real suspense of the Convention was over the selection of the vice presidential candidate. Bill Rogers had driven up from Washington to spend the night and we were watching television together when the first news came over the air that Lyndon Johnson was to be Kennedy's running mate. We agreed that the Kennedy-Johnson ticket was the strongest the Democrats could possibly put in the field. In spite of Johnson's all-out attack on Kennedy during the primaries, I had anticipated that this might be the ticket. Thruston Morton and I had discussed the situation and, acting on my suggestion, he publicly predicted that a Kennedy-Johnson "deal" was in the making. While Morton's claim was categorically denied by both the Kennedy and the Johnson camps, I was still of the opinion that this was the ticket that would probably come out of the Convention.

The Johnson nomination for Vice President was not a surprise to me as far as Johnson was concerned. He has always been a political pragmatist and has never had too much difficulty accommodating his principles to his politics. But Kennedy's selection of Johnson and the way he was then able to ram this choice down the throats of his liberal supporters told a lot more about Kennedy than it did about Johnson. Here, indeed, was a tough-minded, capable political operator, and a formidable opponent.

Many Republicans thought that Johnson's selection was a mistake on Kennedy's part. But they were grossly underestimating both men. Kennedy understood that Johnson might cost him some votes in the North—but only if Johnson campaigned extensively in the Northern states, and Kennedy was smart enough to see that no such thing occurred. While Johnson alienated some of his more conservative supporters by going on the ticket, he was the best available bridge for Kennedy between the Northern liberals and the Southern conservatives.

My estimates of the strength of the Kennedy-Johnson ticket were confirmed by Claude Robinson four days after the Democratic Convention. I had asked him to test this combination against Republican tickets of Nixon-Lodge, Nixon-Morton, and other potential vice presidential candidates. He reported that the best showing any one of the various Republican tickets could make against the Kennedy-Johnson combination was 45 to 55, which would have meant a four-million-vote majority for the Democratic ticket. Part of the margin, of course, could be attributed to the fact that the Kennedy-Johnson ticket had just had massive public exposure on television and radio and in the press through the Democratic Convention. But I was under no illusions whatever about the difficulty of the task before us. We had to regain some of the lost ground immediately and the place to begin was at the Republican National Convention.

My most critical problem was to see that our Convention ended with all Republicans united behind the ticket. If this were to be accomplished, I knew I had to take some decisive action with regard to Nelson Rockefeller. Throughout the spring, while he had not entered any of the primaries, he had continued to snipe away at me. I ignored his attacks—except for one occasion when he charged that I had never stated my position on the key issues and that no one, in effect, knew where I stood. At a press conference in Camden, New Jersey, on June 9, I answered his charges in detail and, by fortunate coincidence, that same week a book of my speeches and public statements[3] was published. The detailed statements in the book, combined with the press conference, pretty effectively demolished his argument.

[3] *The Challenges We Face*, McGraw-Hill, New York.

But my goal was to beat Kennedy—not Rockefeller. Rockefeller had a perfect right and, in my view, a responsibility to contest the nomination and to disagree with positions I had taken. On the other hand, I felt it was essential that he be an enthusiastic rather than a reluctant supporter of my candidacy after the Convention. His differences with Administration policies had to be ironed out.

In his inexperience, he had been the victim of almost unbelievably bad advice during the period of his abortive attempt to launch a campaign for the nomination. But I knew that under present circumstances he would not come to me—I had to go to him.

Consequently, I called Herb Brownell in New York. Brownell had always been a close personal and political friend of mine, and I knew that Rockefeller trusted and respected him. I put the problem directly to Brownell and asked for his advice. He suggested that the two of us —Rockefeller and myself—get together and he agreed to talk to Rockefeller about a mutually convenient time for such a meeting. As a result of these negotiations, I flew to New York on Friday afternoon, July 22, with no publicity whatever, and, at Rockefeller's invitation, joined him for dinner at his apartment. During the dinner hour we reminisced cordially about some of our Washington experiences. After dinner I got right down to brass tacks.

I said that I expected to be nominated the next week at Chicago. I noted the fact that there had been a great deal of speculation as to whether he might consider the vice presidential nomination. I told him also that at the Convention, if he should indicate any interest at all, he would probably be the choice of a majority of the delegates. I did not offer him the nomination or urge him to accept it, because I did not want to put the eventual nominee in the position of being second-choice, in the event that Rockefeller refused it. But I told him of the plans I had for expanding the duties of the Vice President in the international field, as I was later to spell them out in my acceptance speech. The challenge would be great and, if he were to run for Vice President, the chances of the ticket's winning would be increased. If we by chance should lose, he—having put personal considerations aside and acceded to the requests of the party leaders—would be in line for the presidential nomination four years hence.

He replied just as candidly. He said he appreciated my speaking as frankly as I had. He realized that pressures for him to run for Vice President would probably mount after he arrived in Chicago, but he said that he simply did not want to be Vice President and therefore could not put his heart into the campaign if he were to be selected as the candidate. At this point we dropped the subject entirely and I suggested that we discuss the differences we might have on key issues, to see if we could work them out prior to the approval of the platform in Chicago.

Rockefeller said he had been doing some thinking on this score during the afternoon and had in fact prepared a statement of principles which he hoped I would agree to. For the most part, I found the positions he had written down were the same as those I had previously and consistently supported. But there were some major and significant exceptions and, from approximately ten o'clock that evening when we started to discuss his proposed joint-statement, until 4:30 the following morning, we went over the various points of the statement, issue-by-issue, until we finally reached agreement.

This final statement was labeled by some political partisans, as well as by some of the press and the radio-TV commentators, as a "surrender" by Nixon to Rockefeller. Any objective analysis of the statement would lead to exactly the contrary conclusion.

On issue after issue, I found it necessary to refuse to endorse Rockefeller's position because it was not in accord with President Eisenhower's and my own. The most sticky area—one which took us almost three hours to resolve—was the field of national security. I told Rockefeller that I had no objection wherever the statement advocated new or stepped-up programs for the future. But I would not approve any phrase in the statement which even by implication criticized the policies of the Eisenhower Administration. After prolonged discussion, my position prevailed, and all criticism of the Administration was removed from the final statement. Our conclusion on national security— "we can and must provide the necessary increased expenditures for these efforts; there must be no price ceiling on America's security"— far from being a new position on my part, was a reaffirmation of convictions I had stated on many previous occasions.

In the domestic field, our differences were resolved without too much difficulty. Again, it was Rockefeller who did the "surrendering" —on his proposal for financing compulsory health insurance for the aged from social security payments; on his insistence that "compulsory arbitration" be one of the weapons in the arsenal of Federal agencies for the settlement of labor disputes; and on an arbitrary rate of "forced" economic growth of 5 or 6 per cent annually, as the Rockefeller Brothers Fund Report had advocated.

In view of these facts, I was genuinely surprised when later Saturday morning I received frantic calls from my Chicago Convention headquarters urging me to come to Chicago immediately because of reports that I had "surrendered" to Rockefeller in the "Treaty of Fifth Avenue." In retrospect, I think what concerned my friends was that I had gone to see Rockefeller at all. They felt, no doubt, after his abortive bid for the nomination, that he should have come to me. But I believe my decision was the right one. I knew I was in the stronger bargaining position and that Rockefeller was confronted with a very ticklish face-saving problem. By going to see him in New York and working out differences that were more illusory than real, I was able to insure his support for the Republican ticket. I have found, over the years, that Republicans have an almost cannibalistic urge to destroy and consume one another whenever they happen to disagree. If Kennedy and Johnson, for example, had been Republicans, there never would have been a Kennedy-Johnson ticket in 1960. Perhaps by 1964 the political realities will force Republicans to consider the need for greater tactical accommodation.

Nevertheless, when I arrived in Chicago—midday on Monday, July 25—I found the delegates in an angry and rebellious mood. They thought Rockefeller deserved nothing but the back of my hand. But through an initial press conference in which I directly took on all the charges of a "surrender" to Rockefeller and answered each of them, and by meeting groups of delegates on virtually a round-the-clock basis as well as greeting and shaking hands and being photographed with every one of the 2600 delegates and alternates, I was finally able to set the record straight and to prepare the way for a receptive audience for my acceptance speech.

In the meantime, the Convention had been going better than I could have dared hope. The major speakers—Walter Judd, Herbert Hoover, and Tom Dewey—and the Convention officials—Thruston Morton, Charlie Halleck, Cecil Underwood, and Chuck Percy—had carried off their assignments in superb fashion. To cap it off, President Eisenhower had arrived in Chicago on Tuesday and delivered one of the most effective political speeches he had ever made. The reports we received from all over the country indicated that our Convention was having a far more favorable impact than the comparatively inept Democratic performance in Los Angeles two weeks before.

On Wednesday, Governor Mark O. Hatfield of Oregon, one of our few winners in 1958, placed my name in nomination before the Convention and, following my selection as the candidate by acclamation, I called a meeting of the major leaders of the party to consider the decision on a running mate.

For several weeks before the Convention, I had discussed potential vice presidential nominees with President Eisenhower and other close advisers. From the outset, I laid down certain standards that the nominee would have to meet: above all, he must be a man who could, if he had to, assume the duties of the presidency. Beyond that, his major qualification would have to be that he shared the views of the presidential nominee on major domestic and international issues.

There were several potential candidates for Vice President who, in my view, met these standards: Henry Cabot Lodge, Thruston Morton, Congressman Gerry Ford of Michigan, Secretary of Labor Jim Mitchell, Secretary of Interior Fred Seaton, and Congressman Walter Judd. When Kennedy won the Democratic nomination, Jim Mitchell ruled himself out. He recognized that putting him on the ticket would be attacked as a crude attempt to cater to the Catholic vote simply because the Democrats had nominated a Catholic for President.

By the time we reached Chicago, the choice had narrowed down to Lodge, Morton, and Judd. In a talk we had shortly after his sensational keynote address, Judd candidly told me that he felt he could render greater service in the campaign and to the new Administration after the election in his role as a Congressman.

Choosing between Lodge and Morton was difficult. Morton and I had come to the House together back in 1947. We had been close personal friends and he was doing an excellent job as Chairman of the National Committee. I knew he would be a loyal colleague as a running mate and would be a very effective campaigner. We shared virtually the same views on national and international issues. But he agreed with me that Lodge had certain assets which the ticket needed. He was from the East where we most needed support. As our UN spokesman, he had been receiving tremendous nationwide exposure in a very favorable way, most recently during the hot debates over the U-2 incident and spying in general. Morton would add strength to the ticket in the Midwest—where I was already strong. Lodge might add strength in the East—and here my own strength was somewhat doubtful.

Prior to my arrival in Chicago, President Eisenhower had conveyed to me his independent conclusion that Lodge would be the strongest vice presidential nominee we could select. But I did not make the final decision until meeting with the party leaders after my own nomination. The great majority of them agreed that Lodge was the man who would add most to the ticket. John Bricker had perhaps the greatest impact in the meeting when he threw his and Ohio's support behind Lodge. At the end of a long session during which each of the 32 leaders present expressed his views, I announced my decision that Lodge should be nominated. After the session broke up, I phoned Lodge, reaching him around 2:30 in the morning Central Time. He knew that he had been under consideration and that there was a good chance he might be named as the nominee. He made plans to fly to Chicago on Thursday to accept the nomination.

My three days in Chicago had been long and exhausting ones. I had attended delegation meetings, met with the Platform Committee, and posed for photographs with all the delegates and with hundreds of candidates who wanted pictures with the presidential nominee for their own campaigns. But I knew that on Thursday evening I would be making a speech which, next to the Fund Broadcast during the 1952 campaign, would be the most important political address I had ever made. It had to be a speech which would unite the Republicans— and not alienate the Democratic voters. It had to be one which defended the record of the Eisenhower Administration but also pointed the way to future progress. It had to be one which took pride in what we had accomplished in the past eight years in keeping the peace without surrender—but which also would chart a future course designed not just to hold our own but to assure victory for the forces of freedom. Fortunately, this was one of the few occasions in my public life when I had been able to set aside ample time to read, to think, and to write before determining the final form of what I was to say.

The standard of speeches for the Convention had been particularly high. Barry Goldwater had spoken with great effect, calling on his supporters to join him in working enthusiastically for the Convention's nominee. Lodge preceded me to the rostrum and received an enthusiastic ovation. Rockefeller introduced me, gracefully and eloquently. As I walked through the aisle to the podium, the fatigue I had felt as a result of three days with almost no sleep left me completely. As I started to speak, I could sense that this would be one of my better efforts.

In the thousands of speeches I had made in my political career, there had never been a more responsive audience. Because of my speaking experience, I have become a fair judge of how much time a speech will require. I estimated this one at thirty-five minutes, including maximum applause. But I had not reckoned with the enthusiasm of the Convention that evening. When I finally concluded, the speech had run forty-eight minutes, and the extra time was due entirely to applause which I was unable to control.

That speech was to mark a high point of my campaign for the presidency. Even my severest critics gave it high marks for content and delivery. And the reaction of the television audience was more favorable even than that of the audience in Convention Hall.

The audience particularly responded to these passages:

One hundred years ago, in this very city, Abraham Lincoln was nominated for President . . . The question then was freedom for the slaves and survival of the nation. The question now is freedom for all mankind and the survival of civilization.

We shall build a better America . . . in which we shall see the realization of the dreams of millions of people not only in America but throughout the world—for a fuller, freer, richer life than men have ever known in the history of mankind.

What we must do is wage the battles for peace and freedom with the same . . . dedication with which we wage battles in war . . . The only answer to a strategy of victory for the Communist world is a strategy of victory for the free world. Let the victory we seek . . . be the victory of freedom over tyranny, of plenty over hunger, of health over disease, in every country of the world.

When Mr. Khrushchev says our grandchildren will live under Communism, let us say his grandchildren will live in freedom.

Our answer to the threat of the Communist revolution is renewed devotion to the great ideals of the American Revolution . . . that still live in the minds and hearts of people everywhere.

I believe in the American dream, because I have seen it come true in my own life.

Abraham Lincoln was asked during the dark days of the tragic War between the States whether he thought God was on his side. His answer was, 'My concern is not whether God is on our side, but whether we are on God's side.' My fellow Americans, may that ever be our prayer for our country. And in that spirit—with faith in America, with faith in her ideals and in her people, I accept your nomination for President of the United States.

When I returned to Washington from Chicago, I began to realize what a tremendous impact the Republican Convention had had on the country. What was particularly encouraging was the number of Democrats who said they were going to support the Nixon-Lodge ticket in November.

The selection of Lodge as vice presidential nominee was meeting with approval in all parts of the country. Barry Goldwater, who had indicated prior to the nomination that he thought Lodge would help the ticket in the East but would not be an asset in the West and Midwest, spoke to me a few days after the Convention and said he had changed his mind—Lodge's selection was proving popular everywhere.

The impact of our Convention was reflected in the polls. Claude Robinson reported that from the low point of 45 to 55, recorded immediately after the Democratic Convention, our ticket had now moved slightly into the lead—51 to 49. Gallup's first post-Convention poll indicated a similar shift, with Nixon-Lodge at 53 and Kennedy-Johnson at 47 per cent. We knew that some of this gain was simply a reflection of our more recent massive exposure on TV and in the press. The new figures in no way changed the conviction I had had since January— that the race would probably be one of the closest in history, and that consequently it would be decided by which candidate was able to put on the more intensive campaign.

That was why I had announced in my acceptance speech that I would undertake the unprecedented task of campaigning in every one of the fifty states. Many disagreed with this decision, but I believed there were strong reasons for carrying it out. In view of the closeness of the election, the outcome in a state with a very small electoral vote might have determined the result. I also recognized that Kennedy would have a considerable advantage in the big Northeastern industrial states. To balance our anticipated losses there, we needed every Western, Southern, and Midwestern state we could possibly win. I felt it was essential to go to each of the traditionally Republican farm states because we could not safely assume that any one of these states would necessarily be in the Republican column. In the usually Republican states of the Northeast—Maine, Vermont, and New Hampshire—Kennedy had so much reported strength that, again, I felt it was essential to include them in my campaign. And in the South, I felt that as the Republican candidate I had an obligation to encourage and build on the trend, which President Eisenhower's victories had started in 1952 and 1956, toward a real two-party system in the Southern states. In meetings with my campaign staff, we mapped out a tentative schedule, therefore, for a fifty-state tour. Our plan was to visit Hawaii, Alaska, several of the Southern states, and Maine, Vermont, and New Hampshire prior to September 12—which we had set as the opening date for continuous day-to-day campaigning. In the eight weeks after September 12, we would then be able to concentrate our efforts on the states with the big electoral votes and on other states in the doubtful column. We could not know then that a serious crimp was to upset all these careful plans.

My first swing, from August 2 to 6, was highly successful. We flew to Reno, Nevada, for a homecoming rally for Pat, to my own home town of Whittier, and then to Hawaii—the first visit a nominee of either party was to make to the fiftieth state. We stopped at Seattle for an airport rally on the way back from Hawaii, and arrived in Washington four days after we had left, having visited four states and traveled nearly 12,000 air-miles. The crowds everywhere along the way had been bigger than we expected and most enthusiastic.

On our return to Washington I scheduled several conferences in which crucial decisions were made for the campaign ahead.

First, I called on the President to discuss plans for his own participation in the campaign. At the outset of the meeting, he said he wanted to do everything he possibly could to assure a Republican victory. But he felt it was important for me to establish my own identity as the new leader of the party. Consequently he thought he should avoid taking so active a part early in the campaign as to overshadow my own appearances. He also expressed the conviction that his great influence with the American people was due in substantial part to his image of being President of all the people, and not just a partisan as Truman had been. Consequently, he thought his first swing around the country should be non-political in character and that he should reserve his frankly partisan speeches until later in the campaign.

After our meeting, Jerry Persons invited me to his office for further discussions. No one knew Eisenhower better than Persons where political matters were concerned, and Persons summed up his attitude this way: "I believe we should give great weight to the Old Man's intuition on his participation in the campaign. If the party people force him to make political speeches before he believes he should, he simply can't put his heart into them. There is no question about his getting into the campaign in good time. After Kennedy, Johnson, Stevenson, and some of the other Democrats start to get rough, he'll get his dander up and go after them. But until he himself feels that he wants to make political speeches, we should not allow anybody to force him to do so." I agreed with Persons' evaluation and that is how we left it—Eisenhower in control of his own timing.

Next, the question arose as to my policy on appearing with and endorsing other Republican candidates in the states and districts I visited. In many instances, these candidates would have no possible chance of winning—particularly, for example, in the South. Some of my advisers recommended that I campaign on my own in such cases and, in effect, disassociate myself from the Republican candidates unless they had some chance of helping rather than hurting the ticket. But I saw the candidate for President as the leader of the party, with an obligation to do everything possible to build up his party. Consequently, in all my stops throughout the country, I appeared on the platform with each local Republican candidate who desired it, and I endorsed all the major candidates by name.

We also had to determine whether our campaign should be turned over completely to the Republican Party organizations in the various states, or whether we should encourage the setting up of separate, but co-ordinated, volunteer organizations as well. I endorsed the plan for volunteers for a very practical reason: I knew that if we won all the Republican votes in the country we would lose the election by about five million votes. I also knew, from experience in my own state of California, that Democratic and independent voters generally react unfavorably to going into a Republican headquarters and volunteering to work in a campaign. Our Nixon-Lodge Volunteer Clubs in the various states did prove to be irritants to some of the regular party officials, but in retrospect I am convinced they made a great contribution to our excellent showing among Democratic and independent voters. This was particularly true in states like Ohio and California where the party organization not only welcomed but encouraged the volunteers. Ray Bliss, State Chairman in Ohio and one of the best political craftsmen in the nation, set an example in this respect that I wish all Republican State Chairmen would follow. He always kept in mind Will Hays' simple axiom that it is the responsibility of a party chairman "not to eliminate but to assimilate."

The most important of all the strategy decisions we made during this period was with regard to the television debates. I should point out, however, that by this time the question we had to decide was not whether we should have debates—but rather, how should they be conducted.

Before the two conventions, Congress had passed a resolution which made joint appearances by the nominees of the two major parties practically inevitable. The resolution provided that the radio-TV networks could give free time for such appearances without being required to provide equal time to the candidates of the minor parties. Thruston Morton and his Democratic counterpart appeared on a television program shortly after this resolution was adopted. Each was asked whether his party's nominee would agree to participate in joint appearances. Morton, before a nominee had been selected, spoke for the party as a whole and very properly said that the Republican candidate would agree—under the right circumstances. By the time I met with my staff to plan campaign strategy, the pressures for joint appearances in some form or other were irresistible.

Looking at the problem from a purely political standpoint, Kennedy had much more to gain from joint appearances than I did. I was better known than he, and our joint appearances would simply build up an audience for him. Moreover, he had the same advantage over me that I had had back in 1946 when I debated my first political opponent, Congressman Jerry Voorhis: Kennedy was attacking a record and I was defending it. I don't mean to suggest that I was not perfectly willing to defend the record of the Administration of which I had been a part. But I knew from long experience that in debate, the man who can attack has a built-in advantage that is very hard to overcome. Almost automatically, he has the initiative and is the aggressor. Incidentally, in the next presidential election, the shoe will be on the other foot. While Robert Kennedy indicated after the '60 election that his brother would never give his opponent equal exposure, as I had done, my view is that debates between the major party candidates will be a feature of all future presidential campaigns, regardless of the candidates' own desires.

As for my own decision, I felt it was absolutely essential that I not only agree to debate but enthusiastically welcome the opportunity. Had I refused the challenge, I would have opened myself to the charge that I was afraid to defend the Administration's and my own record. Even more important, I would be declining to participate in a program which the majority of the American people, regardless of party, wanted to see.

The decisions that still had to be made, however, at this early-August meeting concerned the subjects of the debates, and the format.

It was agreed that each candidate would keep his schedule open for four possible joint appearances. The first and fourth would be along the lines of a formal debate, with each candidate having an opening and closing statement and with questions from a press panel taking up the balance of the time. The other two appearances were to be, in effect, joint press conferences in which the candidates would alternate in answering questions, with each having an opportunity to comment on the other's answer.

The most critical decision made at this time turned out to be the subject matter of the first and fourth debates. It was readily agreed that one should be devoted exclusively to domestic issues and the other to foreign policy. I believed that I would have a considerable advantage over Kennedy when the subject matter was foreign policy and consequently wanted that subject to be discussed on the program that would have the larger audience.

But our public relations advisers disagreed on the key question: which of the debates would draw the bigger audience? My own view was that the first would be larger and that interest would go down as the novelty of the debates wore off. A majority of our group, however, thought that the audience would build up because of increased interest in the debates and in the campaign generally, and that the fourth debate would outdraw the first. I yielded to the majority and in this case their opinion proved to be wrong. We agreed that foreign policy would be discussed in the fourth debate and domestic policy in the first. When the debates were held, at least 20 million more people listened to and watched the first than any of the others, including the fourth and final appearance. I turned in my best performance before the smallest audience.

Meanwhile, the "rump" congressional session continued to drag along. I was tied down to Washington, except for weekends, when there was no possibility of a sudden vote, while Kennedy could much more safely leave town and get some preliminary campaigning out of the way.

I was, however, able to make two brief swings into the South during this period. The first was a one-day sortie into the state that had been my home for three years while I was attending Duke Law School, from 1934 to 1937. It was in Greensboro, North Carolina, on August 17, that I tackled head-on the civil rights issue—and the political problem of how to handle this issue in the South. I began by saying that I knew many people in the audience, and throughout the state and region, would disagree with my position, but that I felt an obligation to make that position clear. Then I went on to say:

It is the responsibility of every American to do everything that he can to make this country a proud example of freedom and the recognition of human dignity in the world.

I also recognize that law alone, while necessary, is not the answer to the problems of human rights . . . that law is only as good as the will of the people to obey it. That is why it is the responsibility . . . of those of us in positions of leadership . . . to . . . promote within the people in the States the desire and the will to keep the law and to make progress in the solution of these difficult problems.

In every speech I made in the Southern states I touched on the civil rights issue—not because I wanted to lecture the people of the South on what I knew was a difficult problem for them, but because I had always believed it to be the responsibility of a political leader to tell the people exactly where he stands on issues, even when those stands may be unpopular, and to use his influence, wherever possible, to further causes in which he deeply believes. Many of my Southern Republican friends questioned the wisdom of these tactics, but I would follow the same course of action if I had the decision to make again.

The next week—after a one-day quick trip to Detroit to address a VFW Convention—I made my second brief Southern swing, this time to Birmingham, Alabama, and then to Atlanta, Georgia. Record crowds gave Pat and me tumultuous welcomes. I pounded hard, at both stops, on the theme that Democrats who voted for the Republican ticket would not be deserting their party because their party had already deserted them—when it adopted the radical platform in Los Angeles in July. The party of Schlesinger, Stevenson, and Bowles, I said, was a far cry from the party of Jefferson, Jackson, and Wilson.

The best guarantee of freedom is local government and the diffusion of power. And when you allow all the power to be centered in Washington, you attack the very fundamentals of freedom itself.

I am proud to say that our platform is based on that Jeffersonian principle, while the platform of our opponents completely denies it.

As we flew back to Washington late Friday night, I was so encouraged and stimulated by the reception we had gotten that I scarcely noticed a nagging pain in my right knee—I had bumped the knee the week before in Greensboro while getting into a car and then promptly forgotten about it.

I applied a home remedy of hot compresses but the pain became so intense that, on Saturday, I finally asked Dr. Walter Tkach, the assistant White House physician, to take a look at the knee. He had me go out to Walter Reed Hospital for a fluid-tap to test for possible infection. I then returned to my desk at the Capitol for a solid weekend of work on the speeches I planned for my next two campaign swings, to the Northeast—Maine, Vermont, and New Hampshire—and then to Alaska, so that we would have these states covered before the intensive operations began on September 12. All these carefully made plans were wrecked by a call I received on Monday morning, August 29.

The White House phone on my desk rang; it was Dr. Tkach calling. "We want you to come out to the hospital right away," he said. I protested that I had no time for it because of my heavy schedule. He replied, bluntly: "Look, I know what your schedule is, and I'm just as anxious as you are to keep it, but you had better get out to the hospital or you will be campaigning on one leg."

That was enough to convince me. I called for my car and was driven out to Walter Reed. A panel of grim-faced doctors gave me the bad news. My knee was infected with hemolytic staphylococcus aureus, which could be just as serious as it sounded if I did not take care of it immediately. They unanimously recommended—indeed, insisted—that I stay at the hospital and receive massive shots of penicillin and other antibiotics until the infection was cleared up.

I asked them how long all this would take. Their prediction: a minimum of two weeks but with no guarantee that I would be out of the hospital even then. The infection was under the kneecap and very difficult to get at. They would be unable to tell how successful their efforts would be until they had tried several different methods and modes of treatment. I could see that I had no choice in the matter but to follow their orders.

The physical pain I suffered those next two weeks was bad enough, particularly when they lanced the knee to shoot antibiotics into the infected area. But the mental suffering was infinitely worse. My hopes for advance campaigning in the Northeast and Alaska, and possibly in two more Southern states—Mississippi and Louisiana—were out the window. This was also the period that I had reserved for working on my major campaign statements and speeches and for several strategy conferences with key volunteer groups.

I learned during this period to take my misfortune philosophically. I reasoned that, after all, this was the first time in my political career that I had had to cancel engagements because of illness. My luck was bound to run out at some point and it was better to have it happen now than during the critical weeks closer to Election Day. I found, too, that illness has its compensations. Thousands of letters and get-well cards poured into my office and into the hospital. One, from a twelve-year-old girl in Baltimore, provided probably the best lesson of all. "God sometimes makes us lie down," she wrote, "so that we will look up more."

President Eisenhower called on me and, when he saw my loud pajamas, remarked that this was a side of my personality the voters had not seen before. Nelson Rockefeller flew down from New York and came into my room wearing a huge Nixon-Lodge button. I also got a chance to spend more time with Tricia and Julie than would otherwise have been possible. They came to the hospital each evening with Pat and proceeded to acquaint me with some of their favorite television programs.

It was while I was in the hospital that a disastrous political development occurred—one, again, over which I had no control. When the nurse brought me the morning papers on Thursday, September 8, I saw that Dr. Norman Vincent Peale was listed prominently among the signers of a statement expressing concern over whether a Catholic President could disassociate himself from the influence of the hierarchy of his Church. I knew we were in for real trouble. Dr. Peale had been a long-time personal friend and supporter. Pat and I had attended his church when I was stationed in New York toward the end of World War II and, in the years since, we had often visited him there. I knew him as a man of infinite good will and one who had made a great contribution to the cause of religious and racial tolerance during his lifetime. The Democratic politicians knew they had an opening, and they attacked savagely and effectively. The outcry was so great that several newspapers canceled his syndicated column. Protestant ministers who were supporting Kennedy charged that Dr. Peale had "loosed the floodgates of religious bigotry." Wires and letters poured in, urging me to denounce him personally.

I had my staff look into the circumstances of the meeting—which had taken place in Washington on September 7—and discovered that Dr. Peale had attended it immediately upon his return from a European trip, that he had in fact presided only at one brief session rather than the entire meeting, and that he had not personally participated in the drafting of the controversial statement of opinion. He had signed it as a member of the group, doubtless sharing the general opinion expressed but not realizing the full political implications. Under all these circumstances, I decided it would be unfair for me to attack him personally for the statement and that the proper course of action was for me to use my next public appearance—I was scheduled to be on "Meet the Press" that coming Sunday, September 11—to disassociate myself from the position Dr. Peale and his colleagues had taken in the statement. I knew that he was heartbroken over the incident and I felt that while his judgment had been bad, his motives were above question. He had been punished enough and I refused to add to his embarrassment for what would have been purely political purposes on my part.

My hospital siege finally drew to a close on Friday the ninth of September and I went home that evening to begin packing for my first intensive campaign swing and to prepare for Sunday's "Meet the Press" program. My most significant statement on that occasion was on the religious issue. In direct response to a question by Herb Kaplow of NBC News, I defined the issue and my own position in this way. I quote at some length because this sums up my convictions as I was to hold to them through the balance of the campaign:

I have no doubt whatever about Senator Kennedy's loyalty to his country and about the fact that if he were elected President he would put the Constitution of the United States above any other consideration . . . I don't believe . . . there is a religious issue as far as Senator Kennedy is concerned.

In the second place, I believe that it would be tragic . . . for this election to be determined primarily, or even substantially, on religious grounds . . .

The question is not whether Senator Kennedy or I believe that religion is an issue—we don't believe it is . . . The question is, how do you keep it out of a campaign?

. . . The best way . . . is by not talking about it . . .

As far as I am concerned, I have issued orders to all of the people in my campaign not to discuss religion, not to raise it, not to allow anybody to participate in the campaign who does so on that ground, and as far as I am concerned, I will decline to discuss religion . . .

. . . All I can say is that I have made my position clear, and I feel that we ought to have a cut-off date on its discussion. I would hope that Senator Kennedy would reach the same conclusion, because if the two candidates refrain from raising the issue, refrain from discussing it, that means that at least to that extent it won't be in the news.

Before taking off on the first week's swing, I met with Jim Bassett for a run-down of our schedule problems between September 12 and Election Day, November 8. Jim, who was in charge of all my scheduling in this campaign, pointed out that because of my illness there were seven states we had thought we would have covered by this time that would now, somehow or other, have to be crammed into the eight remaining weeks of campaigning. He said he had made up tentative schedules by which I could fulfill my commitment to visit every one of the fifty states—but that it would be a back-breaking assignment. His judgment was that my stay in the hospital gave me all the excuse I needed for leaving out some states which we considered either hopelessly lost or relatively safe. But I felt that I should follow through with my commitment and asked him to set up the schedule accordingly. In retrospect, this decision is open to serious question. Had I followed his advice, I would not have had to put myself through such a brutal schedule before the first radio-televison debate and, in addition, would have had more time to spend in some of the critical states than eventually was possible. But the decision was made and, once the schedules were published, we had to live with them.

At this same time, we took another look at the polls. Claude Robinson, who was doing our private polling, showed the race 50–50. Gallup came up with approximately the same finding. On August 31, he had rated the race all-even, and his release of September 14 showed Kennedy in a hairline 51–49 per cent lead.

What was discouraging and even alarming to us was the continued weakness of the Republican Party in general, as reflected in the polls. On September 1, for example, in answer to the question "Which party would you like to see win the congressional elections in your state?" Gallup reported the break at 58 per cent Democratic, 42 per cent

Republican. This meant that in order for the national ticket to win, we would have to accomplish two objectives during the course of the next eight weeks. Republican Party strength for Congress and state offices would have to be pulled up substantially—by four or five per cent if possible. And even then we would have to run five or six per cent ahead of the congressional and local candidates.[4]

The first week of any campaign is one of the hardest. In this period, the candidate must learn how to pace himself, decide how best to assign functions within his staff, and get the feel of audiences and of the campaign itself. The trips I had taken between the Convention and the end of August had prepared me to a certain extent for this first period of intensive campaigning. But the hospital stay had left me much weaker than I had realized—and, worse still, I found a huge backlog of paperwork on my desk in the plane, all of which had to be handled during the same period that I was preparing and delivering current campaign speeches.

Much of this backlog, incidentally, consisted of issue-by-issue questionnaires submitted by the Scripps-Howard papers, United Press, and other news syndicates. My staff had done an excellent job of sifting down the material into suggested "positions." But I felt it was my clear responsibility to review each answer in detail because they had asked for my views, not those of my staff. The result was that during the first week to ten days of an already heavy schedule, I had to work literally night and day to catch up on this backlog and still keep current on the very important speeches that had to be made daily.

I had told Jim Bassett that we wanted to get off to a fast start— and he had taken me at my word. Cabot Lodge and I were taking off simultaneously on our first tours from Baltimore's Friendship Airport the morning of Monday, September 12. President Eisenhower drove up from the capital to wish us well as we began the big push for victory. A driving rain forced us to cram the big crowd indoors but failed to dampen its enthusiasm. We flew from Baltimore to Indianapolis for a giant rally at Monument Circle where I had spoken in both 1952 and 1956. Our next stop was Dallas, where we motorcaded through cheering thousands in the downtown area, followed by a speech at the Memorial Auditorium. We then went on to San Francisco

[4] An indication of the difficulty of our task was a Gallup Poll published in late-July 1960, showing the decline in GOP support, 1952–60, among various occupational groups. In 1952, 28 per cent of the farmers said the Republican Party "best serves" their interests; in 1960, only 18 per cent. Among white-collar workers, the drop was from 44 to 29 per cent.

for an airport rally and another one downtown in Union Square. It was 11 o'clock Pacific Coast Time (two in the morning Eastern Time, in terms of our take-off) before we finally got to bed.

The following morning I had to be up at 6:30 for a televised press conference at 7:30. We drove to Hunter's Point Navy Yard for a non-political speech dedicating the SS *Hope*—a specially fitted demonstration hospital ship which was about to make its maiden voyage to Southeast Asia. Our next stop was Portland, Oregon, and from there—after a motorcade that took us to Vancouver, Washington—we flew on to Boise, Idaho, for a night rally. The next morning—Wednesday—we again had to be up at 6:30 for a 7:30 take-off and a day that included a noontime stop at Grand Forks, North Dakota, and an evening rally at the Bradley University Field House in Peoria, Illinois. From there, we flew to St. Louis and, while it was past eleven when we arrived, we were greeted by an enthusiastic airport crowd of over 5000. After the long drive into the city from the airport, I still had an hour's work to do at the hotel on a major speech I was making Thursday morning to the National Convention of the International Association of Machinists—my first campaign appearance before a labor organization.

I knew that the Machinists were going to endorse Kennedy and that the audience would not be a friendly one. I had accepted the invitation because I wanted every opportunity to talk over the heads of union leaders to the rank-and-file workers.

As I finished my notes for the Machinists speech and got ready for bed, I looked back over the first three days of the week with considerable satisfaction. The crowds had consistently exceeded our expectations and the campaign was rolling along with good momentum. I felt more tired than usual, but I attributed this to the fact that I had so recently been in the hospital and to the unusually heavy schedule with its early morning departures cutting into my sleep. But when I awoke at about three-thirty in the morning, I knew that there were other causes for my fatigue. I had a raging fever and was shaking with a chill. I woke Don Hughes and asked him to get Dr. John C. Lungren, who was traveling with us and was a veteran of three previous campaigns. When he came to my room, he found that I was running a temperature of over 103, caused probably by a flu virus. I told him that if there was one meeting in the entire campaign at which I had to show up, it was at the Machinists' convention, scheduled for 8:15 that morning. He shook his head and said, "I don't see how you can possibly do it, but let's try to get this fever under control." He gave me an extra-large dose of aspirin, antibiotics, and other assorted pills. Whatever they were, the fever broke, and while I got very little sleep for the balance of the night, I was able to get up at seven and proceed to the Kiel Auditorium for the scheduled meeting.

I don't know when I have ever felt so weak before walking out onto a public platform but I was determined to let no one know my condition. I then proceeded to make what some of the reporters have called my best speech of the campaign.

I had already decided that this was the right time and place to make another frontal assault on the "tell 'em what they want to hear" school of campaigning—as I had done, for example, in Greensboro with respect to the civil rights issue. Kennedy, in fact, had given me a perfect opening in his own kick-off speech in Detroit on Labor Day, and I carried on from there:

I have here a report of a speech made by my opponent in Detroit before a labor group, and this is what it says:

". . . what the American labor movement wants for America is what I want for America, and what the American labor movement opposes I oppose."

If I were solely concerned about votes, I would tell you that today. I would say that I was 100 per cent for everything that the officers . . . [and] delegates to this convention are for, representing a great number of voters in this country. I would say that I was against, 100 per cent, everything that you are against . . . It might win votes, but . . . it would not be good for the labor movement and for labor union members and it would not be good for America for a President of the United States to make that kind of a statement . . .

Then, after spelling out the overriding goals of peace and a widely shared prosperity about which all Americans are agreed, and after specifically rejecting the idea of a blanket endorsement of the particular goals of business or labor or farmers or any special group, I summed it up this way:

It is the obligation of the President of the United States to be President of all the people and not to set one group against another.

From St. Louis, we flew to Atlantic City, New Jersey, then on to Roanoke, Virginia, and then back crosscountry to Omaha, Nebraska. We motorcaded through the Iowa countryside to Des Moines and on to Sioux City. One of the most memorable stops for me was before the smallest audience of the whole campaign. It was an unscheduled stop on a roadside, on the way to Guthrie Center, where I had noticed a small group of students standing at the roadside with a sign: WEL-COME PAT AND DICK NIXON—IOWA SCHOOL FOR THE DEAF. I spoke to the students, standing on the hood of my car, as a teacher interpreted my remarks in sign language. I won no votes, for my listeners were under voting age, but no audience reception moved me more than the looks of delight on their faces when they realized I was going to take the time to speak to them.

The next day—Saturday—included a morning rally in Sioux City, Iowa, an airport rally in Minneapolis, and then a press conference and evening rally in the field house at Macalester College in St. Paul. We left Minneapolis that night at ten but, because of the time difference, arrived in Washington at 4:30 Sunday morning. The milk trucks were moving through the streets as we drove home from the airport.

In that first week of campaigning, we covered fourteen states and more than 9000 air-miles. It had been a successful week from several viewpoints. We had drawn overflow crowds everywhere we went. Most encouraging was our reception throughout the farm belt. The columnists and commentators, as well as many Republican leaders, were predicting that the farm situation would be the most difficult domestic issue confronting us during the campaign. Before the National Convention, every farm state Congressman, Senator, and State Chairman (with only two exceptions) had stated on his own initiative or in response to inquiries made by those working on the farm platform that it was absolutely imperative for me to come up with a new farm program. The Democrats for eight years had done a vicious hatchet-job on Ezra Taft Benson. They had created the impression, not only among Democratic farmers but among many Republicans as well, that Benson had no sympathy for the farmers and their problems and that his attitude was simply that the farmer should "grin and bear it." The Republican farm bloc leaders respected him as a man of high principle. Scarcely a one of them had any alternative to offer. But almost to a man they told me—"the farmer has not been getting his fair share of America's increasing prosperity. He is hurting. He will not vote for a presidential candidate who says, in effect, 'we are doing all we can and things will work out in time.'"

I personally made it clear to everyone concerned that under no circumstances would I repudiate Benson, either personally or in terms of his long-range goal of less dictation to the farmer from Washington. But I knew we would be in grave danger of losing the farm states unless we were able to offer an affirmative program—going beyond what Benson had previously stood for. I insisted to my staff members working on this issue that the program must be one that was honest and sound. On this and every other issue, the admonition I gave to some of those who had a tendency to let their eagerness to appeal to voters overrule their judgment on the substance of issues went something like this: "We must always assume that we are going to win this election. And I do not want to say anything or do anything during the campaign that I will not be able to live with as President."

The farm program we eventually adopted was set forth in the Republican platform, my speech at Guthrie Center, and a second speech delivered during the second week of the campaign at Sioux Falls, South Dakota. It provided for a massive step-up in the program for taking out of production acreage which was yielding surplus crops, and a new five-point program for increased consumption of these surpluses. A basic feature of the program was that there should be more control of farm programs by farmers and their representatives, and less by Washington bureaucrats.

The reception for this program was generally favorable in the farm belt. But what helped us even more was the very unfavorable reaction to Kennedy's farm program. He had never had too much interest in the farm problem and very little acquaintance with it. Consequently, he took his program from the panacea-peddlers who were anathema to the average, practical-minded farmer. The Kennedy plan provided for a massive increase in Federal Government control of agriculture and, in effect, would have made virtually every farmer in America beholden to bureaucrats in Washington. Polls taken two weeks after his farm speeches and mine indicated a substantial shift of the farm vote, away from Democratic candidates and back to its traditional Republican mooring.

My only criticism of the first week's activities was that we had scheduled too many early morning departures which meant, consequently, too little sleep, not only for me but for members of my staff and our traveling press corps. I did not realize how bone-tired I really was until I opened my eyes about noon on Sunday and found that I could hardly pull myself out of bed to get on with the mass of preparatory work that had to be done before we started out on our second week's swing.

The second week took us for the first time into some of the big industrial states, which were so important because of the size of their electoral votes. The pace was even heavier than that of the first week. From Monday through Friday we prop-stopped on a split-second schedule through Pennsylvania, Michigan, Illinois, Indiana, Missouri, Kentucky, South Dakota, Wisconsin, and Kansas. On Saturday we flew south to Lafayette, Louisiana, and Jackson, Mississippi—which, incidentally, was the first time a Republican nominee for President had ever visited that state. We were back in Washington on Saturday at midnight.

For every major stop on the schedule, of course, there were usually half a dozen side-trips and motorcades; there were local press conferences, airport rallies, downtown rallies, auditorium and stadium rallies —and if not a speech, at least a few words at each stop.

During this second week, the size and enthusiasm of our crowds had, if anything, exceeded those of the first. I hammered away, both weeks, at certain basic themes. I pointed with pride to an eight-year record of unparalleled national growth and prosperity in every area of the economy, whether measured by total income or by classrooms and houses and hospitals constructed. But at the same time I warned against smugness or complacency, asserting that this progress must be simply the jumping-off point for still greater future growth, stable and sustained. In any competition with the Soviet Union, I argued, we would win hands down. I also pointed out that, easy as it is to make pie-in-the-sky promises and to offer panaceas for all our remaining problems, the crucial question of how best to move ahead revealed the basic Democratic-Republican split. For every problem, either real or fancied, Kennedy had a ready-made program of Federal action— along with increased Federal outlays, increased bureaucratic control, and increased inflationary pressure. For my part, I contended that the traditional American way has always been to rely on the free choices of millions of individuals and that the role of government must be limited to encouraging and stimulating private initiative and to creating the right climate for the exercise of freedom, with equal opportunity for all. Kennedy had a tremendous advantage here: his approach was simple and easy to understand. It promised something for everyone. And he never had to bother about such details as costs and bureaucratic controls.

During these first two weeks, Kennedy concentrated on building up what I characterized as a "poor mouth" image of America—just barely limping along in second place behind the dynamic Soviets, with the gap widening day by day. He kept insisting we were "stalled on dead-center" and "frozen in the ice of our own indifference" and were fast becoming "second-raters." "Last year," he said, "the Soviet Union exceeded the growth of this country by three times."[5] Kennedy promised, without spelling out the details, to "get America moving again."

He seized on every possible shortcoming and inequity in American life and promised immediate cure-alls. I consistently maintained that we must solve our remaining problems, but always in the tradition of freedom and responsibility, while still meeting our tremendous world-wide obligations and the overriding demands of our national security. I knew I was right. But his approach was simpler and more dramatic.

After two weeks of this intensive campaigning, covering twenty-five states and 15,000 miles, my staff estimated that I had spoken to and been seen in person by crowds exceeding two million. Several millions more had been reached through local radio and television. But I realized that important as these two weeks had been and no matter how big the crowds or how extensive the local coverage, it was a drop in the bucket: the effect up to September 25 would be infinitesimal compared with the first joint debate scheduled for all-network coverage the next evening, Monday, September 26, in Chicago.

All the previous week I had used every spare minute preparing my opening statement and studying the issues that might be raised by the panel of newsmen. I got up early Sunday morning and worked through the day, without interruption, until it was time to go to the airport for a ten o'clock night flight to Chicago. As I pored over my material I wished that I had arranged to have Saturday free as well as Sunday

[5] That this was just campaign rhetoric was demonstrated by President Kennedy himself, barely half a year after taking office. In a late-June press conference he changed his tune and said the United States was outproducing the USSR, that the Soviets won't catch up with us by the year 2000, and that Soviet total product has increased but one per cent in comparison with that of the U. S. in the past 48 years. All of which led Roscoe Drummond to comment: "I thought I was at the wrong press conference or that . . . the man who was talking was President Richard Milhous Nixon . . . One could fairly say that President Kennedy has hurled Mr. Nixon—or at least his arguments—at Mr. Khrushchev and scored a bull's eye."

for this preparation. But it was too late to do anything about the situation now, except to ask Jim Bassett to lighten the schedule somewhat before each of the next three debates so that I could have more time for studying the issues and also for some needed rest after a hard week of campaigning.

Our flight was scheduled for a 10:30 arrival in Chicago, Central Time, which would make it possible for me to get to bed by midnight for a good night's sleep. But our plans did not work out exactly as we had expected. Despite the late hour, we were met at the airport by a crowd of some 5000. And the Chicago Republican leaders had planned street rallies in each of the five wards we would be passing through on our way from the airport to the Pick-Congress Hotel. Only a brief 15-minute stop was required in each case, but it was past one o'clock Monday morning before we finally arrived downtown.

The next morning I made an eleven o'clock appearance before the annual convention of the Carpenters Union, my second campaign speech to a labor organization. While the Carpenters, like the Machinists, were expected to end up in the Kennedy camp, I thought it important to accept their invitation, particularly in view of the fact that Republican strength among the rank-and-file is probably greater in the Carpenters' membership than in any other union.

For five solid hours that afternoon I read through and digested material which my staff had prepared, on every issue that might conceivably be raised during the course of the debate. By the time I had completed my boning and was ready to take off for the television station, I felt that I was as thoroughly prepared for this appearance as I had ever been in my political life up to that time. I had crammed my head with facts and figures in answer to more than a hundred questions which my staff suggested might be raised in the field of domestic affairs.

The tension continued to rise all afternoon. My entire staff obviously felt it just as I did. As we rode to the television studio, conversation was at a minimum as I continued to study my notes up to the last minute.

The presidents of the four major networks greeted me as I walked into the studio and I was immediately ushered onto the set so that the lighting and sound technicians could make their final tests. About ten minutes later, Kennedy arrived. This was the first time we had met each other since the Senate had adjourned. I had never seen him look more fit. I remarked on his deep tan and he jokingly replied that he had gotten it from riding in open cars while touring sunny California. We posed for pictures for four or five minutes and then each of us went to the rooms assigned us to wait for broadcast time.

I had vetoed Ted Rogers' recommendation that I wear makeup and agreed only that Ev Hart of our TV staff might apply some "beard stick" powder to help cover my perpetual "five o'clock shadow" —which the television cameras always pick up, even five minutes after I have shaved. I continued to pore over my notes until Rogers came in the room and told me, with five minutes until broadcast time, that we should move on-stage.

Howard K. Smith of CBS News, Moderator for the evening, stuck to the classic script, said "the candidates need no introduction"—and then proceeded to introduce us anyway—and history's first television debate between presidential candidates, and what may have been the most important and most decisive appearance either Kennedy or I was to make during the entire campaign, was on.

Kennedy had the opening argument. He took roughly the line I had expected and he spoke as effectively as I have ever heard him. He did exactly what I would have done under similar circumstances: he attacked. Depressed and distressed areas, the unemployed, Puerto Rican and Negro victims of discrimination, the downtrodden farmers, the old people who couldn't afford adequate medical care, the underpaid teachers—all these were the fault of the Eisenhower Administration. We wanted to stand still—he wanted to move ahead. We didn't care about these problems—he did. For eight lagging years America had been stuck on dead-center—it is time to get her moving again. The Russians are catching up with us and will soon leave us in the dust— unless we get going.

When he finished, eight minutes later, I realized that I had heard a very shrewd, carefully calculated appeal, with subtle emotional overtones, that would have great impact on a television audience. And particularly it would impress unsophisticated voters who—far from questioning the facts of the matter—would not even ask themselves: How does he propose to do all these things? How much is it going to cost? How is he going to keep all these promises? Whose money is he going to spend anyway—his or ours?

Against this appeal, and in the mood thus established, it was now my turn. Looking back, I suppose the politically expedient course would have been for me to grant without argument that we had been standing still for the past eight years and then to promise, if I were elected, to do everything he had promised, and more besides. But I rejected this demagogic approach and proceeded to answer him, point-by-point. I said that, far from standing still, the nation had experienced eight years of its greatest progress in history under Eisenhower, largely because of his sound policies. I pointed out that there was no difference between us in "caring" about the problems of less fortunate people. We had the same ultimate goals—sustained growth and prosperity widely shared. Our differences—and all-important ones —arose over how best to solve all these problems. Kennedy would do it by primary emphasis on huge and costly Federal Government programs—which would have to be paid for right out of the pockets of the people he was trying to help, and in cheapened dollars to boot. I proposed to solve them with a necessary minimum of government action but with primary emphasis on and encouragement of individual initiative and private enterprise. The great gulf of difference between us, I strongly implied, was that of a bureaucratic society vs. a free society.

The issue had been joined. Now came the questions. One of them— of no real substantive importance actually—was to plague me the rest of the campaign. It was put by Sander Vanocur of NBC. He referred to a statement President Eisenhower had made in a press conference on August 24. Someone had asked him, "What major decisions of your Administration has the Vice President participated in?" Eisenhower had replied: "If you give me a week, I might think of one." Later that same day, Eisenhower had called me on the phone and expressed chagrin at the way this exchange had been handled by the press. He pointed out that he was simply being facetious and yet they played it straight and wrote it seriously. I could only reply to Vanocur's question in the same vein, but I am sure that to millions of unsophisticated televiewers, this question had been most effective in raising a doubt in their minds with regard to one of my strongest campaign themes and assets—my experience as Vice President.

With that teaser out of the way, the panel turned to more important issues—Kennedy's and my farm programs, the probable cost of the "New Frontier," school aid, the seriousness of the internal threat of Communist subversion, Kennedy's prediction as to his probable success in getting Congress to pass all the new legislation he was proposing, especially in view of his failure to get any major legislation passed during the post-Convention congressional session. But because of the format of the program, there was no time for answers in depth. And because the members of the panel jumped from subject to subject with no apparent attempt to provide any continuity, the question period took on a decidedly scatter-shot tone. In our closing statements, both Kennedy and I returned to the basic positions we had taken at the outset, I to the need for sound and stable progress with an emphasis on free choice and private initiative, and Kennedy to a demand that we simply "get moving."

Finally, the hour came to an end. Kennedy and I shook hands. The press asked us who had won. I replied that we would learn the answer to that question on Election Day. We then left the studio and I returned to the hotel.

As we rode back, I tried to analyze the debate objectively. I felt that Kennedy had done extremely well. He had been on the offensive throughout, just as I had expected him to be. I thought that as far as the arguments were concerned, point-by-point, I might have had a little the better of it. But also, from a great deal of experience with television, I knew that appearance may at times count more than substance, and I was anxious to make a check as soon as possible on the key question: how did each of us come through on the TV screen?

When I got to my hotel suite, I asked Don Hughes to get Len Hall, Fred Seaton, Bob Finch, Jack Drown, Jim Shepley, and any others who were available to come by and give me an appraisal. Before they arrived, however, Rose Mary Woods, my personal secretary and also one of my most honest critics, came in with some disturbing information. Her parents had called—from their home in Sebring, Ohio—and asked if I were feeling up to par. They said that on their TV set I had looked pale and tired. I asked Rose what she thought. She said she tended to agree with their reaction, despite the fact that she thought I had had the better of the argument on substance.

This proved to be the unanimous reaction of my campaign advisers. At the conclusion of our post-mortem, I recognized the basic mistake I had made. I had concentrated too much on substance and not enough on appearance. I should have remembered that "a picture is worth a thousand words." I would be the first to recognize that I have many weaknesses as a political candidate, but one of my strengths is that I try to be my own severest critic. In this instance, I realized that the lesson was plain: next three times out we must not make the same mistake. If the picture was bad, it could not be blamed on the technicians. If we felt the technicians were not competent, then it was our responsibility to find better ones.

My growing conviction about how bad I must have looked was further confirmed when my mother called from California, after the program was carried there, to ask Rose if I were "feeling all right."

It would be a most convenient excuse for me to blame my poor physical appearance on the fact that I really wasn't feeling up to par. But this simply is not the truth. I had never felt better mentally before any important appearance than I did before the first debate. My knee still bothered me a bit, but when I am keyed up, as I was on this occasion, I do not notice physical pain at all. What then was the trouble? Some of it was technical, over which I had no control. But in all honesty, I must admit in retrospect that some of it was avoidable. The TV camera is like a microscope: it shows not how one feels but what his physical condition actually is.

Dr. Malcolm Todd, who had joined us by this time, talked to me like a Dutch uncle after the program. He asked me how much I weighed because he had noticed that my shirt—collar-size 16, standard with me since college days—fit loosely. I had to admit that I had not been on the scales since leaving the hospital over two weeks before. I stepped on the scales in the bathroom at the Pick-Congress and realized for the first time how much had been taken out of me, physically, by two weeks in a hospital bed followed immediately by two weeks of intensive campaigning. I weighed 160—ten pounds below normal and five pounds less than I could remember having weighed at any time in the last thirty years. Dr. Todd said, "You looked weak and pale and tired tonight on TV because, in fact, you *are* weak and pale and tired—even though you don't feel that way at all, in your own mind. We have to lighten up the schedule, get more food into you, and get you up to par before the next debate." His prescription, incidentally, was a pleasant one. There happens to be nothing I like better than a rich milkshake but because of trying to keep my weight in check, I had not had one for years. The doctor ordered me to have one with each meal—plus another in mid-afternoon—for the next two weeks. The prescription worked. For the second debate, I had put on five pounds.

During the next few days, as we resumed the campaign, I tried to put the probable effect of the first debate into reasonable perspective. I concluded that it had been a setback—but not a disaster. As far as the television audience was concerned, Claude Robinson and the other pollsters recorded a clear edge for Kennedy. But at the same time, they noted that the debate had in itself had but slight effect on the way people said they were going to vote: rather than changing voters' intentions, in other words, it intensified previous decisions and preferences.

The press, almost without exception, called it a "draw." Typical reactions were: the Philadelphia *Inquirer*—"inconclusive, won by neither." William S. White: "It is impossible to say who won. It is not even easy to say who came out ahead on points." Robert Albright of the Washington *Post:* "A dead heat." The St. Louis *Post-Dispatch:* "We should not say that anybody won." Richard Starnes in the New York *World-Telegram and Sun:* "Neither made a mistake or scored a point." The Denver *Post:* "A draw." But while the press was calling it a draw, I knew that they were basing their conclusions primarily on what had been said, not on how the candidates had looked. I knew, too, that how the candidates looked, to many viewers, was going to be a great deal more important than what they said.

Radio reaction was just the opposite from that on television. All the polls gave me a clear advantage. Ralph McGill of the Atlanta *Constitution*, a Kennedy supporter, had run an actual test. This is what he concluded: "Kennedy looked better . . . But I had a number of persons listen on the radio . . . They unanimously thought Mr. Nixon had the better of it." This information was of very little comfort to me, however. The TV audience ran five-to-six times bigger than the radio audience and it was concentrated in the big industrial states which would be decisive in determining the election outcome. It was, then, essential that we make a comeback, and the time and place to start was October 7 in Washington when we were to have the second debate.

But before then there was campaigning to do. On Tuesday we went from Chicago down to Memphis, Tennessee, and then to West Memphis, Arkansas, and finished out the day in Charleston, West Virginia. Significantly, the crowds were bigger than ever. Regardless of who "won" the first debate, public interest in the election and in the candidates had been tremendously stimulated and this was to hold true for the balance of the campaign.

For the next ten days—the interval between the first two debates —we continued to crisscross the country, and we continued to draw big and enthusiastic crowds. The list of states included New York, Vermont and New Hampshire, Massachusetts, and Maine, then back to New York, Ohio and Indiana, Virginia and North Carolina, New

Jersey and New York again, Pennsylvania, Tennessee, and—for a second swing—Ohio. At every stop I hit the same basic themes: the accomplishments of eight Eisenhower years, the promise of the future, and the fakery of Kennedy's pie-in-the-sky all-purpose panaceas. I hit him on immaturity, on lack of judgment, and on lack of candor with the American people.

One of the most stimulating meetings of this whole swing was my reception at New York's Fordham University where I addressed a student convocation. Attendance was strictly optional and yet the armory was packed and there was an overflow crowd as well. This was typical of the whole campaign: our ticket received strong support from colleges and universities throughout the nation—as the Young Democrats of Texas discovered to their considerable embarrassment when they polled the student body of the University of Texas at Austin. Straw polls among faculty groups generally favored the Democrats, but the students reversed the situation—from Tuskegee to Texas, and even Harvard. This would seem to indicate that America's college youth is more interested in opportunity than in handouts.

The second television debate was coming up on Friday, October 7, in Washington, and it had quite naturally been much on my mind. I was fortunate to have a chat with Louis Seltzer of the Cleveland *Press*, a long-time personal friend and one of the nation's outstanding independent editors, the evening before. I had always found Seltzer's advice especially helpful because he never failed to lay it on the line. He told me, first of all, that he thought my speech that evening in Cleveland had been one of the best of the campaign so far. He said he liked the fighting spirit I had shown, and he urged me to continue in the same spirit right down to the wire. "Don't pay any attention to the critics who talk about a New Nixon and an Old Nixon," he said. "These men are not your friends anyway. The reason they are criticizing you is that they are trying to blunt your attack because they know you are most effective when you are on the attack. Tomorrow night with Kennedy on TV, take him on. Take the offensive from the first, with the gloves off."

We arrived back in Washington at midnight, and early Friday morning I began my intensive boning up for the second debate.

The tension before the first round had been very great, but now it was greater. I knew that Kennedy had made a better impression first time out. While the immediate press reaction had been to call it a draw or to give a very slight edge to Kennedy, as the days had gone by it was more and more being referred to as a "decisive" Kennedy victory. I was thus increasingly in the position of having to make a decided comeback, or of being placed at an almost hopeless disadvantage for the balance of the campaign.

I followed my usual practice of reading as widely as possible and of listening to as much advice as I could cram into my crowded schedule. But in the final analysis, I knew that what was most important was that I must be myself. I have seen so-called public relations experts ruin many a candidate by trying to make him over into an "image" of something he can never be. I went into the second debate determined to do my best to convey three basic impressions to the television audience—knowledge in depth of the subjects discussed, sincerity, and confidence. If I succeeded in this, I felt my "image" would take care of itself.

I arrived at the NBC studios in Washington shortly after six and, following the usual preliminaries, Kennedy and I took our places on the set. A few minutes later, the red light over the camera flashed on and the second great debate was under way. This time, with no opening or closing statements, we went right to the questions put alternately to each of us by the four-man press, radio and TV panel. It was a hard-hitting, sharp contest from beginning to end. When it was over, I knew I had done better than in the first debate as far as substance was concerned—but the verdict was not yet in on the most important question of all: What kind of a picture had come through on the home screens?

I did not have long to wait for the answer. Calls and wires were pouring in when I reached my home thirty minutes later. The consensus was—as different from the first debate as night from day. By the next morning, the messages I had received from my friends and supporters were fully corroborated by more objective critics. A New York *Times* spot-survey in 23 cities showed Nixon over Kennedy, 82 to 65. A poll of the 26 newsmen who had been at the TV studio showed Nixon over Kennedy, 11 to 4, with 11 rating the match even. Lucey and Steele of Scripps-Howard said: "Nixon is back in the ballgame with a sharply improved national impact." Joe Alsop: "The Nixon candidacy got a real lift." The New York *Herald Tribune* editorial: "The Vice President clearly won the second round." The Washington *Star:* "The Vice President this time had a clear-cut edge." James Reston in the New York *Times:* "Nixon clearly made a comeback, came out ahead." And Roscoe Drummond had this to say: "Nixon is now back on even terms. An indispensable lift to his campaign."

What, then, were the major reasons for the difference in impact between the two debates?

First, there was a simple but important physical factor—the milk-shake prescription had done its work. I was back up to my normal weight and collar-size. Second, this time we gave the technical factors the attention they deserved but had not received first time out. The lighting was better. The set was less bleak. I had yielded to Carroll Newton's and Ted Rogers' advice that I use makeup to cover my five o'clock shadow, instead of the powder which had made me appear pale during the first debate.

But most important, this time I had the advantage on substance. The first debate had been fought pretty much on grounds favorable to Kennedy—domestic issues where he was consistently on the attack and I had to defend. In this debate, the questioners moved into the field of foreign policy where I was particularly strong and he had some glaring weaknesses. I was able to hit him hard on his off-the-cuff and, I thought, very foolish suggestion that Eisenhower should have "apologized" to Khrushchev for the U-2 flights and that if he had done so, the Paris Conference would have taken place on schedule. I said that "when the President of the United States is doing something that's right, something that is for the purpose of defending the security of this country against surprise attack, he can never express regrets or apologize to anybody, including Mr. Khrushchev."

At the very end of the debate, I had again been able to attack very sharply, this time on Kennedy's contention that the offshore islands of Quemoy and Matsu be surrendered to the Red Chinese, presumably in order to get a cease-fire in the Formosa Straits. He said they "are not strategically defensible" or "essential to the defense of Formosa" and that therefore we should "work out a plan by which the line is drawn at the island of Formosa" itself. I had only to point up the analogy here to Korea, where another "line" had been drawn and aggression had almost immediately followed. And then I stated the principle involved, and the clear lesson:

These two islands are in the area of freedom. We should not force our Nationalist allies to get off of them and give them to the Communists. If we do that we start a chain reaction because the Communists . . . are after Formosa . . .

This is the same kind of woolly thinking that led to disaster for America in Korea. I am against it. I would never tolerate it as President of the United States.

We received only one piece of discouraging news with regard to the second debate, but it was significant. The audience for the first had been estimated at about 80 million. It had fallen to about 60 million for the second, and it was not to rise above that figure for the third and fourth debates. This meant that, regardless of the fact that I had done better in the second debate and might extend my advantage in the third and fourth, there were 20 million people who saw only the first —and who would carry with them to the polls whatever impression they had gained from that one encounter.

Nevertheless, as we moved West on Saturday morning, we could feel from the size and enthusiasm of the crowds that our campaign had received a real lift from the second debate—and number three was only a week off. Again, we managed to keep up with a rugged schedule, with major stops in Minnesota, Wisconsin, Montana, Utah, and New Mexico. Then, from Tuesday through Friday, we moved into California for our first campaigning in depth on my own home grounds.

On Friday, October 14, I made my first major foreign policy speech of the campaign, before the World Newspaper Forum in Los Angeles. I called for "the total mobilization of all of our national resources and those of the free world" in a crusade for a just and honorable peace. I noted the urgent need for more co-ordination, more unity of purpose and action within the Atlantic Community, and recommended "moving toward confederation." I pledged that as President I would call together the leaders in each major area of the world—in Asia and Africa and in our own hemisphere—to consider "the over-all political, economic, and military problems most susceptible to further common action" and then to encourage the initiation of long-range programs which would preserve and extend the area of freedom.

The third television debate on October 13, in which I appeared in a studio in Los Angeles while Kennedy was speaking from New York, was one in which each of us alternately answered questions put by members of the press corps, with an opportunity for brief rebuttals. The second debate had given me a needed lift and I went into the third confident that if the questions developed subjects of sufficient interest, particularly in the foreign policy field, I was prepared for my best effort in the series to date.

When the hour was over, I felt that this confidence had been well placed, and the overwhelming majority of columnists, commentators, and pollsters agreed. Claude Robinson reported that my advantage in the third round was as great as Kennedy's had been in the first—but again, with this significant difference: 20 million more people had seen the first. Press reaction was pretty well summed up by the Houston *Chronicle* which observed: "Nixon turned in his best performance to date. The third of the debates was the hardest hitting of the three."

But what really was important about the third debate was not so much the superficial aspects—the quality of the picture, the style of delivery, or the fact that Kennedy used notes. It was that the debate developed in some depth a major difference between us on an issue of foreign policy. The issue was whether the Eisenhower policy of not writing off Quemoy and Matsu to the Chinese Reds should, as Kennedy had advocated, be substantially modified. Kennedy, in fact, began to hedge on the issue by attempting to draw an almost invisibly thin line over the use of the word "merely"—in a letter from the President to Senator Theodore Green assuring him that the U. S. did not intend to start a war "merely in the defense of Quemoy and Matsu." Kennedy thus argued:

Now that is the issue. I believe we must meet our commitment to Formosa. I support it in the Pescadores Islands. That is the present American position. The treaty does not include these two islands [i.e., Quemoy and Matsu].

But no one, of course, had ever remotely suggested that an attack on Quemoy and Matsu could represent anything other than the beginning of an attack whose ultimate objective was Formosa itself. Kennedy's attempt to draw this distinction and to insist that he, not I, really supported the President's position—this argument was made of the purest straw. I continued to hammer hard on the general theme that in the struggle against World Communism we could make no greater mistake than to submit to blackmail—that surrendering a relatively small and unimportant area under threat of war would never satisfy an aggressor but would only stimulate and encourage him to step up his demands. And the eventual and inevitable result would be that the area demanded would be so important as to make war—or surrender—unavoidable.

Our polls indicated that voters generally, Democrats as well as Republicans, overwhelmingly supported my position on this issue. Kennedy apparently was receiving similar reports from his own surveys. Shortly after the third debate, at any rate, Fred Seaton received a curious message from Washington. Chester Bowles, who had been chairman of the Platform Committee at the Democratic Convention and who was now one of Kennedy's top foreign policy advisers, had called on Secretary of State Chris Herter at the latter's Georgetown home. The purpose of the call was to indicate Kennedy's concern over the way the Quemoy-Matsu debate was developing. Kennedy, according to Bowles, did not want to give the impression during the campaign that the American people were divided in their support of the Eisenhower Administration's firm stand against Communist aggression. Kennedy had long disagreed with the Eisenhower-Dulles policy on Quemoy-Matsu—a disagreement that went back at least to the Senate debate of January 1955 over the so-called Formosa Resolution and his support of the Lehman-Morse amendment (fortunately defeated) which would specifically have excluded Quemoy and Matsu from the Formosa Straits defense perimeter. But now, Bowles went on, the issue had been raised in the campaign by questions during the debates and not on Kennedy's own initiative. He was prepared under the circumstances to modify his position so that there would be no appearance of opposing Eisenhower on this issue and so that we could present a united front to the Communists.

I asked Seaton what he thought the real purpose of this message might be. His reaction was that Bowles and Kennedy—if Kennedy was aware of what Bowles had done—were using this device for the purpose of getting me to lay off on an issue that was becoming increasingly unpopular for Kennedy. My own reaction was that if Kennedy did modify his position, I would have no choice but to drop the issue—except for continuing to point to the whole "shoot first, think later" approach as indicative of his lack of experience in the foreign policy area. This was the course of action I eventually followed. While I recognized that I had Kennedy over the barrel on an issue which was turning sour for him, I believed that he had a right to change his mind. It was important that the Chinese Communists be given no encouragement to start trouble in the Formosa Straits because of a hassle in the American presidential campaign.

After the debate we put in a final day of campaigning in the Los Angeles area and then went cross-country, with stops in Arizona, Oklahoma, and Illinois, to Hartford, Connecticut.

Rather than return, as usual, to Washington, we had decided to spend Sunday in Hartford so as to be on the spot for Monday's swing through Connecticut. On the schedule, this was to be a day of rest. But in the final month of a campaign there can be no days of rest, as I had learned from previous experience. Cabot Lodge, Len Hall, Bob Finch, and some of our other campaign associates joined the traveling party in Hartford to go over schedules and pin down plans for the last two weeks of the campaign.

We came to several key decisions at our all-afternoon meeting.

The most important new development was that Eisenhower had decided this was the time for him to move into action. He had agreed to make speeches at an airport rally in Minneapolis-St. Paul, on October 18—the next Tuesday—and at a Nixon-for-President Committee dinner in Philadelphia, on October 28. The real climax of the campaign was to be reached on Wednesday, November 2, in New York City, when Eisenhower, Lodge, and I would all meet for a ticker-tape, motorcade parade, and for helicopter stops in some of the key, strategic outlying areas. Our chances in New York, according to the *Daily News* poll, were very slim. At the time we made this decision, the poll indicated we would lose the state by as much as a million votes; but we decided to concentrate our efforts there anyway, for two reasons. First, we could not write off a state as big and as important as New York, or give any appearance of doing so. And second, New York City is the news, TV and radio center of the nation, and we felt we could gain a great deal through the stories and broadcasts which would originate from our visit there. Following the big day in New York, with a climactic rally at the Coliseum, Eisenhower was also slated for a one-day swing on November 4, the Friday before election, to Cleveland and Pittsburgh.

We decided that Lodge would continue to concentrate his efforts in the industrial cities and states of the North and East where he had been drawing exceptional crowds.

Another decision, which derived from an idea I had had before the campaign began, was to whistle-stop through the densely populated areas of Pennsylvania, Ohio, Indiana, Michigan, and Illinois during the second week before election. I felt that we not only would thus reach a great number of people in smaller towns where air-stops were not feasible, but also it seemed to me that the drama of the traditional campaign train would add zest and color to our efforts during this critical period when the nation's attention would be riveted on what we were doing.

There was one knotty problem that I discussed with Lodge privately. We had been receiving a good bit of flak over a statement he had made, October 12, during a talk in New York's Harlem. This is what he said:

". . . there should be a Negro in the cabinet . . . It is part of our program and it is offered as a pledge." (The following week, in Albany, he added that he had meant this only as a "personal prediction" and he amended it to read "qualified Negro" but typically, this clarification made few headlines.)

When I was questioned about this, I of course replied that no pledges had been made for Cabinet appointments and that I would select my Cabinet solely on the basis of personal qualification—without regard to race or creed or color. The background for Lodge's statement puts it in perspective.

When he resigned as Ambassador to the UN, at the beginning of the campaign, Lodge felt that one of the best qualified men in the nation to replace him was Ralph Bunche, long-time member of the U.S.-UN delegation and of the Secretariat. Lodge knew that I shared his own high opinion of Bunche, who had lived and taught in my home state of California and whom I knew well. But there were so many current questions under debate at the time of Lodge's resignation that the decision had been to raise his experienced deputy, Jerry Wadsworth, to serve as Ambassador for the balance of the Eisenhower Administration. When Lodge had arrived in New York the previous week, he was urged by several of the New York Republican leaders to indicate in his Harlem speeches that a Nixon-Lodge Administration would follow a policy of appointing Negroes to any and all positions in government for which they were qualified. Lodge, consequently, made his statement about appointing a Negro to the Cabinet, having particularly in mind that our UN Ambassador sat in as a Cabinet member under Eisenhower and that Bunche might well be named by me to this position.

He could not have been more surprised when the story got the attention and the rather lurid play that it did. He immediately made it clear that he was expressing only a personal opinion and that the new

President, of course, would make all decisions with regard to his Cabinet. But the statement continued to plague us for the balance of the campaign. It hurt us in the South unquestionably. And it did us no good in the North. To Negroes as well as to other voters it appeared to be a crude attempt to woo the support of Negroes without regard to the qualifications an individual might have for high office—something that Lodge had never remotely intended to suggest. Such are the "unpredictables" of any campaign, especially in this day of almost instant mass communication.

Except for this one problem, the reports we received that Sunday were encouraging and we moved into the third week before Election Day with a confidence that the tide was running our way, an impression confirmed by former National Chairman Meade Alcorn as we campaigned through "Kennedy country" in southern New England on Monday, October 17.

At the American Legion Convention on Tuesday in Miami, I fired the opening gun of what was to turn out to be the major subject for discussion in the fourth and final debate, scheduled for Friday, October 21, in New York. Kennedy had been hammering away for weeks at the Administration's Cuba policy—although none too consistently. Early in the year—in a book of his speeches published in January—he was still describing Fidel Castro as "part of the legacy of Bolivar" and as simply a "fiery young rebel." In May, he said in a TV interview that "for the present, I support the Administration" even though "the situation in Cuba . . . continues to deteriorate." But by mid-September, with his campaign in full-swing, he was taking a very different line: the existence of Communism "eight jet minutes from the coast of Florida" was the fault of the Administration, he said on the fifteenth. On a September 30 TV show, he charged Castro up to us generally ("what they did wrong was not to use . . . our great influence . . . on Batista to have him relax his dictatorship and permit free elections"). Kennedy had much to criticize but little of substance to offer in the way of new policies and proposals.

This issue is an excellent illustration of the disadvantage that confronts a candidate who also represents an incumbent Administration. I had long been urging a stronger policy, within Administration councils, against Castro. I had had a three-hour conference with Castro when he visited Washington, back in April 1959. After that conference, I wrote a confidential memorandum for distribution to the CIA,

State Department, and White House. In it I stated flatly that I was convinced Castro was "either incredibly naïve about Communism or under Communist discipline" and that we would have to treat him and deal with him accordingly—under no further illusions about "fiery rebels" in the "tradition of Bolivar." My position was a minority one within the Administration and particularly so within the Latin American branch of the State Department. Trying to "get along with" and "understand" Castro continued to be the State Department line despite my own strong recommendation to the contrary—one, incidentally, which was shared by J. Edgar Hoover and by two of our former Ambassadors to Cuba, Arthur Gardner and Earl E. T. Smith, as well as by William Pawley who had held several diplomatic posts in Democratic Administrations and was a widely acknowledged expert on Latin American affairs.

Early in 1960, the position I had been advocating for nine months finally prevailed, and the CIA was given instructions to provide arms, ammunition, and training for Cubans who had fled the Castro regime and were now in exile in the United States and various Latin American countries. This program had been in operation for six months before the 1960 campaign got under way. It was a program, however, that I could say not one word about. The operation was covert. Under no circumstances could it be disclosed or even alluded to. Consequently, under Kennedy's attacks and his new demands for "militant" policies, I was in the position of a fighter with one hand tied behind his back. I knew we had a program under way to deal with Castro, but I could not even hint at its existence, much less spell it out.

Kennedy had spoken up to now only in vague generalities, and so I decided that here was the time and place—the Legion Convention in Miami—to counterattack. I felt that in addition to our secret operations, we could also substantially strengthen our overt and official policy for dealing with Castro. I urged several courses of action in my talks with State Department officials and finally found an ally in Douglas Dillon, the Under Secretary. In a nutshell, what I advocated and what I announced in my Miami speech was a policy of all-out "quarantine"—economically, politically, and diplomatically—of the Castro regime. I said that the time for patience was over, that we must move vigorously—if possible, in full association with our sister American republics—to eradicate this "cancer" in our own hemisphere and "to prevent further Soviet penetration." Our government was even then, I pointed out, planning "a number of steps" and "will very promptly take the strongest possible economic measures to counter the economic banditry being practiced by this regime against our country and our citizens."

We flew back North late that night and on Wednesday evening, October 19, Kennedy and I were co-speakers at Cardinal Spellman's annual Alfred E. Smith Memorial Dinner. Kennedy spoke first and read a speech which delighted this distinguished audience with its wit but also irritated them with an incredible display of bad judgment. At this strictly non-political, non-partisan affair, he proceeded to raise what were obviously partisan political overtones. When I then spoke extemporaneously, all I had to do to top his performance was to avoid any statement that smacked of partisanship. The effect was easily predictable. He had received polite applause. I received a prolonged ovation.

Kennedy himself referred ruefully to this incident when we met in Miami immediately after the election. He was discussing voting patterns among Catholics and he pointed out that economics rather than religion primarily determined how people voted. And then he added with a smile, "You saw how those wealthy Catholics reacted at the Al Smith Dinner in New York."

I had reserved Thursday for preparations for the fourth and final television debate. Foreign policy was to be the sole subject for discussion, and I knew that this was a major opportunity for me to move ahead—not only in the debate series but in the campaign itself. But Kennedy, recognizing that my Miami speech had taken most of the wind out of his sails on the Cuba issue, chose this day before the fourth debate for a major counterattack of his own. Huge black headlines in all the afternoon papers put it succinctly:

KENNEDY ADVOCATES U.S. INTERVENTION IN CUBA
CALLS FOR AID TO REBEL FORCES IN CUBA

I could hardly believe my eyes. As early as September 23, Kennedy had given an exclusive statement to the Scripps-Howard papers in which he said, "The forces fighting for freedom in exile and in the mountains of Cuba should be sustained and assisted." But he had not followed up by advocating what was, in effect, direct intervention in Cuba in violation of our treaties with other Latin American countries—until now. Now, on October 20, he said:

We must attempt to strengthen the non-Batista democratic anti-Castro

forces in exile, and in Cuba itself, who offer eventual hope of over-
throwing Castro. Thus far, these fighters for freedom have had virtually
no support from our government.

As soon as I saw the story and read the statement I asked Fred
Seaton to come to my hotel room. I knew that President Eisenhower
had arranged for Kennedy to receive regular briefings by Allen Dulles,
Director of the CIA, on all covert operations around the world, as well
as on the latest intelligence estimates—precisely so he would be as
well aware as I of what our policies and programs were. I asked Seaton
to call the White House at once on the security line and find out
whether or not Dulles had briefed Kennedy on the fact that for months
the CIA had not only been supporting and assisting but actually training Cuban exiles for the eventual purpose of supporting an invasion of
Cuba itself.

Seaton reported back to me in half an hour. His answer: Kennedy
had been briefed on this operation.

For the first and only time in the campaign, I got mad at Kennedy
—personally. I understand and expect hard-hitting attacks in a campaign. But in this instance I thought that Kennedy, with full knowledge
of the facts, was jeopardizing the security of a United States foreign
policy operation. And my rage was greater because I could do nothing
about it.

I was faced with what was probably the most difficult decision of
the campaign. Kennedy had me at a terrible disadvantage. He knew,
as I did, that public sentiment in the United States was overwhelmingly in favor of a tougher line against Castro. I had long favored and
fought for this line within the Administration, and the covert training
of Cuban exiles as well as the new overt quarantine policy were programs due, in substantial part at least, to my efforts. Kennedy was
now publicly advocating what was already the policy of the American Government—covertly—and Kennedy had been so informed. But
by stating such a position publicly, he obviously stood to gain the support of all those who wanted a stronger policy against Castro but who,
of course, did not know of our covert programs already under way.

What could I do? One course would be simply to state that what
Kennedy was advocating as a new policy was already being done, had
been adopted as a policy as a result of my direct support, and that
Kennedy was endangering the security of the whole operation by his
public statement. But this would be, for me, an utterly irresponsible

act: it would disclose a secret operation and completely destroy its effectiveness.

There was only one thing I could do. The covert operation had to be protected at all costs. I must not even suggest by implication that the United States was rendering aid to rebel forces in and out of Cuba. In fact, I must go to the other extreme: I must attack the Kennedy proposal to provide such aid as wrong and irresponsible because it would violate our treaty commitments.

This then was the background for the fourth debate. Predictably, the Cuba issue was raised almost at once—and was frequently returned to, both by the panel of questioners and by the candidates. This is what I said:

I think that Senator Kennedy's policies and recommendations for the handling of the Castro regime are probably the most dangerously irresponsible recommendations that he's made during the course of this campaign.

But I could not say why. Instead, I took this tack:

. . . if we were to follow that recommendation . . . we would lose all of our friends in Latin America, we would probably be condemned in the United Nations, and we would not accomplish our objective . . . It would be an open invitation for Mr. Khrushchev . . . to come into Latin America and to engage us in what would be a civil war and possibly even worse than that.

I concluded by returning to my previous recommendation for a policy of strict quarantine—on every diplomatic and economic front. Kennedy suggested, in turn, that a policy of quarantine would be too little, too late, and in every way short of the need for vigorous action.

When the debate was over, I felt that I had made as good a case as possible for my point of view, but I had no illusion about the effect on the public generally. I was in the ironic position of appearing to be "softer" on Castro than Kennedy—which was exactly the opposite of the truth, if only the whole record could be disclosed.

My attack was effective but with the wrong audience. Doug Dillon called from Washington immediately after we went off the air and said he thought it was my best effort yet and that I had handled the Cuban situation particularly well. He knew the handicaps under which I had had to operate on this issue.

Another touch of irony was that the columnists and editorial writers who leaned to Kennedy, for the one and only time in the campaign, gave me the better of the argument because they thought Kennedy had been off-base with his new "tough" line on Cuba. James Reston said, "The Vice President's criticism of Senator Kennedy's program for assisting the anti-Castro forces to regain power in Cuba was approved by well-informed people here tonight." The Washington *Post* said: "Mr. Nixon accused Mr. Kennedy of recklessness and there is a good deal of point to this observation. Mr. Kennedy has been rather extravagant in his criticisms and rather unsatisfying as to just what to do. Mr. Nixon made a sound point about avoiding unilateral intervention."

But I knew that editorial reaction was one thing and that of people around the country would be something else again. The polls taken after the fourth debate for the most part rated it even or gave me a slight advantage. But I was sure then, and am now, that the position I had to take on Cuba hurt rather than helped me. The average voter is not interested in the technicalities of treaty obligations. He thinks, quite properly, that Castro is a menace, and he favors the candidate who wants to do something about it—something positive and dramatic and forceful—and not the one who takes the "statesmanlike" and the "legalistic" view.

My attack registered in another quarter as well. The vehemence of the editorial criticism, particularly from columnists and papers generally friendly to him, was so great that two days after the debate Kennedy changed his position again. This was his new line: "I have never advocated and I do not advocate intervention in Cuba in violation of our treaty obligations. We must use all available communications, and the moral power of the American Government, to let the forces of freedom in Cuba know that we are on their side." This was, of course, a far cry from his original statement that "the forces fighting for freedom in exile and in the mountains of Cuba should be sustained and assisted."

The New York *Times* noted his new statement with approval: "The use of propaganda and diplomacy is immensely different from force of arms. Mr. Kennedy was . . . well-advised to clarify his position."

I got little comfort, politically, out of his change of position. At least 60 million people had seen and heard him on television demanding a tougher stand against Castro than the Administration and I were advocating publicly. Only a very small percentage of that number would note Kennedy's change of position, which was reported in the press on the basis of a formal statement and not even a public speech, much less a national television debate. The general "image" to the end of the campaign was to be one of Kennedy stronger and tougher than I against Castro and Communism.

Nevertheless, despite the Cuban episode, I had come out of the fourth debate at least on even terms, in the opinion of most observers.

Looking back now on all four of them, there can be no question but that Kennedy had gained more from the debates than I. While many observers gave me the edge in the last three, he definitely had the advantage in the first—and especially with the television audience. And as I have pointed out, 20 million people saw the first debate who did not bother to tune in the others.

Charles Lucey and Jack Steele of Scripps-Howard probably summarized the total effect of the debates as objectively as anyone: "Nixon started slow and finished fast in the four debates . . . He thus wiped out Mr. Kennedy's advantage in their first contest. But on balance, the four debates also left Mr. Kennedy with a big political plus. He slugged it out on fairly even terms and gained exposure before vast audiences."

Looking to the future, the incumbent—or whoever represents an incumbent Administration—will generally be at a disadvantage in debate because his opponent can attack while he must defend. But joint TV appearances of candidates at the presidential level are here to stay, mainly because people want them and the candidates have a responsibility to inform the public on their views before the widest possible audience.

In future campaigns, however, I would suggest that debates would be more interesting and would serve a more useful purpose if they were limited to specific subjects with only the candidates participating, and if the time allowed for discussion were two hours rather than one so that a subject could be discussed in adequate depth. This was the pattern of the Lincoln-Douglas debates of 1858, to which the 1960 series was often and quite erroneously compared. Every possible effort should be made from the standpoint of makeup, lighting, and other technical factors, to see that the candidates are on even terms. This last objective is easier said than accomplished. As my television adviser, Ted Rogers, commented after the campaign, "It is almost impossible to get a bad picture of Kennedy because of his coloring. On the other hand, it is difficult to get a good picture of Nixon."

I have no complaints and am doing no second-guessing on that score, incidentally, but one possible improvement would be to have debates in future campaigns conducted as was our third round, with the candidates in separate studios, allowing for the special kind of lighting that is needed and appropriate for each. In essence, what ought to be decisive in selecting a President is what is in a man's head rather than the type of beard he may have on his face. Anything that gets in the way of communicating this mental content ought, if possible, to be eliminated.

With the debates over, we moved our campaign into high gear. Back in Washington on Sunday—another one of those days labeled "rest"—we prepared for our week of whistle-stopping. But that afternoon, I called an emergency strategy conference. In New York I had seen evidences of the use by Kennedy and his associates of a time-worn but highly effective campaign technique—the victory blitz. Kennedy and all of his associates were now talking in terms not just of victory but of a landslide. Lou Harris, his private pollster, was predicting a four-to-five million vote popular margin. Too many Republican leaders and campaign workers, on the other hand, were talking—probably with complete honesty but still with political naïveté—of a "close election." Some evidence of defeatism (with suitable quotes) was creeping into the "dope stories" being written by leading columnists and editorialists. I asked Len Hall, Bob Finch, and our National Committee Headquarters under Thruston Morton's direction, to get the word out to the field to counteract Kennedy's tactics with an affirmative optimism campaign of our own. In fact, we were not just talking. Claude Robinson's polls still showed the race even, with no evidence whatever of Kennedy pulling away in key areas. Gallup and Roper were making the same forecasts: 50–50, take your pick. I recalled to my associates what Jim Farley had been saying at the Al Smith Dinner —that Kennedy was going to carry forty states. Farley as an experienced pro couldn't possibly have reached so ridiculous a conclusion; but he knew that in a close election, those who tend always to "play the winner" might determine the outcome, and he was doing his bit to see to it that everybody he could reach would think that Kennedy was a "sure thing."

Despite our best efforts, however, we were unable to make much impression on the press and radio commentators who were now spearheading the blitz. In the two weeks before Election Day, the newspapers and airwaves were full of predictions of everything from a close Kennedy victory to a Kennedy landslide. NBC's "Election Countdown," on October 20, showed Kennedy having increased his lead during the three preceding weeks. "Three weeks ago," said emcee Leon Pearson, "Kennedy was leading in states representing 180 [electoral votes] and now the figure is 326, according to our boys. Three weeks ago Nixon was leading in states representing 162, and now it is 105." Again on October 27, Elmer Peterson, reporting on trends in the Western states, said, "The tendency has changed rather dramatically to Kennedy." On Election Eve pollster Sam Lubell said: "Kennedy will win in an uneven sweep across the country."

In the press, Rowland Evans' October 31 report in the New York *Herald Tribune* said, "Kennedy's private polls show an increasingly upward trend. Ohio, tipping toward the Senator at better than 52 to 48. California—moving his way." The New York *Times* for October 24: "The reports based on a study of polls and interviews with voters in 50 states suggest that the Kennedy tide, if unchecked, would be enough to elect him." On the same day, Joe Alsop reported "a surge toward the Democrats that may well be strong enough to produce a fairly dramatic vote on Election Day." David Lawrence, commenting on a Gallup forecast of a possible 50 per cent shift in the Catholic vote from Eisenhower in '56 to Kennedy in '60, wrote on November 1 in his widely syndicated column: "This is such a sensational shift that, if corroborated by election returns, it could mean not only a landslide for Kennedy but possibly one of the largest popular vote totals ever given to a presidential candidate in American history." James Reston didn't go quite that far—but in his November 2 column in the *Times* he entered the "sinking ship" note: "Eisenhower is engaged in a rescue operation but it is very late in the game to reverse the forces now moving with Senator Kennedy."

The three mass-circulation news weeklies also followed the same general line. *U.S. News & World Report* predicted "Kennedy-Johnson, with electoral votes to spare." *Newsweek* reported that "forty of the fifty Washington correspondents and political writers predict that Senator Kennedy would win, most by substantial margins. Only ten thought that Nixon would win, most by narrow margins." *Newsweek* also predicted that Kennedy would carry 21 states with 278 electoral votes as against 159 for Nixon, with 100 electoral votes undecided— still enough to win—and Ernest K. Lindley said flatly: "Kennedy will be elected by a substantial margin." *Time* saw a two-to-one Kennedy margin in electoral votes and said "the likeliest forecasts seem to run from a close Nixon victory to a Kennedy electoral landslide." I would say, incidentally, that at least fifteen million Americans read one of these three magazines every week—and usually swear by it as a political authority.

All these reports were brought to my attention. I did my best to counteract them, and I urged my campaign associates to do likewise, but we learned that political reporters often predict with their hearts rather than with their heads. Back in 1952, I recalled, the Washington correspondents covering the Eisenhower-Stevenson campaign had confidently predicted a Stevenson victory (4 out of 5 of them also declared their personal preference for Stevenson). I jokingly told my staff that Sunday afternoon that I knew how Harry Truman must have felt in 1948.

But, like Truman, I was not going to let the Kennedy bandwagon discourage me. I was tremendously buoyed up and encouraged by the enthusiasm of our campaign crowds. As our campaign train moved through Pennsylvania and Ohio during the week of October 23, I stepped up the attack on Kennedy's rash campaign statements and his inexperience:

You have the choice between two men—one who has had the opportunity of dealing with the problems of keeping the peace, and another man who, on occasion after occasion, has indicated that when the chips are down he would have made the mistake which could have led, in my opinion, either to war or to surrender of territory. Let me give you three examples.

In 1955 President Eisenhower had to meet the threat of Communism in the Formosa Straits. He asked for the right to defend that area. Senator Kennedy opposed this policy, he opposed it again in 1958, and he opposed it in our second and third debates. He was wrong. The President was right.

We find that he disagreed with the President in his conduct at the Paris Conference. Senator Kennedy said the President could have apologized to Khrushchev, he could have expressed regrets. The President was right; again Senator Kennedy was wrong.

More recently, in Cuba he says that our policy of quarantining Castro is too little and too late. He advocates a policy which was universally interpreted as intervention in the affairs of Cuba. Again he was wrong, and the President was right.

On all of these points, I recognize that Mr. Kennedy has said he has changed his mind. He now supports the President on Quemoy and Matsu. He has agreed that the President conducted himself properly at the Paris Conference. As far as Cuba is concerned, he didn't really mean what he said.

I know from experience that when a President speaks, when a President makes a decision, it is for keeps. He doesn't get a second chance. He can't call a bullet back after he shoots from the hip. It goes to the target. In these critical times we cannot afford to have as President of the United States a man who does not think first before he speaks or acts.

I could feel the tide running our way. I have often been asked about this by newsmen—how does a candidate "feel" the trend of a campaign? It is hard to describe this emotion, except to say that it is not simply the size of the crowd or the applause that greets a speech but rather the spirit of the mass of people which, some way or other, conveys itself to the candidate.

When 20,000 people stood in a driving rain to hear me speak at midday in downtown Dayton, I knew that at least in Ohio the reports of our early demise were somewhat exaggerated.

When I reached Toledo, I made what I consider to be one of the most significant speeches of the campaign. I had long felt that we should resume our underground atomic testing program—the uncontrolled, uninspected moratorium was at this time two years old—but my views had not prevailed within the Administration. Consequently, I hit the issue head on and announced that if elected I would ask President Eisenhower to send Cabot Lodge at once to Geneva to prod the stalled test-ban negotiations—and, agreement or not, I would order the resumption of underground testing no later than February 1, 1961.[6]

Our train moved triumphantly through Pennsylvania, Ohio, Michigan, and Illinois during the week. Every stop we made, with each crowd far exceeding expectations, raised our hopes higher. The train trip had been so successful that we were sorry when it came to an end at Carbondale, Illinois, where we transferred again to an airplane for more prop-stopping.

Saturday, October 29, took us back to Chicago where we motorcaded through heavily Republican suburban territory in order to stimulate the big turnout we needed on Election Day. I finished the day in the Chicago area with a statewide telecast, after which I held a "background briefing" for the press corps traveling with us. They bombarded me with questions about the "Kennedy landslide." I tried to

[6] This speech was prepared with the assistance of Jim Shepley, the head of my research group, who rates as an expert on the subject of atomic development.

give an honest appraisal of my strength in each of the major states and said I felt that those who were writing in terms of a decisive Kennedy victory were being taken in by a political gimmick. I released the figures on some of Claude Robinson's confidential polls in California, Ohio, and other key states. All those who were present accurately reported that, far from being downhearted and pessimistic, I thought our campaign was going well and was confident about the outcome. But from the reports that Herb Klein gave me later, I realized that most of them—perhaps understandably—thought I was just whistling in the dark and therefore continued to write what was their actual belief— that it was going to be Kennedy, and probably by a big margin.

There was one incident during our week of whistle-stopping which, in retrospect, might have been avoided or at least better handled. Back on October 19—at the time of the Legion speeches in Miami when the Cuba issue fired up—the Reverend Martin Luther King, nationally respected leader and symbol of the anti-segregation forces, had been arrested, along with some fifty others, at an Atlanta restaurant sit-in. The rest were quickly released on bail but King was held and, on October 26, was given a "quick" four-month sentence based on a former charge of driving without a valid license. Robert Kennedy, realizing the tremendous political potential of King's misfortune, wasted no time in calling the judge in the case.

Herb Klein, in response to inquiries from the press, asked me what comment I had on Robert Kennedy's action. I told him: "I think Dr. King is getting a bum rap. But despite my strong feelings in this respect, it would be completely improper for me or any other lawyer to call the judge. And Robert Kennedy should have known better than to do so."[7] Under the circumstances, Klein answered the press query by saying that I had "no comment" on the matter.

This incident was widely interpreted by Negro leaders both North and South as indicating that I did not care about justice in the King case. As a matter of fact, immediately after Klein brought the case to my attention, I took up the problem with Attorney General Bill Rogers, who by that time had joined our campaign train, and asked if this were not a case in which King's constitutional rights had been infringed— thus paving the way for Federal action. Rogers, in turn, strongly recommended that a statement be made by Hagerty from the White

[7] One of the American Bar Association's *Canons of Professional Ethics*, which govern the conduct of attorneys, provides that "a lawyer should not communicate or argue privately with the Judge as to the merits of a pending cause, and he deserves rebuke and denunciation for any device or attempt to gain from a Judge special personal consideration or favor."

House to the effect that the Justice Department had been instructed to look into this question. Had this recommendation been adopted, the whole incident might have resulted in a plus rather than a minus as far as I was concerned. But Rogers was unable to get approval from the White House for such a statement.

The ironic part of the whole incident is that well-informed Washington observers knew that I had been one of the most consistent and effective proponents of civil rights legislation in the Administration. I had made several key rulings in the Senate which were essential in getting such legislation to the floor for debate. As Chairman of the President's Committee on Government Contracts, I had helped develop an effective program, among companies with government contracts, which resulted in providing job and promotion opportunities for thousands of Negroes in Northern and Southern states alike. As far as Martin Luther King himself was concerned, I had met him in Ghana and respected him for his advocacy of non-violence in working for equal rights for his people. But this one unfortunate incident in the heat of a campaign served to dissipate much of the support I had among Negro voters because of my record.

Despite this episode, as I flew home to Washington from Illinois late Saturday night, I looked back on the past week with great satisfaction and with my morale and confidence as high as they had been since the start of the campaign. I was convinced that our campaign had received the lift it needed, and at just the right time. The Kennedy victory blitz which had bowled over so many press, radio, and television commentators, and even some of my own people, had been blunted. The Kennedy campaign had peaked in New York two and a half weeks before Election Day, roughly at the time of the fourth debate. Ours was now moving forward toward the high point which we hoped to reach on Election Day. And the big crowds that had just greeted our whistle-stopping were strong evidence that the tide was running our way. Some of the veteran Washington correspondents on our train, many of whom had gone out on a limb predicting a decisive Kennedy victory just a few days before, were beginning to have second thoughts.

As we started off on our last full week of campaigning, I returned to one of my recurrent themes—the fiscal irresponsibility of Kennedy's promises.

If he says he can keep his promises in the Democratic platform—which would add 15 billion a year to the budget—promising everything to everybody, with the people paying the bill—if he says he's going to do this and balance the budget and not raise taxes, then he is showing such an ignorance of simple economics that he disqualifies himself to be President.

In Pennsylvania and upstate New York, I continued to carry the attack to Kennedy. I said we could not afford "to use the White House as a training school for a man who wants to learn how to be President, at the expense of the United States of America" and I hit out at the Kennedy formula designed to "produce prosperity with a printing press."

During this week, we had not only stepped up the number of rally appearances, but at Tom Dewey's suggestion, we had added a nation-wide telecast each evening at seven in which, for fifteen minutes, I discussed a major issue of the campaign in a "fireside chat" format.

Wednesday, November 2, was our big day in New York, with President Eisenhower, Cabot Lodge, and myself appearing together in huge rallies in the heart of the city and in the suburbs. The highlight was our meeting which overflowed the New York Coliseum in Columbus Circle, ending with the President and I sharing a half-hour of national television time.

It was a long day but a highly gratifying one because of the tremendous outpouring of people—nearly three million all told. I did not get back to the hotel until after ten but, tired as I was, I asked Don Hughes to gather our key staff members for a strategy conference. It was after eleven before we finally sat down in the drawing room of my Waldorf suite. The time had come to discuss a subject which I had deliberately refused to bring up in a staff meeting until now, despite considerable pressure to do so.

What, if anything, should I say on the religious issue during these last few days of the campaign?

I had insisted from the day of my nomination that religion would be an issue in the campaign only to the extent that the candidates themselves talked about it and thus made it one. Consequently, it had been my policy and the policy followed at my explicit direction by everyone directly or indirectly connected with my campaign not to initiate or even engage in any discussion of the religious issue. When the subject was raised by others, as it had been in the Peale incident, I had categorically disassociated myself from any individuals, however strongly they might be supporting me, who based their support on religious grounds.

I had taken this position because I did not believe religion had any legitimate bearing on Kennedy's qualifications for the presidency. I had even gone so far as to exercise a veto over a proposed endorsement that would certainly have given my candidacy a boost. Billy Graham, with whom I had enjoyed a long and close friendship, contacted my campaign staff early in the fall and said that he had been asked to write an article on the election for *Life* magazine. He had prepared an article in which he endorsed me unqualifiedly and enthusiastically, largely on grounds of my experience in world affairs and foreign policy. He had mentioned the religious issue in the article only in order to deny explicitly that it either was or ought to be an issue at all. But he did not want to give *Life* the go-ahead on publication unless I gave my approval. I was naturally pleased to have Graham's support. My staff felt that a Billy Graham public statement might be very helpful in the closing days of the campaign. But I ended up vetoing the proposal because of my fear that, even though he was basing his support on other than religious grounds, our opponents would seize on his endorsement as evidence of religious bigotry, his own forthright denial notwithstanding.

I understood that Kennedy was in a very different position. He was a Catholic and he had not only a right but a responsibility to answer affirmatively any attacks that were made on him because of his religion. But what concerned my staff at this point was not what Kennedy himself had been saying (ironically, he had made a quip about "racism in reverse" in commenting on Cabot Lodge's alleged promise to appoint a Negro Cabinet member)—it was what Johnson, Stevenson, Robert Kennedy, Walter Reuther, and other key leaders in the Kennedy campaign were saying and doing on the religious issue. In a speech before the Houston, Texas, Ministerial Association early in the campaign—on September 12, just one day after my own TV statement on "Meet the Press"—Kennedy had made an eloquent and very proper appeal that he not be denied the presidency on the sole basis of his religion. Touching on all facets of the question, he had pointed out that he had fought in the South Pacific, that his brother had died in Europe in World War II, and that no one had then suggested they might have a divided loyalty in serving their country.

This very effective speech was recorded on video tape, and it was being played and replayed across the country—but, according to our reports, far more often in Northern cities, where it might be expected to appeal to Catholic voters, than in the South and Midwest, where one would expect the heaviest anti-Catholic or simply non-Catholic population. Furthermore, my staff showed me a file of "scare" headlines and news stories from the nation's press. Some of them were:

DEMOCRATS HIT BACK ON RELIGION (New York *Times*). JACK'S BROTHER SAYS RELIGION TOP ISSUE (Columbia, S.C., *State*). RELIGIOUS ISSUE STRESSED AT KENNEDY CONFERENCE (Nashville *Banner*). JOHNSON BLASTS 'HATERS' ATTACKS ON CATHOLICS (Washington *Post*). BOB KENNEDY SCORES STRESS ON RELIGION (Cleveland *Plain Dealer*). CREED ISSUE MUST BE MET, BOB KENNEDY SAYS HERE (Cincinnati *Enquirer*). BOB KENNEDY SAYS CATHOLIC ISSUE WANES (New York *Herald Tribune*). MRS. FDR HITS RELIGIOUS BIAS IN TALK TO NEGROES (Baltimore *Sun*). UAW PAMPHLET LIKENS KENNEDY FOES TO BIGOTS (Washington *Star*).

And it was not just headlines. Stevenson, for example, was quoted as "wondering out loud" why nobody was making an issue of Nixon's Quaker faith, since "many Quakers are pacifists." Governor Luther Hodges of North Carolina, speaking at Charlottesville, Virginia, warned: "We had to choose between a Catholic and a Quaker in 1928. We elected a Quaker and lived to regret it. And if you vote for a Quaker this time, you will live to regret it horribly." Lyndon Johnson—as well as the members of Kennedy's family—almost always referred in their speeches to the fact that the Senator's brother had died in action in World War II without anyone questioning his loyalty. Senator Jackson, the Democratic National Chairman, accused Nixon of "conniving" with anti-Catholics.

Congressman Charles Diggs told his Detroit constituents that "Kennedy has felt the sting of hate; he is feeling it today as the propaganda masters of the Republican Party keep up a continuous, well-financed attack against his religion." Congressman Adam Clayton Powell was saying that "the Klan is riding again and . . . all bigots will vote for Nixon and all right-thinking Christians and Jews will vote for Kennedy rather than be found in the ranks of the Klan-minded."

AFL-CIO's COPE—the Committee on Political Education—distributed nation-wide an unadulterated hate-pamphlet which said the issue in the campaign was not Kennedy vs. Nixon but "liberty vs. bigotry." The Kennedy-Johnson Labor Committee put out its own leaflet—equating a vote for Nixon with a vote for the Ku-Klux Klan.

So it went. At every possible juncture and on every possible occasion, Kennedy's key associates were pushing the religious issue, seeing to it that it stayed squarely in the center of the campaign, and even accusing me of deliberate religious bigotry. They were, in short, contributing all they could to make religion an issue while piously insisting that to do so was evidence of bigotry. And they were using it where it would do them the most good. It was, for Kennedy, a "heads I win, tails you lose" proposition.

The Catholics on my own staff had taken to kidding me that there were probably more Catholics on my payroll than there were in Jack Kennedy's office, right across the hall from us. My aide, Don Hughes, my personal secretary, Rose Mary Woods, my receptionist, Betty McVey, three of my top secretaries, Rita and Jane Dannenhauer and Mary Fenton, and my research assistant, Agnes Waldron—all were Catholics. During my fourteen years in Washington, I had gained the friendship, and I believe the respect, of top members of the Catholic hierarchy in the United States. I had spoken and written publicly on many occasions in commendation of the effective work Catholics have done and are doing, everywhere in the world, to combat the spread of Communism.

It was the Catholics on my own staff and among top officials of the Administration who were now most outraged at the tactics used by some of Kennedy's supporters, and most insistent that I answer their attacks in at least one major television speech before the campaign was over. Secretary of Labor Jim Mitchell, Chairman Bill Miller of the Republican Congressional Campaign Committee, and Peter Flanigan, executive director of the Volunteers for Nixon-Lodge, all urged me to make such a speech denouncing what they called "reverse bigotry." As they well pointed out, I was getting it from both ends: Republican Catholics were being urged to vote for Kennedy because he was of their religion; and Republican Protestants were being urged to vote for him to prove that they were not biased against Catholics!

Our meeting at the Waldorf went on into the early hours of Thursday morning. Arthur Flemming, Secretary of Health, Education and Welfare and a leading lay member of the Protestant Council of Churches, had prepared a draft of a speech on the subject. It was moderate in tone and reasonable in approach, calling on Protestants and Catholics alike to cast their votes on the basis of the real issues and not to be influenced in any way by the religion of the candidates—which had been, of course, my own consistent position.

Everyone in the room that night thought I should make such a speech. In the end, I voted "no"—and since I was the candidate, this was of course a "majority" vote. Kennedy and his supporters were saying "don't vote against Kennedy just because he is a Catholic" and I simply could not see myself saying "don't vote *for* him just because of this fact either." This might be as reasonable a position as his, but I felt it would open me to charges of bigotry and of deliberately inflaming the issue. Also, from a personal point of view, I could not dismiss from my mind the persistent thought that, in fact, Kennedy was a member of a minority religion to which the presidency had been denied throughout the history of our nation and that perhaps I, as a Protestant who had never felt the slings of discrimination, could not understand his feelings—that, in short, he had every right to speak out against even possible and potential bigotry. I felt a responsibility to keep the lid on the boiling cauldron of embittered anti-Catholicism. I still believed that this would probably be one of history's closest elections, and I reasoned that if I made a speech late in the campaign on the religious issue and then won the election, it would inevitably be charged that my victory was the result of my having deliberately injected the issue into the waning days of the campaign. The cause of religious tolerance, which had advanced slowly and painfully for so many years, would be substantially set back.

It was after two o'clock on Thursday morning, November 3, when my disappointed campaign associates filed out and I quite literally closed the door, once and for all, on any further discussion of the religious issue. As I look back on the campaign now, I can think of many things I should have done or might have done differently. But on this key decision, I have never had a moment's regret.

As we completed our last day in New York, there were but five days to go until November 8—the target we had been working toward for almost two years. In those five days we were to cram the most backbreaking traveling and speaking schedule in the history of American political campaigning. This was also the week of President Eisenhower's maximum effort. His wind-up in Cleveland and Pittsburgh, from every report, was a day to remember.

For all his reputation for finding politics distasteful, Eisenhower is a man of irresistible magnetism with great crowds and they, in turn, seem to trigger his own irrepressible vigor—especially when he has his dander up. And "up" it was on Friday, November 4, as a result of Kennedy's recklessly irresponsible charges about America's second-rate military posture, its second-class power status, and all the various "gaps"—from carbines to missiles.

Kennedy, as President, has had to retreat from these campaign charges—has, in fact, been eager to do so because now, with the responsibility on his own shoulders, he can begin to realize how damaging it is to America's negotiating position and to clear thinking about the world balance of power to so downgrade America. But in October and November of 1960, he seemed less concerned with responsibility than with campaign strategy and political advantage. Eisenhower took out after him with no holds barred.

He described Kennedy as "a player who knocks the team all season and then wants to become coach." He referred to him scathingly as "this young genius" who thinks he knows more about defense and weaponry than "the joint chiefs of staff and the dedicated men, military and civilian, who have given their lives to this work." "The White House," he pointed out to a Cleveland luncheon audience, "is one place where we should not depend on on-the-job training of the occupant." By contrast, he said he was "completely committed to the election of Dick Nixon. For eight years he has been immersed in the responsibilities of leadership. He is now prepared to take over national leadership in January."

In Pittsburgh, Eisenhower attacked Kennedy's whole campaign:

The juggling of promises by the inexperienced, the appeal to immediate gain and selfishness, the distortion of fact, the quick changes from fantastic charge to covert retreat—all these are intended to confuse the voter, not to enlighten him.

And he called, in simple contrast, for "woodshed honesty" with the American people. All we could do was wait and see what effect this would have. We knew at any rate that these were the most hard-hitting political speeches that Eisenhower had ever made.

As for my own schedule, after three hours sleep following our important strategy session, I was up again on Thursday morning at six-thirty for a flight to Columbia, South Carolina. I met there with the leaders of our campaign from all over the South and then was eloquently introduced by Governor James F. Byrnes for a televised address from the steps of the State House. A cheering crowd of 30,000 crammed every inch of the space that had been roped off for our meeting. From Columbia, we flew to San Antonio, Texas, for another TV address, in the Plaza of the historic Alamo. We left the Alamo just in time to arrive at the television studio for a 15-minute nationally televised talk on national defense.

Fron San Antonio, our next stop was Houston, where Senate candidate John Tower introduced me to a crowd of 40,000 in Herman Park. Thad Hutcheson, the Republican State Chairman, and Mrs. Oveta Culp Hobby, former Secretary of Health, Education and Welfare, told me after this meeting that Texas was close but they were sure this tremendous turnout had shifted the tide in our direction and that we would carry Texas on Election Day.

It was the same story the next day when record crowds cheered us along our way in Fort Worth; Cheyenne, Wyoming; Spokane, Washington; and Fresno, California. I stepped up the tempo of my attack. I pointed out that Kennedy was a "Pied Piper," saying "give me your money, and I will solve all your problems." I struck hard at his "switch-hit" tactics: he was a "jumping Jack" who promised vast new spending programs but no new taxes and no deficits; who first will not defend Quemoy and Matsu and then will; who sometimes will and sometimes won't "apologize" to Khrushchev over the U-2 incident; who urges "intervention" in Cuba but then says he meant only "moral" influence. I compared him with the old-time medicine man who got out of town just before the people caught up with his quack remedies. Judging from the crowd response, these points were hitting home.

We knew our campaign was going well in my home state when the next day not even a dose of California's "unusual weather"—in the form of drenching rains—dampened the size or the enthusiasm of turnouts in San Jose, Hayward, Oakland, and Van Nuys. After our nationally televised evening rally, before an overflow crowd at the Pan Pacific Auditorium in Los Angeles, some of the reporters traveling with us, who had been conceding California to Kennedy, began to hedge their predictions.

The Saturday night rally traditionally marks the end of intensive campaigning. But I woke up on the Sunday before election to begin what was to be the longest "day" of my life—a stretch of 72 hours during which I was able to manage less than five hours of sleep. Most political professionals say that no votes are changed on the Sunday and Monday before election, but as the candidate, I could take no such chances. Truman fought to the last in 1948. This election, I felt, was going to be just as close as '48 and perhaps more so. I was tired after a campaign that had already probably been too long and too strenuous. But the stakes were high and I was determined to do everything I could, right up until voting began on Tuesday, to swing our way any last-minute deciders.

We attended church services at Immanuel Presbyterian, within walking distance of the Ambassador, and then returned to the hotel where I got down to final preparatory work on a half-hour telecast which I was to tape that afternoon for national broadcast at ten Sunday night. In that talk, which some observers—Frank Holeman of the New York *Daily News* was one—rated the best of my campaign telecasts, I returned to the theme of my acceptance speech at Chicago. I did this deliberately, to complete the circle of three months' effort. I restated the one great and overriding issue of the campaign: how to keep the peace without surrender of territory or principle, and how to preserve and extend freedom everywhere in the world. This, I said, was the supreme challenge to our national purpose and our leadership. And the key was to be found in the moral and spiritual strength of a free people, and in the American idea—the one truly revolutionary idea still abroad in all nations. This idea is a simple one: we believe that all peoples should be free to rule themselves as they see fit and to seek their own destiny. It was to the fulfillment of this promise, for nations and peoples everywhere, that I pledged myself in the Office of President.

At 4:30 Sunday afternoon, we took off for Alaska, a trip which was to mark the fulfillment of the pledge, made in my acceptance speech, to carry the campaign into every one of the fifty states. Not even our most optimistic supporters thought we had a chance to carry Alaska. They urged me to cancel our scheduled trip to Anchorage and instead to cut a television tape which could be played at the Sunday night rally at which I was slated to appear. But for reasons I have already discussed, I was determined to keep my commitment. The warmth of the crowd that greeted us at that rally made the trip worthwhile as far as I was concerned, whether we carried the state or not.

At ten P.M. we left Anchorage for Madison, Wisconsin. Our reports indicated that Wisconsin was close and beginning to lean our way. At eight o'clock Monday morning, with the thermometer at about 5 degrees above, the airport hangar was jam-packed. My talk was put on film, for later telecast throughout the state. And then we flew on to Detroit. I was returning to Michigan because, here again, our latest reports indicated that our chances were improving and I thought that another appearance might tip the scales in our favor.

From a rally before an overflow audience at the Ford Auditorium, we went directly to the studios of WXYZ-TV for a four-hour afternoon nation-wide telethon. I had wanted to have several telethons in the last days of the campaign but funds had not been available. Only three days before air-time were we able to obtain enough contributions to finance this one show.

For four hours I answered questions that were phoned or wired in from all over the country. John Payne, Robert Young, and Lloyd Nolan had come to Detroit to act as questioners-by-proxy and to fill in a few intervals when I was off-screen. Cabot Lodge, by means of split-screen remote techniques, took part from Boston. Thruston Morton, who had been one of our most effective campaigners, flew to Detroit for a five-minute appearance. When we were off the air, I asked him for his prediction about the election outcome and he reflected the feeling that had become unanimous among staff members who had been traveling with me—that our campaign had "caught fire" in the last two weeks and that we would reach our peak just when we needed to, on Election Day itself.

The candidate himself is usually the poorest judge of his performance during the last grueling hours of a long campaign. I knew that I was tired physically, but despite lack of sleep, I had never felt more alert mentally and none of the questions gave me any trouble. Frances Dewey (Mrs. Tom Dewey) was to tell me weeks later that the telethon was my best appearance of the entire campaign. Here again, therefore, was an example of something I had learned from long experience—that in times of stress and crisis, an individual can be at his best mentally even though he is physically exhausted. I had been through a similar experience in a very different situation three years before, when I had my first and last White House press conference after the President had suffered his stroke. I was so tired at the time, for sheer lack of sleep, that I was concerned as to whether my handling of the conference had been anything close to par. Frank Stanton, president of CBS, called me later that night and said he was sending me a recording of the conference because he thought it the very best I had ever had up to that time. I told him of my concern and he observed that it had been his experience, often as not, that an individual is at his best on radio or TV when he is physically tired. Because of his very awareness of fatigue, he raises the level of his mental and emotional concentration even higher, to compensate for the physical factor and thus to meet the challenge.

At six, Eastern Time, the telethon came to an end. I had barely enough time to drop by the switchboard to thank the hundreds of women who had rendered such fine service at the phones before driving to the airport for our flight to Chicago and our final telecast of the campaign, the traditional Election Eve show.

We were scheduled to go on the air at 9:30 Central Time, and we arrived at the studio only an hour before. I wanted to use this period for preparing notes and hoped for some relaxation before making my final nation-wide appeal. But as a campaign nears its end the candidate is permitted no such luxury. A telephone call came in from New York. Nelson Rockefeller, hoarse from a speaking tour which he had just completed, reported that he had just checked with all of his county leaders and that, in their view, the tide in New York had finally turned. He knew that New York had been conceded to Kennedy by virtually all the experts, but he was genuinely hopeful that our last minute campaigning might have moved it into our column.

Then Don Hughes came by and reported that our Volunteers for Nixon-Lodge Committee had whipped up an impromptu rally outside the studio where over 5000 supporters, many of them from colleges and universities in the area, wanted to wish me well before the voting began. I had not been scheduled to appear. But Illinois was close. I could overlook no possible opportunity to do or say something that might be decisive in winning this pivotal state. Because the television time was fast approaching, I could make only a brief appearance. But the ten minutes or so in which I thanked this group of loyal and enthusiastic volunteers was one of the most heartening experiences of the entire campaign.

By the time I got back inside the studio, only fifteen minutes remained before air-time. Eisenhower spoke first from Washington, then Lodge from Boston. This allowed me another few minutes which I needed and used for preparation of my final remarks. I emphasized again, as I had throughout the campaign, my concept of the presidency and the challenge it presented. I urged everyone to vote with but one thought in mind: "Put America first, rather than party or any other consideration." And I concluded this way:

Vote for the man that you think America and the world needs in this critical period. Whatever that decision is, it is one that I know will be best for America. It is one that we will all abide by; one that we will all support. And my prayer and my hope . . . is very simply this: that the next President of this country . . . will be a worthy successor of

Dwight D. Eisenhower and that he will be worthy of the high ideals and the great purpose of the American people.

With that, the campaign had reached its final stages. The program was over at ten and we left immediately for the airport and our flight back to California.

I had planned to sleep on the flight from Chicago to Los Angeles. Tricia and Julie, who had joined Pat and me for the last day of campaigning, dropped off almost at once on bunks that we had had made up for them. But the tension of the last forty-eight hours had taken its toll and I spent the flight reliving the campaign which was now drawing to an end. I did not try to second-guess any of the decisions I had made during its course—all that came later. My thoughts now turned primarily to those who had given so much of themselves for our cause.

Pat fell asleep in her seat across the aisle from me. She had once said that someday she would write a book and call it *I Also Ran*. This was no less than the truth: beginning with my 1946 campaign for Congress, she had been at my side in all the years of campaigning. She had never once lost her dignity or her poise in the face of even the greatest provocation. She had had to go through the indignity of being spit on in Caracas and splattered with rotten eggs in Muskegon, Michigan, just two weeks before. Her physical stamina had been even greater than mine. In the long hand-shaking sessions, it was I, rather than she, who would first have to ask for a break in the line. Roy Howard was to tell me after the election that he had seen the wives of all the presidential candidates for fifty years—and never had he seen one to surpass Pat Nixon as a campaigner and a gracious lady throughout.

I thought of my top campaign associates who had been with me through so many battles before and had rendered service above and beyond the call of duty in this one. (Here was a cliché that for me had been given new luster.) I thought of Bryce Harlow, Gabe Hauge, Jim Shepley, and George Grassmuck who had been working around the clock helping to prepare the key speeches and statements for the campaign. I thought of my own personal staff: Don Hughes, who was officially designated as my aide but had been, in effect, my personal assistant from the time he first joined the staff right after the 1956 elections; Rose Mary Woods, who had been tried in battle during the '52 fund episode and who has that rare and unique characteristic that marks the difference between a good secretary and a great one—she is always at her best when the pressures are greatest. There were literally scores of others—secretaries like Rita Dannenhauer to whom the clock meant nothing when there was work to be done; Bob Cushman, back in Washington, my superbly qualified adviser in the field of national security affairs who had also taken on the assignment of administering my office staff; and Loie Gaunt who, though she lived in California, had turned down the chance to fly to Los Angeles to hear the election returns because "there was too much last minute work to be done in Washington."

I thought of Thruston Morton and all the party workers in state and local organizations; of Charlie Rhyne and his dedicated Volunteers for Nixon-Lodge; of the gifted Voices for Nixon, under the leadership of Ralph Hunter who organized great choruses of volunteer singers—numbering sometimes as many as a thousand—who gave such spirit and lift to our campaign; and of the Nixonettes—1500 of these teenagers had provided us with a guard of honor at our airport reception in Burbank. I thought of those unsung heroes, the advance men and the rally men who, under Bob Haldeman's direction, had done such a superb job that never once during the campaign did we fail to fill an auditorium—one indispensable ingredient of a successful rally.

People like this—from Len Hall to the last anonymous doorbell-ringer—make a candidate proud and humble at the same time: proud that the cause he represents can attract such devoted and competent people, humble because they have placed so much confidence in him.

Why does a candidate add to a schedule that is already too full? Why does he exert himself to the outermost limits of mental, physical, and emotional tension? Certainly he is greatly motivated by his natural competitive instinct—by his desire and will to win. But in a presidential campaign, even more than in others, he wants to win not just for himself but for the literally thousands of people, many of whom he will never know or meet, who have given him their loyal support.

And so, as the plane flew on to Los Angeles that night, I wished I could have done even more than I had done during those last two months of intensive campaigning. I felt that way even though I could look back on a campaign which, from the standpoint of number of states visited, miles traveled, speeches made, and people seen either in live audiences or on television, had exceeded in intensity any in American history up to that time. From the time of the Chicago Convention, I had traveled over 65,000 miles and visited all the fifty states, made 180 major scheduled speeches and as many more impromptu ones—not to mention press conferences, spot interviews, radio and TV appearances. I had shaken uncounted thousands of hands, signed as many autographs; and an estimated five million people had seen Pat and me in person.

But still I could not be sure that I had done enough. I thought we were going to win—but if there had been any other thing I could still do or say I would have put it on the schedule. I thought of all the people I had not had time to call, of interviews I had not been able to grant, of meetings I had not been able to attend—simply because there was no time left in a schedule already overloaded with commitments.

There was, I realized, nothing more I could do. It was in fact now past midnight and Election Day 1960 had begun. I was wrong, however, about the campaign being over: one of the biggest and most inspiring rallies of all was still to come. In our previous visits to California, we had never been able to fit in a trip to the San Bernardino-Ontario-Riverside area, one whose population had doubled since I campaigned the state in the Senate election of 1950. Our supporters there urged us to land at the Ontario Airport instead of the Los Angeles International, and so we had arranged it.

When our plane finally touched down, it was nearly two in the morning, Pacific Coast Time. More than 15,000 cheering people were there to welcome us home to California. The night air was cold and in my brief talk I said I didn't much mind catching cold myself—but I wanted to be sure everyone else was well enough to vote before the day was out.

It was good to be home again after a long journey. Shortly after two we left the platform and made our way slowly to the cars, shaking hands and signing autographs as we went. It was past five in Washington by then, and Tricia and Julie were still sleepy despite their nap on the plane; but they, like their mother, proved themselves good campaigners and signed autographs for scores of teenagers wearing Nixonette costumes.

The ride to the Ambassador was enlivened by college students in sports cars decorated with Nixon-Lodge streamers and bumper strips, who took turns "buzzing" our car as we moved into the city. It was almost four o'clock when we finally reached the hotel—and for the first time in forty-eight hours, I went to bed.

Two hours later, we were up again. First order of business was to go out to our voting precinct in Whittier so that pictures of us casting our ballots could appear in the afternoon papers, both East and West. Even this bit of publicity might swing a critical vote! We voted in precinct 33, located in a house belonging to Roger and Mary McNey. Mrs. McNey happened to be a Nixon supporter, and she had prepared coffee for us and the members of our party. I met her children, and even they had voted for Nixon—in a mock election at school. As we were about to leave and Pat and I thanked her for the coffee, she said to us, "This is one of the most exciting days of my life." I could reply with utter sincerity: "It is for us, too!"

Finally, there was nothing more we could do. The rest of the day belonged to us—until the returns began to come in.

Pat and I knew from experience what a long day this would be. In 1946, 1950, 1952, and 1956 we had watched the hours creep by until the polls closed and the returns started to come in. We knew the best thing to do was, if possible, to get our minds off the election during this period. Pat decided to take the girls to get their hair done for the election night festivities. I suggested that we meet again at the hotel that evening but that we hold off listening to returns until six o'clock Pacific Coast Time, when they would begin to mean something. I knew the suspense would be very difficult on the girls, and we both felt we should compress the evening as much as possible.

When we left the polling place in Whittier, Pat drove back to Los Angeles. With the help of Don Hughes, Jack Sherwood, and John DiBetta of the Los Angeles Police Department, who had always driven me so expertly on my official visits to the Los Angeles area, I was able for the first time in many months to have a few hours to myself —away from the surveillance of the press. I explained my reasoning to Don: "If we win tonight, we will not be able to escape the press or the Secret Service for four years. If we lose—they won't care what happens to us." The four of us got into a convertible, slipped down a side street, and parked in an empty garage while the car with the wire service reporters assigned to follow us went by. Then we headed down the Coast Highway toward San Diego.

Don Hughes had never seen this beautiful drive before and I enjoyed showing off my native state to him. Nobody knew who we were and the only time we were recognized was when we stopped at a service station in Oceanside for gas. We had not expected to drive for longer than an hour or so and then return to the hotel. But as we got closer to San Diego, I learned that Don had never been to Tijuana. I had not been in this border city myself for twenty-five years and so we decided to drive on past San Diego and across the border into Mexico.

We arrived in Tijuana at one o'clock. John DiBetta had asked the Border Patrol for the name of a good restaurant where we could get some authentic Mexican food. On the trooper's recommendation we ended up at the Old Heidelberg—which turned out to be owned by a German who was reputed to serve the best Mexican food in Tijuana. On our arrival in town, I asked Don to call headquarters at the Ambassador so that they could let the press know where we were. He got Bob Finch on the line. Don recounted to us with great glee that when he told Bob—who thought he had seen and heard everything in this campaign already—he realized that this incident topped them all: a presidential candidate having lunch in a foreign country on Election Day!

As we roamed the streets of the city, the word finally began to get around as to who we were. The mayor of Tijuana, Tia Xicotencatl, came into the restaurant during lunch and joined us. This was to be my last "good will visit" to a foreign country as Vice President. The mayor was a gracious host. We discussed some of his problems in governing so unique a city, because of its truly "international" status.

With lunch over and our good-bys said, we took off at two for the return trip to Los Angeles. This time, so that Don and Jack Sherwood could see one of California's most famous landmarks, we turned inland at San Juan Capistrano and stopped at the Mission. There were only half-a-dozen other visitors on the grounds as I led a conducted tour among the points of interest. As we walked by the windows of the grade school on the Mission grounds, the Sisters who were teaching recognized me and one, I recall, held up her fingers in the V-for-victory sign. Before we left, I took Don into the exquisite little chapel which had been completely restored and is now used again for services. For a few minutes we sat in the empty pews for an interlude of complete escape from the battles we had long fought together, and those still to come.

We would have liked to stay longer but it was now past three-thirty, the polls in the East would be closing in thirty minutes, and we were still an hour-and-a-half away from the Ambassador Hotel suite where I was scheduled to listen to the returns. I had been doing the driving from San Diego, but now John DiBetta took over for the last lap into the city.

As we drove from Capistrano to Los Angeles, we deliberately did not turn on the car radio because I had learned from experience that fragmentary first returns have virtually no meaning at all and that it is best to wait until something more definitive is available. But by this time none of us could keep from thinking of how the voting might be going. I expected the first returns to run against us since they would be primarily from the northeastern states in which Kennedy had such great strength. But I knew that the margins by which he carried states like Massachusetts and Connecticut would be some indication as to whether we would be able to recoup these losses when the returns from our own areas of strength—the Midwest and the Far West—began to come in. The South was an enigma. Reports had been mixed as to the effectiveness of Johnson's "corn pone special" but I had learned never to underestimate Johnson's political shrewdness. The major question was whether his last-minute efforts had been effective in his native state of Texas. But this we would not know until hours later. At any rate, we resisted temptation during the drive. The radio stayed off.

Just before five we arrived at the Ambassador, slipped in the back entrance, and climbed up the stairs to my fourth-floor suite. Pat and the girls were in the suite immediately above. I had hoped for an hour's sleep—but just a few minutes after five I called Bob Finch and asked him to bring me an analysis of the first returns.

This was the moment we had been working toward and waiting for—for so many months. Now we were to learn whether our efforts had been successful. No one who has not been a candidate can understand the tremendous tension one feels at this moment, just before he hears the first returns—nor can a candidate really put it into words.

Finch arrived in my room only five minutes after my call, but it seemed like an hour. He handed me the first sheet of tabulated returns. This was just after five, Pacific Coast Time. "How do they look?" I asked.

"About as we had estimated at this time," he replied. "Surprisingly, we were leading on the first returns and now Kennedy has pulled even on the popular vote. But only two-and-a-half million votes have been tabulated so far, out of a probable total vote of 70 million. Reports from the South are mixed: we lead in South Carolina, and Kennedy is pulling ahead in North Carolina. Maine, Vermont, and New Hampshire all seem to be holding to their Republican tradition."

"What about Connecticut?" I asked. (Connecticut is always first in with complete and official returns.) Bob said we should have final returns in the next few minutes.

Five minutes later Herb Klein walked in and handed me the Connecticut returns.

Kennedy had carried the state by 90,000. We had thought he was ahead here, but the margin was somewhat larger than we had expected. On the plus side, the Republicans had picked up two House seats in Connecticut, breaking up a solid bloc of six Democrats.

By 5:30, the computing machines on both NBC and CBS television were making their predictions on the basis of early returns. Walter Cronkite of CBS reported: "Kennedy seems to be lengthening his lead." NBC's RCA computer showed the odds in favor of a Kennedy victory at 7 to 1, but it showed Nixon leading in states-ahead, 16 to 13.

At six—before the polls had closed in the West—CBS predicted a Kennedy victory with 52 per cent of the popular vote. Howard K. Smith commented: "We have established a trend and we now think we are close to being right." At this time only 8 per cent of the votes were recorded, with Kennedy leading in popular vote by 3 million to 2.75 million.

At 6:30, NBC's computer had lengthened the Kennedy odds to 15 to 1. As we had expected all along, Massachusetts had gone for him overwhelmingly.

First Ohio returns showed Nixon leading. But John Chancellor of NBC, reporting from the Midwest, said: "I think Ohio will come out for Kennedy."

At 6:45—still 15 minutes before poll-closing time in the West—Eric Sevareid of CBS reported: "We are pretty confident now of a Kennedy victory. All of the computing machines are now saying Kennedy." Len Hall, interviewed in Los Angeles, fired back: "I think we should put all of those electronic computers in the junk pile so far as election returns are concerned. This one is going down to the wire—a squeaker, a real close election."

At seven, we heard some good news. Kentucky, Vermont, and Oklahoma now joined Indiana in the Nixon column.

At 7:30, we began to get substantial returns from the big states with the big electoral votes, the states that would really decide the election. The states we were watching in this respect were New York, Pennsylvania, Ohio, Michigan, Illinois, Texas, and California. Of these seven states, we figured we would win if we carried three, but that Kennedy could not win unless he carried at least five.

We looked at the trends, state by state. We had very little from New York at that time but, with nearly 50 per cent of the vote in, Kennedy was leading in Pennsylvania by 300,000. In our analyses, we had figured on only a fighting chance in New York, a fair chance in Pennsylvania with the state leaning to Kennedy, a better than even chance in Ohio, a fair chance in Michigan but again leaning to Kennedy, an even chance in Illinois, and both Texas and California close but leaning to Nixon.

John Chancellor reported from the Midwest that Nixon had moved into the lead in that area generally but, with regard to Illinois, he said flatly: "It's a runaway; Kennedy's lead is insurmountable."

At 7:30, NBC reported the odds on a Kennedy victory at 250 to 1. Reports from New York were by no means yet conclusive but Kennedy had a substantial lead—in New York City—and we were not gaining as much upstate as we had hoped.

By eight o'clock (eleven, Eastern Time) we had thought everything would be over but the shouting. But eight came and went, only 20 million of an estimated probable final total of 70 million votes had been recorded—and the fight was far from over.

By this hour, Arizona, Florida, and Tennessee had fallen into the Nixon column. Kennedy had jumped to an early lead in California, based on scattered returns from primarily metropolitan areas. He had carried Missouri and Rhode Island—as expected. NBC's computer predicted a Kennedy electoral landslide, with a final count of 401 electoral votes (out of 537).

At 8:30 we took a close, hard look at the seven big decisive states. Only 40 per cent of New York State was in, but we felt Kennedy's lead there was more than we could overcome. Bob Finch called Tom Dewey and our feelings were confirmed. Kennedy's eventual margin in New York was to be 375,000 votes out of 7.3 million cast—a substantially better showing for us than the 800,000-vote Kennedy margin the usually reliable New York *Daily News* poll had indicated when we were in New York two-and-a-half weeks before election—but not enough.

There was also bad news from Pennsylvania: Kennedy's margin was now 115,000. Before giving up completely on that key state, however, we called Hugh Scott to get his appraisal. He had been confident that we would carry Pennsylvania, though by a close margin, because he believed we would come to the Philadelphia line with a lead of 200,000 votes. We had in fact reached that goal—but a Kennedy landslide in Philadelphia of over 300,000 votes, exceeding even the huge margins that Roosevelt had rolled up in the depths of the depression, had wiped out our outstate lead.

Ohio by this time was safely in our column. We were rolling toward a margin of 275,000 votes in this state which Kennedy's private pollster, Lou Harris, had predicted he would carry by at least 200,000. Only 45 minutes earlier, Stuart Novins of CBS had said: "Whereas Cleveland is delivering for Kennedy, Cincinnati is not doing as well as expected for Nixon. Therefore, it looks like Kennedy in Ohio."

At 8:30, CBS had given Illinois to Kennedy, although less than 50 per cent of the vote was in. Reports from Michigan were still not decisive, but at eight John Chancellor of NBC had observed: "Ohio and Michigan ought to make the Democrats a little bit anxious. The Nixon lead is holding in Ohio; and in Michigan, Wayne County is not as strong for Kennedy as expected."

Then came our most discouraging news. Texas had been a dingdong battle from the beginning but with most all of the vote in, it appeared that Kennedy would carry the state by about 40,000 out of a 2.3 million vote total. And that is the way it ended up: another plus for the "corn pone special."

Less than 10 per cent of the California vote was in, with Kennedy still holding a slight lead. Consequently, no predictions could be made.

I did some quick computing on the yellow pad on which I was jotting down these results. With Kennedy carrying New York, Pennsylvania, and Texas, we had to win three of the other big four—California, Illinois, Michigan, and Ohio. The prospects were not encouraging but we were a long way from giving up. There were still a lot of votes to be recorded.

But the TV commentators were going all out in predicting a Kennedy victory—or perhaps the better word is "conceding." Eric Sevareid, just before eight, had said: "A Kennedy victory is now beyond any reasonable doubt. It would be a very difficult feat for him now to snatch defeat from the jaws of victory." Dave Brinkley, on NBC at 8:15, said: "Kennedy at this moment, on these returns, has well over enough to make it as President." Grant Holcomb of CBS, reporting from the West, commented: "Senator Kennedy is doing very well in the West. It would appear that Kennedy is going to carry California by a very considerable margin." At the time he said this, only 8 per cent of California's precincts had reported. Newspapers that had been supporting the Republican ticket joined in the stampede. Charles Collingwood of CBS reported that the New York *Daily News* had declared Kennedy the winner.

Actually the Kennedy highwater mark had now been reached. At nine o'clock, the western returns began coming in, with substantial leads for Nixon in Idaho, Washington, and Utah. California still showed a slight Kennedy lead with 15 per cent of the vote recorded, and Governor Pat Brown predicted—according to CBS—"Kennedy will carry California by 800,000 votes." Two hours later, he changed this estimate: he raised it to an even million!

What was particularly significant was this: while Kennedy led in the popular vote as well as the electoral vote, his popular margin was not increasing. On the contrary, as the total mounted, his lead narrowed. It was 1.7 million at nine. By 9:45, it was down to 1.6 million.

As the midwestern and western returns piled in, we rolled up victory after victory in the farm belt. Iowa, Kansas, North and South Dakota, and Nebraska joined Indiana and Ohio in our column.

It was now midnight in the East and nine o'clock in the West. In the next hour and a half, I believed a sufficient number of votes would be counted in the West and Midwest for us to make a final determination whether the Kennedy trend was to continue or whether our hopes were still alive. Between nine and ten, "victory statements" and "concession statements" were being recorded, coming from prominent Democrats and Republicans alike. Adlai Stevenson, at 9:30, said: "I am elated at the prospect of a sweeping victory for Jack Kennedy." Five minutes later, Walter Cronkite interviewed Barry Goldwater and reported over CBS: "Well, that's it. Goldwater wrote off Nixon's chances to win in this presidential race." At 9:45, the New York *Herald Tribune*, which had supported the Nixon-Lodge ticket, conceded to Kennedy. At ten, the Chicago *Sun-Times*, another paper that supported our ticket, declared Kennedy the winner. And at 10:15, the New York *Times*, which had endorsed Kennedy, declared that he had won. But as the western and midwestern returns continued to come in, Kennedy's popular vote margin which earlier in the evening had been as high as 2 million, was fading away: by 10:30, it was down to 1.1 million. UPI commented at this point: "This seems mighty close compared with vote counts of previous years." Between 10 and 10:30 we learned that we were doing far better in the West than we had dared hope. We were able to add Washington, Wyoming, and Colorado to our column.

But some commentators were already speculating as to what I

would do after my defeat. David Brinkley of NBC, at 10:15, said: "Nixon is a lawyer. He will probably wind up in some high-paying corporate job." Despite the ever-narrowing popular vote margin and our surprising strength throughout the West, NBC and CBS were still insisting that California was in the bag for Kennedy. Grant Holcomb put it this way: "One of the things about California is that once the trend is established, it very, very seldom changes. It would be surprising indeed if this trend of Kennedy winning California changed." Merrill Muller of NBC went further: "Kennedy has California and the national election." NBC's computer predicted a Kennedy victory in the state at odds of 7 to 3—this at 10:30. Holcomb reported at that time that the San Francisco *Chronicle* and the Los Angeles *Examiner* had both conceded California to Kennedy.

The commentators and observers were now turning to analyses of the vote by racial and religious patterns. Howard K. Smith said at eleven: "Our tentative conclusion would be that Kennedy lost a little by being a Catholic, but he gained a great deal more."

The popular vote margin continued to narrow. As each new batch of votes was recorded, I was gaining more of them than Kennedy.

Shortly after eleven (two o'clock Eastern Time) I decided I had to make a decision, one way or the other, about issuing a statement. I asked Don Hughes to round up our key advisers. First to enter my room were Len Hall and Cliff Folger. These two men had been with me on that cold evening back in November 1958, when we decided to start down the long road which seemed now to be ending at such a heartbreaking destination.

They could not have been more magnificent. Len Hall had a big smile on his face, shook my hand, and—acting for all the world as if nothing more serious had happened than that he had just lost two dollars on a horse race—said, "It's a real squeaker." I knew his heart was breaking. No one had worked longer or harder for our cause. Cliff Folger, my finance chairman, was just as fine. I mentioned that one of my major regrets was that I felt I had let down those who had contributed so generously to the campaign. His eyes flashed as he answered: "Why, don't you think that for a minute. All of these fellows had a real run for their money. We'll try again and next time we'll beat them to a pulp!"[8]

[8] One of our major financial contributors, W. Alton (Pete) Jones, expressed the same thought to me this way a few weeks later. "This was just like a horse race. When you bet on a horse and he loses by a nose after being bumped in the stretch, you are disappointed. But you figure you've had a good run for your money."

Bob Finch, Fred Seaton, and Herb Klein joined us and I told them all that I thought the time had come for me to make some kind of a statement. Seaton was particularly opposed to my making an outright concession. He had just had a call from Jim Worthy in Illinois, and another from Ev Dirksen's top assistant, Harold Rainville. Both agreed that, if the present trend continued there, we were gaining enough in each downstate precinct to overcome the lead Kennedy had built up in Cook County. Worthy, incidentally, was to point out to me several months later that after I made my statement at 12:20, which was interpreted by some as a concession, the Republican poll-watchers downstate gave up and went home. In his opinion this contributed to our loss by the razor-thin margin of 8000 votes.

But I gave the group my own analysis. While we were leading Kennedy in the number of states carried (and it was to end up that way, 26 to 23, with one state uncommitted), he now had New York, Pennsylvania, Texas, and Michigan for sure. With Ohio definitely in our column, we still had to win California, Illinois, and one other state—possibly Minnesota—in order to overtake him. The odds were strongly against that happening. I thought we would win California because I knew there were a quarter-of-a-million absentee ballots out, traditionally heavily Republican, and that they would be decisive in view of the closeness of the vote at that hour. But we were still 40,000 behind in Illinois. Absentees had been opened and counted there and I considered our chances of pulling through very remote, the more so in view of a call we had just received from a good friend and very experienced Illinois political observer, John Drieske of the Chicago *Sun-Times*. He had told us a few minutes before that it just wasn't in the cards for us to take the state.

I felt that by midnight I would have to make a statement of some sort—one in good grace but, at the same time, one that would not let down our legion of supporters who still had hopes we might pull the election out of the bag. Bob Finch brought in stacks of wires and phone messages urging me not to concede until all the votes were in. Herb Klein, on the other hand, said many in the press corps thought I had already waited too long and was being "a poor sport" in not conceding—especially in view of the fact that some of the major Republican papers, like the *Herald Tribune* and the *Sun-Times,* had long since given up.

I finally decided, at about 11:30, that I would make a statement to the group of loyal supporters who had been listening to returns all evening long down in the ballroom and whom I would have greeted much earlier had it not been for the indecisiveness of the result.

Pat was still upstairs in her suite with the girls. We had agreed that they would not join me until we knew what the result would be. As the evening dragged along, I kept putting off calling them in the hope the tide might eventually turn in our direction. Now I could wait no longer. Don Hughes went up to get them. At 11:30, Pat walked into my room with Helene Drown and Tricia. Both Pat and Tricia were wearing the new dresses they had bought for the occasion, Tricia in blue and Pat in a gray-green flowered print. No one could have guessed as they came into the room that things had been going against us. All evening long, Pat had been telling Tricia and Julie—who had gone to bed earlier—that the news would get better as the West came in.

Tricia greeted me with, "Hi Daddy, how is the election coming?"

For a fleeting moment I didn't have the heart to tell them what I had concluded from the trend of the returns. But then I knew I could no longer put off preparing them for the bad news that was to come.

I replied, almost too bluntly, "I'm afraid we have lost, honey."

Tricia, who had been smiling bravely up to this point, began to cry uncontrollably. She said through her tears: "I'm not crying because of myself but for you and Mommy. You have worked so hard and so long."[9]

It was difficult for all of us to keep our tears in check as she spoke.

I then told Pat that I thought the two of us should go down to the ballroom to greet those who had been waiting it out so patiently. She asked me what I intended to say. I replied: "I don't intend to make an outright concession, but the least I can do is to indicate that, if the present trend continues, Kennedy will be elected."

Pat was adamant against my making any kind of a concession statement—even a conditional one. She said: "I have no regrets about all the work we have done in this campaign. But I simply cannot bring myself to stand there with you while you concede the election to Kennedy."

I understood so completely how she felt that I did not press the point. I kissed her and Tricia good night, and they went back upstairs. I asked the members of my staff to leave me alone in the room, and then I sat down with yellow pad and pencil to try and draft some notes which I might use for the statement.

[9] Months later, as I was writing this book, she was to tell me, "That was the saddest day of my life."

It was now almost midnight. In fifteen minutes I would have to go downstairs alone to the Ambassador ballroom and speak not only to the thousands gathered there—my closest personal and political friends who, through the years, had worked so hard in my campaigns—but also to millions across the nation, many of whom had worked and voted for me, and perhaps as many more who had worked and voted against me.

I thought back over other crises which had confronted me as I prepared for speeches or key press conferences: the fund speech in 1952; my White House press conference after the President's stroke in 1957; trying to hold my temper as I met the press in Lima and Caracas after the riots there in 1958; those tense moments when Khrushchev had verbally assaulted me at the American Exhibition in Moscow and I had a split-second to decide whether to remain silent, to retreat, or to fight back.

But this was the greatest test of all. How could I be gracious, and yet not concede outright? On the other hand, how could I avoid disappointing and discouraging over thirty million people who had voted and worked for me and who were now waiting to hear what I had to say? Most important, if the trend were to continue as I expected it would, and Kennedy were elected, how could I best use this opportunity to get those who had voted for me to stand with him—wherever and whenever he would speak in the future as President of all the people and not just as the leader of his party? At least a dozen times I jotted down notes—and then tore the pages from the pad and tossed them in the waste basket.

I thought back on what other men had done under similar circumstances. I recalled Tom Dewey's generous comments "the morning after" in 1948 when he finally had to acknowledge a defeat which was, if anything, harder for him to take than mine would be for me because he had been such an overwhelming favorite to win.

As a student of history, I thought—what an appropriate time for a Lincoln anecdote! But this ground had already been pre-empted by Adlai Stevenson. In 1952 he had compared his feelings in defeat with Lincoln's little boy who had stubbed his toe: "It hurt too much to laugh, but he was too old to cry."

I still had not been able to put down a note that I felt would be appropriate when Don Hughes opened the door and walked in, with Pat beside him. "I have been thinking of all those people in the ballroom who have given so much of themselves to all our campaigns," she said. "I think we should go down together and tell them how much we appreciate what they have done."

It was now 12:15, Pacific Coast Time. Just as we were leaving the room, Bob Finch rushed in to tell me that the popular vote margin was now less than a million—less than 900,000 in fact—and growing smaller as the returns kept piling up. The count by states was now 20 sure states for Nixon—but with only 157 electoral votes—against 19 sure states for Kennedy, with 265—only four electoral votes short of going over the top. Michigan Democrats, according to Stuart Novins of CBS, were still not claiming the state for Kennedy because, while he had piled up a 66 per cent margin in Wayne County, he was running about 3 per cent behind the expected outstate vote. And in Minnesota, it was the same story: "still a horse race."

There was still a bare chance that, if we could win California, which I expected we would do, and two out of the other three critical "undecided" states—Illinois, Minnesota, and Michigan—we could take it all. But the chance was a long one, and it had already been announced that I was on my way downstairs to address the group in the ballroom and the national radio and television audience. I had to go ahead with it.

Pat and I walked together down the long deserted hallway to the elevators. A lone Secret Service man stationed at the end of the hall smiled as we approached him, and then turned away to hide the disappointment he shared with us. Just before we went on-stage we saw Herb Kaplow of NBC, ears covered with headphones. As I saw him, I remembered that he had been the first man to reach my car after we had run the gauntlet of the stone-throwing mob in Caracas. I sensed that he might be remembering the same incident as he smiled at us as we walked on by him and out onto the stage.

Paul Niven of CBS reported our entrance to the ballroom: "The Nixons are headed for the ballroom where presumably Vice President Nixon will concede defeat to Senator John Kennedy. It is a most enthusiastic reception, a tremendous ovation." As we moved to center stage, it seemed like still another campaign rally. Johnny Grant, who had been master of ceremonies at our big California rallies, was leading the crowd in the campaign song, "We want Nixon, we want Nixon! We want Nixon to be our Pres-i-dent"—to the tune of "Merrily We Roll Along." It took us at least two minutes to get everyone quieted down. As we looked out over the crowd, I could see that more than half of them were crying, and we saw literally hundreds who had been personal and political friends since the time, fourteen years before, when I had first run for public office.

And so I tried first to speak to them in personal terms:

I thought we had had the last rally of the campaign, but here we go again!

As all of you in this room know, and as all of you millions who are listening on television and radio realize, it is normally the custom for a candidate for the Presidency . . . not to appear until after the decision is definitely known, and all the votes are counted beyond doubt.

However, I have been keeping some pretty late hours recently as some of you have . . . I know too that many who are listening in the Eastern part of the United States will find that it is now about 3:15 in the morning, and before the evening was over I did want to have the opportunity to speak to those in this room who have been with us during the day, and also to those who are listening on television, to say these things.

First, to express to all of you who have done so much in this campaign, our appreciation. Words are really inadequate at times like this. We can only try to let you feel what we have in our hearts . . .

As I said this, I could see tears welling up in Pat's eyes and, before going on, I put my arm around her.

I can say that we couldn't have had a more wonderful group of people in all of the 50 states than have been in our campaign.

Next, I tried to say something to those who had supported Kennedy:

The other thing I wish to do is this: I am sure that many are listening . . . who are supporting Senator Kennedy. I know too that he is probably listening to this program and, while . . . there are still some results to come in, if the present trend continues, Senator Kennedy will be the next President of the United States.

Here, I very nearly lost control of the situation. Shouts of "no, no, don't concede" filled the ballroom from the emotional crowd in front of me. I tried to quiet them by saying:

I want to say that one of the great features of America is that we have political contests, that they are very hard fought, as this one was hard fought, and once the decision is made, we unite behind the man who is elected . . . I want Senator Kennedy to know, and I want all of you to know, that certainly if this trend continues, and if he does become our next President, he will have my whole-hearted support.

My deep thanks to all of you who are here . . . My congratulations to Senator Kennedy for his fine race in this campaign.

Finally, I felt I should say something which, at the end of so long and hard a campaign, would remind all those listening, Democrats and Republicans alike, that we were all united in a cause far greater and more important than any partisan considerations. And so I said:

And while because of interruptions . . . I have not been able perhaps to make this as coherent a statement as I might have wanted to, I do want to say that having been through all of the 50 states of this nation since the nominating convention in Chicago, having seen the American people . . . by the hundreds of thousands and perhaps millions, in the towns and cities of America, I have great faith about the future of this country. I have great faith that our people, Republicans, Democrats alike, will unite behind our next President . . . in seeing that America meets the challenge which destiny has placed upon us.

That challenge is to give leadership to the whole world which will produce a world in which all men can have what we have in the United States—freedom, independence, the right to live in peace with our neighbors.

And so with that, may I say again, my thanks to you. Having had only two hours sleep last night, and two hours sleep the night before, I am now going to bed—and I hope you do, too.

I had spoken for only five minutes but it seemed like a lifetime. Pat and I walked off the stage, making our way slowly through the crowd of friends who swarmed around us—many of them crying, most of them congratulating us on a fine campaign and wishing us well. As we walked back down the hall to my suite, I thought: "Now, it's really all over. No more schedules. No more crowds. No more handshakes, no more autographs, no more speeches. Now, at last, we can rest."

I took Pat to the fifth-floor suite where the girls were sleeping and then went back downstairs to check over any last-minute reports.

Herb Klein reported that the reaction to my statement had been about what we might have expected. Ed Morgan of ABC called it "a curious bundle of sentiments and statements," and John Daly said: "Fighting right down to the end of the race, Vice President Nixon was unwilling to concede the victory. If the trend continues, he said, Senator Kennedy will be the next President. A gracious speech, but not conceding." Virgil Pinkley called it, "virtually conceding—a sporting speech; the Vice President was in fine form." On NBC, Chet Huntley said, "I don't know whether that was a concession or not," and Dave Brinkley replied: "I suppose it was, but I never heard one just like it before. You can choose your own name for it."

The one o'clock reports indicated Oregon and Washington definitely in our column, with California becoming closer all the time. At 1:30, Kennedy's popular vote margin kept on shrinking: it was now only 800,000 out of 54 million votes recorded.

Len Hall came into the room at 2:30. Illinois, he reported, was getting closer. Kennedy's lead had been whittled down to 35,000, and UPI had reported that in each downstate precinct—with 1700 of them still to go—I had been gaining about 100 votes per precinct. At such a rate, Illinois could not yet be conceded to Kennedy. UPI also began to carry reports out of Chicago on alleged vote frauds in Cook County. Len commented, "The Democrats are holding back about 200 Cook County precincts, waiting to see what the count is downstate. We are trying to get them to throw them in but they refuse to do so. Unless they do, they will be able to count us out, no matter what happens downstate."

After Len left the room, I continued to listen to returns for another hour. At four, Kennedy's popular vote margin was down to 600,000. NBC, which as early as 8:00 on Tuesday evening had flatly predicted a Kennedy victory, now began hedging: "Our best *judgment* is that Kennedy is ahead." CBS, which had made the same sort of prediction, joined in: "Kennedy *apparently* has won." I finally turned off the television set, just as NBC flatly gave California to Kennedy and thus added up his electoral vote total to 296, well over-the-top. I did not accept this conclusion because I knew what any observer of California political trends should have known—that the absentee ballots, if past trends held, would put the state in our column.

As I went to bed at last, a little after four, I realized that if we could win California, gain enough downstate to take Illinois, and come through in Minnesota, we might do exactly what Eric Sevareid had suggested earlier in the evening, only in reverse—"snatch victory from the jaws of defeat." As I dozed off, I recalled what had happened to Charles Evans Hughes in a similar but again reverse situation in 1916. He had gone to bed believing that he had been elected President. California, however, because of an unintentional snub to Senator Hiram Johnson by Hughes, had surprised all the experts and ended up going for Wilson. The next morning, a newsman called to talk to Hughes. A secretary replied, "The President is asleep and cannot take your call until he wakes up." To which the newsman reputedly replied: "Well, when he wakes up, tell him he isn't President any longer."

Perhaps in the morning, I thought, someone might awaken me with a report that the miracle had come to pass—that we had turned the tide by winning California, Illinois, and Minnesota. And with that, I finally did go off to sleep, expecting and hoping to get my first good night's rest since leaving Los Angeles for Alaska almost three days before.

Barely two hours later, I felt someone shaking my arm insistently and urgently. I opened my eyes and saw that it was Julie.

Pat had put her to bed at about ten o'clock the night before, as she was becoming more and more distressed by the early returns. As she tucked her in, Pat had said: "You go to sleep now and don't worry. Things will be much better in the morning." Well, here it was morning and, waking at six and finding her mother and sister still asleep, she had gone to the Secret Service man in the hallway and asked where I was. He had brought her down to my room.

She asked me, "Daddy, how did the election finally come out?"

I could think of no way to make the news easy for her. "Julie, I'm afraid we have lost."

She started to cry and the questions tumbled out through her tears: "What are we going to do? Where are we going to live? What kind of a job are you going to be able to get? Where are we going to school?"

I tried to reassure her and told her there would be no problems that we could not work out—and that she never needed to worry about my ability to provide for my family. I then took her into the drawing room of the hotel suite, called room service, and ordered breakfast for the two of us. We then proceeded to have what was for me the first and probably the most difficult post-mortem of the campaign.

I explained how close the election was and that we had actually won more states than Kennedy—but because he had received a bigger vote in the major cities of the key states, he had won the election. Then she asked a strange and disturbing question: "Daddy, why did people vote against you because of religion?"

"What in the world gave you that idea?" I asked. She said, "That was what they were saying on television last night." Then I recalled that several commentators, appraising the early returns from the big cities, had stressed Kennedy's huge margins in some predominantly Jewish and Catholic precincts.

I tried to explain it to her this way. "Julie, people do not vote for one man or the other because they happen to be Jews or Catholics —or Protestants, as we are. They vote for a man because they believe in what he stands for or because they like him as a person. And you must never think just in terms of the people who voted against us. You must think of those who voted for us."

I reminded her of one of her favorite people—Mr. Wagshall who ran the delicatessen near our home in Washington, and who never failed to bring her and Tricia some special treats from his store during the holiday season. I recalled that she and I had helped Father John Cronin, one of my best and closest friends, celebrate his twenty-fifth year in the priesthood at an anniversary luncheon. And then there were Earl Mazo and Ralph de Toledano, my biographers, who had visited in our home on many occasions and, with their families, had been so close to all of us.

"So you see, Julie," I said, "it isn't a question of a man's religion when he decides to vote for you or against you. It is whether he believes in you and respects and likes you as an individual."

She did not answer for a moment after I had finished. Finally she said, "I think I understand, Daddy." And then: "Well, maybe we didn't win the election, but we won in the hearts of the people."

I had seen many people in tears the night before as they heard the returns, but for the first time I was confronted with the same problem. I told Julie my hay fever was bothering me as I wiped my eyes with a handkerchief.

It began to look as if everyone was up early on the morning of November 9—or, what is perhaps closer to the truth, very few had bothered to go to bed at all—and that all of them had decided at once to drop in for a visit and a good word. From 7:30 on, old friends and members of the campaign staff came in a steady stream: Bebe Rebozo who had flown to Los Angeles from Miami to be with us on Election Day, Jack Drown, Ray Arbuthnot, and many others whom we count among our closest personal as well as political friends—each in his way tried to take some of the sting out of the results of the night before. It was during these hours and days after our defeat that I was to learn not only who were my most loyal friends but also how much such friendship can mean in a period of great emotional, physical, and mental stress. One of the hardest lessons for those in political life to learn is that the rarest of all commodities is a political friendship that lasts through times of failure as well as success. I have seen many men become bitter after an election defeat when they saw friendships melt away; friendships they thought were personal turned out to be purely political. And what usually hurt the worst was that those for whom they had done the most were often the first to desert. I was not unprepared for this reaction because I had already gained that experience during my mercurial career.

I had seen Congressmen and Senators, who politely avoided me when Hiss was riding high after his first appearance before the House Un-American Activities Committee, beg me to come into their districts and states to speak for them—after Hiss was indicted.

The same men who had publicly called on me to resign from the ticket during the early days of the fund attack in the 1952 campaign, heaped praise upon me after my television speech—and after the favorable reactions started pouring in.

When newspaper columnists and radio and television commentators were blaming me for the narrow Republican defeat in the 1954 off-year elections, it was like pulling teeth to get even Senators and Congressmen for whom I had campaigned to come to my defense. But when President Eisenhower had his heart attack in 1955, many of these same men fell over one another trying to get appointments and pictures with the man who might, at any moment, become President of the United States.

Some of my younger and less experienced staff members were bitterly disillusioned by the sudden desertion of some of those we had thought were close and loyal friends, even as the unfavorable returns started coming in. What I tried to tell them was that they, in fact, were the exceptions. Their loyalty through good times and bad was the rarity. Those who reach the top, particularly in the political world, have to develop a certain tough realism as far as friendships and loyalties are concerned.

But what was now to compensate for these understandable defections among my supposed supporters was the overwhelmingly warm and friendly reaction we began getting, by wire and letter the morning after Election Day, from thousands of people in all walks of life. Our appearance on television in the early hours of the morning had created a warm reaction throughout the country. Wires and letters from Kennedy supporters complimented us for our "good sportsmanship."

Those who had supported us thanked us for our efforts during the long and hard campaign and urged that we not be discouraged by this defeat—that we continue to carry on the fight for the principles in which we believed.

At about nine that morning I received what was to be the first among scores of offers of positions after I finished my term of office as Vice President on January 20, 1961. A partner in one of the biggest and best law firms in Los Angeles called to say that he had checked with all his partners by phone, and they were already prepared to offer me a full partnership in the firm if I decided to return to Los Angeles—and with an annual income approximately three times as great as the salary I had received as Vice President.

But I had many things to do before I could even think about such an offer, tempting as it was.

First of all, I called President Eisenhower in Washington. He did his best to try and buck me up, but he could not hide his own crushing disappointment. I had never heard him sound more depressed. But he still had lots of fight left: he had heard early reports of fraud charges in Illinois and Texas and urged me to do everything possible to check them out.

Just as I completed my call to the President, Cabot Lodge reached me by phone from Boston. I knew that he felt our loss just as deeply as I did. He had suffered a great disappointment in 1952 when, after leading the fight for Eisenhower's nomination, he had lost his own Senate seat to John F. Kennedy. Now, in a sense, he had lost again to the same man. Neither of us could think of very much to say. I told him how much I appreciated his untiring efforts in the campaign. He replied: "We can always look back with pride on the fight we waged." But Cabot and I, experienced practitioners of the art of politics, knew that these words meant little to either of us. General MacArthur, in his historic address to the Congress on his return from Korea, had said: "In war, there is no substitute for victory." Cabot and I knew that this is truer still, if that is possible, in politics.

It was now almost ten o'clock and Herb Klein reported that the press was asking him when I would send Kennedy a formal concession wire. I had thought that my statement of the night before would suffice for the purpose; but because of the closeness of the race, Kennedy apparently felt he could not claim victory until a formal concession was received. I asked Len Hall and Bob Finch to work with Herb in preparing an appraisal of the returns to that hour so that I could make an appropriate statement.

While I was waiting for them to get their notes together, Willard Edwards of the Chicago *Tribune* dropped by the room. He had first covered my activities during the events leading up to the Hiss case, back in 1948. Our talk turned to the press coverage during the campaign just concluded. He was aware, as I was, that although a majority of the nation's publishers were Republican, an overwhelming majority of the reporters covering Kennedy and me during the campaign favored Kennedy. Later, *Newsweek* was to report on an informal poll, with these results: for Kennedy, 37—for Nixon, 13. In 1952, a similar poll of 50 top Washington newsmen had shown 40 for Stevenson and 10 for Eisenhower. I told Edwards that, because of this fact, Herb Klein's task had been much more difficult than that confronting Pierre Salinger, Kennedy's press secretary.

I am sure that no candidate is ever completely satisfied with the press coverage given his activities. And I am the first to grant that the candidate is the least objective of critics in this kind of appraisal. But I completely reject the theory, expressed by some since the campaign, that I might have received better treatment from the press had I "courted" them more, or had Herb provided the more elaborate facilities for entertainment that Salinger, with greater funds at his disposal, was able to provide.

I told Edwards that morning that I doubted if any official in Washington had greater, more sincere respect for the press corps than I, or had tried to be more fair in his treatment of them. Kennedy, Salinger, and several top members of the Kennedy staff followed the practice during the campaign of complaining to individual reporters about the fairness of their stories. In several instances, Kennedy himself and members of his staff went over the heads of the reporters to their publishers and to the top officials of the radio and television networks, when they felt they were getting less than fair treatment in news stories or on TV and radio reports. Never once during the course of the campaign did I resort to such tactics, regardless of what opinion I had of the coverage of my activities.

As Edwards and I talked that morning, I told him if I had to do it all over again, I would follow this same course. Going over the heads of reporters to their publishers would only have irritated them more. I have always felt that a reporter has a perfect right to any political bias whatever—provided that he keep it out of what are supposed to be straight news stories. Signed "opinion pieces" are, of course, something else altogether, as are regular editorials.

On my trips to Caracas and to Moscow, the reporters could not have been more fair and generous. Why, then, would some of the same men who covered my trips now take a different point of view during the campaign? The answer seemed fairly plain: When we were abroad, we were all on the same side. During the campaign, however, they quite naturally—and often as not, perhaps, quite unconsciously—favored the candidate of the party of their own choice. Nor do I believe that special favors and flattery, nor all the gimmicks recommended by public relations experts, would have made an iota of difference in their coverage. This kind of treatment may turn the heads of the minor-leaguers. But the men in the Washington press corps are big-leaguers, and the best of them would only have resented such crude attempts to curry their favor—and properly so.

Typical of the problem was the attitude of one of the most highly regarded of the Washington corps—James Reston, chief of the New York *Times* Washington bureau. He had, for example, given me very generous treatment when he covered my Russian trip. But ten days before the election, one of my supporters—Henry Arnold of Philadelphia—had written him, complaining about his coverage of my activities. Reston wrote back: "I'm afraid we differ about Korea, Radford, Nixon, Knowland, Bridges, etc. You like their policy, and I don't."

As Edwards was leaving, he asked me what I thought was the answer to this problem. I expressed my honest opinion: "Republicans will get better treatment in the press only if and when more reporters, like their publishers, take a more favorable or at least a more tolerant view of Republican policies and principles—and not before."

At 10:30, Hall, Klein, and Finch brought in their final analysis of the election returns to that hour. Kennedy's popular vote margin had now been pared to less than 500,000. With complete but unofficial returns from Illinois, his lead there was a bare 8000 votes. In California, he still held on to a 35,000 vote lead—but we knew, with nearly 250,000 absentee ballots yet to be counted, the usual Republican preponderance among these ballots would give us the state, and I specifically authorized Herb to make that prediction after our meeting. With California in our column, our margin in states-ahead was 26 to 23 for Kennedy, but his lead in electoral votes was still decisive—303 to 219, with the balance of 15 unpledged. Even if we were to overturn the Illinois outcome, therefore, we would still need 15 more electoral votes to win. Minnesota held out our only immediate hope, and it was a thin one. We made some phone calls to party officials in Minneapolis and they told us there was no further hope—that Kennedy would probably carry the state by 20,000 (which turned out to be almost on the nose). It was then that I dictated my formal concession wire to Kennedy:

I WANT TO REPEAT THROUGH THIS WIRE THE CONGRATULATIONS AND BEST WISHES I EXTENDED TO YOU ON TELEVISION LAST NIGHT. I KNOW THAT YOU WILL HAVE THE UNITED SUPPORT OF ALL AMERICANS AS YOU LEAD THE NATION IN THE CAUSE OF PEACE AND FREEDOM DURING THE NEXT FOUR YEARS.

Now, it really was all over. Pat, Julie and Tricia, and I walked together down the corridor to the elevator. On the way, we stopped to say good-by to my mother and my brother, Don. Over and over again in the days and weeks ahead I was to find that the hardest thing about losing is not how it affects you personally but to see the terrible disappointment in the eyes of those who have been at your side through this and other battles. It was particularly hard for Don. During the last days of the campaign, the opposition had resurrected the financial troubles which had forced him into bankruptcy two years before and had tried to connect me with a loan he had received from the Hughes Tool Company during that period. They had, of course, conveniently ignored the fact that my mother had satisfied the loan by transferring to the creditor a piece of property which represented over half her life savings and which had been appraised at an amount greater than the loan.

As we left, Don said with his voice breaking: "I hope I haven't been responsible for your losing the election." I reassured him: "The only place the charge meant anything was here in California, and we are going to carry California anyway." For a number of reasons, I was especially gratified when the absentee ballots finally did put California in our column ten days later, by a 35,000 vote majority, but one of the major reasons for my satisfaction was that I did not want Don to have any feeling of responsibility for my defeat.

The elevator took us down to the lobby floor, and there a very warm and wonderful thing happened. Eight years before, Pat and I had walked through this same lobby at a time of great victory. The halls had been crowded with our cheering friends and supporters. This time we had expected them to be deserted—but again they were filled.

People cheered, slapped us on the back, shook our hands as if we had won the election rather than lost. Julie put a book over her face to cover the tears which, in her case, come quickly to her eyes at such times. I looked at Tricia and saw the thin, tight smile which I knew covered emotions deeper than tears could express.[10]

After a two-hour delay at the airport because of mechanical difficulties, we boarded our chartered Pan American 707 for the flight to Washington. I had had less than four hours sleep in the last two-and-a-half days but, while I am usually able to cat-nap in airplanes or in automobiles, I found that now I was too tired to sleep. I wandered up and down the aisle talking to members of my staff, many of whom had flown from Washington to Los Angeles to be with me on Election Night. I could not find words to thank them adequately for their devoted service through the years and all during the campaign. Only a candidate for office truly knows how a campaign brings forth almost superhuman efforts from members of a campaign staff, and especially from those who type the letters, run the mimeograph machines, do the research, expect (and get) no coffee-breaks or long lunch hours or overtime pay, and receive no public credit or recognition. Their only reward is victory for their candidate. I could well understand the tears in the eyes of many of my loyal staff members that night.

Finally I returned to my own seat and, for perhaps the first time since the campaign began, looked down at the lights of the cities below. Always before I had had to use every available minute on my flights preparing speeches or statements for the next appearance.

As I saw the lights, I tried to guess the cities over which we were passing. It seemed now almost like a dream that only a few days and weeks before, Pat and I had motorcaded through the streets of these same cities with thousands of our supporters cheering us on. As we went over Chicago my thoughts turned not to the charges of vote fraud which had begun to reach Los Angeles before we had left—they turned, rather, to my acceptance speech at the Republican National Convention just four months before, probably the highwater mark of my whole political career.

As the plane approached Andrews Air Force Base, across the Anacostia River from the District of Columbia, where we had been spe-

[10] The difference in the personalities of our two girls, who are in many ways, of course, very much alike, was illustrated by their reactions to the motion picture, *King of Kings*. Julie exclaimed, "It was wonderful! I cried so much." Tricia said, "I didn't cry when Christ died—He had suffered so much. I cried during the Sermon on the Mount because it was so beautiful."

cially cleared for landing, Herb Klein brought me a message which
some of the reporters who were returning with us had composed. It
read:

Dear Friends:
You shook us on the Tijuana trail. (But it wouldn't have happened if
you had had a Washington newsman and not a Young Republican at
the wheel of our car.)

You made us stand for an hour and a half in the grim fog in Lima, Ohio,
while your train rumbled back onto the main line.

You told us in Chicago you never delivered the same speech twice,
but some sense we've heard the same phrases once or twice in the
course of the campaign.

You took us from St. Louis to Atlantic City to Roanoke to Omaha in
one nightmarish day and confined us to Convairs for the last two legs
of the journey. And if that weren't enough, you sent Fred Seaton down
at 3 A.M. to explain your farm program to us.

Your entourage in all these travels was a mixed breed. But as this plane
wings eastward it was the majority opinion of the regulars in the press
corps that we have toured the land with a champ. And we double it in
spades for Pat.

                                    [*signed*] YOUR CAMP FOLLOWERS

As I read this I was especially glad that while I had undoubtedly
made my share of mistakes during the campaign, I had never complained to a reporter or to his superior about his stories.

   We landed in one of those dreary, drizzling rains which plague the
Washington area during the late fall. Because of the weather and because our plane was late, we were surprised to see a crowd at the airport. Thruston Morton was first to greet us as he said, "We let you
down." I could reply with all sincerity: "No one could have done more
than you did." John Eisenhower was there representing the President.
Chris Herter led a delegation of Cabinet members and their wives—
all of those who were in Washington at that time. And, in addition,
several hundred friends who had heard of our arrival were standing
there, soaked to the skin but cheering and calling out "Speech.
Speech."

   The mark of a true politician is that he is never at a loss for words
because he is always half-expecting to be asked to make a speech.
This was one of those few instances when I was caught so completely
by surprise that I spoke without any preparation whatever. I was so
tired, in fact, that I literally could not remember ten minutes later

what I had said, but the papers next morning reported it this way:

This is just about the nicest thing that's happened to us in the whole campaign. Because it is in defeat rather than victory that real friendship and loyal support is put to the test—and may I simply say that, in Pat's and my book, you have passed this test with banners flying. And so all we can say, from deep in our hearts, is thank you.

We got into the waiting limousine finally and started for home. The air had been bumpy on our flight's descent and Tricia, who has the same tendency toward air sickness that I had at her age (in my generation, to be sure, it was car sickness), had become quite ill. Several times on the trip from the airport we stopped the car so that she could walk around and get some fresh air. We finally pulled up in front of our house just before midnight. Our long journey—which had, in reality, begun so many years before—was now ended.

Pat put Tricia and Julie to bed at once but, after saying good night, I found I was still unable to sleep. I went down to the library, built a fire, and sat before it to let the tension and fatigue drain away. In the quiet of my own home, I tried to think not of the past but of the future. I knew that the next few days and weeks would probably present me with the greatest test of my life.

In each of the crises of my political career, one lesson stood out: the period of greatest danger is not in preparing to meet a crisis or in fighting the battle itself but rather in that time immediately afterward, when the body, mind, and spirit are totally exhausted and there are still problems to deal with. It had been difficult enough in those past instances, each of which in its way had ended in victory, to avoid making serious errors of judgment once the battle was over. Now, in defeat, I knew the problem would be even greater.

As I sat before the fire, I determined that I would try to conduct myself in such a way that even those who had been most bitterly opposed to me would find nothing to criticize. I knew this would not be easy. We had been through a long, hard-fought campaign. Kennedy's margin of victory was razor-thin. Charges of fraud and demands for recounts had already begun. I realized that what I said and did in the next few days would be observed closely, and not in the United States alone but all over the world.

Apart from considerations involving the nation and my party, it was important now with so many eyes so sharply focused on me that, from a purely personal standpoint, I try to set a proper example of conduct in defeat. Because defeat is a much more common experience than victory. For everyone who reaches the top—in politics, business, the professions, or any other field—there are many more who seek that goal and fall short. I had had more than my share of victories in my lifetime. But I had known, too, the sting of defeat. I knew that defeat was a greater test of character than victory.

It was not that I believed I should accept defeat with resignation. I have never had much sympathy for the point of view, "it isn't whether you win or lose that counts, but how you play the game."

How you play the game does count. But one must put top consideration on the will, the desire, and the determination to win. Chief Newman, my football coach in college and a man who was a fine coach but an even more talented molder of character, used to say: "You must never be satisfied with losing. You must get angry, terribly angry, about losing. But the mark of the good loser is that he takes his anger out on himself and not on his victorious opponents or on his teammates."

Bob Reynolds, who had been chairman of my Sports Committee, and who is now one of the owners of the Los Angeles Angels, put much the same thought this way, in a handwritten letter he sent me the day after election:

Sometimes one loses a battle to win a war . . . I leave you this thought which came to me as the best advice I ever had from one of my college professors, after Stanford's stunning defeat by Howell-Hutson of Alabama—"Bob," he said, "defeats are poison to some men. Great men have become mediocre because of inability to accept and abide by a defeat. Many men have become great because they were able to rise above a defeat. If you should achieve any kind of success and develop superior qualities as a man, chances are it will be because of the manner in which you meet the defeats that will come to you just as they come to all men."

These were the thoughts running through my mind as, sitting before the library fire, I began to relax in the small hours of the morning. I had arrived at no momentous decisions about what I would do or say when finally I pulled the screen in front of the fire, turned off the light, and went up to bed. But I was at peace with myself. I was confident that, knowing the dangers to watch for, I would be able to handle the problems I would be confronted with, without making serious mistakes.

I did not wake up on Thursday until after noon. John Wardlaw, my chauffeur for the eight years I had served as Vice President, drove me down to my office at the Capitol. He is not only an excellent driver but one of the finest men I have known. This was one of those exceedingly rare occasions when he spoke to me as he drove. With an emotion I had never before seen him show, he said: "Mr. Vice President, I can't tell you how sick I am about the way my people voted in the election. You know I had been talking to all of my friends. They were all for you. But when Mr. Robert Kennedy called the judge to get Dr. King out of jail—well, they just all turned to him."

I assured him, as I was to assure scores of others who expressed their regrets as to why this or that group of which they were a member had not given me more support, "When an election is this close, John, no one can say for certain what caused us to lose. If there was any fault involved it was not with your people: it was mine, in failing to get my point of view across to them."

At the office, I found my staff buried in the mass of wires and letters that had poured in from all over the country. Except for the period after my fund telecast in 1952, I was to receive more messages during the next week than in any previous period of my public life—and this was only the beginning. When I saw how much work there was to do, I realized Pat and I would have to put off the vacation that we had planned for right after the campaign. But I felt we should try to get away for a few days at least and—since we had been seeing very little of Tricia and Julie over the past several months—that even a brief holiday with them now would mean more than a longer one later on. So, the next day we flew to Florida for what we hoped would be a complete escape and relief from the tension under which we had been living for so long.

But we were to discover that it was far too early to find even partial escape from what we had been through. The letters and wires and messages followed us and, although Don Hughes and Rose Woods did their best to keep phone calls at a minimum, there had to be exceptions. One round of calls added up to a notable exception.

Two days after our arrival, Pat and I were having dinner at the Jamaica Inn on Key Biscayne. The party included Bob Finch, Herb Klein, Don Hughes, each of them accompanied by his wife, Bebe Rebozo, and Rose Woods. Just as the waitress was taking our order, I received word from the hotel, which was nearby, that former President Hoover was trying to reach me by phone from New York. I knew that he would not be calling unless it was a matter of vital importance; consequently, I asked Don to return the call on the pay phone in the restaurant lobby. Within a couple of minutes he came back to the table with the word that he had Mr. Hoover's Waldorf Towers apartment on the line. I went to the phone, chatted briefly with his secretary, Bunny Miller, and then Mr. Hoover came on the line.

He is like Sherman Adams in one respect—he never wastes a word in a telephone conversation: no introduction, no amenities, just the substance of whatever is at hand. I said, "Hello, Chief." He replied: "The Ambassador[11] has just called me and suggested that it would be a good idea for you and the President-elect to get together for a visit. If you approve of the idea, the President-elect, who is now in Palm Beach, would like to phone you to make the necessary arrangements."

I asked him what he thought I should do. He said: "I think we are in enough trouble in the world today; some indications of national unity are not only desirable but essential." I answered that under the circumstances, I would of course be willing to have a talk with the President-elect and that he could so inform the Ambassador.

After this conversation with Mr. Hoover, I called the White House operator in Washington and asked her if she could get me through to Augusta, Georgia, where President Eisenhower was vacationing. He knew that it was my practice never to call him outside office hours unless the matter was of great importance; and so, within a few seconds, the phone rang in the pay booth and Eisenhower was on the line. I told him of my conversation with Mr. Hoover and said I felt I should report it to him, especially because there had already been newspaper reports to the effect that, because of the closeness of the election, some of Kennedy's advisers were urging him to bring Republicans into the new Administration. There had even been suggestions that he should offer me some kind of a post. Eisenhower, who had made a similar gesture toward a defeated opponent—to Senator Robert A. Taft, at the 1952 Republican Convention in Chicago—agreed that it was only appropriate for me to meet with Kennedy. "You would look like a sorehead if you didn't," he said. He suggested, however, that in any such conversations I should reserve judgment on the advisability of top Republicans going into the Kennedy Administration. "A true coalition government is possible only in a period of national emergency," he said. "And a coalition, to be truly effective, must give members of the minority party who take positions in the Administra-

[11] "The Ambassador," of course, was Mr. Hoover's way of referring to Joseph P. Kennedy, the President-elect's father and one-time Ambassador to Great Britain.

tion independent authority and responsibility. I do not think it would
be in the best interests of the two-party system for Republicans to go
into the new Administration in purely secondary or ceremonial positions which might give the color of coalition and the appearance of
shared responsibility, when that was actually not the case at all."

I talked to Eisenhower for only a couple of minutes and then returned to the table. I was just about to tell the others of these two
conversations when Don Hughes came up hurriedly and said, "Kennedy is calling."

When I picked up the phone, Kennedy was already on the line.
He made no mention of the call I had received from Hoover or of his
father's previous call. He began the conversation pleasantly and informally by asking how the weather was and if we were finally getting
some rest from the campaign. I replied in the same vein and then
quite casually he said, "I would like to fly down from Palm Beach to
have a chat with you—if it won't interfere with your vacation." I replied that I would welcome the opportunity to talk with him, but
added: "I would be glad to come up to Palm Beach to call on you.
After all, that's the proper thing to do in view of last Tuesday's results." He laughed and said, "No, I have a helicopter at my disposal and
it would be easier for me to come to you." I asked him what day
would be most convenient and we agreed to meet at the Key Biscayne
Hotel on Monday, November 14. As I hung up and walked slowly back
to our table, it dawned on me that I had just participated in a probably unprecedented series of conversations. In the space of less than
ten minutes, I had talked to a former President of the United States,
the present President, and the President-elect!

But I found very little appreciation of the historic significance of
the occasion when I reported it to Tricia and Julie the next day. They
both berated me roundly: "How can you possibly talk to him after
what he said about you in the campaign?" I replied, "After all, he
won the election and this is the only proper thing for me to do under
the circumstances." But Julie still protested: "He didn't win. Haven't
you heard about all the cheating in Illinois and Texas?" I could see
that I was not going to win this argument and so, quickly as possible,
I changed the subject.

But for weeks and even months afterward, I was to see repeated
evidence of a lesson I had learned years before in my political career:
women basically find it much harder to lose than do men. This is probably a credit to them. Once they or those they admire and love are

committed to battle, they enter into the contest with all their hearts and souls. They work harder and fight harder than men. Their commitment is generally more total and their loyalties more lasting.

Tricia, Julie, Pat, and my mother, typically, were to find it terribly difficult to reconcile themselves to the fact of defeat—and the same was true among the secretaries on my staff. Not a day was to pass until after Kennedy's inauguration on January 20 but that Julie would ask me: "Can't we still win? Why can't we have a recount in Chicago?"[12] When some of our friends sent the girls small checks with which to buy presents for themselves at Christmas, they insisted that I forward the proceeds to the Chicago Recount Committee.

Their attitude was far from an isolated instance. In my travels around the country over the next several months, I was to meet scores of couples who had supported me in the campaign where the husband had adjusted to the fact of defeat but where the wives insisted that "they would never give up." And they meant it, too. The best advice I can give to those planning to run for public office is simply this: get a corps of dedicated women committed to you and working for you— and you have it made!

Florida's weather was at its fabled best on Monday the fourteenth, when Kennedy came to see me at the Key Biscayne Hotel. It was a warm day, but a light breeze kept the heat from being oppressive. I stood at the hotel entrance with Bob Neale, the manager, surrounded by scores of reporters and photographers, waiting for Kennedy to arrive. Finally the Dade County police escort came up the drive. Behind them was the Secret Service escort car, traditionally used to protect Presidents and Presidents-elect. Kennedy was in the next car—riding in the back of a convertible and, despite the officials surrounding him, looking almost lonely.

As the car pulled up, I opened the door for him and we shook hands for the photographers. Then we walked together through the hotel grounds to a private detached villa where I had often stayed before on my visits to the Key Biscayne and which Bob Neale had made available for our conference. I insisted that Kennedy walk on my right as his new rank now entitled him to do. As former naval officers, we joked about the protocol involved.

[12] Tricia's reaction was similar. When I was in Washington briefly in May, right after the Cuban disaster, Kennedy asked me to come to the White House to discuss the situation. I first learned that he wanted to see me when I came back to the house after a visit to the Capitol and found a message for me by the telephone. It was in Tricia's handwriting and read: "JFK called. I knew it! It wouldn't be long before he would get into trouble and have to call on you for help."

When we reached the villa, we decided to sit on the porch so that we could get the benefit of the balmy air. There were some soft drinks in the refrigerator and I fixed one for each of us.

He started the conversation by saying, "Well, it's hard to tell who won the election at this point." I agreed that the verdict had been close but that the result was pretty well determined, despite the fact that California would end up on my side. He asked what, for me, had been the biggest surprise of the election and I answered, "Probably Texas. I really thought we would win there." He said that Ohio was the most surprising result as far as he was concerned. His polls had indicated that he would carry the state decisively, he had been in the state more than I had, and his crowds had been big on every occasion. He asked me how I evaluated Claude Robinson—who had done my private polling. I told him that "Robinson called the election even from the beginning, right after the national conventions, and his polls in individual states were almost miraculously accurate."

He went on to say that, for him, the farm problem had been the most difficult of the domestic issues. His polls indicated, as ours had, that two weeks after our speeches at the Plowing Contest the farmers were leaning my way. "It is terribly difficult to develop a farm program that is both politically appealing and economically sound," was his comment.

I asked him whether he was getting any rest after the hard campaign, and he replied that for the first time he was feeling real fatigue. "During the campaign, some way or other, you are sustained and inspired by the crowds. But now that the campaign is over I find that even driving from the airport to the hotel today, standing and waving to the crowd was tiring." I told him that that had been exactly my own reaction after each of the national campaigns in which I had participated.

Another aspect of the campaign about which we found ourselves in agreement was the great difficulty of adequately tapping and then making good use of the scholars' groups that each of us had set up for preparing basic research and speech material. We had had the same trouble: the material prepared by Washington staffs, with whom we could not have day-to-day contact, proved less and less useful as the campaign proceeded. "In the end," he said, "I found myself relying more and more on Sorensen, who was with me on the campaign tour and who therefore could react to and reflect up-to-the-minute tactical shifts in our basic strategy." I told him I had run into the same difficulty, and that one of my major regrets was that I had not been able to make better use of the fine group of scholars who prepared material for my speeches and statements.

Then we turned to more current issues. He asked for my opinion of the career people in CIA, USIA, and the State Department. I told him very candidly the conviction I had reached after my very first trip abroad in 1953, and from which I had not deviated—that our careerists in these agencies are for the most part devoted, loyal, and efficient public servants. But many times they lack imagination, or are fearful of using it. All too often they are more concerned with keeping a good job than with doing one. I made two recommendations.

As far as CIA was concerned, I felt that its assignment was presently too broad. It should continue to have primary responsibility for gathering and evaluating intelligence, in which it was doing a good job. But I said it had been my plan, had I been elected, to set up a new and independent organization for carrying out covert para-military operations.

I also expressed my strong opinion that under no circumstances should he follow the line of appointing only career people to top ambassadorial posts. "The foreign service," I said, "needs a leavening of top-notch, hard-driving, none-career people who will not be completely controlled by the more rigid, even stodgy, career officers. It needs an element with no vested interests."

I then brought up an issue which I told him was one on which I had particularly strong views—the recognition of Red China and its admission to the UN. I did so because just the day before, Senator George Smathers had told me that Chester Bowles and some of Kennedy's other foreign policy advisers were urging him to reappraise our position on that issue. Kennedy said that he was opposed to recognition of Red China. He indicated, however, that strong arguments had been presented to him in favor of the so-called "two Chinas policy." Under this policy, Nationalist China would retain its seat on the Security Council, and Red China would have only a seat in the Assembly. This would mean that Red China would have only one vote out of about a hundred in the Assembly and would not be able to block UN action by veto. Kennedy said that proponents of this policy were contending that Red China could not do any damage in the UN under such circumstances.

In expressing my strong opposition to this policy, I pointed out that the issue wasn't whether Red China had one vote in the Assembly, or even the veto power. What was really at stake was that admitting Red China to the United Nations would be a mockery of the provision of the Charter which limits its membership to "peace-loving nations." And what was most disturbing was that it would give respectability to the Communist regime which would immensely increase its power and prestige in Asia, and probably irreparably weaken the non-Communist governments in that area.

Kennedy expressed some concern about the probable fate of his domestic programs, in view of the makeup of the new Congress. His observation, I thought, was acutely perceptive on this score. He said: "A Republican President can probably get more out of a Congress where his domestic policies are concerned because of his ability to get support from the natural coalition of conservative southern Democrats and most of the Republicans, who also have conservative views. On the other hand, a Democratic President, unless northern and western Democrats make up a clear majority of the House and Senate—which, of course, will not be the case in the new Congress—will find that his more liberal programs will fall short because of the strength of the conservative coalition arrayed against him."

Finally, Kennedy touched briefly on the subject I had expected might be a major topic of conversation during our visit. He said: "In view of the closeness of the election, there have been several suggestions that it might be well for me to appoint some Republicans to positions in the Administration. I am not thinking at this time of appointing Republicans to Cabinet posts, because I realize that there cannot be divided responsibility as far as major policy decisions are concerned. What I had in mind were appointments to posts abroad which would create an impression of unity and bipartisanship as far as our allies and potential enemies are concerned."

He indicated that Lodge and Dillon were among those he had considered for such posts and then added, "I wondered, in fact, if after a few months you yourself might want to undertake an assignment abroad on a temporary basis."

I thought I could sense that he was making this suggestion mainly because he thought it was expected of him—"the thing to do"—and not because he had become convinced in his own mind that the idea was a useful one. In any event, I replied: "I appreciate very much your thinking of me in this connection, but it seems to me the very fact that the election was so close makes it all the more imperative for me not to accept an assignment in the new Administration, even on a temporary basis, unless there should be a real national emergency. Any other course of action would be widely misinterpreted and could be a very damaging blow to the concept of a two-party system and party responsibility." I sensed that he was considerably relieved when I answered his suggestion in this way; he readily dropped the subject.

We had talked by this time for almost an hour and, as he got up to leave, our conversation again turned to a lighter vein. I told him that he wouldn't have to bother about making news in the next few weeks because the new baby they were expecting in December would probably turn out to be a bigger story than anything that had happened in the campaign. He laughed and said that while he had a great deal of work to do in selecting his Cabinet, he did hope to get some rest before undertaking what he knew would be the very arduous duties that would be his after January 20.

As a parting comment, I urged that he take off whatever time he felt was necessary for relaxation after he became President. I told him how enjoyable I thought he would find Camp David and recounted the fact that I had written my acceptance speech there. And I said: "In the months ahead, I will from time to time try to offer constructive criticism of policies you may be following. But of one thing I can assure you: I shall never join in any criticism of you, expressed or implied, for taking time off for relaxation. There is nothing more important than that a President be physically, mentally, and emotionally in the best possible shape to confront the immensely difficult decisions he has to make." Kennedy seemed to be deeply appreciative of this comment and, with that, we asked Pierre Salinger and Herb Klein to come to the villa so that we could find out what arrangements had been made for his meeting with the press. I escorted him back to the hotel, to the room where the press and TV reporters were waiting, and we parted on cordial terms.

After two more days in Florida and then three in Nassau, I returned to Washington. We had planned to make this a longer holiday. But we had found that it was too soon after the campaign to unwind.

This had been my experience in previous campaigns. My layman's analysis of what happens is that an individual gears up his mind, body, and emotions to run at double or triple speed during a campaign. Once the job is done, the system just won't slow down to a walk instantly. A runner at the end of a race jogs a few more yards to taper off, and I find that the same therapy is called for after a campaign or any major crisis. That is why a vacation immediately after a battle is not nearly so enjoyable as one taken a week or a month later, when one has had time to adjust to a more normal pace of activity.

In addition, daily calls to my Washington office made me realize that this was no time to take a vacation. In just two more months, on January 20, 1961, and for the first time in fourteen years, I would be without an office, a staff, or a job. And there was what looked like a solid year's work still to be done in those two months.

I had to close my office and dispose of a fourteen-year accumulation of files. There were now over 100,000 letters and wires in the office which had to be answered. Most important, I felt a personal responsibility to see that all these post-campaign details were handled properly. This meant the preparation of letters to those who had contributed to and worked in the campaign. It meant helping to find jobs for members of my own staff and of the campaign staff who, like myself, would shortly be "at liberty."

When I got back to Washington I was faced with the immediate necessity of making one vital decision. What should I do with regard to the mounting charges of voting frauds and the demands that I ask for a recount in Illinois and other states where the outcome had been particularly close? In order to make this decision, I spent a day with my staff analyzing the final election returns.

The popular vote margin had now been whittled down to 113,000, out of 68,800,000 votes cast. A change of half-a-vote per precinct, nationwide, would have shifted that margin to me. One enterprising statistically minded commentator even pointed out that if the votes for Alabama's six uncommitted electors were subtracted from Kennedy's total, I would have led in the popular vote count.

I had received 49.6 per cent of the total vote, while Republican candidates for Congress had received 44.8 per cent. One gratifying aspect of the returns was that we had gained a net of 22 seats in the House and two in the Senate. We had made substantial gains in the state legislatures. And my staff pointed out that I could, perhaps, take some credit for this achievement in view of this fact: of the 27 Congressional Districts that returned a newly elected Republican, I had run ahead of the successful congressional candidate in all but four.

The electoral vote count was 303 to 219 (there were 15 votes pledged to neither Kennedy nor me). But a shift, for example, of 4000 votes each in Illinois and Missouri, and of a total of 3000 to 5000 votes in any two such states as New Mexico, Nevada, or Hawaii, would have changed the electoral result as well. Thus, a swing of between 11,000 and 13,000 votes—properly distributed in a few states—and the election results would have been reversed.

We then turned to the fraud charges. From the evidence I examined, there was no question but that there was real substance to many of these charges. To cite just a few of them—each one sworn to and widely published:

(1) Fannin County, Texas (which went 3 to 1 for Kennedy): there were 4895 voters on the official "poll tax list" but 6138 votes were counted.

(2) Angelia County, Texas, 27th Precinct: 86 individuals were officially recorded as having voted—but the final tally was Kennedy, 147–Nixon, 24.

(3) Fort Bend County, Texas, two adjoining precincts: in one, which voted Nixon over Kennedy, 458 to 350, 182 ballots were declared void at the "discretion of the judges." But in the other, 68 to 1 for Kennedy, not a single ballot was declared void.

(4) Chicago, 6th Ward, 38th Precinct: after 43 voters had cast ballots (by machine), the machine tally read 121 total votes. This precinct returned a final count for Kennedy, 408 to 79.

(5) In another Chicago precinct, one that voted for Kennedy by 451 to 67, the initial registration of a husband and wife was challenged on grounds of "false address." On Election Day, both voted. On recanvass, it was found that there were no such persons at the address listed.

(6) Chicago, 2nd Ward, 50th Precinct: there were only 22 voters on the official list but 77 individuals voted. At this polling place there were three judges present, all Democrats, although the law prescribes that there be five judges, at least two of whom must be Republicans.

(7) A Chicago *Tribune* reporter and her husband found on Election Day that their names had been removed from the voting list despite the fact that both had legal residence in the precinct and both had voted from that address in 1956.

But substance or not, when I looked into the legal aspects of the situation, I found that it would take at least a year and a half to get a recount in Cook County, and that there was no procedure whatever for a losing candidate to get a recount in Texas.

Many of my close friends and associates urged, nevertheless, that I demand a recount. They felt it was important for me to continue fighting so long as there was any hope whatever of winning. They also thought that, even should the effort fail, the publicity which would result from my taking the lead in demanding a recount would carry over and be most helpful to Republican candidates in the 1962 and 1964 elections. This was a compelling appeal in view of my responsibilities as a party leader.

But I finally made the decision against demanding a recount for what appeared to me, on balance, to be several overriding considerations. If I were to demand a recount, the organization of the new Administration and the orderly transfer of responsibility from the old to the new might be delayed for months. The situation within the entire Federal Government would be chaotic. Those in the old Administration would not know how to act—or with what clear powers and responsibilities—and those being appointed by Kennedy to positions in the new Administration would have the same difficulty making any plans.

Then too, the bitterness that would be engendered by such a maneuver on my part would, in my opinion, have done incalculable and lasting damage throughout the country. And finally, I could think of no worse example for nations abroad, who for the first time were trying to put free electoral procedures into effect, than that of the United States wrangling over the results of our presidential election, and even suggesting that the presidency itself could be stolen by thievery at the ballot box. It is difficult enough to get defeated candidates in some of the newly independent countries to abide by the verdict of the electorate. If we could not continue to set a good example in this respect in the United States, I could see that there would be open-season for shooting at the validity of free elections throughout the world.

Consequently, I made the decision not to support the contest and recount charges. I know that this greatly disappointed many of my best friends and most ardent supporters—but I could see for myself no other responsible course of action.

With this question decided, I turned to the mountain of correspondence that had to be answered before January 20. This is perhaps the most difficult of all the tasks a defeated candidate has to face. Writing notes of thanks and appreciation to friends and supporters after a successful campaign is, of course, a thoroughly enjoyable assignment. This same assignment for a losing candidate is like burying a dead horse. But I considered it far more important in defeat than in victory. Literally thousands of people across the nation had worked as hard as I had in this campaign. Their disappointment was just as great. The least they should have, then, was some recognition from the candidate that their efforts were appreciated. In the eight weeks between November 20 and January 20, my small office staff did a herculean job. We got out more than 160,000 letters—individually typed and signed —acknowledging messages we had received and thanking key workers for what they had done in the campaign. And my staff addressed and mailed over 500,000 cards, containing a personal message from Pat and me, to our volunteer workers and contributors.

As I worked through this mountain of mail, I found some real satisfactions in reading and answering it. And the thousands who wrote us will never know how much their letters and messages meant, not only to me but even more to Pat and the girls, the members of my staff, and others with whom I shared the sentiments expressed.

Dictating all these letters took many hours of time and thought. But my effort was nothing compared to what my small vice presidential staff did during this period. Without a break—except for Christmas Day itself—right on up to January 20, they worked at a back-breaking 80-hour-week pace. And for the two days before January 20, Rose Woods, Loie Gaunt, Marilyn Matthews, Don Hughes, and Bob Cushman worked literally around the clock.

Despite the fact that we got out a tremendous volume of mail, a few of the names of those who had contributed to and supported our campaign did get overlooked in the shuffle—but they were the exceptions. I had always been proud of my staff's reputation for being one of the hardest working groups on Capitol Hill. But this time they broke even their own records for dedication, efficiency, and sheer productivity— and in a difficult period after defeat when it was so hard to maintain spirit and morale.

During the Christmas holidays, Pat and I had a brief respite from the killing pace when we took Tricia and Julie up to New York. For months they had been wearing out their recordings of the scores of some of the top Broadway musicals on our stereo-phonograph. We had promised that after the campaign we would go to New York and see some of the shows "live." It turned out to be one of the most pleasant trips we had ever taken—not least because of the warm hospitality of such people as Walter and Jeanne Thayer whose guests we were at a performance of *Fiorello!* The show on-stage exceeded even the high expectations we had built up from hearing it on records. But an incident occurred which made it mean even more. As we entered the Broadhurst Theatre just before curtain time, several people recognized us and started to applaud. Before we could find our seats, the entire audience rose and joined in. This was as unexpected for a typically blasé New York audience as it was heartwarming. It obviously meant a great deal to Pat and me. But what we appreciated most was that it meant so much to Tricia and Julie. As we rode back to our hotel from the theater, Tricia said to us: "You see—the people still like you."

Back in the Capital, we had before us a particularly heavy social and official schedule. There were two White House dinners over which Mrs. Eisenhower presided with all her friendly graciousness and poise. The President, on each occasion, proposed toasts in which he spoke warmly of the contributions Pat and I had made to his Administration and of our efforts during the last campaign.

Pat and I hosted a number of receptions and dinners for friends in Washington and for those who had been most closely associated with us during the campaign in other parts of the country. Governor and Mrs. James Byrnes paid us the high compliment of coming from South Carolina to Washington for one such dinner. In his toast, the Governor said: "If the Vice President had won this election, I would not be here tonight. But because he lost, Mrs. Byrnes and I wanted to come to Washington to assure him and Mrs. Nixon of our continued friendship and support." Afterward, he told me that he well recalled his own feelings when he lost his first election campaign. "Only a man who has suffered a close defeat," he said, "can possibly know how someone else feels under the same circumstances."

I had only one more test as far as my official duties were concerned before January 20, and it was a minor one. On January 6, as Vice President and President of the Senate, I was to preside with Speaker Rayburn over a Joint Session of Congress for the now obsolete but still constitutionally required ceremony of counting the electoral votes. Earl Mazo, an hour before the session was to begin, called my office to suggest that in view of some comments in the press gallery that this would be an embarrassing moment for me, I might well make some statement at the time I announced the official outcome. This was, in fact, a most unusual occasion. Only once before had the defeated candidate had the responsibility of presiding over his own "funeral" by announcing his defeat in a Joint Session, and this had occurred exactly one hundred years before when John C. Breckinridge announced the election of Abraham Lincoln. I thought the idea was a good one and made a few mental notes as to what I might appropriately say.

When the counting had been concluded and announced—to no one's very great surprise it came out 303 to 219, with the balance of 15 cast for Harry Byrd—I added these remarks:

Mr. Speaker, since this is an unprecedented situation I would like to ask permission to impose upon the time of the members of this Congress to make a statement—which in itself is somewhat unprecedented. I promise to be brief. I shall be guided by the one-minute time rule of the House rather than the unlimited rule that prevails in the Senate.

This is the first time in 100 years that a candidate for the presidency announced the result of an election in which he was defeated and announced the victory of his opponent. I do not think we could have a more striking and eloquent example of the stability of our constitutional system and of the proud tradition of the American people of developing, respecting, and honoring institutions of self-government.

In our campaigns, no matter how hard fought they may be, no matter how close the election may turn out to be, those who lose accept the verdict, and support those who win. And I would like to add that, having served now in Government for 14 years . . . as I complete that period it is indeed a very great honor to me to extend to my colleagues in the House and Senate on both sides of the aisle who have been elected—to extend to John F. Kennedy and Lyndon Johnson, who have been elected President and Vice President of the United States, my heartfelt best wishes, as all of you work in a cause that is bigger than any man's ambition, greater than any party. It is the cause of freedom, of justice, and peace for all mankind.

It is in that spirit that I now declare that John F. Kennedy has been elected President of the United States, and Lyndon B. Johnson, Vice President of the United States.

The effect was electrifying and, to me, unexpected. The ovations from both Democrats and Republicans lasted so long that I had to stand and acknowledge it again. Sam Rayburn, at whose side I had often sat as he presided over Joint Sessions of the Congress during the past eight years, broke personal precedent and joined in the applause himself. He grasped my hand warmly as I left the Speaker's Rostrum and said: "That was a fine speech, Dick. I will miss you here. Good luck." We had been political opponents for years, but he had always been one who had great respect for fellow practitioners of the art of politics—even when they were in the other party. Neither of us knew at that moment that these were to be our last personal words together.

Two weeks later, at just a few minutes past noon, John F. Kennedy took the oath of office as the 35th President of the United

States. As he repeated after the Chief Justice the words required by the Constitution—*I do solemnly swear that I will faithfully execute the office of President of the United States, and will, to the best of my ability, preserve, protect, and defend the Constitution of the United States*—my own period of fourteen years service in Washington came to an end.

There was a brief afterglow which lasted through the balance of the day. Admiral Lewis Strauss gave a luncheon immediately after the inaugural ceremony which we attended at the F Street Club along with the President and Mrs. Eisenhower and the members of the Cabinet. John Wardlaw then drove us home and, as we got out of the official car, told us that it would continue to be at our disposal as long as we wanted it through the evening. After dinner, I asked him to drive me one last time down to the Capitol. The gay crowds attending the inaugural balls crowded the streets but we were able to drive by unnoticed. When we arrived at the Capitol, I got out of the car and looked once again down what I believe is the most magnificent vista in the world—the Mall, now completely snow-covered, with the Washington Monument and the Lincoln Memorial in the distance.

John then drove me home and I said good-by to him for the last time. As I went into the house, I recalled something that Alben Barkley had said to Pat and me shortly after inauguration day, eight years before: "The hardest part about leaving the vice presidency was losing my car. One day—I'm met by a car, a chauffeur, and a Secret Service man. The next day I'm completely on my own—and it takes time to get adjusted to it!"

For us, too, the next day was different. Don Hughes thoughtfully came to the house to pick us up in his station wagon for the trip to the airport. Pat and I finally were going to get that month's vacation we had been planning so long. My entire office staff and many from the campaign staff were there to see us off. Earl Blaik had generously offered us a ride in the AVCO company plane which was scheduled for a flight to Florida. While I was Vice President, I had always declined similar offers to use private planes because of the possible criticism that the corporation or individual owning the plane might thereby be trying to get special favors from the government. We were learning already that there were some benefits, after all, to being just plain "private citizens."

We could not have asked for more hospitality and consideration than were lavished on us during our stay in Nassau. Lindsey Hopkins made his house available to us at Coral Harbour, and Perkins McGuire did so at Eleuthera. We could go golfing, swimming, yachting, fishing—do anything we wanted, or nothing at all. Elmer Bobst brought his luxurious yacht, the *Elisa V*, to Nassau so that we could get relaxation cruising among the picturesque Caribbean islands. Our close friends, Roger and Louise Johnson, were with us, and Bebe Rebozo flew over from Miami to join the party. In the past fourteen years it seemed we could never find time enough for a real vacation—our longest, in all those years, had been limited to ten days. But now we could make up for lost time and opportunity.

As I soaked up the sun on those warm and peaceful Caribbean days, my thoughts turned back time after time to the campaign.

What could I have done differently—what were the things that would have brought victory rather than hairline defeat?

The Christmas season "of good cheer" had scarcely ended before the sniping and the second-guessing had begun. I understood this and, indeed, expected it. The election had been virtually a dead-heat. It was to Kennedy's advantage—as well as in the interests of those who might want the Republican nomination in 1964—to discredit my campaign. And, ironically, their task was made easier by the very reason that the election was so close. Had I lost by two million votes, or more, no one could say "if you had just done this or that you would have won." But when a shift of ten or twelve thousand votes in three or four key states would have overturned the result, anyone could make a pretty good case for the proposition—"if only you had taken my advice, you would have won."

Among the claims—"sure roads to victory"—that were most commonly made were these:

I should have refused to debate Kennedy.

I should have used Eisenhower more in the campaign.

I should have been more "liberal" (particularly on civil rights), as Rockefeller supporters wanted.

I should have been more "conservative" (again, particularly on civil rights), as Goldwater people argued.

I should have personally repudiated Norman Vincent Peale, so as to win more Catholic votes.

I should have made a speech at the end of the campaign attacking Kennedy for his systematic exploitation of the religious issue, so as to win more Protestant votes.

I should have catered more to the working press.

I should have complained directly to the Republican publishers, as Kennedy did, whenever the reporters appeared to be biased against me.

Lodge should not have promised that there would be a Negro in the Cabinet, and should have been slapped down hard for saying so.

I should have called the Judge, or done something similarly "grandstand," in the Martin Luther King case.

I should have campaigned only as a "regular Republican" and not tried to appeal, as I did, to independent and Democratic voters.

I should not have campaigned for and been associated with weaker Republican candidates in states like Illinois and Texas.

I should have asked the Justice Department to appoint special U. S. Marshals to police the polls in Cook County, as Senator Dirksen had requested a few days before the election.

I should have requested the Justice Department to impound, the day after election, all the ballots in Cook County and other areas where there was evidence of fraud.

My campaign was "me too"—I had not attacked Kennedy hard enough.

I should have exposed and exploited Joe Kennedy's background.

Anyone who holds to one or another of these views no doubt believes that if only I had followed his advice, the election would have been in the bag. Each could be right. Who can say, after all, what would have effected a change in a few thousand votes in just a few states?

The one claim to which I take real exception, though, is that I waged a "me-too" campaign and failed to attack Kennedy. I did not attack him or members of his family personally. But on the issues, I drew the line between us coldly and clearly and could not have hit him harder than I did, with any sense of responsibility.

Perhaps part of the reason for the growth of this campaign myth is explained in a letter I received after the election from Willard Edwards. He wrote me:

This letter represents the startled and indignant reactions of a reporter who came back to normal life in Washington to discover some unexpected reactions to your campaign.

The first thing that aroused my anger was to hear the statement that you had lost because you conducted a "me-too" campaign. I'd expected some such thing from the extremists who would be satisfied only with a Republican candidate who called for abolition of the income tax and social security. But I was dumbfounded to hear this sentiment from sensible moderates until the facts dawned upon me. They had never read an accurate report in the press reflecting the strength and depth of your attacks upon Kennedy and his program. . . .

When I first heard this remark, I indulged in a tirade. How could anyone, with a glimmer of common sense, make such a statement, I raged, in view of your continual slashing at Kennedy as reckless, irresponsible, dangerously impulsive, immature, obsessed with fear, a breast-beating imitator of Adlai Stevenson, a distorter of facts helpful to communist propagandists, putting politics above relief of misery, a downgrader of America, confused, uncertain, imperiling the cause of peace, a planner of inflation, a blundering advocate of retreat and defeat, etc., etc., etc.

The impression of "not much difference" between two candidates was fostered by the press coverage of your campaign. The staggering extent of that slanted reporting was not brought home to me until I began consulting newspaper files to check up on how the campaign was reported.

I think this is one of the most, if not the most, shameful chapters of the American press in history. The literal truth, and it can be documented, is that your strongest attacks on Kennedy were soft-pedaled by the pro-Kennedy press attached to your campaign. Why blame the voters for thinking that it didn't matter too much who was elected when they read, day after day, dispatches subordinating your strongest points and playing up frivolous details? . . .[13]

The decision not to drag Kennedy's father and other members of his family into the campaign was one for which I take sole responsibility and for which I have no regrets. Throughout my political career, I have always held that a candidate's public record should be exposed and at-

[13] The answer, of course, to Edwards' charge, assuming it has some validity, is that the fault was mine for failing to get across my views more effectively to the press. As far as "fairness" of coverage is concerned, my attitude is summed up by a statement Governor Munoz-Marin made when we visited Puerto Rico in 1955. Mrs. Munoz-Marin, at dinner, had complained bitterly about what she thought was a particularly unfair attack on her husband in one of the San Juan papers. She turned to Pat and said, "Wouldn't it be wonderful if we could get up in the morning and not have to read such unfair attacks on our husbands?" Munoz-Marin responded quickly, "No, it wouldn't. Above everything else, a free press is the greatest guarantee of our freedom. And if the press is to be truly free, those who write have a right to be unfair. Because who is to judge what is fair or unfair? Only the readers have that right."

tacked in as hard-hitting a fashion as possible. But his personal life and that of his family are not fair subjects for discussion unless they somehow bear directly on his qualifications for office.

I put this policy into practice at the time of the Republican National Convention, and I stuck to it throughout the campaign. At the time of the Convention, some of my Chicago supporters reported to me that the Merchandise Mart—which is owned by Kennedy's father and his brother-in-law Sargent Shriver, now head of the Peace Corps—hired no Negroes at anything above the very lowest, most menial level. They reported that there was great resentment over this policy in the Negro community of Chicago. And they suggested that this issue be dramatized during the Convention by means of a mass-picketing demonstration at the Mart. I rejected the proposal on the ground that I was running against Jack Kennedy, not against his father and brother-in-law.

As far as the religious issue is concerned, I must admit that I am at a loss to know how I could have treated it differently. Gallup, Roper, and the other pollsters reported after the election that I got the lowest percentage of the Catholic vote of any Republican presidential candidate in history (22 per cent) and that there was not a corresponding and balancing shift of Protestants away from Kennedy. But I still believe my decision was right, and I can take some satisfaction from the fact that this was probably the last national election in which the religious issue will be raised at all. One of the most gratifying postelection comments on this score, as far as I was concerned, was made by Cardinal Cushing of Boston when, in a speech in Baltimore on January 13, 1961, he nominated me "good will man of the year." He said: "During the recent campaign which tested and taxed all his powers, physical and mental, he never exploited the religious or any other issue that would tend to divide the American people."[14]

Except in these three instances, I do not intend what I have written to be a justification for every decision I made during the campaign. All I have tried to do is to set forth the reasons for those decisions, with the thought that others can look at the record more objectively than I and perhaps can avoid making the same "mistakes" in the future.

It may be, of course, that what both Kennedy and I said and did during the campaign had, in the end, very little effect on the outcome

[14] Cardinal Cushing and I have enjoyed a personal friendship which goes back several years. When I called on him in Boston in 1955, after my first trip to Latin America, he greeted me with the Spanish word *"tocayo"* which means, in effect, "your name is the same as mine." His first name, of course, is Richard.

of the election. David Lawrence has often expounded the theory that people have pretty much made up their minds several months before an election and that, unless some great national or international event occurs, what the candidates say and do merely tends to confirm opinions previously reached. There is some support for this theory in the polls taken last year. On September 14, Gallup reported the split at Kennedy 51 per cent, Nixon 49 (actually 48–47, with 5 per cent undecided and then redistributed). This was just before each of us began two months of intensive campaigning. Two months and several million words later—not to mention the back-breaking, nerve-racking travel schedules—the vote on Election Day came out in approximately the same proportion.

Looking back on it all, in addition to the observations I have already made, I have reached these general conclusions:

The campaign was too long, from all standpoints—in terms of time spent, miles traveled, and the number of speeches made. In these days of mass communication when huge audiences can be reached by television and radio, the candidates should not have to put themselves through the physical, mental, and emotional wear-and-tear that both Kennedy and I experienced in the last campaign. This would mean that both candidates would have more time for thinking and planning, and spend less time traveling and speaking.

My second conclusion is that a candidate must save himself for the major events—and his staff must never forget this. Wendell Willkie's experience in 1940 is an example in point. He was a magnificent whistle-stopper but, after wowing audiences of thousands during the day, he was hoarse and virtually voiceless by the time he was slated to speak to millions by radio at night. With the advent now of television, adhering to this principle becomes infinitely more important.

My third conclusion is one that I have reached regretfully. I believe that I spent too much time in the last campaign on substance and too little time on appearance: I paid too much attention to what I was going to say and too little to how I would look. Again, what must be recognized is that television has increasingly become the medium through which the great majority of the voters get their news and develop their impressions of the candidates. There are, of course, millions of people who still rely primarily on newspapers and magazines in making up their minds on how they will vote. But the fact remains, one bad camera angle on television can have far more effect on the election outcome than a major mistake in writing a speech which is then picked up and criticized by columnists and editorial writers. I do not mean to suggest that what a candidate says is not important; in a presidential election, in particular, it should be all-important. What I do mean to say is that where votes are concerned, a paraphrase of what Mr. Khrushchev claims is an "ancient Russian proverb" could not be more controlling: "one TV picture is worth ten thousand words."

These were some of the thoughts which ran through my mind as I soaked up the warm Caribbean sun. I had never dreamed it would be possible to get enough of this relaxation. We enjoyed ourselves immensely. But after about two weeks of it, I began to get restless. Through the years I had been so busy in Washington, I had thought that it simply wouldn't be possible to get tired of a vacation. Not to see a paper, not to be under attack, not to have to worry about the problems of the world, to be able to play golf, swim, do anything else I wanted—all this, I thought, would be practically the millennium. But much as I enjoyed it at the outset, after a few days the shallow talk, the lack of interest in subjects of importance, grew more and more boring. Perhaps part of the problem was that I was still too tired to relax. I realized it would take me some time to get adjusted to a more leisurely pace than that of the past fourteen years. I could hardly wait to get back to work.

Back in Washington, I began for the first time since the election to appraise my personal financial situation so that I could plan for the future.[15] After four years in the House, two in the Senate, and eight in the vice presidency, all that Pat and I owned was the equity in our Washington house. We owned no stocks or bonds, and we had just enough cash in the bank to take care of current expenses. My life insurance had been acquired so recently that its cash value was minimal. And as a former Vice President, under the law, I had no allowance for an office staff and no pension—except for the Congressional retirement plan to which I had contributed and for which I would not become eligible until age sixty-two.

We had two girls growing up who would soon need funds for college. My problem, in a nutshell, was an acute one—I had to find a job and start saving some money.

15 It was Tom Dewey who had urged me to delay any decisions with respect to the future for at least sixty days after the election. "This is one area where I can speak as an expert," he said. "A candidate who has lost an election for the presidency, after all he has gone through in the campaign, is literally in a state of shock for at least a month after the election. He should make no decisions of importance until after that period has passed."

But there was a much brighter side to the picture. Since the election, several very generous offers had reached my office, coming from all parts of the country. Jack Dreyfus, with whom I had developed a warm friendship during the campaign, urged that I come to New York because of the greater opportunities for high income available there, more so than in any other part of the country. Others thought I should become affiliated with a foundation or a university. But I finally decided to return to California and to the practice of law. This was my profession and, while I was tempted by some of the more remunerative offers of executive positions with corporations, I felt I was more qualified in the field in which I had been trained.[16]

As I write these words, just a year after November 8, 1960, I can say that private life has been good to me, materially at least, far beyond anything I had ever expected. My income tax alone this year will be twice as great as my salary as Vice President last year. And Pat and I have often remarked since returning home that we had almost forgotten how superb the California climate can be and how wonderfully varied are the recreational and cultural opportunities in my home state.

Why, then, would anyone risk these advantages of private life and decide to re-enter the political arena?

Because, as President Eisenhower once told me, "an individual who desires to remain in public life must never reject what he senses to be a sincere desire on the part of a majority of the rank and file voters, as well as the officials of his party, for him to lead them in battle."

And because, once a man has been in public life for any period of time, his interests and ambitions change. Naturally, he wants and needs enough income to take care of his own and his family's needs. But acquiring money and property, as an end in itself, has no appeal for him. It is what he does rather than how much he makes that counts. This does not mean that he is in some way better motivated than others who concentrate on building an estate, or that he is necessarily a more useful citizen. In fact, one of the major reasons for America's phenomenal growth has been that our system, based on economic

16 An interesting sidelight is that Earl Adams, senior partner in the firm with which I am now associated—Adams, Duque & Hazeltine of Los Angeles—had offered me a position in that firm fifteen years before. At that time I was running for Congress and the prospects were not bright. He was one of my earliest supporters and he told me one day that he wanted me to have the assurance in the back of my mind, should my candidacy fail, that a position in his firm would be available for me. It was an extremely thoughtful gesture on his part at that time and my association with his firm now, therefore, became a very natural and pleasant one.

incentives, has unleashed and stimulated the creative energies of the most talented group of business and professional executives the world has ever known. But the public man—and I include in this category not only elected officials but also those who work in government and for public institutions at all levels—federal, state, and local—has simply chosen to make his contribution to society in another manner. The nation needs qualified men and women in both categories. It just happened, because my fate sent me to Congress in 1946, that I became primarily a public man and must, therefore, remain in that channel—so long, of course, as the public wants to keep me there!

Whittaker Chambers put the case perceptively in the last letter he was ever to write me, one I received after my return to California at the end of February 1961. He wrote:

It seems possible that we may not meet again—I mean at all. So forgive me if I say here a few things which, otherwise, I should not presume to say.

You have decades ahead of you. Almost from the first day we met (think, it is already 12 years ago) I sensed in you some quality, deep-going, difficult to identify in the world's glib way, but good, and meaningful for you and multitudes of others. I do not believe for a moment that because you have been cruelly checked in the employment of what is best in you, what is most yourself, that that check is final. It cannot be.

On the other hand, speaking in wholly different (and, by contrast, superficial) terms, it seems to me that executive office has passed to the other party for a long time to come. I should find it hard to believe that you have not drawn the same conclusion. If true, that changes your routing and precise destination. It does not change the nature of your journey. You have years in which to serve. Service is your life. You must serve. You must, therefore, have a base from which to serve.

Some tell me that there are reasons why you should not presently run for Governor of California. Others tell me that you would almost certainly carry the State. I simply do not know the facts. But if it is at all feasible, I, for what it is worth, strongly urge you to consider this. There would be a sense and an impression of political come-down? Great character always precludes a sense of come-down, greatly yielding to match the altered circumstances. The public impression will then take care of itself—may, indeed, become an asset. I believe you to be, rather uniquely, a man who can do this.

Chambers' assumptions as to the political prospects of the Republican Party, nationally and in California, are subject to question. But he showed an acute understanding of why men who have been in public life seldom leave it voluntarily and, more often than not, are drawn irresistibly to return to it.

But probably the greatest magnet of all is that those who have known great crisis—its challenge and tension, its victory and defeat—can never become adjusted to a more leisurely and orderly pace. They have drunk too deeply of the stuff which really makes life exciting and worth living to be satisfied with the froth.

I do not know what the future holds for me. But whatever happens, I shall have no regrets about the past.

When I was talking with President De Gaulle on his visit to the United States in April of 1960, he commented philosophically on the fact that he was one of those rare individuals who was seeing some of his greatest days late in life. He quoted the Greek poet, Sophocles, as having aptly characterized his own situation: "One must wait until the evening to see how splendid the day has been."

For me, the evening of my life has not yet come. But for the boy who, forty years ago, used to lie in bed in Yorba Linda, California, and dream of traveling to far-off places when he heard the train whistle in the night, I can say even now that the day has indeed been splendid.

Appendix

THREE PUBLIC SPEECHES OF RICHARD NIXON

For Release AM's, Thursday, 11/27/58

TEXT OF ADDRESS OF
THE VICE PRESIDENT OF THE UNITED STATES OF AMERICA
BEFORE
THE ENGLISH-SPEAKING UNION OF THE COMMONWEALTH

November 26, 1958, Guildhall, London, England

In the six years in which I have had the honor of serving as Vice President of the United States, it has been my privilege to visit many countries and to participate in many significant events. I can assure you that no occasion in that period will live more indelibly in my memory than the dedication of the American Chapel at St. Paul's which I attended this morning and the gathering in this historic hall which I am privileged to address this evening.

This meeting of the English Speaking Union dramatizes the enduring character of the friendship and alliance of our two countries. The activities of this organization have been most vital in cementing our bonds of comradeship.

I consider it a particular privilege to pay tribute to the thoughtful and inspiring leadership of His Royal Highness, Prince Philip, who has spared no sacrifices in this dedicated work. His recent visit to Canada was only one of many activities which indicate his vital interest.

You all may be justly proud, not only of the contribution you have made to better understanding between our two countries, but also the even greater work of building an enduring basis of friendship among all English-speaking peoples.

The dedication at St. Paul's this morning dramatizes the unity you have worked so hard to achieve. It was symbolic of the enduring ties that bind us. It brought to mind the dramatic events of earlier and more trying days—the magnificent leadership and the great sacrifices that made possible our victory in the Second World War.

Our thoughts went back to our great national leaders, Sir Winston Churchill and President Roosevelt, working together in intimate harmony. They will receive the ungrudging tribute of history for their capacity to marshal the forces of democracy.

Our thoughts turned also to our incomparable Generals and Admirals—Eisenhower and Montgomery, Cunningham and King. They were more than brilliant strategists and commanders. Because of their unwavering devotion to the concept that military ingenuity must be combined with recognition of civilian authority, they rank indeed among the great military leaders of all times.

But above all, today, we honored brave men—whose names are legion and whose sacrifices can never adequately be repaid. British and American—farmers and laborers, from cities and countryside, from offices and classrooms—these were the men who made possible our victory in the greatest war in history. Many events of that war will be forgotten as we turn our eyes to other tasks, but their deeds will live forever. They bequeathed to us a spirit, a sentiment, a national memory that will never fail to capture our admiration as we move side by side in the path of friendship and alliance.

As Abraham Lincoln said at Gettysburg, "The world will little note nor long remember what we say here, but it can never forget what they did here. It is for us, the living, rather to be dedicated here to the unfinished work which they who fought here have thus far so nobly advanced."

What is the unfinished work they leave for our generation? I believe that two American Presidents speaking in this same Guildhall have simply, but eloquently, answered that question.

Woodrow Wilson on December 28, 1918 said: "The peoples of the world want peace and they want it now, not merely by conquest of arms, but by agreement of mind."

And Dwight D. Eisenhower, twenty-seven years later on July 12, 1945 said: "To preserve his freedom of worship, his equality before law, his liberty to speak and act as he sees fit subject only to provisions that he trespass not upon similar rights of others, a Londoner will fight. So will a citizen of Abilene."

To preserve freedom, to keep the peace, not only for themselves but for all people—this, then, is the cause for which the brave men we honored today gave their lives. It is the challenge and opportunity of our generation to further the ultimate realization of this noblest goal of mankind.

Let us examine the policies we should follow if this goal is to be attained. We begin by recognizing that the Free World must be militarily stronger than any potential aggressor. The existence of our military strength and our determination and ability to maintain it are the basic elements without which the objectives we seek would be impossible to realize.

But we recognize that military strength in and of itself will not keep peace unless it is combined with a wise and judicious diplomatic policy. Let us see what some of the guidelines for our policy should be.

We must retain the armed strength needed for security in a troubled world, but we should speak with the calm assurance of those who are not afraid.

We know that to the extent the law of the jungle prevails in any area of the world, weakness and indecision lead to disaster. Yet, firmness is not and should not be arrogance.

We will shun assurances based merely upon naive hope or even self-deception. But we must never tire in our search for enforceable agreements which will reduce tension.

We know that little is lost by discussion but that all may be lost by war. Yet, even in our tireless striving for peace, we must always be prepared to say that freedom and the rights of man are even more ultimate values.

Above all, our policies must represent the best thinking the Free World can produce. We are indeed fortunate in the fact that in men like Macmillan and De Gaulle, Adenauer and Spaak, Fanfani and Eisenhower we have the kind of dedicated and experienced leadership which is superbly qualified for the difficult task of keeping the peace with honor for the Free World.

In this connection, I wish to pay special tribute to your Prime Minister for his initiative in developing the enlightened concept of interdependence which has proved so useful in bringing about closer understanding between our two nations and which points the way for improving consultation and cooperation among all the countries in the Free World.

If the struggles for peace and freedom were to be decided solely by the adequacy of our military strength and by the quality of our diplomacy, we could look to the future with justifiable confidence as to the prospects for our eventual success. But we must recognize that this is only one phase of the struggle.

Our military strength and our diplomatic policies are designed to avoid a war we might otherwise have to fight in the future. We must not overlook the fact that other policies must be designed to avoid losing the non-military battle which has already begun and which is being waged in many areas of the world today.

Let us examine the battleground where this conflict is taking place—in Asia, in the Near East, in Africa, and in parts of Latin America. A great revolution is taking place among the people in these areas of the world. What I refer to is not a military or political revolt, but the revolution of peoples' expectations—the assertion of all peoples of their claim to a greater share of this world's goods.

Millions of people in these newly-developing nations are determined to break the bonds of wretchedness and poverty that have enslaved them through the centuries. They wish to achieve in this very generation a decisive breakthrough in the struggle against misery and disease.

They would prefer to attain these objectives and retain their freedom. But we must make no mistake about it—if they believe they are offered no other choice, they will choose progress even without freedom.

What is their choice? On the one hand, they have the example of the Soviet Union and the Communist satellites. Here is a pattern that promises quick results. Thousands of leaders of these countries are being invited to visit the Soviet Union to see the very real changes accomplished in the forty years since the Communist Revolution.

It is not an adequate answer to this challenge to cite the far higher material standards in most Western nations. To the newly-developing nations of the world, this is not the point. They are not particularly impressed by achievements primarily accomplished in the century of the Industrial Revolution. They are far more interested in what can be accomplished in the last half of the Twentieth Century.

What must be made clear and unmistakable for all the world to see is that free peoples can compete with and surpass totalitarian nations in producing economic progress. No people in the world today should be forced to choose between bread and freedom.

To shape the world of tomorrow in a pattern compatible with freedom and human rights we must all take our part in a great offensive against the evils of poverty, disease and misery. We cannot, for example, afford to allow the free government of India to fail in its heroic effort to produce economic progress and retain freedom at the same time.

We need to apply in this field the same determination, willingness and cooperation which enabled us to build the military strength which deters aggression today.

We must not be miserly, small-minded and negative in our approach to this problem. And while it is wrong to favor change solely because it is change, it is worse blindly to insist that we have nothing better to offer than maintaining the status quo.

We must associate ourselves with the decent aspirations of people everywhere for the better life to which they are entitled.

Just a few weeks ago, Premier Khrushchev promised his people a revolution in living standards within the next twelve years. He claimed that the Communist system would overtake and surpass the economies of the Western World.

We should be happy that such claims have been made. We would be eager to match the Soviet leaders in putting less emphasis upon armies, military research and the costly lethal weapons of modern warfare and more stress upon better housing, food, clothing and the other necessities for a good life.

If Mr. Khrushchev wishes to consider these steps as a form of competition or contest, I am sure that all of us would be delighted to accept the challenge. In such a contest no one could really lose. The world would be infinitely better off if man's energies were used for the welfare of families rather than the building of armies.

But our answer to the Soviet challenge should not stop here. We say—broaden this competition and include the spiritual and cultural values that have distinguished our civilization.

Material achievements, while necessary, do not meet the deeper needs of mankind. Man needs the higher freedoms, freedom to know, to debate freely, to write and express his views.

He needs the freedom that law and justice guarantee to every individual so that neither privilege nor power may make any man subservient before the law.

He wants the freedom to travel and to learn from other peoples and cultures.

He wants freedom of worship.

To us, these are the most precious aspects of our civilization. We would be happy if others were to compete in this sphere and try to surpass our achievements.

The Free World is too often made to appear to be relying on our superior military power and economic strength. It is not worthy of those with the heritage of freedom we share to appear to be resting our case on materialism alone.

I know of no better example to illustrate the point I am trying to make than through an analysis of that much-maligned institution— British Colonialism. It is understandable in view of the surging rise of nationalism that we have heard all that is bad and little that is good about colonialism in the past few years.

Colonialism has had its faults, but it also has had its virtues. I speak from some knowledge on this subject. I have visited twelve countries which at one time or another have passed through the status of British Colonialism.

I have known personally and admired the dedicated and effective work of your superb colonial administrators. You can indeed be proud of the contributions that have been made by men like Grantham in Hong Kong, Templer in Kuala Lumpur, MacDonald in Singapore, Crawford in Uganda, and Arden-Clark in Ghana.

Let us examine some of the benefits British colonial policy has produced in the areas in which it has operated. It brought the military strength which provided the security from external attack. It brought in many areas the technical training which assured economic progress.

But more important than either of these, it brought the great ideas which provided the basis for progress in the future—ideas which will live on for generations after the nations concerned have acquired the independent status for which an enlightened policy has prepared them.

The common law, the parliament, the English language, freedom of speech, assembly, press and religion—these are the institutions which are the proud legacy of the British people in lands throughout the world.

And so today let us never forget that in the momentous struggle in which we are engaged our major advantage is not in the strength of our arms or even the productivity of our factories. It is in the quality and power of the great ideals of freedom which have inspired men through the ages.

Our responsibility then is clear. Here is a cause worthy of the descendants of brave men and women who crossed boundless oceans and settled in every area of the globe.

Once again we must venture forth not to seek untilled lands, but rather to bring encouragement, aid, guidance and partnership to those peoples who want to live in freedom and decent prosperity.

We come to them as friends, as brothers in a shrinking world. We do not seek to impose upon them our economic system or our culture. It is theirs to choose the path to the future. But it is our responsibility to see that this choice is an informed one and a free one.

Let it never be said that because of our failure to present adequately the aims and ideals of freedom others chose the often irreversible path of dictatorship.

Let us speak less of the threat of Communism and more of the promise of freedom.

Let us adopt as our primary objective not the defeat of Communism but the victory of plenty over want, of health over disease, of freedom over tyranny.

With such a goal we shall give the lie to those who proclaim that we are witnessing the twilight of a dying western civilization. Rather we shall see the onset of a glorious dawn of a new world based on the immortal ideals for which men have sacrificed their lives through the ages.

In this very hall, a century and a half ago an English Prime Minister gave a brief address that has been ranked by Lord Curzon as one of the indisputable masterpieces of English eloquence. After the news of Nelson's glorious victory at Trafalgar, William Pitt was toasted as "the saviour of Europe." He responded in these words: "I return you many thanks for the honor you have done me. But Europe is not to be saved by any single man. England has saved herself by her exertions and will as I trust save Europe by her example."

Here is a challenge worthy of the brave men we honored today. May we, the English-speaking peoples, proud in the heritage we share, join with the friends of freedom everywhere and by our example save the cause of peace and freedom for the world.

The Vice President returned to Moscow July 31 to prepare an unprecedented radio-television address to the Soviet nation. As the press throughout the world reported, Mr. Nixon brought home, through an interpreter, facts never before revealed to a Soviet audience.

RADIO-TELEVISION ADDRESS
FROM MOSCOW

August 1, 1959

I first want to express my appreciation to the government of the USSR for giving me an opportunity to speak to the people of this country by radio and television just as Mr. Kozlov and Mr. Mikoyan spoke to the American people on their visits to my country.

I realize that nine days is much too brief a time for a visitor to spend in this great country. But in that period I have had the opportunity of having extended and frank discussions with Mr. Khrushchev and other leaders of your government. I have visited Leningrad, Siberia and the Urals and I have had the privilege of meeting thousands of people in all walks of life.

What I would like to do tonight is to answer for the millions of people who are listening to this program some of the questions which were asked me over and over again on this trip so that you may get a true picture of the policies of the American government and people.

I should like to begin by answering a question which I often heard: What are my impressions of this country and its people?

While my visit was brief I did have a chance in addition to visiting this great capital city of Moscow to see the beauty and culture of Leningrad whose brave people won the admiration of the world for their heroic defense of their city during the war; to savor the inspiring pioneer spirit of Novosibirsk; to witness firsthand the thriving productivity of the factory complex of the Urals. I was greatly impressed by the efficient modern equipment of your factories; your magnificent ballets in Leningrad and Novosibirsk; by the competitive drive for progress which is evident on every side.

But most of all I was impressed by your people; after all, the greatest asset of a country is not its forests, its factories or its farms but its people.

These are some of the characteristics of the Soviet people which I particularly noted on this trip.

First, their capacity for hard work, their vitality; their intense desire to improve their lot, to get ahead, is evident everywhere.

There was another feature about the Soviet people which I noted that may surprise you and that is in how many respects you are like us Americans. We are similar in our love of humor—we laugh at the same jokes. The people of your frontier East have much the same spirit of what was our frontier West. We have a common love of sports; the name of Vasily Kuznetsov, your great decathlon champion, is known in the United States as well as it is in the Soviet Union. We are both a hospitable, friendly people. When we meet each other we tend to like each other personally, as so many of our soldiers who met during the last great war can attest.

Above all, the American people and the Soviet people are as one in their desire for peace. And our desire for peace is not because either of us is weak. On the contrary, each of us is strong and respects the strength the other possesses.

This means that if we are to have peace it must be a just peace based on mutual respect rather than the peace of surrender or dictation by either side. Putting it bluntly, both of our peoples want peace but both of us also possess great strength and much as we want peace neither of us can or will tolerate being pushed around.

That is why I was so surprised at a question that was asked me by a worker on the new scientific center outside of Novosibirsk. My heart went out to him as he told me that he had been wounded in World War II and that his father and mother had been killed by bombs. But then he said, "I don't believe you when you say America is for peace."

Nothing he could have said could have astonished or saddened me more.

And so to the millions of Soviet people who suffered or lost their loved ones in war, and to all of those in this great country who want peace, I say tonight, if you doubt that the American government and the American people are as dedicated to peace as you are, look at our record, examine our policies and you can reach only one conclusion—only aggressor nations have anything to fear from the United States of America.

We have fought in two World Wars and have demanded and received not an acre of territory or a cent in reparations. We enjoy the highest standard of living of any people in the world's history, and there is nothing whatever that we want from any other people in the world except to live in peace and friendship with them. No leader in the world today could be more dedicated to peace than our President. As his brother, who has honored us by making this visit with us, can tell you, President Eisenhower's whole life is proof of the stark but simple truth—that no one hates war more than one who has seen a lot of it.

We know as do you that in this age of nuclear weapons it is impossible for either of our nations to launch an attack which would not bring terrible destruction to itself.

In this age any leader who is so insane even to think of starting a war should well heed your proverb—"Do not dig a pit for another; you may fall into it yourself."

Why then is there any doubt that the American government and people are just as dedicated to peace as the people of the USSR? I think part of the answer is to be found in another question which was often asked of me on this trip and which Mr. Khrushchev, himself, raised in this manner in his speech on July 28 at Dnepropetrovsk. "If you believe in the peaceful intentions of our country, why do you continue the arms race, why do you construct new military bases around our borders?"

In answering this question, let me first point out that these bases are not maintained for purposes of attacking you but for purposes of defending ourselves and our allies.

Why did we think it was necessary to set up bases? Let us look at the record. We disarmed rapidly after World War II. Then came a series of events which threatened our friends abroad as well as ourselves. The Berlin blockade and the war in Korea are typical of the actions which led the United States and our allies to rearm so that we could defend ourselves against aggression.

We must also remember that these events occurred before the 20th Party Congress changed the line to the one Mr. Khrushchev enunciated again in his speech at Dnepropetrovsk—that Communism will now try to achieve its international objectives by peaceful means rather than by force. I could cite statement after statement made by previous leaders of the USSR which advocated and threatened the use of force against non-Communist countries in order to achieve Communist objectives.

A striking illustration of why we maintain bases and strong military forces is the fact that one-fourth of the entire production of the USSR goes into armaments. This, in effect, means that every worker in the Soviet Union works one day out of four for armaments. And we in our country are also bearing a heavy burden of armaments. Think what it could mean to both of our countries if we could lift this burden from the backs of our people.

Some may ask, why don't we get rid of the bases since the Soviet Government declares today that it has only peaceful intentions? The answer is that whenever the fear and suspicion that caused us and our allies to take measures for collective self-defense are removed, the reason for our maintaining bases will be removed. In other words, the only possible solution of this problem lies in mutual rather than unilateral action leading toward disarmament.

Another question which was often asked was—why won't the United States agree to stop the tests of atomic weapons? The answer in a nutshell is that the question is not whether we both should enter into an agreement to stop tests but whether that agreement is one which will make sure that the tests actually are stopped.

That is why we say that if both sides honestly want to stop tests, we must first agree to set up inspection procedures in both of our countries which will make certain that the agreement is not violated. We believe this position is the only one that gives assurance of accomplishing the objective of stopping tests rather than just signing an agreement to do so.

We are encouraged by the fact that at least in this area we are presently engaged in serious negotiations which have made some progress. I know that I express the sentiments of the people of both of our countries when I say that I am hopeful that these negotiations will finally end in agreement.

Another question that has often been asked me went something like this: "The United States says it is for peace, but what the world wants are deeds not words, and the United States is short on deeds and long on words."

Nothing could be further from the truth. It is possible that many of you listening to me are not aware of the positive programs the United States has proposed which were designed to contribute to peace. Let me tell you about just a few of them and what happened to them:

We had a monopoly on the atomic bomb when on June 14, 1946, we submitted the Baruch plan for international control of atomic energy. What happened? It was rejected by the USSR.

Under Article 43 of the United Nations Charter, provision was made for the establishment of the United Nations Armed Forces to keep the peace. On June 4, 1947, we made the first of many requests that agreement be reached. What happened? All have been rejected by the USSR.

At the Summit Conference in Geneva on July 21, 1955, President Eisenhower made his offer of open skies aerial inspection. What happened? It was rejected by the USSR.

On May 1, 1958, the United States offered an Arctic aerial inspection plan to protect both nations from surprise attack. What happened? It was rejected by the USSR.

I realize that your government has indicated reasons for its rejection of each of these proposals. I do not list these proposals for the purpose of warming over past history but simply to demonstrate the initiative that our government has taken to reduce tensions and to find peaceful solutions for differences between us.

I realize that my answers to these questions indicate that there are some very basic differences between us. But let me emphasize at the same time that the very fact that we have not made as much progress as we would like in the past in settling our differences is the strongest reason for us to redouble our efforts to create better understanding between our two countries; to remove fear, suspicion and misconception where they exist, and thereby, to pave the way for discussions and eventual settlement by agreement of some of the basic conflicts between us.

We should both frankly recognize that we have some very real differences; that they are not easily settled: But two men who are friends can settle an argument between them without using their fists and two nations who want to be friends can do so without war.

I should like to suggest tonight some practical steps which will contribute to the cause of peace to which we are both dedicated.

First there are some positive things we can do which will create better understanding between us.

We can start by removing the language barrier. Here is one place where you are ahead of us. I was amazed at the number of people I met on this trip who were studying English. What we need are millions of American students who understand Russian and millions of Soviet students who understand English.

Both the exchange of persons and the cultural exchange programs should not only be continued but sharply expanded. The more Americans who visit and get to know firsthand the people of the Soviet Union and the more Soviet citizens who do the same in the United States, the better understanding we shall have.

I believe also that visits by officials like the ones Mr. Mikoyan and Mr. Kozlov made to the United States and which I have just concluded can provide the means of frank and full discussion of some of our problems and the development of solutions for them. Consequently, we should explore ways of increasing contacts of this type.

Most important of all, we need a much freer exchange of information between our two countries so that misconceptions we may have about you and that you have about us may be removed. I was rather surprised that Mr. Khrushchev should raise a question about the failure of the Western press to report adequately one of his recent statements. I would estimate that at least 100 of Mr. Khrushchev's words are printed in our American press for every one word of President Eisenhower's speeches that are printed in the Soviet press.

Perhaps this is an area where the cause of better understanding would be served if we had a more equal exchange. Let us agree that all of Mr. Khrushchev's speeches on foreign policy be printed in the United States and that all of President Eisenhower's speeches on foreign policy be printed in the Soviet Union.

Why not go further and set up regular radio and television broadcasts by Mr. Khrushchev to the American people in return for President Eisenhower having the same privilege to talk to the Soviet people?

Let us put a stop to the jamming of broadcasts so that the Soviet people may hear broadcasts from our country just as the American people can hear forty hours of broadcasts a day from the Soviet Union. And let us have a freer flow of newspapers and magazines so that the Soviet people can buy American newspapers and magazines here just as we Americans purchased over one and one-half million Soviet publications in last year alone.

I recognize that freedom of information can be abused and that neither of us is free from blame in this respect. The press, radio, television and other means of communication such as film studios, have a heavy responsibility for maintaining the spirit of truth and for preventing misinformation. In the final analysis the misrepresentation of facts or distortion of the truth defeats itself. Let me give you an example from an experience that occurred to me on this trip.

There was a report in *Pravda* to the effect that on the morning after I arrived in Moscow I tried to give money to a poor Soviet citizen, with the hope that American press photographers might take pictures of the incident and send them around the world. There was not a shred of truth to this story.

Here is what actually happened. On an early morning visit to the Danilovsky Market, I had talked to scores of people and received a most friendly welcome. As I was about to leave, several of the people asked me for tickets to the American Exhibition. I told them I did not have any with me, but that I would be glad to buy some tickets for those present who wanted to attend the Exhibition. One of the group explained that it was not a question of their not having money for the tickets, but simply a question of their not being able to obtain them. I told him I would be glad to check into the matter and see if I could get tickets for him.

These are the simple facts as far as this incident was concerned, and I can only add that all irresponsible reporters should never forget that in the end the truth always catches up with a lie.

Through this greater exchange of information between our two peoples we not only learn from each other and improve our way of life but we reduce the suspicion, the mistrust, the fear and misunderstanding and assure the understanding and friendship which will lead to the peace we all want. That is why, to me, the concept of co-existence is completely inadequate and negative. Co-existence implies that the world must be divided into two hostile camps with a wall of hate and fear between.

What we need today is not two worlds but one world where different peoples choose the economic and political systems which they want, but where there is free communication among all the peoples living on this earth.

Let us expand the concept of open skies. What the world also needs are open cities, open minds and open hearts.

Let us have peaceful competition not only in producing the best factories but in producing better lives for our people.

Let us cooperate in our exploration of outer space. As a worker told me in Novosibirsk, let us go to the moon together.

Let our aim be not victory over other peoples but the victory of all mankind over hunger, want, misery and disease, wherever it exists in the world.

I realize that this era of peaceful competition and even cooperation seems like an impossible dream when we consider the present differences we have between us. But the leaders of our countries can help make this dream come true. So far as the leader of our country is concerned, I can assure you that President Eisenhower has no objective to which he is more dedicated.

As far as Mr. Khrushchev is concerned, as I am sure you know, we disagree sharply on political and economic philosophy and on many world problems. But these characteristics are evident to anyone who meets him—He is a self-made man who worked his way up from the bottom; he is an articulate spokesman for the economic system in which he believes; he has immense drive; in sum, he is one of those individuals who, whether you agree with him or disagree with him, is a born leader of men. Because he has these unique qualities and because the decisions he makes will affect not only the 200 million people of the USSR but the 3 billion people on this earth, he carries a tremendous responsibility on his shoulders.

I would not be so presumptuous as to try to give him advice on how he should fulfill that responsibility. But could I relate something that I noted on the trip I have just completed? In every factory and on hundreds of billboards I saw this slogan, "Let us work for the victory of Communism."

If Mr. Khrushchev means by this slogan working for a better life for the people within the Soviet Union that is one thing. If, on the other hand, he means the victory of Communism over the United States and other countries, this is a horse of a different color. For we have our own ideas as to what system is best for us.

If he devotes his immense energies and talents to building a better life for the people of his own country, Mr. Khrushchev can go down in history as one of the greatest leaders the Soviet people have ever produced. But if he diverts the resources and talents of his people to the objective of promoting the communization of countries outside the Soviet Union, he will only assure that both he and his people will continue to live in an era of fear, suspicion and tension.

The Geneva conference is a case in point. It would not be proper for me to comment on the specific proposals that are pending before that conference at this time. But agreements between great powers cannot be reached unless they take into account the views and interests of all parties concerned. I was encouraged to note in my conversations with Mr. Khrushchev that he recognizes this fact and agrees that a successful outcome of this conference could be a great step forward in settling some of the problems I have discussed tonight.

I have one final thought to add. Mr. Khrushchev predicted that our grandchildren would live under Communism. He reiterated this to me in our talks last Sunday.

Let me say that we do not object to his saying this will happen. We only object if he tries to bring it about.

And this is my answer to him. I do not say that your grandchildren will live under capitalism. We prefer our system. But the very essence of our belief is that we do not and will not try to impose our system on anybody else. We believe that you and all other peoples on this earth should have the right to choose the kind of economic or political system which best fits your particular problems without any foreign intervention.

As I leave your country, I shall never forget an incident that occurred as I was driving through your beautiful Ural Mountains. A group of children on the side of the road threw wild flowers into my car and cried in English the words "friendship," "friendship." Mr. Zhukov told me that the first word children who study English are taught is the word "friendship." There could be no more eloquent expression of the attitude of the Soviet people, an attitude which we share in common with you.

Finally, may I express on behalf of my wife and I, and all the members of our party, our deep appreciation for the warm friendship and boundless hospitality we have found everywhere we have gone in the Soviet Union. I pledge to you that in the years to come I shall devote my best efforts to the cause of peace with justice for all the peoples of the world.

This address was reprinted, as agreed, in Soviet newspapers.

Before departing from Moscow for Poland, the Vice President held a news conference where he was questioned by representatives of the press of several nations, including the United States and the Soviet Union.

The Vice President's News Conference
Spaso House, Moscow, August 2, 1959

Vice President Nixon: Ladies and Gentlemen: There has been a request that the questions and answers be translated into Russian and I believe that is the fair thing to do in view of the fact that we are guests here and we have a number of correspondents who will be reporting in Russian. As each question is asked in English, it will be translated into Russian (by Yuri Lepanov of the Soviet Foreign Ministry) sentence by sentence as I answer it. Incidentally, I might say that Mr. Lepanov, along with Mr. Troyanovsky, did a superb job of translating at the Dacha when Mr. Khrushchev and I held our talks.

Ernest Barcella of United Press International: Have you recommended or will you recommend to the President that he invite Mr. Khrushchev to the United States?

Vice President Nixon: The President in his press conference indicated that I did not issue an invitation to Mr. Khrushchev to come to the United States. As far as any decision as to whether he should come and as to when he should come, the President, of course, should and will make that decision. I will give my own opinion as to whether such a visit should be made, but I emphasize that whether such a visit should be made, and when, is the President's decision.

There are a number of factors to be taken into consideration, some on the plus side, some on the minus side. On balance, I believe that at some time Mr. Khrushchev should be invited to come to the United States. I think on such a visit, clearly apart from the discussions he would have with the President on an official basis, the visit would serve other useful purposes. He would have a chance to see firsthand the United States.

In my conversations and those of others who have talked to Mr. Khrushchev from the United States, we have, of course, tried to tell him about our policies, our people, and the attitudes of our Government on various issues. But, in my view, he still has some very real misconceptions with regard to both our policies and the attitudes of our people. And I think that his going to the United States, and seeing it firsthand, would serve to reduce and remove those misconceptions which may exist.

He would see, for example, that our people, regardless of party, overwhelmingly support the President in the field of foreign policy. He would see that our economy is strong and productive. And, while his visit would of course not convert him to capitalism, any more than my visit here has converted me to Communism, it would serve to change his ideas, I am sure, as to how our system works.

Edward P. Morgan of the American Broadcasting Company: Mr. Vice President, on the basis of the talks and the observations that you made on this trip, could you tell us in general what you will recommend to Washington when you go home, in terms of a continuation or a change in any way of our policy toward the Soviet Union. Would it be for a firmer policy, a softer policy, or a continuation of the present policy?

Vice President Nixon: I can well understand the interest in this question. But I am here as the representative of the President, and I am to report to the President when I return. And any recommendations or views that I might have on this particular question should be made to him in the first instance.

Carroll Kilpatrick of the Washington Post: Have your talks with Mr. Khrushchev brought us any nearer to a summit conference?

Vice President Nixon: I have been out of touch with the developments in Geneva and consequently I could not give a helpful answer to that particular question. I have emphasized publicly, as you know, how important we feel some progress in Geneva is in creating a basis for agreement on some of our basic differences. Whether what I said publicly and what I may have said privately has had any helpful effect with regard to stimulating progress I, of course, am unable to say.

Vladimir M. Menshikov of the Moscow New Times: As you have probably seen during your travels in the Soviet Union, the establishment by the United States of military bases in foreign lands, especially near the Soviet Union, evokes among Soviet people mistrust with regard to the policy of the Government of the U.S.A. You know, Mr. Vice President, that the Soviet Union has eliminated military bases in foreign lands. Why shouldn't the United States of America follow the example of the Soviet Union in this respect, and by so doing help create an atmosphere of mutual understanding and confidence between nations?

Vice President Nixon: I, of course, discussed our position with regard to our bases in considerable detail in my speech last night. In essence, the problem of bases cannot be dealt with until we deal with the overall problem of disarmament at the same time, and until the threat and the fear which brought about the setting up of bases by our collective security group is reduced.

I would further question the gentleman's reference to the elimination of bases by the Soviet Union because his statement that bases in foreign lands have been eliminated would be true only if East Germany, Poland and Hungary were considered part of the Soviet Union.

Ray Sherer of the National Broadcasting Company: Of all the places that you could have visited on your way home, why have you singled out Poland?

Vice President Nixon: The visit to Poland grew out of an invitation that was extended to me two years ago by the Polish Government to visit that country, and when we made the plans for this trip we found that we would have the time to make this visit on this particular occasion. The Polish Government re-extended the invitation and we accepted it.

Charles Mohr of Time, Inc.: The President has repeatedly said he would not attend a summit conference unless there was progress at Geneva. Since any visit by Mr. Khrushchev to the United States would amount in effect to a sort of summit conference, do you think an invitation should come before there is any progress at that conference, or if the conference broke down?

Vice President Nixon: The decision as to whether or not a visit should be made by Mr. Khrushchev to the United States and the timing of such a visit is the President's and his alone to make. For me to comment on that question would therefore be uncalled for.

Preston Grover of the Associated Press: Do you feel that the press, radio and television attention given in the Soviet press to our visit here has been as full and fair as that given the visits of Mikoyan and Kozlov to the United States?

Vice President Nixon: I think any of us can always find reasons to object at times to press coverage that we may have received on a trip of this type, but I have been very pleased with the amount of coverage that has been given to my activities by the Soviet press and particularly pleased, may I say, and somewhat flattered, that both my speeches were carried in full by the Soviet press. I can assure you that many speeches I make in the United States do not receive such coverage.

Correspondent of the Moscow New Times: It was with satisfaction that we read repeatedly your statements about the necessity of peace and friendship with the Soviet Union. But how are we to understand in the light of those statements the policy pursued by the American Government in respect of trade with Communist countries?

Vice President Nixon: Do I understand that he would want me to comment on our policy with respect to trade?

Correspondent: I just wanted to know how we can understand the policy of discrimination in trade, in view of the statements about the necessity of bringing our two nations closer together?

Vice President Nixon: I could comment in considerable detail on some of the technical reasons why trade between the Soviet Union and the United States is at the relatively limited level it presently is. For example, in the field of strategic materials we cannot expect any substantial trade or any change in policy, I should say, until the political tensions and political differences are solved.

Now, as far as peaceful trade is concerned, it has always been and is now the policy of the United States to encourage and favor such trade. But in this field it is not only necessary to have something to sell, it is necessary for the purchaser to have something to sell back, and the difficulty is that we can no longer buy from the Soviet Union some products with which the Soviet Union could purchase commodities that they might want in the United States.

Manganese and chrome, for example, are two commodities we used to buy from the Soviet Union, but this market was cut off by the Soviet Union several years ago. Consequently, the United States had to develop new sources for these commodities. Now we buy manganese, for example, from India and Turkey, among other countries.

This difficulty is just one aspect of the whole complicated problem. But I emphasize again that we should explore ways in which peaceful trade can be indulged in between our two countries. But even with respect to peaceful trade, the settlement of political differences will contribute greatly to the possibilities in this field.

Nielsen of Deutsche Press Agentur: You probably noted the comment made by Mr. Khrushchev about Adenauer and the West German Government. What is your opinion about this comment?

Vice President Nixon: I think it is well known that our attitude toward the West German Government and toward Chancellor Adenauer differs from that of Mr. Khrushchev. I should emphasize that I know Dr. Adenauer personally and have had the opportunity to talk to him at length on several visits and particularly on his last visit to the United States. He is a man who is dedicated to peace and he is a man who speaks as eloquently and emphatically on disarmament as any man today.

I could only add, with regard to the comments made in reference to the German people generally, that it is difficult for me to see that the Germans who live in West Germany are all devils and the Germans who live in East Germany are all saints.

Alexander Parkson of the Jewish Daily Forward of New York: Mr. Vice President, in your talks with Khrushchev and the other leaders did you have a chance to touch on the reported discrimination against the Jews in the Soviet Union?

Vice President Nixon: I recognize that there is a legitimate interest among members of the press in the subjects that I did discuss with Mr. Khrushchev and the other leaders, but I have always followed the practice of not disclosing the substance of such talks or indicated the subjects covered. I think this is the only proper course to follow, and this way we encourage a very frank exchange of views when talks of this type do take place.

Zorin of Moscow Radio: Mr. Vice President, I have the impression that the conditions are such that representatives of the Soviet press have less opportunity of putting questions to you than foreign correspondents. The foreign correspondents you have with you on the trip have better opportunity of putting questions to you than the Russians.

I want to insist that you give us Soviet correspondents the same opportunity to put questions to you. I am a representative of Moscow Radio and my name is Zorin. I have a question. The Soviet Union has repeatedly suggested a ban on nuclear weapons, to eliminate the arms race among the states, and to put an end to war. The Soviet Union had made the same proposal after 1949 when it became known that the Soviet Union was the possessor of a nuclear weapon. The demand became stronger after 1953 when the Soviet Union became the possessor of thermonuclear weapons. Why, then, does the United States so persistently not want to put an end to all the atomic and nuclear weapons and eliminate all stocks of such weapons?

My second question is closely connected to the first one. In your television speech last night you touched on the "open sky" plan. Why, since the Soviet Union accepted that suggestion in a form which excluded the using of that plan for intelligence purposes, would the United States not hear of it?

Vice President Nixon: As far as tests are concerned, I discussed this at considerable length in my speech last night. I think the record will show that in regard to both tests and the "open skies" proposal, we have taken a position which is unassailable and the only one which will assure the real objective: not simply the writing of an agreement and signing a piece of paper, but the stopping of tests. And I can only say what I said last night, that I trust that we can make a breakthrough at some reasonable time in the future in this area where discussions are going on and some progress has been made.

Evgeni Litoshko of Pravda: My question is mostly related to the previous one from your television and radio speech last night. We get the impression that the Government of the United States of America was putting out proposals which were rejecting those of the Soviet Government. But you must be well aware of the fact that on several occasions the Soviet Government put out the right proposals for both concerning the ban on nuclear weapons and the reduction in conventional weapons. And you must also know that, in those Soviet proposals due regard was given to the position of the Western powers and in particular to that of the United States.

Why then is the impression created in this country that the Government of the United States rejects effective measures in the field of disarmament and goes back on its own proposals after they are accepted by the Government of the Soviet Union?

Vice President Nixon: We can spend a great deal of time in discussing the proposals of the Soviet Union in these fields and the proposals of our Government. I can only say that, speaking for our Government, I believe that the proposals we have made have been put forward in good faith and that they are proposals that will accomplish the objectives in each instance rather than merely the signing of a piece of paper, which might not accomplish these results.

It has been charged that we did not let the Soviet press ask questions. Now I believe we should let the ladies ask a question.

Miss Grenier of The Reporter: Mr. Vice President, I would like to know whether you have had any official or unofficial Soviet reaction to your speech last night that the Soviet Union is spending one-fourth of its budget on defense?

Vice President Nixon: I have not had an opportunity of getting any Soviet reactions except, of course, the newspaper comments. Now I think I can answer another American.

James Reston of The New York Times: Mr. Vice President, in view of the questions put to you here by our Soviet colleagues, may I ask whether during your conversations you discussed with Mr. Khrushchev the aggressions in Korea or Indochina, or the Hungarian uprising?

Vice President Nixon: For me to answer that question would again break my rule of not disclosing the specific substance of conversations. But I will say this. As those of you who witnessed our public discussions know, Mr. Khrushchev is a man who likes to get down to brass tacks early in conversations. And I can assure you that in this instance the diplomatic language which is usually used to describe talks—full and frank—should be assumed to mean exactly that. And from that I think you can draw conclusions that we discussed a number of very controversial issues.

John Scali of the Associated Press: Thank you, Mr. Vice President.

Vice President Nixon: The last question should be by a member of the Soviet press.

Chayev of Moscow News: Mr. Vice President, during your tour of the Soviet Union, you could see the desire on the part of the Soviet people for peace and friendship with the United States of America, and in your speech you admitted that fact. Why then has the Government of the United States of America rejected the proposals put out by the Government of the Soviet Union about the conclusion of a treaty of peace and friendship with the Soviet Union which was made in January, 1956? (There was a discussion as to whether the translator had translated the entire question.)

Vice President Nixon: May I make clear that our translator is from the Soviet Government and so there is no discrimination intended. And he's good!

The question is now complete?

Here again we get into the question of proposals that have been made by each of our governments in this general field. And I could reply by raising questions as to why the Soviet Government has turned down so many of the proposals we have made. I don't think this serves any useful purpose. I think what is important is that we find a proposal that each of us can agree upon.

And now if I can make a final statement, since I understand our time limit is up. I mentioned last night the great friendship and warm hospitality that I found every place we went in the Soviet Union.

I particularly want to mention the consideration that has been shown by the members of the Soviet press during the course of this visit. And I also want to mention the fact that I realize the problems presented to cities like Novosibirsk and Sverdlovsk in handling an immense press corps of this type were extremely difficult. And I think that the government officials concerned in the various cities that we have visited deserve our thanks for their cooperation and the efforts they have made to take care of our press party during what I know has been a very arduous journey for the press corps and a difficult task for their hosts. Thank you very much.

AN ADDRESS BY RICHARD M. NIXON, VICE PRESIDENT OF
THE UNITED STATES, ACCEPTING THE REPUBLICAN NA-
TIONAL CONVENTION'S NOMINATION AS CANDIDATE FOR
THE PRESIDENCY OF THE UNITED STATES

Mr. Chairman, delegates to this convention, my fellow Americans:
I have made many speeches in my life, yet never have I found it
more difficult to find words adequate to express what I feel.

To stand here before this great convention, to hear your expressions
of affection for me, for Pat, for our daughters, for my mother, for all of
us who are representing our Party, is, of course, the greatest moment of
my life.

I want you to know that my only prayer as I stand here is that in the
months ahead I may be in some way worthy of the affection and the
trust which you have presented to me on this occasion—in everything
that I say, in everything that I do, in everything that I think in this
campaign and afterwards.

May I also say that I have been wanting to come to this convention,
but because of the protocol that makes it necessary that a candidate
not attend the convention until the nominations are over, I have had to
watch it on television.

I have never been so proud of my Party as I have been in these
last three days as I compared this convention and the conduct of our
delegates and our speakers with what went on in my native state of
California just two weeks ago. I congratulate Chairman Halleck, and
Chairman Morton, and all of those who have helped to make this convention one that will stand in the annals of our Party forever as one
of the finest we have ever held.

Have you ever stopped to think of the memories you will take away
from this convention? The things that run through my mind are these:
That first day, with its magnificent speeches—Mr. Hoover with his great
lessons for the American people; Walter Judd, with one of the most
outstanding keynote addresses in either Party in history; our platform
and its magnificent presentation by Chuck Percy, the Chairman; and
last night our beloved, fighting President, making the greatest speech
I ever heard him make. All of this is part of our convention.

For these and for so many other things, I want to congratulate you
tonight and to thank you from the bottom of my heart on behalf of
Americans—not just Republicans, but Americans everywhere—for making us proud of our country and of our two-Party system.

Tonight too, I particularly want to thank this convention for nominating as my running-mate a world statesman of the first rank, my

friend and colleague, Henry Cabot Lodge of Massachusetts. In refreshing contrast to what happened in Los Angeles, you nominated a man who shares my views on the great issues and who will work with me and not against me in carrying out our magnificent platform.

During this week we Republicans with strong convictions about our Party and about our country had our differences—but as the speech by Senator Barry Goldwater indicated yesterday, and the eloquent and gracious remarks of my friend Nelson Rockefeller indicated tonight, we know that the differences that divided us were infinitesimal compared to the gulf between ourselves and the Democrats as a result of what they did at Los Angeles during their convention two weeks ago.

It was only eight years ago that I stood in this very place after you nominated as our candidate for the Presidency one of the great men of our century. Now, I say to you that for generations to come Americans, regardless of party, will gratefully remember Dwight Eisenhower as the man who brought peace to America, as the man under whose leadership Americans enjoyed the greatest progress and prosperity in history; and above all, they will remember him as the man who restored honesty, integrity and dignity to the conduct of government and to the highest office of this land.

My fellow Americans, I know now that you will understand what I am about to say. Because the next President of the United States will have Dwight Eisenhower's great example to follow in confronting new and challenging world problems of utmost gravity, this truly is the time for greatness in America's leadership.

I am sure you will understand why I do not say tonight that I alone am the man who can furnish that leadership. That question is not for me to decide, but for you—and I only ask that the thousands of you in this hall and the millions of you listening to me on television make that decision in the most thoughtful way you possibly can, because what you decide this November will not only affect your lives and your future, it will affect the future of millions throughout the world. I urge you to study the records of the candidates, to listen to my speeches and my opponent's, and Mr. Lodge's and his opponent's, and then, after you have studied our records and listened to our speeches, decide. Decide, on the basis of what we say and what we believe, who is best qualified to lead America and the free world in this critical period.

To help you make this decision I would like to discuss tonight some of the great problems which will confront the next President of the United States and the policies that I believe should be adopted to meet them.

One hundred years ago, in this very city, Abraham Lincoln was nominated for President of the United States. The problems which will confront our next President will be even greater than those that confronted Lincoln. The question then was freedom for the slaves and survival of the nation. The question now is freedom for all mankind and the survival of civilization. The choice that each of you listening to me makes this November can affect the answer to that question.

What should your choice be? Let us first examine what our opponents offered in Los Angeles two weeks ago. They claimed theirs was a new program, but you know what it was. It was simply the same old proposition that a political party should be all things to all men, and nothing more than that. They promised everything to everybody with one exception: they didn't promise to pay the bill.

And I say tonight that with their convention, their platform, and their ticket, they composed a symphony of political cynicism which is out of harmony with our times today.

Now, we come to the key question, what should our answer be? Some might say to do as they do—and even out-promise them because that is the only way to win. I want to tell you my answer.

I happen to believe that their program would be disastrous for America, that it would wreck our economy and that it would dash our people's high hopes for a better life. So I serve notice here and now that whatever the political consequences, we are not going to try to out-promise our opponents in this campaign. We are not going to make promises we cannot and should not keep, and we are not going to try to buy the people's votes with their own money.

To those who say that this position will mean political defeat, my answer is this: We have more faith than that in the good sense of the American people, provided the people know the facts.

I pledge to you tonight that we will bring the facts home to the American people, and we will do it with a campaign such as this country has never seen before.

I have been asked all week by the newsmen sitting on my right and left, "When is this campaign going to begin, Mr. Vice President? On Labor Day or one of the other traditional starting dates?" This is my answer: This campaign begins tonight, here and now, and this campaign will continue without letup from now until November 8.

I have also been asked by my friends in the press, "Mr. Vice President, where are you going to concentrate? What states are you going to visit?" This is my answer: In this campaign we are taking no states for granted, and we are conceding no states to the opposition. I announce to you tonight—and I pledge to you—that I personally will carry this campaign into every one of the fifty states of this nation between now and November 8.

And in this campaign I make a prediction—I say that, just as in 1952 and 1956, millions of Democrats will join us in 1960; not because they are deserting their Party, but because their Party deserted them at Los Angeles two weeks ago.

Now, I have suggested to you what our friends of the opposition offered to the American people. What do we offer? First, we are proud to offer the best eight-year record of any administration in the history of this country. But, my fellow Americans, that isn't all and that isn't enough. We happen to believe that a record is not something to stand on, but something to build on. In building on the record of this administration we shall build a better America. We shall build an America in which we shall see the realization of the dreams of millions of people not only in America but throughout the world for a fuller, freer, richer life than men have ever known in the history of mankind.

Let me tell you something of the goals of this better America toward which we will strive. In this America, our older citizens shall have not only adequate protection against the hazards of ill health, but—rather than sitting on the sidelines—they shall have a greater opportunity to lead useful and productive lives by participating to the extent they are able in the nation's exciting work.

And in the better America, young Americans shall have not only the best basic education, but every boy and girl of ability, regardless of financial circumstances, shall have the opportunity to develop intellectual capabilities to the fullest.

Our wage earners shall enjoy increasingly higher wages in honest dollars, with better protection against the hazards of unemployment and old age.

For those millions of Americans who are still denied equality of rights and opportunity, there shall be the greatest progress in human rights since the days of Lincoln one hundred years ago.

America's farmers, to whose hard work and almost incredible efficiency we owe the fact that we are the best fed, best clothed people in the world, must and will receive what they do not have today, and what they deserve—a fair share of America's ever-increasing prosperity.

To accomplish these things we will develop to the full the untapped natural resources, our water, our minerals, our power with which we are so fortunate to be blessed in this rich land. We shall provide for our scientists the support they need for the research that will open exciting new highways into a future in which we shall have progress which we cannot even dream of today.

Above all, in this decade of decision and progress we will witness the continued revitalization of America's moral and spiritual strength, with a renewed faith in the eternal ideals of freedom and justice under God which are our priceless heritage as a people.

Now, I am sure that many of you in this hall, and many of you watching on television, might well ask, "But Mr. Nixon, don't our opponents favor just such goals as this?" And my answer is, "Yes, of course." All Americans regardless of Party want a better life for our people.

What is the difference then? I will tell you what it is. The difference is in the way we propose to reach these goals. The record shows that our way works and theirs doesn't, and we are going to prove it in this campaign. We produce on the promises that they make. We succeed where they fail.

Do you know why? Because, as Governor Rockefeller said in his remarks, we put our primary reliance not upon government but upon people for progress in America. That is why we will succeed.

We must never forget that the strength of America is not in its government, but in its people. And we say tonight there is no limit to the goals America can reach, provided we stay true to the great American traditions.

A government has a role, and a very important one. The role of government is not to take responsibility from people, but to put responsibility on them. It is not to dictate to people, but to encourage and stimulate the creative productivity of 180,000,000 free Americans. That is the way to progress in America.

In other words, we have faith in the people, and because our programs for progress are based on that faith, we shall succeed where our opponents will fail, in building the better America that I have described.

But if these goals are to be reached, the next President of the United States must have the wisdom to choose between the things government should and should not do. He must have the courage to stand against the pressures of the few for the good of the many. And he must have the vision to press forward on all fronts for the better life our people want.

I have spoken to you of the responsibilities of our next President at home. Those which he will face abroad will be infinitely greater. But before I look to the future, let me say a word about the past.

At Los Angeles two weeks ago, we heard the United States—our government—blamed for Mr. Khrushchev's sabotage of the Paris Conference. We heard the United States blamed for the actions of Communist-led mobs in Caracas and Tokyo. We heard that American education and American scientists are inferior. We heard that America militarily and economically is a second-rate country. We heard that American prestige is at an all-time low.

This is my reply: I say that when the Communists are running us down abroad, it is time to speak up for America at home. Let us recognize that America has its weaknesses, and that constructive criticism of those weaknesses is essential—essential so that we can correct our weaknesses in the best traditions of our democratic process. But let us also recognize this: while it is dangerous to see nothing wrong in America, it is just as wrong to refuse to recognize what is right about America.

No criticism should be allowed to obscure the truth either at home or abroad that today America is the strongest nation militarily, economically, ideologically in the world; and we have the will and the stamina and the resources to maintain that strength in the years ahead.

Turning now to the future. We must recognize that the foreign policy problems of the '60's will be different and they will be vastly more difficult than those of the '50's through which we have just passed.

We are in a race tonight, my fellow Americans, a race for survival in which our lives, our fortunes, our liberties are at stake. We are ahead now, but the only way to stay ahead in a race is to move ahead; and the next President will make decisions which will determine whether we win or whether we lose this race.

What must he do? He must resolve first and above all that the United States must never settle for second best in anything. Militarily, the security of the United States must be put before all other considerations. Why? Not only because this is necessary to deter aggression, but because we must make sure that we are never in a position at the conference table where Mr. Khrushchev or his successor is able to coerce an American president because of Communist strength and our weakness.

Diplomatically, let us look at what the problem is. Diplomatically, our next President must be firm on principles; but he must never be belligerent. He must never engage in a war of words which might heat up the international climate to the igniting point of nuclear catastrophe.

But while he must never answer insults in kind, he must leave no doubt at any time that in Berlin or in Cuba or anywhere else in the world, America will not tolerate being pushed around by anybody. We have already paid a terrible price in lives and resources to learn that appeasement leads not to peace but to war.

It will indeed take great leadership to steer us through these years, avoiding the extremes of belligerency on the one hand, and appeasement on the other.

Now, Mr. Kennedy has suggested that what the world needs is young leadership; and, understandably this has great appeal. It is true that youth does bring boldness and imagination and drive to leadership, and we need all those things. But I think most people will agree with me tonight when I say that President De Gaulle, Prime Minister Macmillan and Chancellor Adenauer may not be young men—but we are indeed fortunate in that we have their wisdom and their experience and their courage on our side in the struggle for freedom today in the world.

And I might suggest that as we consider the relative merits of youth and age, it is only fair to point out that it was not Mr. De Gaulle, Mr. Macmillan, or Mr. Adenauer, but Mr. Kennedy who made the rash and impulsive suggestion that President Eisenhower could have apologized or sent regrets to Mr. Khrushchev for the U-2 flights which the President had ordered to save our country from surprise attack.

But formidable as will be the diplomatic and military problems confronting the next President, far more difficult and critical will be the decisions he must make to meet and defeat the enemies of freedom in an entirely different kind of struggle. Here I want to speak to you of another kind of aggression, aggression without war, where the aggressor comes not as a conqueror, but as a champion of peace, of freedom, offering progress and plenty and hope to the unfortunates of the earth.

I say tonight that the major problem confronting the next President of the United States will be to inform the people of the character of this kind of aggression, to arouse the people to the mortal danger it presents, and to inspire the people to meet that danger. He must develop a brand new strategy which will win the battle for freedom for all men and win it without a war. That is the great task of the next President of the United States. And this will be a difficult task, difficult because at times our next President must tell the people not what they want to hear, but what they need to hear. Why, for example, it may be just as essential to the national interest to build a dam in India as in California.

It will be difficult, too, because we Americans have always been able to see and understand the danger presented by missiles and airplanes and bombs; but we have found it hard to recognize the even more deadly danger of the propaganda that warps the mind, the economic offensive that softens a nation, the subversion that destroys the will of a people to resist tyranny.

Yet while this threat is, as I believe it to be, the greatest danger we have ever confronted, this is no reason for lack of confidence in the outcome.

Do you know why? Because there is one great theme that runs through our history as a nation: "Americans are always at their best when the challenge is greatest." And we Americans shall rise to our greatest heights in this decade of the '60's as we mount the offensive to meet those forces which threaten the peace and the rights of free men everywhere.

There are some things we can do and some things we must do, and I would like to list them for you tonight:

First, we must take the steps which will assure that the American economy grows at a maximum rate so that we can maintain our present massive lead over the Communist bloc. How do we do this? There isn't any magic formula by which government in a free nation can bring this about. The way to assure maximum growth in America is not by expanding the functions of government, but by increasing the opportunities for investment and creative enterprise for millions of individual Americans.

At a time when the Communists have found it necessary to turn to decentralization of their economy, and to turn to the use of individual incentives to increase productivity—at a time, in other words, when they are turning our way—I say we must not and we will not make the mistake of turning their way.

There is another step that we must take: our government activities must be reorganized to take the initiative from the Communists and to develop and carry out a world-wide strategy and offensive for peace and freedom. The complex of agencies which have grown up through the years for exchange of persons, for technical assistance, for information, for loans and for grants—all these must be welded together into one powerful economic and ideological striking force.

What we must do is wage the battles for peace and freedom with the same unified direction and dedication with which we wage battles in war. And if these activities are to succeed, we must develop a better training program for the men and women who will represent our country at home and abroad. We need men with a broad knowledge of the intricacies and techniques of the strategies of the Communists, with the keen knowledge of the great principles for which free people stand, and, above all, men who with a zeal and dedication which the Communists cannot match will out-think, out-work and out-last the enemies of freedom wherever they meet them anywhere in the world. This is the kind of men we must train.

We must recognize that government cannot do this job alone. The most effective proponents of freedom are not governments, but free people; and this means that every American—every one of you listening tonight—who works or travels abroad, must represent his country at its best in everything that he does.

The United States, big as it is, strong as it is, cannot do this job alone. The best brains, the fullest resources of other free nations, which have as great a stake in freedom as we have, must be mobilized to participate with us in this task to the extent they are able.

But do you know what is most important of all? Above all, we must recognize that the greatest economic strength that we can imagine, and the finest government organization—all this will fail if we are not united and inspired by a great idea, an idea which will be a battlecry for a grand offensive to win the minds and the hearts and the souls of men. Do we have such an idea?

The Communists proclaim over and over again that their aim is the victory of Communism throughout the world. It is not enough for us to reply that our aim is to contain Communism, to defend the free world against Communism, to hold the line against Communism. The only answer to a strategy of victory for the Communist world is a strategy of victory for the free world.

Let the victory we seek be not victory over any other nation or any other people. Let it be the victory of freedom over tyranny, of plenty over hunger, of health over disease, in every country of the world.

When Mr. Khrushchev says our grandchildren will live under Communism, let us say his grandchildren will live in freedom. When Mr. Khrushchev says the Monroe Doctrine is dead in the Americas, let us say the Doctrine of Freedom lives everywhere in the world.

Let us welcome Mr. Khrushchev's challenge to peaceful competition of our systems; but then reply, "Let us compete in the Communist world as well as in the free world," because the Communist dictators must not be allowed a privileged sanctuary from which to launch their guerilla attacks on the citadels of freedom.

Instead, we say, extend this competition, extend it to include not only food and factories as he has suggested but extend it to include the great spiritual and moral values which characterize our civilization.

Also, my friends, let us welcome the challenge, not be disconcerted by it nor fail to meet it, but welcome the challenge presented by the revolution of peaceful peoples' aspirations in South America, in Asia, in Africa.

We must not fail in this mission. We must not fail to assist them in finding a way to progress with freedom so that they will not be faced with the terrible alternative of turning to Communism with its promise of progress at the cost of freedom.

Let us make it clear to them that our aim in helping them is not merely to stop Communism, but that in the great American tradition of concern for those less fortunate than we are, we welcome the opportunity to work with people everywhere to help them achieve their aspirations for a life of human dignity. And this means that our primary aim must be not to help governments but to help people—to help people attain the life they deserve.

In essence, what I am saying tonight is that our answer to the threat of the Communist revolution is renewed devotion to the great ideals of the American Revolution, ideals that caught the imagination of the world one hundred and eighty years ago and that still live in the minds and hearts of people everywhere.

I could tell you tonight that all you need to do to bring about these things that I have just described is to elect the right man as President of this country and leave these tasks to him. But, my fellow Americans, America demands more than that of me and of you.

When I visited the Soviet Union, in every factory there was a huge sign which read, "Work for the victory of Communism." What America needs today is not just a President, not just a few leaders, but millions of Americans working for the victory of freedom. This means each American must make a personal and total commitment to the cause of freedom and all it stands for. It means wage earners and employers must make an extra effort to increase the productivity of our factories. It means our students in schools must strive for increasing excellence rather than adjustment to mediocrity.

It means supporting and encouraging our scientists to explore the unknown, not just for what we can get but for what we can learn. And it means assuming a personal responsibility for making this country which we love a proud symbol of freedom for all the world.

Each of us, for example, should be doing his part to end the prejudice which one hundred years after Lincoln, to our shame, still embarrasses us abroad and saps our strength at home.

Each of us should participate in this and other political campaigns not just by going to the polls and voting but by working for the candidate of his choice.

Also, my fellow Americans, it means sacrifice—not the grim sacrifice of desperation but the rewarding sacrifice of choice which lifts us out of the humdrum life in which we live and gives us the supreme satisfaction which comes from working together in a cause greater than ourselves, greater than our nation, as great as the whole world itself.

What I propose is not new, it is as old as America, and as young as America, because America will never grow old.

You will remember that Thomas Jefferson said, "We act not for ourselves alone, but for the whole human race."

Lincoln said, "In giving freedom to the slave, we assure freedom to the free—honorable alike in what we give and what we preserve. We shall nobly save or meanly lose the last, best hope of earth."

Teddy Roosevelt said, "Our first duty as citizens of the nation is owed to the United States, but if we are true to our principles we must also think of serving the interests of mankind at large."

And Woodrow Wilson said, "A patriotic American is never so proud of the flag under which he lives as when it comes to mean to others, as well as himself, a symbol of hope and liberty."

We say today that a young America shall fulfill her destiny by helping to build a new world in which men can live together in peace and justice and freedom with each other. But there is a difference today, an exciting difference, and the difference is because of a dramatic breakthrough in science. For the first time in human history we have the resources, the resources to wage a winning war against poverty, misery and disease wherever it exists in the world.

And upon the next President of the United States will rest the responsibility to inspire and to lead the forces of freedom toward this goal.

I am sure now that you understand why I said at the beginning that it would be difficult for any man to say that he was qualified to provide this kind of leadership.

I can only say to you tonight that I believe in the American dream because I have seen it come true in my own life.

I know something of the threat which confronts us and I know something of the effort which will be needed to meet it.

I have seen hate for America, not only in the Kremlin, but in the eyes of Communists in our own country, and on the face of a mob in Caracas.

I have heard doubts about America expressed, not just by Communists, but by sincere students and labor leaders in other countries searching for the way to a better life and wondering if we had lost the way.

And I have also seen love for America in countries throughout the world, in crowds in Accra, in Bogota, in the heart of Siberia, and in Warsaw—250,000 people on the streets on a Sunday afternoon singing, crying with tears running down their cheeks and shouting: "Niech Zyje America!"—Long live the United States!

My fellow Americans, I know that we must resist the hate, we must remove the doubts, but above all we must be worthy of the love and the trust of millions on this earth for whom America is the hope of the world.

A hundred years ago, Abraham Lincoln was asked during the dark days of the tragic War Between the States whether he thought God was on his side. His answer was, "My concern is not whether God is on our side, but whether we are on God's side."

My fellow Americans, may that ever be our prayer for our country. And in that spirit, with faith in America, with faith in her ideals and in her people, I accept your nomination for President of the United States.